IN THE SERVICE
OF THE CROWN

The Story of Budge and Nancy Bell-Irving

RAYMOND EAGLE

The Golden Dog Press
Ottawa – CANADA – 1998

Copyright © 1998 by Raymond Eagle.

ISBN 0-919614-83-3

All rights reserved. No part of this publication — other than in brief form for review or scholarly purposes — may be reproduced, stored in a retrieval system, or transmitted in any form or by any means, electronic, mechanical; photocopy, recording or otherwise, without the prior premission of the copyright holders.

Canadian Cataloguing in Publication Data

Eagle, Raymond
    In the service of the Crown : the story of Budge and Nancy Bell-Irving

    Includes index.

    ISBN 0-919614-83-3

    1. Bell-irving, Henry, 1913- . 2. Bell-Irving, Nancy. 3. Lieutenant governors – British-Columbia – Biography. 4. Canada. Canadian Army – Officers – Biography. I. Title.

FC3828.1.B43E23 1998   971.06'092   C98-901411-8
F1088.E23 1998

Cover design by The Gordon Creative Group, Ottawa.

Layout and printing in Canada by Arrimage of Montreal.

The Golden Dog Press wishes to express its appreciation to The Canada Council and the Ontario Arts Council for current and past support of its publishing programme.

I dedicate this book to the memory of Nancy Bell-Irving, whose patience, graciousness and gentle humour won the hearts of all who knew her, in peace and war.

ACKNOWLEDGEMENTS

MY THANKS TO Dr. Reginald Roy for his kind permission to quote from *The Seaforth Highlanders of Canada 1919-1965*, (copyright the Seaforth Highlanders of Canada) and to Dr. Robert MacDougall for his kind permission to quote from *A Narrative of War – From the Beaches of Sicily to the Hitler Line with the Seaforth Highlanders of Canada, 1943-1944*, (The Golden Dog Press). My thanks also to Ms Sue Bapte and the staff of the Vancouver City Archives for their assistance with the Bell-Irving papers; to General B.M. Hoffmeister, D.S.O., for help with information relating to the war; to Mr. Robert Bonner Q.C., Mr. E.A. (Smoky) Smith V.C., Mr. Duncan Manson, Mr. John Stagliano and Mr. Frank Wood for sharing their wartime memories; to Mrs Arlene Graham for allowing me to quote from the frontline dispatches of her father, Corporal Roy Thorsen, he sent to the Victoria Daily Times; to the Hon. Grace McCarthy and the Hon. Hugh Curtiss for their assistance with Government House/Provincial Cabinet communications between 1978 and 1983; to Admiral Michael Martin, R.C.N. (retired) and Captain Neil Boivin, R.C.N. (retired), for information relating to the annual coastal cruises; to Mr. Michael Roberts, personal secretary to the Hon. H.P. Bell-Irving at Government House (and three subsequent officeholders) for giving his time so readily with questions relating to protocol and events between 1978 and 1983; to Hal Bell-Irivng, Roderick Bell-Irving, Ian Bell-Irving and Elizabeth O'Kiely for assistance with Bell-Irving family matters. Lastly, my special, warmest thanks to the Hon. H.P. (Budge) Bell-Irving and his late wife, Nancy, for their patience, encouragement and good humour. Also my thanks to them for providing unlimited access to family papers and other information sources. My special thanks to Mr. Fred Shiffer for so kindly allowing me to use his portrait of Budge and Nancy.

TABLE OF CONTENTS

FOREWORD VII

PREFACE I

PHOTOGRAPHS (between page 174 and 175)

CHAPTER ONE Wartime childhood in Dover; Henry Bell-Irving's action in the English Channel; Budge's early schooling in Vancouver. 11

CHAPTER TWO Attends Shawnigan Lake School on Vancouver Island and Loretto School in Scotland—tough times for a new boy; exciting holidays and a first visit to the Highlands. The death of H.O. Bell-Irving. 31

CHAPTER THREE Attends U.B.C.—briefly; works in the west coast canneries; meets H.R. MacMillan—joins the H.R. MacMillan Co.'s Vancouver office; commissioned in the Seaforth Highlanders of Canada militia; Nancy goes to Cambridge 59

CHAPTER FOUR West Coast winter, 1934/35; Nancy makes an important decision; Budge returns to family business and more adventures on B.C. coast; the Seaforth Armoury is built; the Depression affects recruiting; Budge and Nancy marry; a last sailing holiday; outbreak of war. 83

CHAPTER FIVE Wartime in England; appointed to company commander; coastal defence role; intensive training for overseas role in unspecified invasion. 109

CHAPTER SIX   Final preparations in the west of Scotland; The Sicily landing; the Sicilian campaign; Budge awarded the D.S.O. at Agira.   139

CHAPTER SEVEN   The Italian campaign begins; return to England as Lieutenant-Colonel; C.O. of Battle School; death of brother Roderick over France; return to Italy to command Loyal Edmonton Regiment.   175

CHAPTER EIGHT   Into battle with Edmonton Regiment; the Arno River and Florence; the San Fortunato Ridge; return to command the Seaforth Highlanders of Canada; Private 'Smokey' Smith's V.C.; capers on the Senio River; a D.S.O. for Padre Durnford.   189

CHAPTER NINE   The Seaforths move to northern Europe; Budge's last battle; the liberation of Amsterdam; promoted to Brigadier; sailing on the Ijssel Meer; the Kurt Meyer war-crimes trial; return to Canada.   223

CHAPTER TEN   Joins the British toy manufacturer Lines Bros. Ltd. to represent them in Canada and the U.S.; establishes a manufacturing plant in Montreal. Budge is fired and returns to Vancouver; establishes Bell-Irving Realty; growing success in real-estate business. Various appointments as President of the Vancouver Real Estate Board, President of the Canadian Real Estate Association and President of the Vancouver Board of Trade.   247

CHAPTER ELEVEN   Becomes British Columbia's 23rd Lieutenenant-Governor; coastal cruises with the R.C.N.; convenes Northern Tribal Council meeting on H.M.C.S. *Yukon;* guest of the Canadian army in Germany and Cyprus; takes salute at Edinburgh Tattoo; helps Victoria 'street kids'; appointed to 'Visitor' status for British Columbia universities; designs new personal flag for Lieutenant-Governors; attends Repatriation of the Constitution ceremony in Ottawa; problems with the Soocred Government's financial crisis; farewll to Government House.   275

POSTCRIPT   333

APPENDICES   337

INDEX   349

BIBLIOGRAPHY   361

FOREWORD

DURING THE YEARS OF THE SECOND WORLD WAR, as a young boy I lived in the town of Eastleigh, in the county of Hampshire, England. It was an important railway manufacturing town, but it also contained the Pirelli cable works, and close-by was the Supermarine Spitfire factory. Only five miles due south were the busy Southampton docks. The area became a major target for the Luftwaffe, so its citizens had an ever present reminder of the war. In the build-up to the invasion of Europe, troops from all parts of the British Empire passed through as they marched from the railway station to the army camps that ringed the town. I have never forgotten one glorious summer evening hearing the sound of the pipes in the distance and, running to the end of the street, which joined the main road out to the country I encountered a column of Canadian troops with a piper at their head, marching to join their battalion.

Little did I know then that I would one day become a Canadian citizen, and a member of the Royal Canadian Legion, having done my own stint, albeit in the peace-time British Army in Hong Kong. Even more remote was the knowledge that I would write the biography of one of the well-known Canadian soldiers of the Second World War. Getting to know Budge as we worked together on the manuscript has been a rare privilege. As we developed a working relationship, compromises became easier. He was a hard taskmaster, but we persevered on the text and there was always Nancy to adjudicate and break the tension as only she could with her wonderful charm.

The stories they told of their lives, in peace and war, made the effort worthwhile, with its British Columbia backdrop, especially during the 1930's when Budge worked up the coast in the canneries of the Anglo-British Columbia Packing Company (the A.B.C.), begun by his grandfather, H.O. Bell-Irving. If ever a man had a sense of destiny it was H.O., and he impressed it upon his family. More importantly he impressed upon them a sense of duty, so that their contribution, not just to B.C., but to Canada has been immense. It soon became clear that the Bell-Irving name has taken on a certain mystique, moreso than with most families and interest in them remains high. For that reason I have included more about individual members and events surrounding them than might normally be found in a biography.

In World War I (WW I) the very young Budge had a ring-side seat of the action in or near the English south-coast town of Dover, where his father, Lieut. Henry Beattie Bell-Irving, R.N.V.R. was in the Dover Patrol commanding a fleet of herring drifters converted for anti-submarine operations in the English Channel. Throughout the war there were visits from Budge's five uncles, one an officer with the 16th Battalion, Canadian Scottish (the only one killed) and two of them fighter pilots in the Royal Flying Corps. By 1918 four of H.O.'s sons, including Budge's father, had between them won nine major bravery decorations. Little wonder Budge grew up with an intuitive sense that there would be another war and he would play a part in it.

After attending Loretto school in Scotland Budge spent a summer at one of the A.B.C. canneries, followed by a brief time at UBC before taking a job in the lumber trade, where he came under the influence of the great H.R. MacMillan. He then returned to the Bell-Irving canning business. Early in the 1930's he joined the Seaforth Highlanders of Canada militia and after the required training was commissioned as a 2nd-Lieutenant, beginning a long association with the regiment. His meeting, courtship and eventual marriage to Nancy Symes began a sixty-year partnership which ended with Nancy's death in July 1997.

In November 1939 Budge received orders to embark for England ahead of the unit along with three N.C.O.s to take a small-arms course there. On two hours notice Nancy made the decision to accompany Budge and remained in the U.K. until 1944. As the war progressed, from the landing in Sicily in July, 1943, to the cessation of hostilities in May, 1945 Budge had a series of promotions, eventually leading to the command of two Canadian battalions, firstly the Loyal Edmonton

Regiment and then his own Seaforth Highlanders of Canada. In that time he earned a D.S.O. and bar and the O.B.E. Toward the end of the war he was promoted to Brigadier, commanding the 10th Canadian Infantry Brigade, in the 4th Canadian Armoured Division.

Back in Canada after demobilization he was employed by the British toy-makers, Lines Bros Ltd., setting up a manufacturing plant for them in Montreal. Budge was billeted with chairman Walter Lines and his family early in the war and later, while fighting in Italy Budge conceived the idea of representing them in North America. Walter Lines accepted his proposal. When, after a couple of years the job ended suddenly, Budge returned to Vancouver and set up a real-estate company, Bell-Irving Realty, later A.E. LePage Western.

The culmination of Budge and Nancy's life together came in 1978 with his appointment as British Columbia's 23rd Lieutenant-Governor. They treated the job as a great adventure, and their humility and friendliness quickly won the hearts of people everywhere. Budge kept a detailed daily diary of his five years at Government House, filling nine large hard-cover exercise books. He jokingly claimed that all they contained were references to the ferry rides between Vancouver and Victoria, but they are a treasure-trove of observations, demonstrating a broad perspective of Canada and Canadians. There are many self-deprecating comments, showing Budge's wry sense of humour and that far from having any sense of self-importance, he suffered from what Mike Grenby, one-time Vancouver Sun reporter, referred to as his "embarrassed modesty."

Budge's life has spanned two world wars; he was born when Canada was still a part of the British Empire and the Union Jack flew above Parliament Hill. Vehicles drove on the left-hand side of the road. There have been momentous developments in science and technology, but through it all, while acknowledging the changes, Budge has stuck rigorously to the standards set by his parents and grandparents. These standards have kept him at the forefront of community service, well beyond his Government House tenure and he still continues to serve Canada in many ways.

Raymond Eagle, FSA Scot.,
West Vancouver, B.C.

PREFACE

BRIGADIER THE HON. HENRY PYBUS (BUDGE) BELL-IRVING, O.C., D.S.O. and bar, O.B.E., O.B.C., K.St.J., E.D., C.D., was Lieutenant-Governor of British Columbia from 1978 to 1983. On January 12, 1980 he held a 'clan gathering' of Canadian Bell-Irvings at Government House in Victoria. For the benefit of the many relatives who attended, a family tree of the British Columbia Bell-Irvings was drawn up. It showed that the growth of the family in Canada began when Henry and Duncan, two of the seven children of Henry Bell-Irving (1819-1864), came here in the 1880's. Their widowed mother, Williamina, soon followed with her youngest son, William, and her four daughters, Jane, Margaretta, Sarah and Adriana, all unmarried. Margaretta returned to Scotland to marry Col. E.A. Fraser. Within four generations the Canadian Bell-Irvings had grown to more than 150 members.

The origins of the family began in Scotland with the marriage of Mary Irving to Thomas Bell in 1743. The following year a son was born, christened William. His parent's surnames were combined and William became the first Bell-Irving. His successors were prolific and prospered as landowners in the Scottish Border country. The joining of the Bells and Irvings brought together the estates of Milkbank (originally called "The Strands") and the properties of White Hill and Bankside, all near Lockerbie.

William, who inherited Milkbank, had a son, John, who was born in 1771 and in due time married Margaretta Ogle. It was from their son,

Henry, that the British Columbia Bell-Irvings emerge. Henry was born in 1819 and in 1851 married Williamina McBean. They had seven children, beginning with Jane, born in 1852 and the last, William, born in 1862. Their first son, born in 1856 was also christened Henry and given his grandmother's surname as his second given name, thus becoming Henry Ogle Bell-Irving.

H.O. (as he became known) and his siblings would, in the normal course of events, have had a life like other family members, as Lowland lairds. For generations the land owned by the Bell and Irving families included tenant farms whose occupants had held them for successive generations for an annual rent. The Bell-Irvings participated in country pursuits such as riding to hounds; otter hunting; hosting shooting parties; fishing, and greyhound coursing*. They took a lead in local affairs, acting as Justices of the Peace and becoming officers in the various county volunteer regiments. For H.O. and his siblings their lives were changed by a financial catastrophe that ruined their father, whose wealth came from an import business, primarily textile manufacturing in Guyana. Two tragedies occurred, the first when fire destroyed his warehouse there, which the manager had forgotten to re-insure, and with it went much of Henry's fortune. The second was the Glasgow Bank failure of 1862. He died soon after, in 1864, aged 45. Williamina was left as a comparatively young widow with seven children and now limited resources. There were sufficient funds to provide an annuity of £300 annually from her late husband's estate. A separate sum was provided for the upbringing and education of the children.

An unusual instruction in the will stipulated that Milkbank must not be sold and should be held until the eldest son, Henry Ogle attained majority, when the trustees "shall convey the same to him, if he desires it, at the price of £11,000, which sum will form part of the estate." If Henry was unable or unwilling to take up the offer then it would be passed to Duncan under the same conditions. If he did not or could not take up the option then it would be passed to William. Only after that could the estate be sold outside the family. The other two family estates, White Hill and Bankside had been inherited by two of their father's brothers. For a family already in an impoverished state it would not be easy to find the means to accomplish the purchase of Milkbank for any

---

* Budge remembers the Milkbank greyhound kennels and he has two coursing silver pot trophies in his possession dated 1865.

of the boys. In the meantime the house was let to a cousin until such time as decisions could be made about its future. The agreement would end in 1895.

H.O. was enrolled at Merchiston Castle School in Edinburgh and while he was there, in a letter to her late husband's trustees, his mother said that he was "anxiously desirous to begin the duties of life." He stayed there until he was fifteen, when Williamina took her family to live in Germany. Living was cheaper there, but it also provided adventure and a chance to learn a new language and to acquire different cultural tastes. The trustees of Henry Bell-Irving's estate disagreed about this move but Williamina was a spirited woman and frequently clashed with them over the allocation and spending of the income. She managed to bring up and educate her family in a very satisfactory manner.

They remained in Germany, where H.O. enrolled at Karlsruhe University and took a degree in civil engineering, graduating in about 1878. For many years raising the required sum to purchase Milkbank was his overriding concern. His twenty-first birthday was past, but his brothers were in no better financial shape than he was to purchase the estate.

In 1882, after working on engineering projects in England, he and his younger brother William sailed for Canada, where H.O. found employment with the Canadian Pacific Railway. Engineers and surveyors were in demand for the construction of the Railway and H.O. had no difficulty in finding employment with the company. As the line progressed west so did he, across the rocky Canadian shield and the prairies, having to endure the intense cold of the winters and the heat of summer, which brought mosquito swarms. This was at a time when much of the land was raw wilderness, especially the Rocky Mountains and most of British Columbia. When he reached Shuswap Lake in central British Columbia he walked 50 miles to join the construction gangs working on the line from the coast, at one point being robbed of most of his possessions. H.O. made a decision to leave the railway once he had acquired enough money to strike out on his own. Through his brother Duncan he had heard of the land speculation taking place on the coast and made his way to the small settlement of Granville on Burrard Inlet (the forerunner of Vancouver), which he reached in October 1885.

Duncan had studied medicine at both Heidelberg and Glasgow universities. After obtaining his M.D. he went to British Guyana for two years where he took part in jungle exploration before returning to

Britain. In 1883 he obtained a post on the West Coast of Canada as Medical Officer for the Federal Department of Marine and Fisheries. In 1887 in London he married Ethel Hulbert and brought her to the newly incorporated City of Vancouver where they settled.

Duncan's advice to H.O. was timely. There were many men who, at the time, saw enormous possibilities in this west coast frontier town and became successful in ways that would not have been possible in the places from which they originated. Henry Ogle Bell-Irving though, would do more than simply make money. He had drive, enthusiasm and talents in many directions, but in addition to these he had a sense of destiny, which soon began to unfold. He also had the advantage of education and was able to use it in this new land. He was an accomplished water-colour artist, painting many pictures in the Canadian Rockies as he travelled through with the construction gangs; he was a first-class figure skater, a yachtsman, big-game hunter and a keen rugby player. (There is a collection of H.O.'s watercolours in the British Columbia Provincial Archives in Victoria. The ones of the Rockies are particularly interesting as they were painted under the most primitive conditions, but have survived well.)

Over the next few years he worked as an architect, real estate agent and land developer. In 1886 H.O. returned to Britain to marry Marie Isabel del Carmen Beattie (Bella), who came from a wealthy Torquay family. They had first met at Lucerne twelve years before and were so mutually attracted that, according to family belief, they made a vow to marry as soon as circumstances allowed.

They were married on February 11th, 1886 and returned to Canada via New York and San Francisco, crossing the U.S. on the already completed transcontinental railroad, then by steamer from San Francisco to Vancouver. Bella had as much spirit as her husband or she would not have undertaken such a long voyage to share an uncertain future with him. Even so, she was not at first taken with Vancouver, despite the natural beauty of the west coast. It was still a rough place and entering George Black's hotel she tripped over a corpse lying on the floor. A hulking logger at the bar jokingly told her "Don't 'urt 'im Ma'am; 'e's dead!" It was not a good start. When they got to their room H.O. drew aside the drapes to show her a wonderful sunset filling the western sky. Her only remark is alleged to have been, "Damn the sunset; take me home!" It is to her credit that she stayed and became a tower of strength to her husband, despite increasing ill-health.

Her consolation was needed when, on June 13, 1886, the still infant town was consumed by fire. Along with most of the other businesses and many homes, H.O. and his partner Robert Taplow lost their office and everything in it. Fortunately neither lost their homes or families. The fire was started by a slash burn fanned by a high wind. The courage shown by the citizens was remarkable and soon the town was a hive of activity as the buildings were replaced.

While H.O. looked for more business opportunities, on May 23, 1887 he was invited to be present when the last spike was driven in at Craigellachie to complete the Canadian Pacific Railway.

In the same year Duncan, H.O.'s brother returned to Vancouver with his new bride. Their first son, Duncan Peter (known as Peter) was born in 1888. Two daughters and another son, Robin, followed. Duncan was totally different in nature to H.O. Easy going and affable he was a great socialiser and was involved in several fraternity organizations. Budge is sure that he acquired a Scottish accent, which he did not possess when he first came here, and he was a leading figure in the St. Andrews and Caledonia Society.

In 1889 H.O. chartered from the Hudson Bay Company, the 879 ton sailing ship *Titania* to bring a mixed cargo from London to Vancouver, via Cape Horn. She arrived in Vancouver on July 25, the first ship to sail directly between the two ports. Her cargo included plumbing supplies, lead pipe for water and gas lines, coal sacks, Rose's lime juice, salt and a good supply of Usher's whiskey.

The two over-riding industries in British Columbia were fishing and forestry and the former appealed to H.O. The salmon numbered in millions and runs were to be found on every river up and down the coast from Oregon to Alaska. He organized a return shipment of sockeye from the Fraser River to be sold in the United Kingdom. With the success of this behind him, by 1889 H.O. was prepared to expand to other areas of the coast, but wanted to ensure sufficient capital for the purpose.

He knew that by returning to Britain he could excite business people there to look at investment opportunities in B.C. First, H.O. acquired options on nine canneries, seven on the Fraser River and two on the Skeena River in northern B.C. On April 14, 1891 he issued a prospectus and by the end of the year he had raised £200,000, capital to begin his venture, a portion of the funds coming from Scottish relatives, especially cousins, brothers John and James Jardine (J.J.) Bell-Irving. Their mother was Mary (nee Jardine) whose forbear, William Jardine founded the far eastern trading company Jardine Matheson. Both John and J.J. Bell-Irving had spent several years in the Shanghai and Hong Kong offices of the firm.

In December 1891 H.O. incorporated the Anglo-British Columbia Packing Company Ltd., known throughout its long history as the A.B.C. Packing Company (or simply the A.B.C.), with its head office in London. Henry Ogle's business acumen is revealed by the fact that while other people in London were elected as directors, he found a partner, Robert Horn Paterson (another Scot), and formed Bell-Irving & Paterson Ltd. It was appointed management and selling agent in British Columbia. Instead of taking a salary from the A.B.C. Packing Co., H.O. drew large commissions based on production, plus of course, options to purchase company shares. In 1895 the partnership with Paterson was dissolved and it became simply H. Bell-Irving and Co. Ltd.

The A.B.C. Packing Company soon became one of the largest salmon packing enterprises on the west coast. While most of the salmon went to the United Kingdom other countries purchased shipments, including France, China, India, Australia and New Zealand. In 1895 the Anglo-British Columbia Packing Company moved into the United States and established the Fidalgo Island Packing Company, which in turn managed five other companies, Lopez Island Fishing Co., Orcas Island Fishing Co., Lummi Island Fishing Co., the Bellingham Bay Fishing Co. and the San Juan Fishing Co.

By this time, although H.O. had made sufficient money, he had decided not to return to Scotland to claim Milkbank. There is no doubt that it would have presented no financial difficulties, but he no longer desired the life of a Lowland Border laird after his free and adventurous life in British Columbia. Neither Duncan or William wished to return to Scotland and the estate was sold to a cousin, William Ogle, at least keeping it in the family.

This single decision of H.O.'s has had a profound effect on British Columbia's history and the contribution that his progeny have made to the province has been immense. As he succeeded in building his fortune, Milkbank was not forgotten though. He built a large house on Harwood Street in what is now Vancouver's West End and called it The Strand's, the original name of the Scottish house. It was also partly modelled after Milkbank. The centre-piece was a large hall, similar to the one at Milkbank, complete with a massive stone fireplace with a stag's head above it. Here much of the family activity took place. When completed it would play a vital part in the family for many years. It was a grand house and equalled the homes of many other aspiring families. Once the family was settled a housewarming dance was arranged for 150 people. H.O. was on the floor for every dance.

Today the original house at Milkbank is a barely recognizable ruin, the roof having been removed years ago to avoid paying taxes on the property. Likewise in the West End, The Strands was demolished years ago.

It has already been mentioned that H.O.'s mother, Williamina also came to Canada with her four daughters sometime after her sons had arrived. She settled near Cochrane, Alberta where William had leased government land to create a ranch. Life was hard on the prairies and it is another example of her toughness. An accomplished horsewoman, she frequently won prizes at local gymkhanas. Williamina is buried on the Stoney Indian reserve at Morley, near Cochrane. This came about when the reserve was enlarged and the cemetery came within the new boundary. Her daughter Adriana married rancher William Duncan Kerfoot, a U.S. born rancher and they had a large family. William Bell-Irving married Bella's sister, Mary Helen and they also had a large family.

On the coast H.O. and Bella also began to raise a family. Despite a list of ailments in H.O.'s notebook which, allowing for the less exact diagnostic capabilities of the time included arthritis, Parkinson's Disease, epilepsy and neuritis, Bella bore H.O. ten children, six of them boys. First came Henry, in 1887 (second name Beattie, from his mother's surname—a practice continued for the first-born son for the next three generations); Richard was born in 1888, Isabel in 1889; Roderick in 1891; Malcolm (Mick) in 1892; Anita in 1893; Alan Duncan (always known as Duncan) in 1894; Mary in 1896; Aeneas in 1898 and Helen Beatrice (always known as Beatrice) in 1904.

Bella's spirit was indomitable and it was said of her that far from lowering her standards to meet those of this new, still rough town, she was determined that it would rise to meet hers. Through it all she kept a keen, though sardonic sense of humour. Once she was unceremoniously spilled from her wheelchair while being pushed by three of her children and they lost control. She wrote of the incident: "Fortunately I was not hurt and when the children saw me laughing they started to laugh too and we continued our walk and listened to the band."

H.O. was the undisputed family head, but Bella nevertheless made her presence felt and on occasion could be as tough as her husband. He had very little sympathy for illness and even when the first world war came and two of his sons were critically wounded he could not remain by their bedsides for very long. There are many diary references to Bella's illnesses and the weeks that she was confined to bed. Despite her incapacity, she wholeheartedly supported his endeavours and was not above reminding her children of this when she thought it was needed. In a letter to Henry when he was placed in charge of a northern cannery she demonstrated a rare prescience. She told him: "You must not expect to settle down for ever as a cannery manager. You must attain greater things than this before you rest content!!! Father is building up a great future for his sons, [and] if they are willing to grasp the situation, they should in time all become very important men both in this, and the old country."

As well as his business ventures, H.O. took a great interest in community affairs in the rapidly growing city of Vancouver. He became an alderman and chaired the Board of Works. He was a member of the Vancouver Board of Trade and its president through 1894/97. When he heard that a group of expatriate Scots wished to found a Highland regiment in the City of Vancouver he was anxious to assist. The idea came from members of the Gaelic Society at a meeting in May, 1909. Other Scottish Societies were invited to participate in subsequent meetings.

It was inevitable that a man with the force and energy of Henry Ogle Bell-Irving would tread on a few toes and this was the case with the founding of this now famous militia regiment in which his family has served with such distinction. One of the groups represented at the early meetings was a pipe band formed under the direction of Pipe Major Hector MacKenzie, a proud Highlander who was born at Lochcarron in 1866. Interviewed in October 1939, by the indefatigable Major J. Matthews, Vancouver's first city archivist, Mackenzie had this to say of H.O.:

"John Hendry, owner of the Hastings Sawmill was a wealthy man and we were going to ask him to defray the cost of raising the regiment. At a meeting to discuss this H.O. Bell-Irving—you know how important he thought himself—took it upon himself, much to the disgust of many, to steal the whole show and just rode right over everybody. He was very domineering."

According to MacKenzie, the nucleus of the regimental pipe-band was formed from the Vancouver Pipers' Society with headquarters in the 1100 block of Seymour Street. H.O. was a regular attender at these meetings.

In 1910 Major R.G. Edwards Leckie was nominated as its first Commanding Officer and was subsequently accepted by the various Scottish societies. The regiment was designated the 72nd Highlanders of Canada and in a short time it was given the title, 72nd Seaforth Highlanders of Canada. Their first public appearance was on June 22nd, 1912, Coronation Day for King Edward VII. The event was held in Recreation Park. H.O.'s third son, Roderick Bell-Irving, was one of the first members to receive a commission in the regiment.

Henry Ogle Bell-Irving continued to mastermind the company he had founded and it weathered many critical times, from price crashes through oversupply or competition, to shortages caused by over-fishing or natural fluctuations. During most of those years the company continued to pay handsome dividends to its shareholders. Despite increasing age H.O. was reluctant to give up the reins to his sons, preferring to make all decisions himself, which did not sit well with the more ambitious ones. It was a shock to many when, at age 75 H.O. became ill with cancer and died in February 1931. He remained active almost to the end and was skating in Switzerland just a few weeks before he died. The leading obituaries called him 'Dean of the West Coast Salmon Industry'.

CHAPTER ONE

IN THE PERSONALITY OF HENRY OGLE BELL-IRVING there was an unusual mixture of the practical man and the dreamer. His notebooks were written up methodically year after year and acted both as diaries and a place for his thoughts, practical and philosophical. There were notes about the canneries, and in one were rough plans for The Strands. He often jotted down inspirational quotations from famous writers and poets. From Disreali: "The secret of success is continuance of purpose." From Emerson he copied "Discontent is the want of self-reliance—it is the infirmity of will."

As an artist he could not have been unaware of the scenic quality of the Fraser River and its estuary, but other things dominated his mind on visits to the river. In 1893 a threatened fishermens' strike was narrowly averted and the company was forced to increase pay to get enough boats out. The season was extended by one week, which helped to increase the catch. In the 1900-1901 season there was a partial failure of the salmon run on the river, which called for the Fraser River Cannery Association to regulate the number of boats.

In 1903 H.O. took his family back to Britain to provide better educational opportunities. Henry was already attending Loretto, a well-known Scottish public school, where he became a piper in the school's Officers' Training Corps band. The other boys were sent either to Loretto or a preparatory school, according to their age, and the girls were sent to private schools too. Bella was carrying their last child,

Helen Beatrice, who was born in 1904. They remained in England until 1908 and rented a house in Devon, though H.O. spent only about three months of each year there. The rest of the time he was in Vancouver. Duncan and Aeneas remained at Loretto to finish their education.

With the growing success of the A.B.C. it was natural that H.O.'s sons, beginning with Henry, would be offered employment if they so wished and in 1905 Henry left Loretto to return to Vancouver where on April 14 he began work with the A.B.C. He had shown himself to be in the same stubborn mold as his father—and possessing very much the same self-reliance. This had developed in his early years when he and his friends took their canoes and paddled to all the deserted places that subsequently became well-known beauty spots; Lynn Canyon, the Capilano River, Spanish Banks and Jericho beach. They camped and fished and explored, occasionally warding off an inquisitive black bear.

An opportunity to explore further afield came when, in November 1909, H.O. purchased Pasley Island from an eastern American, Anson Stokes. Pasley is situated in the southern approach to Howe Sound, with glorious water and island views, and of mountain ranges encircling the Sound to the north. Together with a small attachment to the south shore, the island contains two hundred and forty-seven acres. It is named after Admiral Sir Thomas Pasley who, as a young officer had accompanied Captain George Richards on a naval expedition to the British Columbia coast between 1858 and 1863. In the latter part of the last century it was crown-granted to Ralph Gibson, after whom Gibson's Landing was later named.

The Bell-Irvings had camped on the south of the island on several occasions and its purchase, for $10,000, was to be of enormous value to their steadily growing family, as it has been to more recent additional owners. Over the years the value of Pasley has steadily increased. With its sheltered bays and good anchorages, Pasley offers a combination of privacy, yet easy access from Vancouver; a locally rare mix of level meadow-land with surrounding forest, and an adequate supply of fresh water.

Despite the problems and growing competition for the Anglo-British Columbian Packing Company, profits continued and dividends of 10% were paid consistently. Chairman James Whittal had died in 1904 and for the next twenty years, H.O.'s cousin, John Bell-Irving chaired the company. In some years the profits well exceeded the forecast; for 1910 the assured profit was forecast at £31,000 but the actual figure was £44,934. A dividend of 12% was paid on ordinary shares. In that year the commission paid to H. Bell-Irving & Company was £9000, which at that time translated to $40,000, a not unusual amount in following years. At the 1910 annual general meeting John Bell-Irving told the shareholders:

"Gentlemen, this is the 20th year of the company and I would just mention that shareholders have, during that time received no less than 160% on preference and 168% on ordinary shares." Two years later the dividend payment was 40%.

In December 1909, Henry was recruited at very short notice to act as 4th Officer on the *Empress of India*, sailing from Vancouver to Hong Kong, via Japan. It happened that he was competing with his friend Charles Oxlade, 3rd Officer on the liner, for the hand in marriage of Miss Annie (Nan) Hylda Pybus. Oxlade did not want to leave Henry with an advantage while he was away on this long voyage and so conveniently arranged the offer. As it happened Henry won her hand soon after returning, with the added benefit of a wonderful paid 'holiday' as well. Nan was the eldest daughter of the Bell-Irving's neighbour, Captain Henry Pybus, who had served both in the Royal Navy Reserve and as a master-mariner on the C.P.R. Empress liners, and was a good friend of H.O.'s.

The great far-east trading company, Jardine Matheson and Co., was at the height of its power. The Bell-Irvings are related to the Jardines and are well represented on the board. As soon as Henry arrived in Hong Kong and made his presence known at the company headquarters he was entertained royally, including some good snipe shooting with the Governor of Hong Kong.

Henry required permission from his father, which was given, but H.O. could not resist a parting shot: "Remember" he told Henry, "a rolling stone gathers no moss." When he returned home, heeding his father's words, Henry quickly put his mind once more to the everyday problems of salmon fishing and canning. He had a very practical streak and was much more at home on the wharves and with the fishermen than sitting behind a desk in the company office. He became a familiar sight in the canneries up and down the coast, where he put in long hours when needed, which did not escape his father's eye. He soon became a trouble-shooter and problem solver. By 1910 both Richard and Roderick were in the company employ, though just before the outbreak of war Roderick moved on to Balfour Guthrie, one of B.C.'s forest product companies. By this time Malcolm, the fourth son, more commonly known in the family as Mick, was also working for his father.

In 1912 Henry married Nan Pybus. The following year, on January 21st, their first son, Henry Pybus was born. A cryptic note was made by H.O. "Henry's wife had a son, born 5.30 p.m." On March 16 came "Henry's boy baptized." Nan was not yet twenty but she soon proved to be a very capable wife and mother. For reasons known only to her the name 'Budge' came very early on and has stayed with him ever since, in peace and war. Before the First World War began a second child, Ruth, was born. Only days before Budge was born, his father was spoken to severely by H.O. for 'talking back.'

Henry and Nan engaged a nanny, Kate, a young English woman who remained with them for several years. Henry was often away on company business and in the few months of peace that remained his family sometimes accompanied him to the canneries. Frequently accommodation was non-existent and they camped nearby. By early 1914 the news from Britain indicated that war with Germany was almost inevitable and in the Dominions there was great excitement among the young men at the prospect of going to Europe to fight for the mother country. All the Bell-Irving sons were of military age excepting Aeneas and Duncan, who were still at Loretto, though Duncan, the fifth son was in his last term and looking forward to returning to B.C.

When the First World War (WW I) commenced Henry was 27 years old and was encouraged by his father to join up, as were other company men. Even though H.O. knew it would make things difficult at the canneries he was determined to do his bit for the war effort. Henry was at one of the northern plants when war was declared. His father wrote to him:

> "There is a movement here to increase the Naval Reserve Volunteers to 1000 men and that would be a good branch for you to take up. Doubtless part of the force will be for service in B.C. only, and part would go elsewhere. You might make preliminary inquiries as to what young men at the cannery would like to join up."

The sons who were of military age; Henry, Richard (Dick), Roderick, Mick and now Duncan, volunteered immediately. Roderick and Dick already held commissions in the Seaforth Highlanders of Canada militia. Duncan had returned immediately to Vancouver, but even with his father's influence he could not obtain a commission, as there were no vacancies remaining. He went to Europe as a private—

with his own motorbike, which his father had purchased for him—and for the first year of the war was a despatch rider. Mick went to England and took private flying lessons before joining the Royal Flying Corps. In 1917 Aeneas joined the Royal Artillery straight from Loretto. Dr. Duncan's sons, Peter and Robin joined the armed forces also, both of them in the Royal Canadian Engineers. Peter was killed in action in France on February 26, 1915.

H.O. was frustrated by the failure of the government to ensure adequate defences on the west coast and in a letter to his cousin John Bell-Irving in September 1914 he wrote, "I am busy trying to secure formation of a stronger naval reserve here, but the government is slow to respond, while New Zealand is showing us the way. A good hammer by a German cruiser would do us good."

In finding ways to help the war effort, H.O. sought practical solutions. He wrote a letter to the A.B.C. board in which he suggested purchasing an armoured car to present to the army. Knowing there was a shortage of suitable craft on the west coast he offered three fish packers to supplement the few naval vessels at Esquimalt naval base. The offer was turned down by the base commanding officer, but not to be put off by this, H.O. cabled the British Admiralty in London, and his offer was accepted. He accused the Dominion Government of a "narrow minded cheese-paring attitude" towards both the militia and the R.N.V.R., saying it made him wary of them.

Henry was granted a Royal Naval Volunteer Reserve commission as a sub-lieutenant and placed in charge of this small packer flotilla, the *Holly Leaf, Ivy Leaf* and *Fir Leaf*. The document granting Henry's commission has no reference to the Royal Canadian Navy on it, as all activities came under the British Admiralty. The Royal Canadian Navy came into being in 1910 under the Naval Services Act and at the outbreak of war it had only two ships, the twenty-three year old light cruisers *Rainbow* and the equally elderly *Niobe*. The former on the west coast and the latter on the east coast. What few officers there were had transferred from the Royal Navy, with hopes of quicker promotion in the fledgling service.

While waiting for Henry to receive his commission, H.O. agreed to provide his salary until the Admiralty began to pay him. Even though Henry was in an acting capacity, Budge recalls that his father had to shave-off his "rather fearsome moustache" as he was now a naval officer.

Henry also arranged the initial contracts with the navy and was chastised by H.O., who said, "It looks as though they got the better of you on the contract. I had figured on financing you personally, but not doing so for the boats and crews. It would have been well if you had rung me before signing. The contract was a one-sided affair. This is not a time to quibble, it is true, but one does not like to be made a convenience of in such a way." In a contrite shift of mind he ended, "They probably mean well." The boats were on loan free of charge on the condition that they would be replaced if damaged or lost.

In early October 1914 the three A.B.C. Co. packers were added to the Esquimalt strength. They were fitted with torpedoes that were, according to one source, taken from H.M.S. *Rainbow*. A release mechanism for the torpedoes was designed by the chief engineer of the Esquimalt yard. They were secured just below the gunwales and held in place by shaped wooden brackets and secured by a chain. A lanyard was pulled in the wheelhouse which released the weapon and activated the propulsion.

On October 5th Henry was ordered to take his boats from the company's Phoenix cannery at Steveston to Esquimalt and on the 10th the packers sailed, with white Ensigns flying from Esquimalt to Alert Bay on the inside passage at the north end of Vancouver Island. Here they remained for some weeks, ready for action.

The reason for their presence at Alert Bay was a belief by the naval authorities that two enemy warships, the *Nurnberg* and *Leipzig*, would enter the inside passage and work their way down past Nanaimo to Vancouver and Victoria. One official report talked of a fear that they would then 'demand ransom' from these cities. To prevent this from happening, as well as the presence of the packer flotilla, Captain Powlett of the Esquimalt based cruiser, H.M.C.S. *Newcastle*, ordered mines to be laid around Malcolm Island, he deployed a battalion of militia on nearby Ellen Island and mounted a 4" gun at Seymour Narrows.

Sub-Lieutenant Henry Bell-Irving's flotilla remained at Alert Bay through December where he was joined by his wife Nan and their children, Budge and Ruth. On December 8 there was a decisive battle near the Falkland Islands in which Von Spee suffered the loss of six of his seven ships taking part in it. Among them were the *Nurnberg* and *Leipzig*. This led to a lessening of the fear of infiltration on the west coast and by Christmas the need for the A.B.C. packer flotilla was gone. (See Appendix 1)

The packers returned to their original role, but Henry Bell-Irving remained on active service and on January 9, 1915 he left Vancouver for the United Kingdom to report to the Admiralty. His wife and family, complete with nanny Kate, sailed with him to England. Even at the age of twenty-eight, Henry was not away from the influence of his father. On January 7th, 1915 H.O. wrote to him:

> "I have withdrawn my veto to your taking your wife and family home with you, on the assurance by Annie and yourself that you have the cash necessary or are ready to provide it.
>
> Though I think it is a great error of judgment and contrary to the dictates of common sense, I am ready to acquiesce and pay your personal expenses on the journey there and back, and also £50 for uniforms; £30 on arrival in London and £35 for each month thereafter while in Europe."

Aside from revealing the control that H.O. still had on his sons, and all of them received generous allowances while in the armed services, it also shows that he still thought of Britain as home despite his success in Canada. Also at that time there was a very popular belief on the British side that the war would be over by Christmas, or not long into 1915 at the latest, so he felt safe in being so generous, especially as profits from the A.B.C. were doing well and his agent's fees for 1915 were £14,730.00 (close to $73,000).

Budge was not quite two years old at this time and was six when he returned to Canada. He has retained very distinct impressions of those Great War years in England. Dover is situated on the English Channel and in a strategic location, therefore the town and vicinity saw more action than most other British cities. With only twenty miles of water separating the English and French coasts, naval engagements were frequently witnessed by the townspeople. Often the frontline guns in Belgium or France could be heard if there was a large offensive going on.

Early in 1915 the Royal Navy formed the Dover Patrol and when Henry's experience on the British Columbia coast was discovered he was attached to the Dover Drifter Patrol and promoted to full lieutenant. These small vessels were in peacetime the mainstay of the British fishing fleets. Most of the crews, like Henry had been civilians just a few months before and nearly all of them had been employed as fishermen in the drifter fleet.

By June 1915 the Dover Drifter Patrol had reached a strength of 135 vessels including two yachts, with a strength of 1500 officers and men. The drifters were engaged in mine-laying and putting in place anti-submarine nets, made of thin, galvanized steel wire and 120 feet in depth. The drifters also protected the marked channels known only to Royal Navy and allied vessels. Frequently the drifters met and engaged enemy submarines while laying mines or nets and several of Henry's colleagues won their decorations while engaged in this action.

Frequent gales were encountered. A gale in the Straits of Dover is fierce, and the power of the sea must be seen to be believed. It is at the junction of the English Channel and the North Sea and with wind and wave fighting the tide in a 20 mile wide channel the seas can be wild. At many points where there are houses just yards from the beach it is common for spray from a breaking wave to reach the roof of a three story house. The task of keeping position in a drifter flotilla, when most of the time the other nearby ships were lost from sight in a giant wave-trough required incredible skill.

Although Henry lived at home he was away for many hours at a stretch, both day and night. The strain of hours at sea and engagements with the enemy could not be hidden from his family. There were visits from his brothers in the Royal Flying Corps and from Roderick, by this time a front-line officer in the 16th Battalion, Canadian Scottish. There were, as well, the wartime activities of a garrison town with the dramatic outline of the massive castle high on the eastern side of the town. It is little wonder that as the war progressed, young Budge began to carry several memorable impressions. Dover suffered from both air-raids and shelling by enemy ships, and he remembers many hours spent in the cellar with his mother, his sisters and nanny Kate.

From February 1915 to October 1917 Henry was at sea almost continuously, often in dangerous conditions. The drifters suffered high losses and in one engagement over October 26-27, 1916, no less than seven of them were sunk and two severely damaged. Fifty-five crew members died and several were taken prisoner. Tragically, several drifters were sunk by their own mines when a crew became over-confident in handling them. Constant vigilance was needed and one careless move would result in the destruction of a vessel and the loss of her crew.

One of Henry's crossings to Ostende was undertaken in fog and when he returned his senior officer accused him of not having gone the whole way. He did not believe that Henry could have completed his mission and returned in the time it took. Backed by his crew, Henry angrily protested and asked for a court of inquiry to clear his name. He invited his accuser and the court President to accompany him on the next occasion of fog, which they could hardly refuse. What they had not reckoned with was a trick that Henry had learned on the B.C. coast from the Union Steamship captains. This was to use a whistle when nearing the coast and timing the echo to gauge the nearness of land. It is a method that Budge learned from his father and has used several times over the years to navigate in the B.C. coast's Inside Passage. Henry's naval colleagues were duly impressed and he was completely exonerated.

There were occasional unexpected rewards. It was not unusual to find barrels of wine or hogsheads of port floating in the sea, which were shared among a grateful crew. Other booty was occasionally found and Budge has in his possession a large oak chest which his father found floating in the English Channel from the S.S. *Port Nicholson* after she had foundered.

By the end of 1916, British coastal forces had no fewer than 3,000 vessels, from small armed yachts, drifters, sloops, torpedo boats to destroyers, all engaged solely in anti-submarine work. This was as well, because in late 1916 Allied intelligence received reports of a new submarine offensive, which came into effect on February 1, 1917. The area of operation included the North Sea, English Channel and the Western Approaches.

German seaplanes took on a more important role in activities around the eastern end of the English Channel. Some carried torpedoes, which according to Admiral Sir Reginald Bacon, Senior Officer in Charge of the Dover Patrol, were not always used effectively, as those used against drifters frequently missed by a wide margin. The Admiralty would not believe that these aircraft were responsible for the destruction of anti-submarine nets by firing at the glass supporting buoys. Henry set out to see if he could catch them red-handed and it was in an action on June 11, 1917 against five German seaplanes that Henry won his first D.S.C. (see Appendix 2)

Although Nan constantly wrote of being so lucky in having her husband home between patrols, she was fully aware of the danger he underwent every time he put to sea. She knew that any explosion, near or far, might herald news of his injury or death. In the midst of such uncertainty Henry and Nan found solace in their increasing family. In the course of the war they added two more girls, Mary McBean (Molly), born November 20, 1915 and Wendy, born on May 22, 1917. In letters from Henry and Nan either to Bella or Nan's parents there are many descriptions of Budge and his activities which showed he was very intelligent—and a shade precocious. He was at times a handful and letters home ranged from Nan telling his grandmother he possessed a 'sweet nature' to his father proudly saying he was a 'wee devil' who was never out of mischief for a minute if he could help it. By the spring of 1915 he was often treated to rides on the motor-bike which his Uncle Duncan had left behind for Henry's use when he could obtain petrol. Budge enjoyed these very much despite the precariousness of the ride.

He was only two and a half years old when his father brought down the sea-planes yet he has a distinct recollection of seeing the prisoners come ashore in an oddly assorted change of clothes after their rescue from the English Channel. Another memory is of one of the seaplane's floats, the only piece that was rescued, being split in half and a section being placed in the large garden playpen as an extra 'toy'. Later Henry's crew shot down an observation balloon, towed by a German boat. The material, a light green oil-cloth was used to make raincoats for the family.

Zeppelin raids were frequent in south-east England, mainly at night. One night in August 1916 a zeppelin tried to get directly over the town but the defence batteries prevented this and his bombs dropped harmlessly in the surrounding cornfields. Henry took his family outside to have a look at this massive object which appeared to hang in the sky, caught in the glare of the searchlights. With the noise of the sirens and the guns firing, it must have presented a surrealistic picture to the fertile imagination of a child. In a more successful raid during which fourteen bombs were dropped on the town, creating a 'fearful row', and forcing the family to take shelter in the cellar, Budge announced "I don't feel very well and I'm not friendly with the Germans."

The black-out was very effective and was observed in the whole of Britain, even the most remote areas of Wales and Scotland. It was achieved with curtains made of heavy black material or by fitted wooden frames covered in thick paper. People who showed the smallest wedge of light were suspected of signalling to the enemy. The Bell-Irvings were well aware of non-compliance. Henry complained that it was almost impossible to light his pipe at night outdoors without being jumped on by a policeman or army sentry. One night a policeman knocked at their door and charged them with sending Morse signals from their home. Henry thought the wind was blowing one of the window curtains just enough to let light through intermittently and someone had reported it.

He wrote, "every speck of light has to be covered after dusk and cars and bikes are used at night without lights and at the drivers own risk."

It was difficult for the people in Vancouver to picture the Britain in which Henry and Nan found themselves. Their first rented house was surrounded by the most peaceful countryside and Nan was pleased with her garden, which was filled with roses of every type from the hedge-rose to climbers on the house wall. She wrote: "The fields are simply yellow and white with buttercups and daisies and the hedges are covered in flowering thorn. There are plenty of shady lanes and fields with large trees in them. The babies play outside and have their tea there on warm afternoons and enjoy themselves thoroughly."

In contrast to this idyll the countryside was interlaced with trenches and in four years of letters to their families in Vancouver at very regular intervals there is hardly one where Nan or Henry do not mention some indication of the war's impact on Dover, either a raid by sea or air or local defence guns firing for practice. Living in the country proved to be impractical and despite the increased risk from air-raids they moved to a rented house in Dover. (See Appendix 3)

It was inevitable that with so many Bell-Irvings serving in Europe, including Isabel, who was nursing in London, there would be occasions for them to get together. One was on December 9th, 1916 when Roderick married Nora Benwell of Vancouver, with Duncan as best man. H.O. was not above using his influence to bring the family together, although even he was thwarted in March 1917, when Isabel married Ben Sweeney. H.O. and his second daughter, Anita, travelled from Vancouver to attend the wedding. They were stopped at New York because the U.S. had severed diplomatic relations with Germany, heightening the dangers of passage by sea. There was also at the time a submarine scare because of the February declaration. The wedding went ahead as planned, Henry gave his sister away in place of his father and Budge was the page boy.

When, on May 22, 1917 Wendy was born, the name came from a suggestion of Budge's, who had become fascinated with the story of *Peter Pan*. One of the first Bell-Irvings to be killed in action was Henry's cousin Peter, son of Dr. Duncan Bell-Irving. Had Nan produced a boy he would have received the name Peter, so naming a girl Wendy, from the main female character of the popular pantomime was a logical choice.

Nan was by this time doing war-work in a local government office. Fortunately she had the faithful Kate to rely on as well as nurses who came in to help after her pregnancies. By the summer of 1917 the war was making things more and more difficult for civilians. Food prices were increasing every week and rationing was becoming tighter, especially dairy products and meat. A burglar broke into the cellar and stole a sack of potatoes. Butter too, was both scarce and expensive and Henry and Nan were shocked when they went for a holiday to St Michael's, Bella's family home near Torquay, to see the amount of food that was served to them, more in one day than they would consume in a week at Dover.

Another problem was keeping the house warm. Central heating was unknown in the type of house they could afford to rent and coal was becoming increasingly expensive. Anyone who has experienced the raw cold of a British seaside town will know the importance of keeping warm, especially with three young children to keep from getting colds, or worse still bronchitis. One Christmas Budge got a lesson in shortages and high prices when he decided to hang up a pillowcase instead of a stocking. He was thrilled the next morning to see it bulging and opened it with great excitement to find it filled with coal! Crying in disappointment did not move his father one bit.

Dover was becoming like an armed camp, with only the railway and three roads open, all of them strictly guarded. Passes had a photo I.D. inserted and movement was restricted. Henry now had a sidecar for the motor bike and fortunately was entitled to enough petrol to take his family on outings once in a while. Because of Nan's war work she had an identity card to show when stopped by sentries, as they frequently were. Once Budge tumbled out of the sidecar but aside from giving his mother a nasty fright he was not hurt and his only concern was being left behind. His uncles Mick and Duncan miraculously survived their exploits in the Royal Flying Corps despite grievous wounds and injuries. Looking back at the frailty of the machines they were flying and the number of times they plunged to earth, the fact that they both survived is unbelievable. (See Appendix 4)

Although he remained in Dover, Henry's war was no less exciting than that of his brothers. One particular episode in which he played an active part was to have repercussions that went on into the early 1920's and showed his great tenacity. Late in the day on November 24, 1916 while returning from patrol in a full south-west gale he spotted a large ship which was drifting on the tide. Though she was flying the Red Ensign of the Merchant Navy it was clear that she had been abandoned. The vessel was the Glasgow registered *Ernaston*, of 6000 tonnes.

If left alone the ship would founder on the Goodwin Sands or be driven into a minefield not far away. As either location would lead to her destruction, Henry decided to board her. He was accompanied by another drifter commander, Lieut. David Watson and Seaman Latta. They found some damage to the bow and one of the forward compartments had been punctured and held 16 feet of water. The log confirmed the ship had been abandoned after hitting a mine while en-route from Rouen to South Shields. By first light, with sufficient steam and a running north-east tide, very cautiously the ship made weigh, as with great skill this small crew overcame steering problems caused by the ruptured compartment. Aided by the tide she was taken into sheltered waters.

With a salvage value calculated at £120,000, reckoned at 1/3 the ship's value (though in wartime this was halved), Henry and his assistants could look forward to sharing £20,000, a claim that was unequivocally acknowledged by the Admiralty, who expressed "their Lordships' appreciation."

It was then discovered that the ship was under direct Admiralty orders and therefore in Royal Navy service, which precluded them from claiming salvage. Even so, Vice Admiral Sir Roger Keyes of the Dover Patrol proved a true supporter and did not let the matter rest, pointing out to their Lordships that a very dangerous situation was averted by the action of these men. Neither did Henry give up; he continued corresponding with the Admiralty and the insurance underwriters for several years. Finally, in 1921 he and Watson were awarded £1000 each and Latta received £400. It was a vindication for Henry, even though it took almost five years to receive this reduced amount, which the Admiralty named a 'gratuity.'

On November 2, 1917 with Lieut. Alexander Daniells he was awarded a bar to his D.S.C. The citation read: "For gallantry when one of H.M. mine sweepers struck a mine." By this time Henry had been given a new job. Some technical advances were being made in submarine detection, one of them being the use of Hydrophones to detect underwater sounds. Henry was selected to teach this to other crews. His job was to select the best sailors on each ship and teach them to distinguish between different underwater sounds and thus detect the presence of a submarine nearby. He was not required to go to sea as much, and was getting a well-earned rest after almost three years of continuous patrolling.

Nan was concerned about the continuing raids on Dover. In a letter to Bella she said: "... the raids over Dover have been very tiresome and not good for the kiddies. Not so much the danger from bombs as the nerve-wracking noise and dreary old noisy sirens, though I must say we are all quite used to it."

As though to confirm her fears, a few days later there was a raid which lasted from 11 p.m. to 3.30 a.m. All of that time they were in the cellar, though Kate declared that she would henceforth stay upstairs despite the raids because a mouse had run over her face in the night and she said this scared her more than the bombs and gunfire!

Budge was still being a 'wee Devil' and gave his sister Ruth a half-bottle of Friar's Balsam to drink. Her parents had to make her take Epicakana to induce vomitting and Henry gave Budge a 'good leathering.' Ruth was none the worse for the ordeal and showed no ill effects afterwards. Budge is sure that about this time they woke up one morning to find that snow had fallen overnight and he convinced Ruth to climb out of the nursery window onto the roof to gather some up. She slipped and fell to the ground. How far it was he cannot remember, but perhaps a combination of snow and a soft flower-bed broke her fall and she was again unharmed. He was still too young to begin school and badly wanted the company of other boys to play with, but this would have to wait for a while.

In late November 1917, Henry wrote to his parents about the hospital trains with the wounded from the Battle of Cambrai steaming past his Dover dockside office. They met up to five hospital ships coming and going every day. He mentioned the organization that went into the transport of the wounded and men going to and from leave, 3000 per day each way. He also noted that after the capture of Vimy Ridge the previous April by the Canadian Corps there was a change of opinion in Britain towards the Canadian armed forces. It was a feat both British and French troops had failed to do.

While his sons were fighting valiantly in their respective services, 1917 had not been a good year for either H.O. or the A.B.C. The Fraser River salmon run had been a complete failure. The same applied to their Puget Sound canneries in Washington State. In Alaskan waters it should have been one of the years for a periodical big run, but there had been earthquakes and violent storms that stirred up volcanic sand in shallow waters, causing the salmon to keep out in the deep beyond the reach of nets.

A Federal Fisheries Commission was appointed to inquire and report upon all matters connected with British Columbia canning. H.O.

was credited with "rendering most valuable assistance in bringing to the commission the many defects and abuses connected with the industry and offered suggestions for remedying the situation." The paper continued, "Should his advice be followed it will go a long way towards placing the fishing interests on a more satisfactory footing than they have been for many years."

In January 1918 H.O. planned a dinner in London for his six sons. They were widely scattered; Roderick was at the front with his unit, Duncan came from hospital, where he was recovering well after a crash (Appendix 4) and Henry was back on seagoing duties temporarily and had been on the French coast before going up to London. It was a good example of H.O.'s pull that early in the fifth year of the war he was able to assemble all his sons in London. They were a great credit to him and to this point in the war, eight decorations for bravery had been won between four of them. Roderick would add a ninth posthumously.

A few days later H.O. travelled to the front line; one of the few civilians to receive permission to do so. He was accompanied part way by Roderick. The reason for his visit was to see first-hand the machine guns that he had donated to the 16th Battalion, Canadian Scottish. He also visited the 72nd Seaforth Highlanders of Canada before returning to England. H.O. witnessed some of the preparations by the 16th Battalion for an assault on the Hindenburg Line. Even while H.O. was present there was heavy shelling by the enemy and several casualties. Here Roderick parted company with his father to return to regimental duties. Just before H.O. left for France, Mick was seriously injured in a flying accident at Gosport, where Duncan had just taken command (Appendix 4).

The war was not going particularly well and the fact that a German offensive was expected at any time made it all the more surprising that H.O. received permission to visit the front and to get so close to the action. Roderick was by this time one of the longest surviving officers in the 16th Battalion and at times had talked of his own disbelief at this fact. Since joining the 16th Battalion in 1915 he had seen its officer strength replaced twelve times,

He had frequently taken over command of the battalion in the absence of Colonel Peck who, although a fearless soldier and a Victoria Cross holder, suffered poor health and was often struck down with high fever. When the German army, relieved of having to keep men and equipment on the Eastern front, began to build up in the west, Roderick was in the thick of things all through that last summer.

The Germans held off their major offensive until March 21 and over several weeks they routed several Allied divisions, and all but obliterated the 5th Army. The assault continued with varying intensity on a wide front into June, but though the Germans succeeded in retaking a few miles of long-desolated land it was their last large scale offensive and slowly the war turned in the Allies favour.

Air raids were still continuing over the south of England but an unpleasant surprise came in late February when the Dover dockyard was attacked by enemy destroyers and several officers and over 100 men were killed. The next night the Germans came back and this time shelled the town. Returning home Henry found that his wife and children had headed for the country and Nan had found a farm where they could stay. The intention was to let the children remain there and he and Nan would give up the house and rent a small flat. As it happened the situation was taken care of when Henry was given a posting to the Naval Depot at Crystal Palace in South London. Although he hated the idea of being away from the action, Henry's talent at instructing was recognized and he was put in charge of a new school to teach the use of hydrophone technology to increasing numbers of naval personnel, including women who were selected from various shore stations.

By the end of March Henry and his family were installed in a rented house on South Norwood Hill, a comfortable bicycle ride from the Crystal Palace. His first intake was 40 men, but when the course was fully established it would build to 200 men and 50 women. He was amused that Dick, Duncan and himself were all 'schoolmasters', because Dick had been promoted to Lieutenant-Colonel and commanded a large air-gunnery school at Turnberry in south-west Scotland, while Duncan was in command of the advanced flying school at Gosport. Mick was improving slowly, but was having difficulty recognizing people when they first came into the room and had poor recall of events. Isabel was credited with doing more than anybody to improve his physical and mental health.

Much less was known then about the brain and its functions and the care of brain-damaged people had a quaintness that sounds strange today. Henry wrote a progress report to his mother in which he said: "Malcolm appears as though he was being spoken to when he is half-asleep and the doctors had to be very careful to make the progress very slow so that what little brain is good will not be injured by a relapse caused by it being overworked." He was at the time in a room with several other officers which, in contrast to what the doctors had decreed, must have provided quite a bit of mental stimulation. It probably did much more to help him than was realized.

With his family established in South London, Budge began nursery school for the first time and enjoyed having other children to play with. Henry was proud as his son "marches cheerfully off to school at 8.45 every morning and returns full of what he has learned." One day as he was walking with his father he suddenly stopped dead in his tracks on the street and said to Henry, "Its 12 o'clock Daddy." Asked how he knew, Budge replied "Because my shadow is pointing to the Crystal Palace." Nan told Bella that he was very sturdy now, with a quaint way of talking—'rather slowly, very distinctly and using very long old fashioned words.'

At a sports day in the Crystal Palace Naval Depot, Budge ran his first ever race. He was leading, but kept looking over his shoulder to see if he was being overtaken and instead came in fifth out of thirty.

Roderick was now the only one still at the front, although Aeneas was acting in a support role in a heavy artillery unit. The tide was now turning in the war and the Allies began a major offensive on August 8th with Canadians playing a vital part. The attack began at dawn and by mid-morning a very decisive victory was reported in that sector. Field-Marshal Haig was anxious not to lose the momentum of this August victory. The German General Ludendorff said that August 8th 1918 was a black day for the German Army and marked the decline of its fighting power.

By September enemy resistance was declining, many soldiers were surrendering without a fight and 77,000 prisoners and six hundred guns had been captured. It seemed that nothing could stop the allied advance and on the 27th several Canadian battalions crossed the Canal Du Nord, though fighting was fierce. On the 30th the Hindenburg Line fell, but there was still some resistance around a number of small villages. Orders were given to the battalions of the 3rd Infantry Brigade to attack these, with Cuvillers as the objective of the 16th Battalion, Canadian Scottish Regiment. It was led by Roderick in the absence of Colonel Peck, who had been ordered away from the front for a rest. Roderick went to examine the forward positions for himself just before the German counter-attack began. He was accompanied part way by the Assistant Adjutant,

Lieut. Kerans. When they reached the outpost line Roderick told Kerans "I'm going to push on to the men on the road at (map reference) M36c" This was the exploitation limit and after instructing Kerans to "see to the flanks" he set off. It was the last time he was seen alive.

For several days after the action there was a strong hope that he had been taken prisoner, but a few days later his body was found where he had fallen, only a hundred yards from the place where he and Kerans had parted. When the circumstances of his death became known he was awarded a posthumous Distinguished Service Order. (See Appendix 5)

It was a cruel blow to his brothers that Roderick had died just as the generals were declaring that the war was, to all intents and purposes, over. Five days after his death an armistice proposal was drawn up, which was at that time rejected but in just over a month a revised proposal was accepted.

War brings out a coping mechanism for grief that is quite different to peacetime loss of loved ones and this was particularly so in the Great War when, for the first time there was a need to grasp the sheer scale of the carnage. There was a belief that those men who took part were getting rid of evil and the war itself was an act of cleansing. Many letters from one next of kin to another expressed this belief and it served as a balm to cope with the loss. The uncle of a young Guard's officer from the Scottish border country wrote to his mother:

"For them it is all right—they go out in the full flower of their manhood, but for us who loved their bright young lives it is terrible. We are fighting not only that materialism with which Germany is associated but a desperate amount of selfishness at home, and I am sure this country will arise after the war in a purer and nobler state. These young lives will not then be wasted. This helps one to bear the sorrow does it not?"

This hope was echoed in many homes and was similar to a letter written by Tsarina Alexandra to Nicholas II:

"I do wonder what will be after this great war is over... shall once more ideals exist, will people become more pure and poetic, or will they continue to be dry materialists? But such terrible misery as the whole world has suffered must clean the hearts and minds and purify the stagnant brains and sleeping souls."

Both writers saw war as a way of turning people from materialism to purity and nobility. These wishes must have dwelt in the minds of many people, if only as a means to help them understand why so many young men had to die. It is difficult to grasp the full measure of grief that the terrible loss of life brought to every corner of Europe and beyond. Grief that could only be, in part, assuaged by attempting to explain the reasons for the slaughter. It gave something to hang on to, and a hope that mankind could really be set on a new path.

The Bell-Irving family was no exception. On October 25 Nan wrote to his mother, "We are all so proud of dear old Roderick and Nora has behaved in a worthy way as his wife. Nobody could be braver and yet feel it as deeply as she has done. She is looking forward to coming back to you, as you will be able to understand better than anyone else exactly how she feels."

Henry wrote to Bella on November 4 "You will by now have heard the full details of Roderick's death and I know you are proud and brave about it. We are very sorry for Nora, but she is looking on the right side of things and is holding her head high. All the B.I.'s have now given a son to the Great Cause. I am sending splendid photos of the funeral, which must have been very impressive and was a great honour to our brother and your son." (Copies of the photograph still hang in the officers' mess in the Seaforth Highlander's of Canada Armoury in Vancouver and the 16th Canadian Scottish mess in Victoria. It was used for many years on Armistice Day on the front cover of the Times of London. Altogether five Bell-Irvings gave their lives in WW I, two from Canada and three from Scotland.)

The A.B.C. Annual Report, dated October 30, 1918 says: "We continue to be short-handed in London and Vancouver. The younger generation is still on duty at the front, and those most closely connected to us have suffered severe losses since we met a year ago. Thanks goes to H. Bell-Irving & Co. Ltd., our Vancouver Agents, for their able conduct of our affairs through a year of great anxiety and difficulties."

H.O.'s notebooks show a peculiar detachment over Roderick's death. There are intense notes about the canneries and their fish catches. There is a note about an operation on Duncan's ankle and the fact that Anita had appendicitis, but the only mention of the loss of his son was of a letter from Aeneas on November 12, who was present at the funeral. The conclusion of the war is underlined in red.

While the world waited for the armistice to be signed, the scourge of influenza that killed thousands of civilians and returning servicemen had already begun. The Crystal Palace Naval Depot was closed down by the second week of October because so many personnel were ill with it. Henry escaped the flu and took leave at Milkbank but was back in time to celebrate the Armistice Day celebrations and on the 13th of November wrote to describe the scenes in London. Henry wrote that Nan, Isabel and he were among a crowd of 50,000 in the pouring rain as the King, the Queen, the Princess Royal and Prince of Wales came out onto the Palace balcony with their umbrella's up. He told his parents, "All London has gone mad and never have such demonstrations gone on before."

Part of the euphoria was the knowledge that there had been a total collapse in Germany. It was not just that the country had surrendered unconditionally and the Kaiser had abdicated on the 9th, fleeing to Holland. The navy that Henry and his colleagues had fought so long and hard against was in chaos, with many of the ships' crews engaged in mutiny. Perhaps even he did not know the full truth of the situation because in the above letter Henry said, "If the Huns surrender their subs at once, as they are supposed to do, our job will not be very long in winding up. With luck you should see us home sometime early in the spring."

When the Kaiser abdicated, General Ludendorff wrote, "Germany collapsed like a house of cards. All that we had bled four long years to maintain was gone. State and society vanished. All authority disappeared. Chaos, Bolshevism, terror, have made their way into the German Fatherland."

By the time Henry was able to return with his family to Canada, six year old Budge had several times seen his uncles in various stages of convalescence and his uncle Roderick had been killed in France. Over the next few years as his surviving uncles and his father settled back into civilian life it would be impossible to forget their contribution to Canada's war effort*; neither would those formative years in Dover be forgotten. The idea grew that there would be another war and that he would be in it. For one so young this idea seems preposterous, but one cannot always explain the premonitions that some people carry.

---

* A list of decorations won by four of H.O.'s sons in WW I:
Henry Beattie Bell-Irving: Distinguished Service Cross and bar.
Roderick Ogle Bell-Irving: Distinguished Service Order (Posth); Military Cross.
Malcolm McBean Bell-Irving (Mick): Distinguished Service Order; Military Cross.
Alan Duncan Bell-Irving (Duncan): Military Cross and Bar; Croix de Guerre.

CHAPTER TWO

THE ONE FAMILY MEMBER UPON WHOM the armistice had the greatest impact was Bella Bell-Irving. She had remained in Vancouver while her husband and most of her children had spent all, or part of the war in Europe. She had seen tantalizing photographs of her grandchildren with letters from Henry and Dick saying how much they longed to return to Vancouver so that she could hold the children herself.

Four of the grandchildren, Henry's daughters Molly and Wendy; Dick's son (also Dick), and Isabel's son, Sedley, she had never seen. Budge and Ruth had left Vancouver in January 1915 as babies and were coming to her as young children with developing personalities, especially Budge, who had been the most frequent subject of his parent's wartime letters. However, Henry and Nan did present her with another grandchild in December 1919, named Roderick Keith Falconer Bell-Irving, named after his late uncle, killed just the year before in France. Six year old Budge now had a brother, but it would be several years before they found a common bond—in the comradeship of war. Like Budge and their father, Roderick was destined to have a fine war record.

H.O. had the advantage that he had seen his grandchildren almost every year on his visits to Britain. Now the war was behind them and miraculously all but one of his sons had survived. The two eldest boys returned to H. Bell-Irving & Co., Richard to his administrative job, while Henry was once more in charge of production and maintenance at the canneries. Mick's disabilities prevented him from taking on full-time work and he endured a lot of pain. Despite this he remained fun-loving and everybody warmed to his outgoing personality. It brought joy to his parents when he married Nora Jones of Mechosin on Vancouver Island, the daughter of a Victoria doctor. They had a very happy partnership until his death in 1942 and she helped considerably in his overcoming and facing his disabilities.

Duncan, whose left leg was 1-1/2" shorter than the right one, nevertheless continued to fly as a civilian and like Mick, drove fast. He married Nan's sister, Mary, and for two or three years they lived in Cuba where he managed the Beattie sugar business. It did not work out, mainly because of depressed sugar prices and with a new son, Gordon, they returned to Vancouver. He did not seek employment in his father's company and instead built a career with other companies in engineering, ocean towing and, much later in the insurance arm of H. Bell-Irving & Co.

Aeneas also decided against joining the company and trained as an accountant. He then joined the Brunner Mond Company (an affiliate of the British Chemical Company) in China. He remained there for five years, in the interval returning to marry Patricia Cowan, who died during childbirth in Shanghai in 1926. Aeneas returned to Vancouver where he became a partner in an investment company, O'Brien, Bell-Irving, Stone and Rook, which did not survive the depression. For the rest of his working life, other than service in WW II he was an accountant with Western Bridge and Steel, which became Canron Company. In 1929 he married Monica Marpole and they had two children, John Darg and Monica Ruth. H.O. was protective of his three younger daughters, Anita, Mary and Beatrice, but during the 1920's they all found husbands that met with his approval. Anita married Archie Kerfoot of the Alberta branch of the family, Mary married Hugh Robb, an Englishman and old Etonian. Their five children were born in Canada but eventually the whole family went to live in England. Beatrice married John Abercrombie.

Henry remained with H. Bell-Irving & Co. Ltd. throughout the 1920's and was constantly on the move from one cannery to the next, while Dick took on more and more responsibilities in the administration of the company. He was in his father's presence for much of the time and had a much more harmonious relationship with H.O. than Henry. Unlike his older brother, Dick was much more content to follow H.O.'s dictates on the-day-to day running of the business.

Isabel returned with Ben Sweeney and their two year old son, Sedley and they lived in a small house that stood in the grounds of The Strands. Ben was offered a job as secretary to H.O., which he turned down. He was a very able man and had served with distinction in the war as a Royal Engineers officer, but he had great difficulty in finding work to match his talents.

Given the state of the business in 1919 it is doubtful if there would have been room for all the sons, even if they had wanted to join the company. It was in a depressed state when Henry and Dick returned despite the best efforts of H.O. He had seen problems coming two years earlier and had tried to warn the government that controls were needed. The 1919 Annual Report told a tale of woe—and some of it has a familiar current ring:

> "... the Directors are well acquainted with the Fraser River. When our company was first registered in 1891 we had acquired nine canneries in total. The seven Fraser River canneries, which then cost £60,000 are now, as fishing stations practically valueless. This is partly due to obstructions up the river, and partly due to the short sighted policies of the authorities, who allowed over-fishing to continue until the run of salmon dwindled to almost nothing. We transferred the equipment as far as we could to other points, but most of our capital expenditure on the Fraser River was lost.
>
> When attention is drawn from outside of the industry, to the apparently large profits earned in salmon fishing, it is too little realized how precarious the situation is and how large a proportion of profits have to be set aside to provide fresh canneries in substitution of those that have become unprofitable. It is only by pursuing this course that your directors have been able to maintain the company as a good, dividend paying concern. But even the selection of new cannery sites is a very hazardous enterprise.
>
> ... our Alaska runs suffer great shortages of both reds and pinks and are not expected to exceed 50% of last year's run."

The profit that year exceeded £55,000, but if the Chairman's words are to be believed, most of this would have been allocated to building new canneries along the coast, where suitable conditions could be found. Nevertheless dividend payments were 20%, with a tax-free 10% bonus. H. Bell-Irving and Co. Ltd were paid commissions of just over £12,000 ($60,000 approximately).

The ever-growing Bell-Irving clan divided its activities between The Strands and Pasley Island. Parties and social events continued at The Strands and one of the first post-war parties was a dance attended by one hundred and twenty-five guests for the coming out of B.T. Rogers' daughter, Mary. H.O. could still out-dance them all, although he preferred the more conventional ballroom dances and did not like the dance crazes of the period.

Vancouver's West End was filled with large houses, the owners reading like a who's who of old Vancouver families, though two and three storey apartment blocks were gradually invading. Across English Bay the population was growing as small subdivisions were built in South Vancouver and Point Grey, though much of the land beyond was still bush and would remain so for many years to come.

One or two wealthy West End families were building mansions in Shaughnessy and as far away as the University Endowment Lands, but H.O. remained in the West End. This may have been partly because he did not want to put Bella through the strain of moving, but more likely because it would not have occurred to him to move. His house was much closer to downtown than these other locations and had the advantage of immediate access to Stanley Park where H.O. liked to ride early in the morning with Budge, or one or more of his daughters.

Budge's development continued and he began attendance at a series of schools. He was enrolled at a private school run by a Miss Seymour in the West End—briefly. Although it was chiefly for girls, the school took small boys, which did not sit well with the precocious Budge. He proudly recalls being expelled in short order for being a nuisance. (Years later, when the Seaforth Highlanders went to war, a number of officers were amused to find that they had also attended Miss Seymour's school.)

From here Budge was moved to a preparatory school run by Mr. St. John Davies and his assistant, Mr. Moody. Some of Budge's energy found an outlet in the 6th St. Paul's Cub Pack. It was run by 'Gramps' Milne. He was a great success as cub master and had a beneficial influence on his boys. Their camps were held on the Rogers family property at Cowan's Point, on nearby Bowen Island. Milne had a dog called 'Dyb'(an acronym for 'Do Your Best', the Cubs' motto) that accompanied him at all times. Budge became a 'sixer', which was his first taste of responsibility.

From the Davies preparatory school he moved on to Lord Roberts School, then on Denman Street. This provided him with his first taste of mixing with students from a more general background, some of them from poorer parts of the city. The school's long-time principal, Mr. Alfred Rines, held the job from 1918 to 1947. In his early days he had a piece of leather, like a razor strop, which was in common use then and he used it to apply to the palms of recalcitrant students. Once in a while Budge had an appointment with Mr. Rines for sundry misdeeds. It stood him in good stead a few years later when he followed in his father's foot-steps to Loretto School, in Scotland.

Once he got into a fight with another boy at Lord Roberts. A crowd gathered round and began sympathizing with the loser—who was not Henry Pybus Bell-Irving. Finally the two broke apart and things looked ugly as the crowd moved in. Budge took off up Davie Street with several boys in pursuit, taking several side alleys to lose them. Back on Davie Street, he found himself in front of the B.T. Rogers' large house. Budge ran up to the front door, opened it, entered the house and ran through to the back door from where he made for home. He knew the house well enough from previous children's parties there. In those days the West End was entirely single family homes with gardens and lanes to dodge pursuers and Budge had no difficulty in keeping them guessing.

Other parties that Budge attended were different from the usual kind. His father maintained an interest in the navy and was an active member of the Naval Officers' Association. There were regular visits by warships from Britain and the Dominions, and he particularly recalls the battleship H.M.S. *Hood*, and the cruisers H.M.S.. *Repulse* and Australian H.M.A.S. *Adelaide*. Budge remembers a boisterous childrens' party on board the *Repulse,* with organized entertainment for the young visitors. The ship's mascot was a Kiwi bird and while it was in port Budge became the bird's official feeder. He would dig up worms in the garden and a ship's boat would be sent to take him aboard. There were a visit to the gunroom and other parts of the ship and generally enjoying his privileged role of feeder.

There were visits by many U.S. Navy ships as well. Henry made sure that all visiting officers were entertained while in port and many functions were put on for them, especially dances and invitations to Pasley. H.M.C.S. *Discovery,* the naval establishment on Coal Harbour was home to a naval reserve squadron and he was a member of the wardroom.

Like many grandparents, H.O. indulged his first grandchild and admired his aggressive spirit. Budge's early years in Dover were quite unlike any that other Vancouver children would have experienced and this may have added to his independence. H.O. agreed to pay for Budge's education, both at Shawnigan Lake and Loretto, and taught him to become competent in outdoor pursuits, such as skating, shooting and fishing.

As H. Bell-Irving's trouble-shooter, Henry began spending more and more time at the canneries scattered along the many inlets of the B.C. coast. Although H.O. appreciated his abilities, there was a growing strain between them which would soon come into the open, a most unfortunate situation when Henry and Nan had a growing family to feed. In 1926 their last child, Anne Helen (Nancy), was born.

By this time Budge was enrolled at Shawnigan Lake School on Vancouver Island. The school was founded in 1916 by Christopher Windley Lonsdale (C.W.) who remained its Headmaster for many years. By the mid 1920's the school had established a good reputation and boys were enrolled from across North America. C.W. had attended Westminster School, a well-known old school in London, England and Shawnigan Lake was modelled along the same lines.

In today's world, some of the principles which he applied to the education of the boys in his care, might seem trite: honesty, fair play and wisdom. With it went, inevitably, a portion of discipline. The belief that 'sparing the rod would spoil the child' was then still in vogue, though its application might today shock many educators. Many people today find corporal punishment abhorrent and yet most of those who received their share of it grew up with self-discipline and a sense of duty. The arguments for and against have been raging for years and will not diminish for a long time to come.

An oral history of the school, *Rough Diamond*, was published in 1992. Author Jay Connolly contacted hundreds of former students and those who were present during the headmastership of Lonsdale have very fond memories of him. His school, at the time the young Budge Bell-Irving arrived, was a collection of older buildings, of no particular architectural merit, yet the teaching staff was dedicated and knowledgeable.

Towards the end of his time there a fire destroyed most of the school buildings. Budge was actually the first person to spot the fire, which began in the gym changing-room. It was during evening prep and he was looking out of the window when he saw the flames and shouted "Fire!" For his pains he was given a cuff with a ruler by the duty master, who doubtless thought it was a practical joke. It was close to the Christmas holidays and all the students trunks had been sent to the dorms for packing. They were given a brief time to return to their dorms and throw in whatever they could. Budge's recollections include the sound of shattering glass as the boys helped each other throw the trunks through the windows onto the ground below. He made light of the incident in his interview for *Rough Diamond*:

> "I suppose my age group were approaching puberty and I was not alone in looking for the young matron, Miss Parmiter, who was the nearest thing available as a damsel in distress. Unfortunately she did not have the good grace to show any sign whatsoever of being in distress!"

In the morning only a few chimney stacks and some twisted plumbing pipes remained to show where the buildings had been. Despite the fact that nearly all the major school buildings were destroyed there were no injuries and no loss of life. Another old boy, D.C. Douglas, recalls the calm leadership of C.W. Lonsdale. In a lengthy recollection he attributes the fact that there were no casualties to Lonsdale's leadership and organizing ability. It was heartbreaking to see his school going up in flames but he did not let it show and began planning to rebuild immediately. Douglas remarked that many of the masters had been on active service in the first war and were well prepared mentally for just such emergencies.

After the Christmas holiday the school was fortunate in being able to rent the Cadboro Bay Hotel in Victoria for the junior school. At that time it was only open in the summer. So successful was Lonsdale in his re-building efforts that by the next summer term several buildings were ready. He had selected a Tudor design for the new school buildings and they have weathered well over the years.

Budge left Shawnigan before the juniors returned to their new accommodation and after the passage of time remembers little of the academic program there. He does remember the more practical elements of his time at the school. The grounds were being constantly cleared to make way for more playing fields and the students were encouraged to take part in this work. The trees were felled professionally but their removal, along with large rocks were left to the staff and the boys. The method was the same used at the time in the logging industry; horses combined with steel hawsers and pulleys to free the roots and pull them from the cleared area. Budge says of this effort, "We probably didn't appreciate it then, but it was good training for future British Columbians."

Building forts in the surrounding trees was another occupation and Budge has a good reason to remember one such effort. He was sitting on one of the logs, with his legs resting on another log a few feet away, when his friend Bill Merritt, without warning threw an axe from above. It struck just below Budge's knee and slid down the shin, taking a slice of skin with it. Tearing off his shirt he wrapped the skin-flap back against the shin bone and walked down the hill to the school sick-bay, accompanied by a concerned Bill Merritt.

At the sick-bay, as well as the doctor putting in some metal staples to re-attach the skin, he was given a dose of 'Dr. Gregory's Powder.' What this foul-tasting concoction was for, no one recalls, except that it tasted vile and may have been given simply to discourage any thoughts of malingering. Among the common but equally obnoxious treatments such as castor oil, cod liver oil, sulphur and molasses, D.C. Douglas describes 'Dr. Gregory's Powder' as a thin, gritty, pink mud which was dispensed generously. He thought it was made from rhubarb ash!

One incident above all others stayed in Budge's mind. Several boys were told to report to the headmaster's study after tea. Budge arrived to join a queue of boys, all of them in trepidation as they waited. Those who had already seen C.W. were coming out rubbing their backsides and in tears. It was not the first time that he had faced the head's thin cane and entering the study he was told: "It has been reported that your table manners were bad this term. Do you want to stay in school for an extra week or take six of the best?" Budge chose the latter, whereupon the head struck a cushion with six loud smacks and grinning pointed to the date on the wall calendar—April 1st. He then said, "cry on your way out!"

Budge left after two years at Shawnigan, before the summer term of 1927 began. He has one other recollection and that is of the food. He was glad that he was an accomplished fisherman because he needed to supplement the meagre food with crayfish and the occasional trout.

His summers centred around Pasley Island, to which most of the wives and children had departed and would remain during the warmer months. It was the custom for businesses to stay open until noon on Saturday mornings and the men-folk had to be ready for a speedy departure from the Royal Vancouver Yacht Club, in Coal Harbour, precisely at 2 p.m. Once H.O. had arranged a time to depart no one dared be late. He had owned a number of boats, the two favourites being the *Beatrice* and later the *Emoh* (simply home spelt backwards). By the 1920's this was the most frequently used to ferry family members and guests to and from the island.

It is to the credit of the Bell-Irvings that the island has been used continuously, generation after generation. Each member of the family had their own dwelling, all with a water view and in a wooded setting, though with varying degrees of comfort. Budge remembers the livestock then comprised of four Jersey cattle and a bull; thirty sheep and a ram; there were white Leghorn chickens and at North Bay a four acre vegetable garden had been created under the fruit trees. Milk, cream, butter, chicken, eggs and lamb, plus a wide variety of fruit and vegetables contributed to feeding a great many Bell-Irvings and their guests. There was a variety of berries in the garden and there was great rivalry between the families to be first to start picking as soon as they ripened.

H.O. took great pleasure in walking around the island trail on Sunday mornings with a sickle to keep the trail in order. It was on Pasley that he taught his grandson to shoot—with a .22 rifle at a can floating on the water. Budge added:

> "A certain pique was sometimes added to the scene in the clearing when the bull came trotting from one direction and the ram came galloping from the opposite direction. No one is known to have been gored by the bull and the ram was eventually banished to Mickey Island, which had only limited success as, following some inter-island love bleats, the ram found little difficulty in swimming back for a party! The cattle were loaded onto a scow and towed to Steveston by an A.B.C. fish packer, to spend the winter there. The horses that rivalled the deer in eating the flowers, came much later."

After a search for reliable caretakers, H.O. employed Chung, a Chinese man and his son Louie who became long-time dedicated caretakers. As Budge and his siblings grew, H.O. made sure that they and any visiting young friends were kept busy helping with the weeding and trail-clearing. It can never be said of the Bell-Irvings that they were spoiled. Discipline was a part of family life from the time that H.O. and Bella had their first children. The reason for going back to Britain in the years just before the first war was to give his children, particularly the boys, a more disciplined education, although even Loretto came under his criticism. Despite making it his choice for his sons and one grandson he once complained of "the low academic standards prevalent at Loretto." This opinion might have been difficult to sustain, but H.O. had to have his say in the matter.

In 1927 Budge was fourteen years old and the time had come for him to enroll at Loretto. As the first grandchild, he was the only one to receive this privilege of being sent out of the country to be educated. Henry's salary and annual bonus from his job in the company was adequate, but not to pay the fees and all the other requirements for attendance there, although H.O.'s own income from H. Bell-Irving & Co. was not as high as it was before the First World War. By 1923 he had accepted the necessity of a reduction. Fishermen and cannery workers up and down the coast were demanding more cents per fish caught and it was at a time when Britain, one of A.B.C.'s biggest importers, was buying a larger quantity of Siberian salmon. In an effort to diversify, the A.B.C. bought an Okanagan jam manufacturing company, King Beach Ltd., which included a berry farm and a large inventory of sugar. When a serious drop in sugar prices occurred it made worse an already unsatisfactory arrangement and the business was sold to the B.C. government for $40,000. From 1923 to 1926 dividends were reduced or eliminated altogether although in 1926 the ordinary shares once more reached 10%. This was due to domestic sales improving and sales to Australia and New Zealand picking up. The United Kingdom no longer held the No. 1 position.

All this took place as Budge left Vancouver to become a British public schoolboy. He arrived at Loretto at the start of the summer term in 1927, the eighth Bell-Irving to attend the school. His father and all of his uncles had attended, as well as his great-uncle Duncan's son, Peter.

Loretto was an old school, with many traditions. It was founded in 1827 and its name came from the site of a chapel, "Our Lady of Loretto", built on the bank of the Pinkie Burn, east of the town of Musselburgh. The chapel was named from Loreto, a holy shrine in Italy.

A neighbouring estate, Pinkie House, is now part of the school and has historical connections with Prince Charles Edward Stuart, 'Bonnie Prince Charlie'. The prince slept here after his success at the Battle of Prestonpans in 1745, when he routed General Sir John Cope. The next morning the Prince led his Highlanders past Loretto on their way to Edinburgh.

The school began when Loretto House was taken over by the Rev. Dr. Thomas Langhorne who, to add to his stipend as a minister took in boys to tutor. Within a few years there were up to fifty boys which, in the early years he ran as a preparatory school. In 1862 Loretto was taken over by Hely-Hutchinson Almond, who at one time had taught math at the school. The number of students soon grew to more than one hundred and several buildings were added. Like Dr. Lonsdale at Shawnigan, Almond believed in a Spartan existence. Coats had to be removed when the temperature reached 60 degrees and a cold bath had to be endured every morning.

The train ride across Canada and the Atlantic voyage on the *Ascania* were a great adventure for a fourteen year old travelling on his own. Budge was an engaging boy and had no trouble making friends. He could also be very persuasive; he asked the purser if it was possible to have an outside cabin and he was given one. His main complaint was the small portions of food served compared to the train and he was afraid that he would soon starve on the ship. However he summoned enough energy for dancing lessons from the gym instructor and then danced away each night until midnight. There was, of course, the inevitable costume party and he went as a pirate, showing considerable initiative in collecting suitable attire—and in his approach to acquiring it. He borrowed the purser's brilliant silk dressing gown, a pair of silver coloured bloomers from one of the lady passengers and a pair of gaily coloured garters from a girl passenger. On board was an opera singer named Mariska Aldrich, whose voice Budge admired when she sang in the ship's concerts. In a mock-auction he bid $5 for her signed photograph—which he still has.

Loretto's Headmaster from 1926 to 1945 was Dr. James Greenlees. Budge's early letters from the school show an engaging simplicity in his reaction to his new environment. He admitted to being 'muddled' for the first few weeks and was anxious to put the new-boy image behind him. School work was easier than he had expected and he found math especially easy, as he had at his previous school. Budge humorously claims that he was placed in Form IIIC and as, before his arrival the lowest was Form IIIB, it was especially created for him! In fact it was simply done before testing the boys and streaming them.

He showed a canny ability to handle money and was, as they say in Scotland 'careful.' He offered to help out with the cost of fitting out his clothing requirements with money left over from his journey from Vancouver. He told his father, "Don't bother to send me any money because after buying a good bike which cost only £8, I have £11 left over, which will last me a long time."

Upon an inquiry from H.O. asking the headmaster if it was worth the expense of sending Budge to the school, the head replied that he was in fact 'doing quite well!' It would have been typical of Dr. James Robertson Campbell Greenlees, D.S.O., M.A., Ch.B., O.L., (known affectionately to the boys in his charge as 'Sunny Jim') to defend Budge. His selection as Headmaster was unusual in that he was a practising physician in Glasgow, though he was a member of the school Board of Governors. His strength for the job was a keen interest in youth psychology and as a leader in the Boy's Brigade, a quasi-military organization with overtones of character building, yet very different in its aims to the Boy Scout movement.

James Greenlees' long term as Headmaster was an indication of his ability and the only difference of opinion between him and the Board of Governors was over the size of the school's enrollment. Greenlees wished it to remain small enough that he could know every boy well, particularly those in the Upper School, while the Board, through economical necessity wanted the enrollment to grow. The doctor's popularity ensured a healthy waiting list throughout his term of office. He offered his resignation in 1939, but with the start of WW II decided to stay on until the end of hostilities. By 1945 the school had lost ninety old boys to the war, and Dr. Greenlees would have had the pleasure of seeing many of his former pupils, including Budge, achieve first-class war records.

In his first few weeks as a new boy, Budge told his parents, "I have tried hard not to blow the horn of Canada, but I evidently have, because the boys are always asking me about the wonderful things there." This is an interesting comment because on recent reflection he felt that the British boys knew little about Canada. There was only one other boy in the school from across the Atlantic, Gordon Winter, who was from Newfoundland and was in the same age group. Budge said, "They thought of us as mere 'colonials'. I didn't mind very much in those days whether they thought Canada and the States were all one , or wondered why I didn't have feathers sticking up at the back. It was really complete ignorance except for what they read in the *The Boy's Own Paper* and *Chums*, both of these having many articles on the Royal North-West Mounted Police. They knew about that." During the First War *The Boys' Own Paper* had carried items about the exploits of both Mick and Duncan Bell-Irving.

Water sports were considered an important exercise at Loretto and Budge passed all his preliminary swimming tests. He swam 25 yards under water and was soon on the water-polo team. But although also on the Colt's cricket team, he admitted to being rotten at it at first. When the streaming test was completed, H.O. must have been pleased to learn that his grandson was top in math and geography amongst the new boys.

Later in the first term, Budge rebutted an accusation by his father that he was slacking, replying: "... I haven't had ten minutes to spare. We do not have more than one hour a day off and then I have to practise for the diving competition or for boxing. In fact I should be boxing now." He was able to prove that school work was not neglected when the end of term marks were released. Budge came top in English and third in math, geography and history.

Boxing was compulsory, but he was soon good enough to represent his house, Newfield, in an inter-house match. It was a sport that was particularly useful in self-defence and Budge had to quickly become proficient at this. In one letter to his parents he said "I have absolutely no complaints, except perhaps that my backside is fast turning into leather. There are twenty-nine boys in Newfield and I am the youngest, but by no means the smallest, and able to hold my own."

Punishment at Loretto was carried out by the prefects rather than the masters and was specific according to the misdemeanor. A mild one resulted in a caning of 'two-in-blue'—two strikes while wearing blue shorts, which had a lining. At the other end of the punishment scale was 'six-in-white'—six of the best dressed in white shorts with no lining. Looking back, Budge has recognized this custom as a valuable learning process in the administration of discipline.

A term used then at the school was 'hardening', more commonly known as 'hazing' in Canada and the United States. It was separate from formal punishment and was an unofficial activity among the boys for the purpose of putting bumptious new boys into their proper place. As

Budge was possibly stronger and certainly less submissive than most new boys he was a prime candidate for this process. He said:

> "We were worse than nothing in the eyes of the well established boys. I was bullied unmercifully, physically and, more seriously, mentally. I was beaten and given a bad time by boys who were very little older, if at all, than I was. The chief reason was that I was physically capable of looking after myself quite well. I could take on any one of them, if not two of them at any time. So I had to be put down to size and made to realize the pecking order where I belonged—which was way down at the bottom.
>
> It didn't knock me down, although it could have. It went on with me for about a year. I was put head first in a wastepaper basket in the form room and they had ink in a teapot which they poured over me. I was laid over a bed with arms and legs firmly held and beaten on my bare back with boots. Hardening had its moments, but no lingering ill-will.
>
> We were twelve to a room and there was a head of the room and a second head. On Tuesday nights the head took half the boys to the tubs, a big bathroom and on Thursday nights the other half would go with the second head. When half the room were away with the head, I took on the other one and won the fight thoroughly. When it was the turn of the second head to take his section I took on the head, with the same results. That was the end of it, but it seems extraordinary that there were no repercussions to these outrageous episodes. About this time the hardening, or hazing, was beginning to die out throughout the British public school system and, coincidentally, at Royal Military College, Kingston. By the time I became a senior at Loretto these unkindnesses were past history."

Participation in the Loretto Officers' Training Corps (O.T.C.), was a compulsory activity. Before the first term ended Budge took part in the O.T.C. annual inspection. An unusual feature of the school O.T.C. when his father and uncles were there was that the cadets wore Australian style bush hats. They also wore the kilt, which made an unusual combination when they were on parade. In Budge's day the hat had been replaced with a 'Balmoral' bonnet. It is now called the Combined Cadet Force and dress is more on regular army lines with a Glengarry bonnet, camouflaged battle-dress fatigues and a web belt. There is still a first-class pipe-band. With his memories of Dover and the premonition of future involvement in an armed struggle, Budge became very keen on his O.T.C. activities.

In his first year the summer holidays began on July 28 and Budge was invited to spend a large part of them with the Bell-Irvings of White Hill, near Lockerbie. Although letters home indicated that he missed Pasley and family activities there, his first holiday in Scotland made up for it in freedom to roam. A cause for some excitement was that part of the time would be spent in the West Highlands at Arnisdale, on Loch Hourn, where the Bell-Irvings spent the stalking months. It is on the coast between Mallaig and Kyle of Lochalsh opposite the Isle of Skye.

At this time the laird was Captain John Bell-Irving. Milkbank was let to an American tenant and John and his wife Dollie, lived at White Hill. He had succeeded his father, also John, as head of the Bell-Irving family upon his father's death in 1925.

While at White Hill, Budge's life-long interest in fly-fishing commenced, catching trout in the Milk River, which ran through the estate. John Bell-Irving's elder sister Bella, known affectionately to Budge as 'cousin Shum' had seen Budge as a small boy in Dover, and took an immediate liking to this now 14 year old boy. He spent much time at her nearby house, Bankside and they went fishing for sea-trout and flounders on the Solway Firth, with good success. Although Shum had never married, possibly because like so many women she had lost her fiancé in the first war, she had a sense of fun. This was demonstrated by her willingness at age forty to practice a new popular dance with Budge, to music on her drawing-room gramophone. The dance was the 'Black Bottom.'

Because of the close family connection with Jardine Matheson, cousin John had been a partner in the company, like his father, uncle and grandfather before him. He had served both in Hong Kong and Shanghai. Jardine Matheson's presence in Honk Kong dated back to 1842, when the territory became a British Colony. Shanghai was also an important base for company activities and trading offices were opened in many of the world's major cities. Jardine Matheson had weathered many economic storms from its beginnings as a player in the opium trade but later, when the Japanese invaded China in 1937 the company received some of its worst set-backs. Many of the company executives in Shanghai were imprisoned and its factories and textile mills were deliberately damaged. This was followed barely three years later, early in

WW II, with the Japanese invasion of Hong Kong, bringing Jardine Matheson's activities there to a standstill until 1946.

John Bell-Irving was Master of the Dumfries-shire Otter Hounds, an inherited responsibility and tradition of the Bell-Irvings. Although otter hunting was new to Budge he enjoyed several 'meets' on the rivers of both Dumfries-shire and Ayrshire, following the hounds along the banks and through rivers. It appealed to his enjoyment of physical challenges and test of stamina, revelling in the discomfort of wet clothes. He was made an honorary 'whipper in' or assistant to the huntsman, John Scott. His job was to keep the hounds in control, particularly wayward young ones. With the recent change in attitude towards wild creatures, otter hunting was banned in England and Scotland in about 1980, though the Bell-Irvings of White Hill remained active throughout the '70's.

The journey to the Highlands was taken in style, in a 1st class saloon coach, rented from the railway company. It contained five bunks and a separate compartment for twelve servants. The coach was shunted between trains, as part of the journey was over tracks of the London, Midland and Scottish Railway (L.M.S.) and then onto those of the West Highland Railway from Glasgow to Mallaig. They did not have to leave the coach while the change-over took place. At the fishing port of Mallaig, at the end of the line, and the end of 'The Road to the Isles' they were transferred to a small motor launch for the last stretch to Arnisdale. It is perhaps ironic that Arnisdale is close to Camusfearna, where Gavin Maxwell lived with tame otters. His book "Ring of Bright Water" did so much to turn the tide in favour of preserving these creatures.

Again Budge recorded his impressions for his parents: "This place is supposed to be a shooting lodge, but it is much more like one of the large hotels on Vancouver Island. It has a big hall with a verandah and lots of windows looking over the sea. There are lots of nice bedrooms, all with hardwood floors."

It is a wild and remote spot, with some of the most glorious scenery in all the Highlands, surrounded on all sides by mountains. The lodge faces onto Loch Hourn, across which is the peninsula of Knoydart. The westerly view to the mouth of the loch has glimpses of the Sound of Sleat and the Cuillin Hills of Skye beyond. There are few places in the world where light provides the drama to the scenery as it does in the west of Scotland and the Hebrides. Much of it has to do with the wind-driven, rapidly changing cloud formations, so that shafts of sunlight constantly move across the landscape to form new images. One moment a hill-side is illuminated in bright golden light and the next it is in deep gloom and the shaft has moved to another place. The heather and bracken combine to give off a soft luminosity and a late afternoon or evening westerly view, especially across water, has a depth to it which is like looking into another dimension.

Budge felt the magic of the area, romantically associated with many of the west coast clans: Cameron, MacDonald, MacLeod, McCrea and MacDonell to name a few. While sitting on a hillside one day, with Skye and the serrated Cuillin Hills off to the west, he realized that the country around was a part of the 'Road to the Isles', named after a stirring 'tramping' song written by the Rev. Kenneth Macleod in 1917 to remind Scottish troops of home:

> *By Tummel and Loch Rannoch and Lochaber I will go,*
> *by heather tracks wi' heaven in their wiles,*
> *If its thinkin' in your inner heart the braggarts*
> *in my step, you have never smel't the tangle o' the Isles.*
> *O' the far Cuillins are pullin' me awa' as step I wi' my*
> *cromack to the Isles.*

A few miles down the coast at Loch nan Uamh is a cairn erected to the memory of Bonnie Prince Charlie. It was the place where he left Scottish soil for the last time after he and the Highland clans were defeated at the Battle of Culloden. He roamed the Hebrides and West Highlands for months with a few loyal followers and a price £30,000 on his head. No one gave him away. Recalling his thoughts as he sat on that hill long ago, Budge said, "I think that the Canadian Scot has a much deeper love of Scotland than the Scot at home. The [White Hill] Bell-Irvings and their guests were not, as far I could tell, at all aware of this. I was very conscious of the history of the 1745 Rising and my proximity to the location."

Budge was far too active to be a total dreamer and filled his hours at Arnisdale with fishing, catching sea-trout on the river of the same name, a few hundred yards from the house. He told his parents, "I have been fishing all day in the pouring rain and didn't catch anything over six inches, chiefly because I was too excited. There is also a lot of sea-fishing and we troll for mackerel and fish for cod, haddock and whiting. There is a small motor boat which we can use."

He also accompanied cousin John out 'on the hill' for stalking and he was surprised to find that a Highland deer forest is not a forest at all, but mainly open moorland with a few Scots pine here and there. The local keepers were nearly all Gaelic speakers and had very little English for conversation.

The letters home give no indication that Budge was not always on good terms with his hostess, 'Dolly' Bell-Irving. She considered him a wild colonial and was not pleased that he spent time fishing with the cockney chauffeur while they were at Arnisdale and berated him for doing so, though he got on well enough with cousin John. For Budge the holiday came to an abrupt end when he heard Dolly say, in a loud aside one evening; "If that damned boy doesn't leave here soon I'll go crazy", or words to that effect. He packed his bags, somehow made his way to Mallaig and took the train to Glasgow, eventually reaching the borders where he stayed for the rest of the time with Shum, before returning to school. He resumed fishing locally with a borrowed rod and Shum was very amused to hear that he had been poaching on her brother's land.

By November in Budge's first year it had been established that he would spend Christmas in Switzerland with his grandfather, with a few days in Paris enroute. Dr. Greenlees was, on the whole pleased with his progress and told Henry that Budge had the makings of a first-class athlete. On December 18 Budge joined H.O. and his very young aunt, Beatrice, who was only nine years older than himself. They stayed at the Park Lane Hotel in London before flying out of Croydon airport in a fourteen-seater biplane.

Budge's letter from Paris is a good example of his droll, self-deprecating sense of humour and the self-reliance that he was developing. He told his parents: "I am getting intensely annoyed with Paris, because they don't approve of my beautiful French accent. A few minutes ago I telephoned downstairs for the time, and said very politely, 'Quel heure a-t-il s'il vous plait?' The answer came back very politely, 'half past one!'

> "I went to get my hair cut and they took three-quarters of an hour. It is most annoying that when you try your French you get a reply in perfectly good American, but when you don't know a thing everybody doesn't know a word of English. The barber left the top alone and, of course, he didn't know a word of English. I had the

dickens of a job to get him to cut it. Once started he wouldn't stop and by the time he finally realized that 'Arretez-vous!' was a request to stop, I was beginning to look like a monk."

Budge complained that food in the hotel was only passable and one night when he was served fish for dinner, none of the waiters could tell him what variety it was. He said, "I didn't go beyond smelling the fish, which must have been caught in a drain in the middle ages!"

Arriving in Switzerland they checked into the Kroninhoff Hotel in Pontresina. Beatrice was a good skier, whereas Budge was at that time a beginner and trying to imitate her prowess he went over a small cliff, ending up with a badly dislocated knee and ankle. Although confined to bed for a few days with pressure bandages and anti-swelling medication he was well looked after. The room attendants were at his beck and call and a Maharaja who occupied a whole floor of the hotel provided Budge with a movie projector on which he watched the latest silent movies, especially the antics of Charlie Chaplin.

On December 31 H.O. wrote to Henry from the hotel. He said that Budge was a fine lad and shaping up very satisfactorily, with excellent manners and a fair amount of common sense. He also told Henry that he would continue to pay the educational costs and "... should he shape out as he is doing now, and you approve, he might take up a billet at the A.B.C. office later on."

He went on to say that Budge was having an active time, skating and bob-sledding all day and dancing at night. He was now recovered from the spill, though not yet able to ski, but could skate without a problem. This led to him being selected as an alternative on a Pontresina ice-hockey team for a tour of local towns. Budge was chosen for the simple reason that it was taken for granted that all Canadians played ice-hockey. His figure skates were unsuitable but he played nevertheless and enjoyed the challenge.

There was however, another underlying matter which H.O. broached in his letter. He alluded to the 'recent difficulty' and his feeling of deep regret, hoping that in the end the result will make happiness for both himself and Henry. He stressed his fondness for his eldest son and his family and said "... it would be a misfortune were the recent business trouble to disturb that feeling."

Mention has already been made of the differences in personality between H.O. and his eldest son and it is not unusual that two strong, determined personalities should find it difficult to work together in harmony at the top. The eventual choice of a more compliant heir was inevitable and Dick, who had remained an inside man, was chosen. He had not been near a cannery since his return from the war, but knew the administrative side of the business. Duncan and Mick took sides with Henry, which caused their father some distress, but he would not change his mind.

On June 1, Henry left H. Bell-Irving & Co. and took up a position offered him by the Canadian Fishing Company. His responsibilities were similar to those he was leaving. Nan took a job as manager of the antique department of a local store. Through it all H.O. remained at least outwardly unperturbed and in total control of his company and of A.B.C.'s British Columbia interests.

Throughout this period, with the continuing financial support of H.O., Budge continued at Loretto. He spent the Easter break at Makerstoun, on the River Tweed near Kelso, the estate of James Jardine Bell-Irving (J.J.) and his wife, Eva. They had two daughters, Marda and Ivy. The latter had married Ian Maitland, 15th Earl of Lauderdale. Although the Maitland family seat was nearby Thirlstane Castle, Ian and his family lived at Makerstoun. The Lauderdales had played an important part in Scottish politics for several hundred years. John, the 2nd Earl, had been secretary to the Privy Council of Charles II and the 10th Earl, Anthony, in about 1795 to 1780 was a member of a social reform group. Now Ian and Ivy and their children lived with her parents.

Whenever Budge was there he spent time in the company of the Maitland's son, Ivor, and daughter Sylvia, who were similar in age to Budge. He found Sylvia to be a good companion and they had many interests in common.

He was given a room in the attic next to the 2nd footman who, as Budge put it "showed me the ropes about what I should put on and when, etc." Sometimes after dinner Budge was able to slip out, change, and go down to the river to fish for grayling in the moonlight with a silver-bodied fly. Returning to his attic room, on at least one occasion his friendly footman brought him half a roasted grouse and a bottle of beer. On another outing Budge went to the races with cousin J.J. and came away 'five bob up'.

Like his late brother, J.J. Bell-Irving had been a partner in Jardine Matheson and served in both Shanghai and Hong Kong. In addition he had been a member of the Executive and Legislative Councils, Hong

Kong's government. Shortly after his return to the United Kingdom he bought Makerstoun House and its lands bordering the River Tweed, though business interests were still maintained, including a directorship in the A.B.C. He had married Eva Piercy, whose father was Benjamin Piercy of Marchwell Hall, Wrexham. Eva was a character and Budge thought her very amusing, if rather eccentric. She had a great interest in Italian culture and having spent much of her adolescence there she could speak the language fluently. She had met and befriended the Fascist leader Benito Mussolini and had a picture of him displayed on her dressing table. Budge wrote to his parents and told them that Eva was anxious to get her son-in-law, Ian Lauderdale, a seat in Parliament and was keen to go out electioneering on his behalf. She read one of her prepared speeches to Budge, which she was to make to some labourers. He said that it was partly in Italian and was mainly about Roman society!

When Budge returned to Loretto for the summer term he was placed in the third senior cricket side, which he now suggests was the side for those boys never likely, ever, to reach the First XI. He had turned fifteen and during the latter part of the spring holidays he shared the driving of another boy's motorbike from Edinburgh to Lockerbie and back. He was very keen on obtaining a motorbike for himself but managed to ride one occasionally, once achieving 70 M.P.H. on a dirt track. He thought it much more exciting than flying because 'you are so near to the ground.' In a minor spill he burnt his leg on the exhaust, but made light of it. Despite his father's uncertain situation he managed to get him to agree to buying a motorbike. The machine cost £20 and was a "New Imperial" one cylinder model with a carbide headlight. It proved to be a faithful machine and took Budge all over Britain, from the Orkneys to Cornwall. When he left Loretto the bike returned to Vancouver with him as "Settler's effects on leaving school." When the customs officer asked how a settler could possess a Canadian passport, he seemed content with Budge's reply—"I got it when previously in Canada." Remembering this long ago encounter, Budge pointed out, "Loretto always instilled honesty, but not to absurd lengths."

The 1928 summer holidays provided Budge with one pleasant stay after another, a summer filled with activity that most boys could only dream about. First with the Griersons (Major Grierson was an old friend of his father) on their estate at Murthly, near Dunkeld in Perthshire, then at Makerstoun, followed by a brief return to White Hill before going on to some elderly aunts at Blackyett, close to the Solway

Firth. The holidays finished with a return to the Highlands where he stayed with the widow of Dr. Greenlees' immediate predecessor, A.R. 'Sconnie' Smith.

His visit here provided an opportunity to do some dinghy sailing. A neighbour of his hostess, Sir William Joynson-Hicks, M.P. (a one-time Home Secretary in James Ramsay MacDonald's first Labour Government), had two sailing dinghies and invited Budge to race him on a nearby loch. They were well matched and Budge was more than able to hold his own. It was perhaps his closest reminder that summer of far away Pasley and the boating pleasures that he was missing there.

The Griersons had really taken to Budge and he wrote glowingly of his stay. They made sure that he saw areas of the Highlands that were new to him, such as the Pass of Killiecrankie and the remains of the Ardoch Roman camp near Stirling. He spent time shooting snipe and rabbits on Major Grierson's moor. He had acquired some new fishing tackle and put it to good use that summer everywhere he went, gradually improving his skill.

The following year Budge returned to Vancouver and Pasley for the summer holidays, the first time since he left in 1927. He was given a double welcome; a dance in his honour at the The Strands and another on Pasley. One pastime enjoyed by the children while on the island was raft building, simple contraptions for paddling about on and usually made from two logs with planks nailed across them. As he approached the island, Budge was delighted to see a flotilla of rafts, gaily decorated for the occasion, coming to meet him. It was a touching home-coming and a dance was arranged later on the wooden-decked tennis court. Suitably dim lighting was provided by Japanese paper lanterns with a candle in each, strung around the perimeter of the court. A gramophone provided music from Broadway melodies such as the "Pagan Love Song" and "Stormy Weather." After the dance there was a moonlight cruise by means of a string of small boats towed one behind the other by the *Emoh*.

At The Strands, Bella (Granny Bell-Irving to the ever increasing grandchildren), gave a supper dance. It was an opportunity for Budge to renew friendships with some of the girls and boys he had known before leaving to attend Loretto. They had all grown while he was away—especially the girls, who proved to be a very attractive lot. One of his Loretto friends had claimed to be in love with a Glasgow cinema usherette and Budge decided that he must find a Canadian girl to be in love with.

When the dance ended there was one very pretty girl who accepted Budge's invitation to drive her home. He was allowed to take H.O.'s car for the purpose. It was Budge's great moment, but when they arrived outside her home all he could do was look longingly at her across the space of the front seat for a few moments before opening the door and escorting her to her door. He had, however, achieved his objective. He said of that night: "I fell in love with her and stayed in love for several years. She went on to MacDonald College in Montreal and I returned to Loretto. Our only contact was by letter and it was pure 'calf-love.' She eventually got engaged to someone else and I went to his stag dinner in Vancouver."

Budge returned to Loretto and soon after his father left the Canadian Fishing Co. when he was presented with an opportunity to go into partnership in a pilchard reduction plant on the west coast of Vancouver Island. The equipment was designed to extract oil and meal from fish by pulverizing them. They purchased a barge in order to give greater flexibility in locating the pilchards and Henry installed some innovative equipment for which his new company held the patent.

Unfortunately the great depression was taking hold and some of the promised capital did not emerge. Their operation was begun on a shoestring and when the equipment broke down there was not sufficient capital to repair and maintain it. This led to a contrite letter at the end of 1930 to H.O. in which Henry had to admit to failure. He had though, received another offer to join a cargo brokerage company in partnership with a friend, Alistair Forbes, but delayed making a final decision until he had talked to his father about it. A meeting was requested to seek his father's advice, which would suggest that things were a little more amicable between them. Henry joined Forbes in the venture.

By 1930 Budge was in the 6th Form and beginning to give thought to his future. Life at school was much different. He had his own room, to decorate to his own taste and

as a 6th Former he was allowed to have a pint of beer, especially welcome after participating in the 'long grinds,' a twenty-five mile cross-country walk. The rules were that the student must have turned 17 and parental permission had been given. He explained, "On holiday we had wine and drinks with everybody else so that we eased into social drinking gradually." Budge remembers buying his first pipe and a tin of 'John Cotton' mild tobacco on Edinburgh's Princes Street.

Studies were going well and he was obtaining good marks in chemistry and science, though they varied from term to term. He gave thought to taking aeronautical engineering and was advised of a very good course at Toronto University. He asked his father to obtain information on entry requirements and apologized for being in such a hurry, saying he 'wished to get on with the job.' Another area of extra curricular study he began was commercial book-keeping, taught by an accountant who came out from Edinburgh every week. The course included business principles and insight on how businesses were run.

H.O. made his wishes known that Budge should begin preparing for Toronto University as quickly as possible, to take two or three years of engineering (though not necessarily in the aeronautical branch). Budge promised that he would study hard towards that goal. As a sixth-former he was preparing for his Certificate "A" in the Officer Training Corps and in a letter to his brother Roderick he said "I am taking an exam tomorrow which will enable me to be an officer in the army in the case of war. I do not intend to join the army anyway, but it is something to do." In his next letter Budge wrote, "The laddie who came from the army to examine us, had been to stay with J.J. at Makerstoun, so he knew who I was. He passed me although I didn't know the difference between a railway cutting and a railway embankment on the map. He said my answers were 'original'."

An explanation of why he did not express keenness about an army commission is that Budge was at this time determined to join the navy in the event of another war. Nevertheless he not only passed the examination but went to the O.T.C. camp that summer and wrote enthusiastically about it. It was a well organized camp and as well as regular troops with a machine gun platoon, there was an R.A.F. squadron on attachment. There were mock battles in which the cadets took part and Budge wrote that he had learned a great deal about war in general.

A visit to the Orkney Islands completed the summer. Budge was a guest of friends of his parents, a Dr. and Mrs Newton, who provided him with good shooting and fishing. There were several Pictish archaeological digs which Budge visited and salvage work was also being done on the ships of the German High Seas Fleet that at the end of the Great War were scuttled by their crews at Scapa Flow. Budge sailed out to watch the activities there in a dinghy belonging to his hosts. He discovered that some of the local fishermen used lifeboats taken from scuttled blockade ships that had been placed at the harbour entrance in 1914.

One small piece of gloom came in the form of a letter from his father. It was partially in response to the news about an exam Budge had sat, which produced mixed results. Budge defended the steps he was taking to pursue a career involving aircraft:

> "You mentioned among other things that I haven't shown any keenness yet for my proposed profession. Well, I am very keen on it and have already assimilated quite a number of technical details and ideas from the periodicals I get; the *Aero Digest* from New York and *Flight* magazine from London.
>
> There is a very interesting series of articles on aerodynamics appearing in the *Aero Digest*, from the theory of heavier than air flight, to the different wing sections and the relationship of lift, drag, thrust and power, etc.
>
> I don't see how I could convince you that I am keen unless I was at home, but I have just told you all I have learned. At the present moment, however, I haven't much time for aeronautics as I am still trying to get through matriculation. Your letter has thoroughly depressed me, but it won't do me any harm. I will return to school early to begin swatting for my university exam."

Budge was so keen on aeronautics that he began drawing outlines of aerofoils for the pleasure of doing it. When he wrote again in September, he had, as promised returned to school early and was putting in at least five hours a day swatting. However, the truth was stretched a little. Going back to school early meant boarding with Edinburgh University medical undergraduates because the school was not yet open. They took great delight in dressing up young Budge in a white coat and in the emergency room he was given a pair of pliers to remove nails and other sharp objects from the bare-feet of the urchins who came in from the back-streets of the town. They deferred to him as 'doctor'. In the evenings, on Leith Walk he was introduced to the Scottish custom of holding a whisky in the left hand and a beer chaser in the other. Between whiles a little light swatting was undertaken.

By this point in his life Budge's letters were now starting to show a very lively mind, full of interest in the world events. He had just received some Vancouver papers and expressed pleasure in learning that the Conservative party had been elected in Canada. He told his father that he was becoming interested in British politics, even though he thought they were complicated. The Prime Minister was now James Ramsay MacDonald and the Labour Party was in power. The great depression was at its height, there were three million unemployed and MacDonald was getting the blame for the ills of the country. Budge's succinct comment was: "Something drastic must happen soon, as none of the parties are strong enough to do anything at all." He was right. Soon after, a National Government was formed, in effect a coalition of parties. MacDonald remained as Prime Minister but his powers were no better because the Conservatives held a majority and in 1935 Stanley Baldwin replaced him as Prime Minister. The economy remained poor and the depression continued until the outbreak of war in 1939.

While swatting for exams and reading aeronautical journals, Budge wondered whether, if he returned to Vancouver instead of going to the University of Toronto, he could apply to Boeing Aircraft in Seattle for a job. Another possibility was to apply to an aircraft factory in the U.K. In due course he sat the Oxford and Cambridge Certificate and gained honours in five subjects. This was sufficient to give him entry to the U of T School of Engineering. He had passed with the required honours and was delighted with his success—though not of his sheer good luck. Having been bored in dull history classes—his only unhappy memory of teaching standards at Loretto—he knew little history, but had swatted on one historical event, the Peninsular War. When he opened the examination paper by sheer chance it requested a lengthy essay on that very subject. The odds of that happening were enormous—but he had passed. He just scraped through French but passed the other four handily.

Any thoughts for the future were put aside temporarily when Budge again joined his grandfather for a holiday in Switzerland. It was equally enjoyable and the Christmas holiday sped by, with skiing, skating and dancing. With so much to enjoy he may not have been aware that H.O. was not showing his usual vigour and refrained from taking part in many of the activities with his grandson. Budge left the resort to return to Loretto and H.O. remained on the Continent for a few days on business commitments.

When H.O. returned to London he kept an appointment with a Harley Street specialist who confirmed that he was suffering from cancer and the prognosis was not good. He was advised against having an operation as the doctor did not think it would serve any purpose in prolonging his life. Before returning to Vancouver he went north to see

Budge and at the same time had a long meeting with Dr. Greenlees. After H.O. departed from Loretto, Budge was called to see the headmaster and told the news of his grandfather's illness. The fact that he was told the true situation is most remarkable because it was at a time when cancer was almost a forbidden subject and people simply did not discuss it.

H.O. returned to Vancouver and in true style he and Bella asked Isabel to arrange a dance at The Strands to celebrate his 75th birthday on January 26. It was his last gesture. Against the advice of the London specialist he underwent an operation. It was not successful and he became weaker with each passing day, finally, by early February being confined to bed. His sons were sent for and they gathered around his bed. It was once again H.O. and his boys. Whatever rancour may have remained between Henry and H.O. was put aside in these last hours. The womenfolk were not in on this meeting, although they came later to say good-bye to their father.

Henry Ogle Bell-Irving died peacefully on February 19, 1931 at 8.30 a.m. His contribution to Vancouver and indeed to British Columbia was immense and was acknowledged in the newspapers. Each one had several columns on his attributes and the front page of the Province had a large portrait style photograph of him. He was referred to as the "Dean of the Salmon Industry" and the "Father of Imperial Preference." The funeral service was held at The Strands, with his five sons as pallbearers. A piper and officers from the Seaforth Highlanders of Canada were present.

H.O. had made a will the previous summer and had updated it just before he left for Switzerland in early December. This update concerned mainly personal effects which he intended distributing between his children and grandchildren. It is ironic that H.O., who had led a life of great physical fitness, was survived by Bella, who had been an invalid for more than twenty years. She bore her husband's death with her usual courage and lived another five years.

Richard Bell-Irving took over from his father as head of H. Bell-Irving Co. and represented it on the Board of the A.B.C. Co. There had been some changes, as the longtime Chairman, E.S.H. Corbett had died a few months before H.O. and now Dick's cousin, Major John Bell-Irving was in the Chair. Also on the Board was the Earl of Lauderdale, making sure that the family was well represented.

When Budge returned to Vancouver in the spring of 1931, he lost no time in going up to Pasley and helping with improvements and repairs. The absence of H.O. was much felt by his family, but the tradition of the weekend visits and the much longer summer stays had been too ingrained for there to be any let-up. Budge had acquired some woodworking skills at Loretto and began helping out with construction jobs on the island. The winter winds had blown trees over, one of them on a cabin. New foundations were required on some of the buildings and repairs to roof and walls were necessary.

He was still trying to decide whether to enter U of T and follow a career in aeronautics, but things did not turn out that way and his life took a totally different turn.

CHAPTER THREE

DESPITE PASSING THE OXFORD AND CAMBRIDGE school certificate with honours in five subjects as required for the aeronautical engineering course at the University of Toronto, Budge had begun to develop doubts about his mathematical capability for a career in that profession. He had further doubts about his financial ability to afford a U. of T. education and most importantly had failed at the time to realize that a career in aeronautics would inevitably mean being away from B.C., which he wished to avoid. He decided instead to take Commerce at the University of British Columbia (U.B.C.) to see where that might lead.

He was pleased to be home again, among his family with old friendships to be rekindled and Pasley Island beckoning. Before long he began to notice among some of his peers a tendency to consider him something of a foreigner. There was some comment on his clothes and the way he wore them, as well as his manner of speaking. Despite four years at a Scottish school, had they made him an Englishman? All this did not bother Budge in the least. He had been well trained four years earlier, having survived unscarred the 'hardening' process as a rather bumptious Canadian new boy, and he brought home with him unforgettable memories of four happy years at Loretto.

After a few weeks of leisure at Pasley, it was time to go to work. Looking back to that time, Budge said, "I realize now that it would have been the moment for some expert career counselling but it did not occur to me to seek it. I had made a perhaps incorrect decision to take a Commerce degree at U.B.C. and I would stay with that decision."

In that first summer home from Loretto, he was given a job in the family company at the far northern Arrandale Cannery on the Nass River, sailing on the Union Steamship *Catala*. The Union Steamship Company in those days provided an invaluable service to the variety of settlements up and down the British Columbia coast, from Vancouver to the Alaska border. Canneries, logging camps, a variety of mills and other enterprises were scattered among the bays and inlets, all requiring incoming and outgoing freight and passenger services. Their schedules were determined by the amount of freight carried and stops were made both day and night. There could be no better way to see these fascinating activities and to appreciate the beauty of the coast than passage on a Union Steamship vessel. The mix of characters usually found among fellow passengers could be always counted on for further interest and sometimes considerable entertainment.

The early Union ships were designed and built in Scotland. Three of the smaller ships had their hulls and engines built on the Clyde in sections and shipped to Vancouver for assembly at a plant in Coal Harbour, part of Vancouver's waterfront. Their names had a west-coast flavour, *Capilano*, *Cassiar* and *Comox*. Other ships, launched in Scotland made the long trip through the Panama under their own steam. Many old timers have fond memories of these vessels that seemed to retain a wisp of Scotland about them, well matched to the frequent Scottish brogue among their crews.

For passengers in cabin class there was a dining saloon with linen tablecloths and good china in which four meals per day were served. Stationery was provided in the lounge and the envelopes had on the left-hand side a scenic picture of tall trees and mountains on either side of a body of water with—of course—a Union steamship on it. The envelope caption was, "Coast trips from one hour to one week—From $1.00 to $50.00." In fact for people 'down on their luck' steerage accommodation might be free. At Arrandale, Glendale and the many similar communities up the coast the cry would go up, "The Union boat is coming!" and the population would react like a disturbed ants' nest.

Budge arrived at Arrandale, located on the south-eastern entrance to the Nass River, where the Alaska border is less than ten miles to the north. Opposite is the native Nisga'a village of Kincolith and he would soon learn to respect and maintain an interest in their traditions. Once ashore he reported to Walter Walker, the widely respected manager who, like all of the A.B.C. managers held warm memories of his friendship with Budge's father, Henry.

The cannery was, typically, on the water's edge at the foot of a steep, heavily wooded mountain. In front of it the dock, built of heavy planks on piles, extended over the water to a sufficient depth for the Union Steamship vessels to come alongside at all tides. The dock accommodated a variety of activities and functions; bluestone tanks containing copper sulphate to sterilize the gillnets; racks on which to dry and repair them. Nearby was a motley collection of buildings, most referred to as shacks, which housed the cannery crews, Chinese, Japanese, native people and a small number of whites; each with their own quarters. The centre of activity, common to all canneries, was the company store, where it was possible to buy almost anything, the currency being script coupons issued by the A.B.C., to be settled up later. Upstream from the cannery dock there were numerous floats in constant use by a variety of boats, large and small, coming and going at all hours. Above it all, with the first indications of some privacy was the manager's house with its small garden. It was the domain of Walter Walker and his family.

In the early 1920's Budge had occasionally accompanied his father to the Phoenix Cannery at Steveston, so he was not a total stranger to the inner workings of a cannery. Now, with this wilderness mountain backdrop as a setting, and so far from the constraints of civilization, young Budge looked forward to the months ahead. The diversity of races and the variety of tasks they accomplished, the efficiency of the cannery under Walter Walker's guidance actually filled him with excitement. He was aware of his good fortune to be a part of such a worthwhile and fascinating enterprise. During this first visit to the north, Budge developed a great love for the British Columbia coast, which he came to know well.

The cannery foreman, Pete Fotheringham, was a big man, excellent at his job, but with very fixed ideas on some things. One was that Budge's collection of gramophone records was not, to his thinking, appropriate to the cannery environment. They were much too classical and within a few minutes of the first record's strains being heard, like a pile of one-way frisbees, they were consigned to the river. The fact that Budge was not unduly upset by this act of desecration on his musical taste might have had something to do with his early Loretto training, which had quickly instilled a liberal dose of "C'est la vie."

One of his first jobs was moulding the small lead weights onto replacement lead lines for the bottoms of gill-nets. Working beside a tub of molten lead was a warm job, not immune to some blisters. It was not too difficult for the new boy, but foreman Pete just could not restrain himself from having another dig at this new arrival. He told Budge, "As long as your hand is wet you can stir the molten lead with it because the steam will form a barrier." Showing either a disarming trust or an appalling lack of judgment, Budge dunked his hand in a nearby pale of water and made a very quick pass through the surface of the molten lead. It was fortunately true and he suffered no damage, but he never did it again.

The first-aid room was another place where Budge was put to use. He had an interest and some proficiency in first-aid dating back to his cubs and scouting days, so this was a good opportunity to be useful. As it turned out, there were virtually no first-aid requirements during that season.

Many of the Arrandale workers were characters in their own right, making a most interesting cross-section of west-coast humanity. One of the most notable of these was Albert Allan, the Native boss. He was a large man with no hint of fat or flabbiness, and he had an aura of power which he carried quite unconsciously. His size almost cost him his life one day crossing to Kincolith, when he fell overboard. Strenuous efforts to get him back on board were to no avail and finally he was simply towed the remaining distance, with no ill-effects despite the freezing temperature. Albert's particular gift was the great fund of Native legends and stories he told in vivid detail, no doubt with some poetic licence, from a time well before the first white men sailed into the Nass. In recalling his conversations with Albert, Budge is sorry that he did not have the benefit of a tape recorder then.

One day a child died in the Native bunkhouse. A small coffin was made and after the body was placed in it a hole was cut in the wall to remove the coffin and so prevent bad spirits from entering through the door. Placed on the hatch cover of a seine-boat, the coffin was surrounded by Nisga'a mourners in their Salvation Army uniforms. With musical instruments playing suitably sad music they proceeded up-river to Graveyard Point.

Budge had been happy to discover the Arrandale brass band, which these B.C. Native people had created despite their own ancient culture, selecting the instruments from a T. Eaton mail-order catalogue. They had then, with little outside help, learned to play them. Not infrequently at night the sound of a single instrument might be heard across the water from the direction of a twinkling light as the lone musician drifted in his boat down river at the end of a gill-net. Sometimes on weekends the whole band played together, producing fine music with particular skill, including tunes from Gilbert and Sullivan. In good weather they performed outside on the dock. It was another reminder to Budge that the art of these people is by no means confined to carvings, sculptures and paintings.

The second job given to Budge for several weeks was the gas wharf. Running the gas station was not very exciting, but it did provide an opportunity to meet a lot of fishermen and to watch their comings and goings. It had its moments, one of them when a baby seal, rescued from a gill-net was given to Budge. The company store provided a bottle, teat and a few cans of Pacific condensed milk. The seal thrived and after a while was placed in the water with a dog collar on the end of a fishing line. After it was released the seal continued to come back for some time.

Once a truculent fisherman remained too long with his boat secured to the dock. When Budge politely asked him to move it he replied, "You make me." Recalling that it was some time since he'd had a decent scrap and it might be fun, Budge invited the man onto the dock. To the delight of onlookers the matter was quickly settled and the fisherman appeared glad to be able to move his boat.

An unusual event that caused some disruption around the gas wharf was the arrival of a boat with a fully grown trussed-up bald eagle on board. It had been found at sea with its talons fully locked into the back of a large spring salmon. The fish was too big even for the powerful eagle to lift from the water and take to the nearest beach to devour. Now the large bird sat regally on top of an oil drum with the appearance of having adopted ownership of the whole cannery. Rescued from his predicament by the fisherman it would be a suitable end to the story to say the eagle flew gratefully away. This, however, was not to be. Some time during the night the bird ended its life's journey through the kitchen entrance of the Chinese bunkhouse where, as Budge put it: "To the well-known culinary reputation of the Chinese might be added their fondness for an interesting variation!"

However large the run of fish might be, fishing was closed on weekends to allow sufficient escapement up river to the spawning beds.

When the time came to set the nets again, all the boats would be out and ready to fish, awaiting the moment when the Fisheries Patrol boat sent up a rocket. Upon the bright flash and accompanying bang, seen and heard all over the Nass estuary, there was a frenzy of activity.

Budge witnessed his first strike, with its inevitable days of haggling and bad temper. There was a belief that it could be settled in time for the following Sunday evening opening and in great anticipation the boats put out. The rocket was seen to explode and the fishing began—but it had not come from the Fisheries vessel. It was too late to stop the fishing so the strike came to an end anyway, even though by default. An irate Fishery Patrol Officer discovered that two rockets were missing from the locker and a warrant was issued for the arrest of the person or persons responsible. No one was identified and fishing continued without further interruption to the end of the season. The Fisheries Officer never found the second rocket, but a later incident at U.B.C. might have had something to do with its loss.

The Caucasian cannery crew, though small in number were all old hands and very proficient. They were always willing to help Budge understand the way things worked and within a short time discovered that he was friendly, eager to learn and to be one of the crew. Their bunkhouse was a friendly meeting place, and added to this were the three sumptuous meals per day, well up to the high standards for which canneries and logging camps along the B.C. coast have become famous.

Poker was a popular pastime here and one evening a visitor who had arrived that day to sell religious books came to the bunkhouse door. He was not given an over-warm welcome but he persisted and to everyone's surprise he took a place at the poker table. It was not his night; within an hour he had lost his books and, if Budge's memory can be trusted, his shirt as well.

By way of contrast, on one visit to the Japanese bunkhouse, while Budge was sitting talking to the Japanese boss, his wife was quite unselfconsciously bathing herself in a tin tub placed in the middle of the room. While Japanese moral standards were always strict, there was no emphasis on unnecessary modesty. Budge also recalls a properly set dinner table, with a clean white table cloth ready for the incoming fishermen. The whole place had an air of clean efficiency as the women went about their chores in readiness for the meal.

The Japanese gill-net fleet fished steadily all week from opening to closing. In the early part of the season, even in the occasional snow storm he recalled their fishermen working with nothing over their yellow woollen undershirts. Their stamina was probably bolstered by an occasional swig from the sake jug (Budge would remember it many years later when, after thirty-six hours in action on the hills of Sicily he was still on his feet—with an army issue water-bottle on his belt filled with rum). From the overall results of the Japanese fishermen he was not surprised that the major packing companies were always competing for the maximum number of Japanese fishing licences.

Within the plant itself the 'Iron Chink' was the most exciting piece of equipment. This invention had taken the place of lines of Chinese workers who in seconds skillfully dressed the fish. Nevertheless they were no match for the machine and that is where the name arose. In the early days the hard-working Chinese labourers in B.C. were most often referred to with unwarranted contempt as 'Chinks'—hence the name given to the new machine that took over in preparing salmon for the cans. In these days of political correctness the name may be seen as derogatory rather than an historic reminder of those displaced industrious people.

After the advent of this machine the Chinese crew still looked after all other aspects of the processing before and after the canning. They tended the machines and kept the premises up to scratch. When Budge worked at Arrandale in 1931 most, if not all the cans were hand-filled by the wives of both Native and Japanese fishermen. They sat side by side in two long rows facing each other on either side of a long table. In between them a moving belt brought a constant supply of salmon washed and pre-cut by the 'Iron Chink.' A second belt moving in the same direction brought a constant line of cans. With remarkable efficiency each woman took a can and a portion of salmon off the belt and placed it in the can. It was nearly always necessary to add to, or trim to fill the can neatly, using great dexterity with only a sharp knife. The filled can was then put back on the moving belt.

At the end of the line, before the cans received their pinch of salt and sealing by the vacuum closing machine, an inspector stood watching the constant procession of cans. The job required constant vigilance to ensure that nothing but salmon went into the can. Budge filled the task from time to time and he remembered it years later when a news story caused world-wide attention—reporting that a mouse had been found in a bottle of beer from a well-known Scottish brewery.

When the season ended it was with regret that Budge returned to Vancouver to become a U.B.C. freshman. As a final comment on that summer he noted that the Chinese cannery crew on their way back showed their addiction to gambling. Before Vancouver was reached most of their summer pay ended up in the hands of one or two particularly skilled participants.

After this eventful summer at Arrandale, at the age of eighteen Budge enrolled in first year arts, the necessary preliminaries to a Bachelor of Commerce Degree. An early U.B.C. memory is of a large bonfire which the engineering students had built on the main Mall. Budge saw it as a suitable resting place for a certain Fisheries rocket. When the bonfire was lit it exploded mightily and he was blamed, captured and convicted without trial.

All in all Budge had an interesting evening. He was de-bagged and the gentleman who had made good his own deficiencies by wearing the said trousers was later booked by the police for some misdemeanor under the name of Bell-Irving—from a piece of paper found in the pocket. Meanwhile it had been thought appropriate to give the real Bell-Irving a 'hair-do' with plaster of Paris mixed with green shingle stain. His evening of fun finished at home in the small hours sitting on the lowest of the basement steps while his father, sitting two steps above attacked the now dry mess with a hammer and chisel and a bottle of Javel water—a none too efficient solvent.

Budge had a considerable fondness for Shakespeare's plays and no doubt would have been spell-bound by the lectures of the famous Dr. Sedgewick but they were not given in first-year arts. The available English courses did not inspire him and though he also had a wish to become proficient in conversational French, he found no inspiration there either. He had enjoyed all his work in the Upper Sixth form at Loretto but he did not succeed in becoming enthusiastic about his first-year Arts courses at U.B.C.

Having passed the required subjects for entrance into Engineering at U of T it would seem likely that he might have been excused first-year arts, but that didn't occur to him. Commencing in the second year programme might well have encouraged his remaining at U.B.C. to emerge with a degree and some useful knowledge.

Budge had played rugby throughout his time at Loretto. He now continued to enjoy the game at U.B.C. even though getting to practise meant a streetcar ride in the early morning dark for a 7 a.m. start. He continued playing in later years with the ex-U.B.C. 'Occasionals.' Fraternities and sororities were also important in providing an opportunity for young men and women with similar interests to be together and forge lasting friendships. In 'rushing season' the 'frat' and sorority houses sought prospective members, entertaining them to foster their interest in joining and also to check them out. Budge was glad to be 'rushed' by two fraternities and was happy to join Zeta-Psi, feeling rather pleased with himself after the initiation ceremony.

A chance encounter that first term in the University bookstore was, to Budge, a foretaste of life to come. Miss Nancy Symes, Arts '34 and future president of the U.B.C. Players Club heard his voice and rather liked it. As she was looking for new club members she suggested that he join, which he did. The club functioned well under the expert guidance of English Professor, F.G.C. Wood. The spring play was put on for four nights on campus and then went on a provincial summer tour. Nancy went on two tours, putting on plays in the small interior towns, using any hall or auditorium that was available—all the while the cast chaperoned by an elderly lady whose other role was make-up artist. Budge remained a humble scene shifter. A lifetime partnership would not be thought of for several years and this chance meeting in the bookstore gave no clue that she would become a Colonel's lady and sometime Chatelaine of Government House in Victoria, B.C.

Nancy was born in 1912, the only child of Reginald and Aileen Symes, who had come out from England the previous year. Reginald was the son of London stockbroker Alfred Symes of Thorpe Hall, Thorpe-le-Soken, and had attended Marlborough, one of England's distinguished public schools, before taking law at Pembroke College, Cambridge. Reginald was called to the Bar by the Society of the Inner Temple in 1905 and in 1910 had married Aileen Hatchell, daughter of Jane and Charles Hatchell, a surgeon-major in the Indian Army.

They settled into furnished rooms in London, knowing that as a fledging barrister, advancement would be slow. At about this time Alfred Symes passed through Vancouver on a world tour and returned to U.K. with glowing reports of the potential of this comparatively new city. He suggested to his son that he look into the possibilities of emigration. Reginald took his advice and in June 1911 he and Aileen set sail for Canada. They headed west for Vancouver , where things went well and Reginald entered into practice with another young lawyer, Charles Wilson. The firm expanded over the years, at one time being known as

Robertson, Douglas and Symes. It continues today as Douglas, Symes and Brissenden. In due course the Symes built a house at 2810 S.W. Marine Drive on five acres of land stretching down to the Fraser River flats.

Nancy grew up at a time of somewhat privileged but small social circles in Vancouver, reflecting the predominating influence of the original British settlers of which H.O. Bell-Irving was one of the most influential. Life in the 1920's could be very pleasant for a young girl whose parents were reasonably well-off.

The stock-market crash of 1929 changed all that and life became more serious and uncertain for many of these young people, though Nancy felt that the 'halcyon years' stood them in good stead when in later years life brought them some tough challenges. Budge and Nancy escaped the worst deprivations. With the help of H.O. Budge had remained at Loretto, while Nancy continued at Crofton House girls' school and they were able to go on to U.B.C. where she studied English Literature and History.

Budge remained there for only one year and said of that period in his life: "Come spring I had no trouble passing every exam because in the Upper 6th Form at Loretto I had been doing much more interesting work. This first year had not given me the spark of enthusiasm to carry on into more interesting studies and an eventual degree. Again, this would have been an appropriate time for some wise consultation as to my future, but it did not occur to me to seek it. After only two terms I decided to 'call it a day' and go out to work."

Uncle Dick agreed that he could spend another summer up the coast which, while looked forward to, was in some ways simply delaying long-term decisions about the future. An indication of how unsettled he was is found in a letter dated April 20, 1932 from his old headmaster, Dr. Greenlees. Budge had written to find out if it was worth returning to Britain to seek work in a shipping office. The depression in Britain was at its worst and the reply was not encouraging:

> "... quite frankly it is no earthly good in this country just now as far as I can find out—there is simply nothing doing in shipping.
>
> Now look here, please realize that Vancouver may be over-crowded but it less so than the Old Country. While I cannot tell you what they are, there must be chances for somebody with initiative to make good out there; certainly far more opportunities than can be

found here, so keep your eyes open for something you can start on your own and the chance will come along. Finish your B. Comm. degree and if you really know the stuff it may help you later."

By the time this letter was received Budge was ready for his return to the cannery. He was pleased to be heading north again for his second summer on the Nass. It was a return to a life which he had learned to enjoy, this time to be skipper of the collector boat *Daisy Leaf*. She was smaller than the other boats of the 'Leaf' series that had been under the command of Budge's father at the outbreak of WW I, though she did not lack power. With her large Hall-Scott engine, set well forward to leave room aft for the salmon, she had a tendency to put her nose well down into a head sea unless the stern was well loaded. Budge was both captain and engineer and his deck hand and general duties man was Colin Collison, son of the Indian Affairs doctor at Kincolith. Doctor Collison, a fine and caring physician, lived in harmony with the Nisga'a people and their culture. His family had served on the B.C. coast for several generations back to Archdeacon Collison, who was among the first Europeans on the Nass.

A few days after Budge arrived at Arrandale he was involved in his first emergency. On the cannery dock was a 45 gallon gasoline drum that had been empty for at least nine years. One of the cannery crew was instructed to cut it in half to make two tubs for some purpose within the cannery. The worker, a popular Irishman with a fund of stories, lit his acetylene torch and had no sooner cut into the drum when there was a loud explosion as the drum ripped apart. The Irishman was found lying on the dock with one foot blown off, other than a few remnants of connecting tendon. A tourniquet was immediately applied and he was laid on a stretcher, warmly wrapped, with his foot still in the boot beside him.

The stretcher was lowered to the hatch cover of the *Daisy Leaf*, abaft the wheel-house and Budge put to sea with great haste for Dr. Collison in the village of Kincolith. On board were Walter Walker and the store keeper, plus two others to accompany the unfortunate man. Dr. Collison immediately went to work with a pain killer and interim dressings then the party set off for the hospital at Anyox, about thirty nautical miles up Observatory Inlet.

The town site served a copper mine and was a bustling place then with fair hospital facilities. A memory of that trip is of the Irishman bravely telling a succession of outlandish stories to distract one of the accompanying crew from being violently ill. The patient was admitted for surgery and would remain there until well enough to be transported south. Budge remained on board to await a preliminary report on his condition, while the crew took off to visit the town. There was no question of saving his leg and weeks later it was learned that the man was to return to Ireland with a company pension and a wooden leg, where Budge hoped he continued his repertoire of outlandish stories.

On the return to Arrandale, an increasing wind blew up Observatory Inlet and the waves grew with it. "Daisy Leaf" headed into a heavy sea as Budge noticed with some alarm that the hatch cover of the engine room was loose and in immediate danger of being washed overboard. He scrambled out of the wheel-house and threw himself on the hatch cover just as a large wave crashed over the bows. Budge caught the full force but the cover was saved from washing away—and avoided the possibility of *Daisy Leaf* achieving her occasional desire to become a submarine. Walter Walker immediately produced a 'dram' of good Scotch, poured into a half-flat salmon can—which did much to revive the young skipper in his near-drowned condition. They made it safely home to Arrandale.

Kincolith was, at the time, typical of the many native villages that dotted the B.C. coast. A gill-net that had seen better days was strung across the small Kincolith River to catch whatever species of salmon might run from time to time. In season, long lines of oolichans were suspended to dry in the sun, contributing to the tell-tale aroma so readily identifying such villages on the B.C. coast.

The oolichan is a small fish that returns in the millions to certain B.C rivers to spawn in the spring. They are particularly oily, though good to eat when fresh and properly cooked. Their oiliness has led to the alternative name of 'candlefish'. The principal native use has been for the rendering and production of oil, commonly referred to as grease—hence the historic 'grease trails' over which certain coast native peoples traded this rich oil with tribes in the interior. Just fifty years later, when Budge was Lieutenant-Governor of British Columbia, at a ceremonial dinner given by the Nootka People on the West Coast, Nancy mistook a jug of 'grease' for salad dressing—an experience not likely to be forgotten.

Surrounded by outstanding scenery and a cultural mix of people, Budge found himself more and more at home. This second summer was spent almost entirely with the boats of the gill-net fleet, at a time when gill-net gas boats were in a minority. The majority were sail boats, twenty-seven feet long "Columbia River" boats with a low 'cuddy' cabin forward, open aft of it to the stern. A mast was stepped right into the bow with one gaff-rigged mainsail, and a thwart amidships. Each boat had a crew of two, one of whom might crawl into the primitive cabin where, lying down he would have perhaps an 18 inch clearance above him. Though not comfortable it provided a comparatively dry place for the off-duty man to sleep.

The gill-net boats, made fast one behind the other on a long line, were towed in the evening across and up-river with each one letting go in his own time until all were free. An oil lamp was lit on the boat and a second one on a small float at the end of the net. Each boat moved across the tide by sail or oars, paying out the net in a more or less straight line until fully extended. The boat and its net then drifted during the night, out towards the open sea. In daytime a flag replaced the lamp on the end.

Each morning at first light, Budge put out to find his drifting fleet. The boats would make fast in turn along-side in line with the open fish-hold abaft the wheel house. The two-man crew had usually finished hauling their catch into their boat in readiness for transfer to the *Daisy Leaf*. In a heavy salmon run they might have emptied the net several times during the night. Using a fish-pike, the fishermen threw each salmon up and over into the hold. Sitting atop the wheel house with his legs dangling, Budge held a small press-button counter in each hand plus one, or sometimes two others placed beside him. Each counter represented one species of salmon, and each fish had to be identified in mid-air as it passed over. The unloading completed, the boat's catch-record book was made up, signed and returned. The fisherman cast off and Budge went on to the next gill-netter.

More than sixty years later, Budge cannot imagine how it was possible for him to have correctly identified each salmon species as they passed in front of him in such a short arc. Perhaps an occasional error might have been excused by the fact that at the time salmon were paid for, not in dollars per pound, but 25 cents each for sockeye, 5 cents each for pinks and 10 cents for bright chums. Prices for big chinooks, cohoe or those of an occasional steelhead have been forgotten in the mists of time.

Of all the boat crews that Budge dealt with in that summer of 1932, there are two he remembers particularly. Coming alongside the first he noticed a large, strong, obviously blind black man and his partner a very small wizened white man. Kneeling, facing each other across the centre-thwart, they were saying grace before breakfast. Between them was half a loaf of bread visibly green with mold, and a dead crab. The second and happier memory is of a jolly Norwegian who owned one of the few gas-boats. He always gave Budge breakfast, a bowl of cornflakes and a glass of rum.

When the loading was completed some of the boats chose to be towed back to the dock, there to indulge in some well earned rest while others remained out, to catch every extra fish they could. It was a hard life, out in their small open boats often in miserable weather, though there were compensating days. After returning to the loading dock the Chinese crew went to work unloading the *Daisy Leaf*'s hold and then washed her down. The working days were long, from dawn till after dark but Budge and young Collison thrived on it.

On some weekends he and Colin were able to take advantage of relaxing pursuits, especially fly-fishing up the Kincolith River. There was thick bush on both sides so Budge took the water route by Native canoe. Though not remembering any particular day—or the catch, he does recall thinking that the stream quite possibly had never before been fished with modern fly-fishing tackle. He was aware that bear were in the vicinity and concluded that early in the season before the salmon spawned, a young bear might be good to eat.

About this time Budge found that his $75.00 monthly captain's pay could become $100.00 if he were to feed himself. Colin agreed it would be a good thing too so the possibility of taking a bear became of some interest to them. A day's hunting was planned up the Kincolith River with H.O.'s .33 Winchester lever action bear rifle, that had been left to Budge in his will. The deed was soon done—and Budge was liberally covered with the wicked little barbed spines of the infamous Devil's club—but he was learning fast.

With the bear safely back at the cannery, a hind-quarter was cooked ashore and the balance was put to good use. The Chinese got the pads and certain internal organs on their prize list. Bear meat in the right season, though a shade on the dark side, is very good to eat. The bear meat supplemented with a generous contribution from the sea and fresh eggs for Sunday breakfast, fed the young crew of the *Daisy Leaf*. The bill for food from the store was only $11 for two months and, most satisfying to Budge, a higher salary as well.

Towards the end of the season Budge and Colin took a small boat up river to Iceberg Bay for some duck shooting. None were bagged but two events were recorded. The first one Budge thought was extremely funny. A bear was seen through the tall rushes at the edge of the marsh and Colin went ashore to see how close he could get to it. Budge lost sight of them—and then, suddenly both stood up, facing each other at a short distance, before running away in opposite directions. The second event was not so funny. Colin's shotgun discharged in the boat, only just missing Budge. The hole in the boat was repairable.

At summer's end the time came for Budge to head back to Vancouver to face whatever lay ahead for him. However, he was to go out in style, skippering the *Getty*, a larger seine boat to Alert Bay with two Nisga'a as crew. Fuel, rations and personal gear on board, the final farewells were said and off they went with Budge facing the task of charting the course through waters that were mostly new to him. Somewhere off Port Simpson the Thorneycroft engine began to run hot, signs that a bearing was overheating. Budge made the wise decision to put into Prince Rupert for a check and to make any necessary repairs. It was two days before the boat was ready to continue.

The repairs completed, the *Getty* continued south with the delightful coastal scenery always in sight until halfway across Queen Charlotte Sound they ran out of scenery and, in fact out of sight of anything at all. The reason for this predicament was fog and the approach of dusk. Budge will never forgot his horror at finding the appropriate chart was missing, that of the north end of Vancouver Island; Cape Scott, Hope Island, Nigei Island and the entrance to Queen Charlotte Strait. He had neglected to check that all the required charts were on board. It was a lesson not to be forgotten but he did not panic. The compass was working and he had a general idea of the lay of the land. It was a situation that called for caution and finding the land and close-in rocks—before they found the *Getty*.

He had the advantage of a father who had distinguished himself as a skipper both on this coast and in the English Channel. He recalled Henry's stories of using a whistle-blast and timing the echo and was also aware that Union Steamships used this procedure in some of the narrow passages along the coast. Budge put the boat's horn to work with brief blasts every few minutes. Eventually an echo came back and the gap between blast and echo shortened each time. Finally pointing the horn to port, then starboard produced echoes from both directions. He put the engine into dead-slow and one of the Nisga'a swung the depth sounding lead-line until a suitable anchorage was found. Daybreak would confirm a good anchorage and that they were on course.

The general lay of the northern entrance to Queen Charlotte Strait was comfortably familiar and Alert Bay was reached in a few hours. An overnight stay here and Budge caught the next Union ship to Vancouver. It was the end of a second wonderful summer and a few years would intervene—plus a few of life's uncertainties—before he would see that part of the coast again. Where was that land-fall? Many years later, from his own cabin cruiser, *Shieling*, Budge recognized it as almost certainly Cascade Harbour on Nigei Island.

Once more in Vancouver, a decision had to be made about his immediate next step. Budge was within a few months of his twentieth birthday and had not yet found a career to replace his youthful interest in aeronautical engineering. Now he was again just one of the multitude looking for a job. His father, Henry, after years in the fishing business had formed a small company booking passengers on freight ships bound for distant ports; arranging export grain shipments on a cargo space-available basis as well as some foreign exchange business, buying and selling foreign currency as required for both exporters and ships. It was an interesting mix of activities and Budge was glad to join him, though realizing that it was not a permanent billet. The pay was modest, but he still remembers buying a good lunch each day in a nearby restaurant—for twenty-five cents.

After a few months Budge left his father's company and joined the Alberta Pacific Timber Co., as a trainee salesman, selling lumber from a downtown office where, to begin with, orders were few and far between. It was difficult to visualize a prosperous future. Later on things got better, but it became evident that the company itself was not on a firm footing and should not be depended upon for a secure future.

Following his years of discipline and constant activity at Loretto, Budge's life as a junior in a downtown office was not enough. Apart from his skiing, Pasley and the various outdoor activities he enjoyed, he was missing this discipline he had long been accustomed to. In short, he was bored.

However, since early childhood in the Dover of WW I Budge had retained a built-in belief that the next war would be his turn, and it was inevitable that he would join one of the services. If he chose to follow in his father's footsteps the Navy would, of course, be his first choice. On the other hand, his grandfather had played a part in raising the Seaforth

Highlanders of Canada, and it had been well-served by at least two of his uncles. Also he had some friends among the junior officers.

One day in May 1933 as he passed the Vancouver Club, Budge met Colonel Blair, the Commanding Officer coming out. On impulse Budge asked if he might have a commission in the regiment. The Colonel invited him to drop by on a parade night, which he did. He applied for his commission, though with the private thought that he would transfer to the Royal Canadian Navy on threat of war. On July 15, 1933 Budge was gazetted 2nd Lieutenant, Seaforth Highlanders of Canada. His first of many memories as a Seaforth was the simple order from the Adjutant, Captain (later Brigadier) J.R.S. (Johnny) Lough, D.S.O., M.C.—"Bell-Irving, go out and get your hair cut!"

Budge remained a 2nd Lieutenant until August 1935 when he took a qualifying course with the P.P.C.L.I. (Princess Patricia's Canadian Light Infantry) at Work Point Barracks in Esquimalt and soon after he received his second pip.

In the month following his joining the Seaforths there was a small bridge party at the Shalcross home in Shaughnessy, to which both Budge and Nancy Symes were invited. During the evening he came to the conclusion that he and Nancy had something in common and invited her to come to Pasley for the following weekend. Her immediate liking for the island helped their budding friendship immensely.

Budge had known and loved Pasley since childhood and it was still a magical summer home for the many Bell-Irving mothers and their children, where they remained summer long. Their fathers continued to arrive on Saturday afternoons to be greeted by the children watching from Pilot Rock. Though over the years there were numerous changes, the great joy of Pasley was much enhanced by sharing it with Nancy.

Sometimes they paddled a canoe in the early morning to then uninhabited Worlecombe Island for some salmon fishing followed by a swim before returning for breakfast. In the evening they would paddle in the opposite direction, past untouched forest behind Silver Beach to Bruce Boyd's house on Hermit Island, where there was often a good party in progress. As time went on, Budge and Nancy developed an ability to walk across Pasley in the dark without a light, feeling their way safely in bare feet. They both enjoyed this caper and years later taught their sons to do the same. Nancy enjoyed Pasley from the first time she stepped ashore, but especially later when she had her own house and family.

Nancy had remained at U.B.C. and graduated after four very busy and fulfilling years. In her final year she was president of the University Players Club and with university activities behind her, by the Spring of 1934 she was searching for another outlet to replace them. She had no immediate plans and no thought of training for a particular career. On the other hand filling her days with tennis, golf, bridge games or tea parties with her contemporaries did not appeal either.

Her father had always encouraged her to read English history and literature and suggested that further studies at an English university might be a valuable addition to her education. Recalling his own years at Cambridge he suggested that she apply for a place in one of the two womens' colleges there, Newnham or Girton. Competition was intense and the chances were even slimmer for overseas applicants. However for someone from an approved university and with the required marks it was possible. In July news came that she had been accepted at Newnham College to study modern history.

In August 1934 Nancy and her mother left Vancouver bound for the British Isles. After staying in Edinburgh they moved into the West Highlands, from where she wrote to Budge, telling him of her reactions to the beauty of the area. They had the same effect on her that he had experienced and he replied: "I'm so glad that you liked Scotland and that the Highlands hold the same inspiration for you as they do for me, for which I am very glad. I am sure their wonderful romance will appeal to you even more as you get to know them better."

Nancy first saw the Highlands in glorious weather, with the heather in full bloom. Just as they approached Loch Katrine in the Trossachs, a lone piper stood against the evening sky. It was very impressive—until she saw several more next day within a few yards of each other. Still, her first impressions remained and she took a long lone walk across the hills till she looked down the length of Loch Katrine. She did not see another person and revelled in the beauty and solitude of her surroundings.

Arriving in Cambridge, Nancy reported to the Principal of Newnham College, Miss J.P. Strachey, sister of the well known author and historian, Lytton Strachey. At the same time she obtained a list of the University's recognized 'digs' as she did not wish to take a room in college, with its boarding school atmosphere.

Separate digs was a much more attractive alternative, even though students were still subject to all the rules applicable to in-college residents, such as a midnight curfew and proof of the requisite numbers of nights spent in residence during the term. The house Nancy chose provided a sitting room and separate bedroom. They were small and far from luxurious, the sitting room on the ground floor and a bedroom above, with shared bathroom facilities. There was no electricity and lighting was by gas. A coal-fire warmed the sitting room and a geyser heated the bath water. There was no heat in the bedroom. All meals were served in her sitting room. These quarters though Spartan by North American standards were as good as others she had seen and the family made her welcome.

Nancy purchased an 'Aladdin' coal oil lamp for extra lighting to study by. The wall-mounted gaslights were quite inadequate for reading or writing. Unfortunately the lamp gave off strong fumes when burning for any length of time, forcing her to choose between opening the window to the cold night air or falling asleep over her books. The lamp eventually did service in the Pasley Island cottage for many years.

The preferred method of transportation at both Oxford and Cambridge is the bicycle. Her initial reaction was not to use one but she soon realized that it was the only practical and convenient way to get around the city. One of Nancy's most cherished memories was of returning to her rooms on Maid's Causeway in the soft, spring evenings when the work-day world of the town had ceased. As she quietly pedalled along the almost deserted streets she was enveloped in a spirit of the past, conjured up by the beautiful old buildings around her. Lectures were of a very high quality, quite often given by the elite of Britain's historians and writers, such as G.M. Trevelean, A.E. Houseman, J.C. Runciman, Lord Rutherford, A.D. McNair and others equally stimulating.

The social side of university life became very busy and interesting. Introductions from family and friends to other undergraduates—almost exclusively male—led to frequent invitations to tea in college rooms, where crumpets were toasted in front of gas-fires. There were numerous 'sherry parties'—the British equivalent of a cocktail party; there were debates (on a visit to the Union Debating Society, Nancy was impressed with the standard of debate and thought that Canada did not measure up nearly as well); there were mock trials; theatre and drama groups. Occasional breakfast parties were given by tutors and at the first of these that Nancy attended she disgraced herself by arriving late, at 11 a.m., while the other guests had assembled at 9 a.m. It was quickly explained with an apology—a similar invitation in Canada would have meant 'brunch' and 11 a.m. would have been a respectable time to arrive.

Budge had written to a Loretto friend, Ronald Murray, in his last year at St. John's College, where he studied medicine. Budge had asked him to 'keep an eye' on his rather special friend Nancy Symes, who was about to enter Newnham College. Among many attributes, Murray had two Cambridge blues for swimming and rugby and was to be capped for the Scottish XV in 1934. He did indeed 'keep an eye'—Budge quickly realized both eyes—on Nancy and introduced her to a new, wide circle of friends and a number of university activities. Nancy grew to like him very much and he soon became an important part of her university life.

In the meantime, despite Budge's concerns over the fate of the Alberta Pacific, he had decided he liked the lumber trade enough to seek the advice of some lumber executives as to what his next move should be to remain in the industry. The general advice was that some practical mill experience would be invaluable. He was offered several jobs and gave consideration to the Port Alberni mill, the Chemainus mill, both on Vancouver Island, or the Powell River Company north of Vancouver.

Before he had made a choice, Budge was fortunate to have a lengthy conversation one evening with timber magnate, H.R. MacMillan. H.R., as he was known, told him about a young man of modest background who had just been moved from the 'green chain' into the office of the Canadian White Pine Company, a MacMillan subsidiary on the Fraser River. His name was Bert Hoffmeister and H.R. forecast that he would become company president in twenty years. (In 1949, Major-General B.M. Hoffmeister, C.B., C.B.E., D.S.O., E.D., was duly appointed president of the now much expanded company, MacMillan Bloedel Ltd.)

H.R. suggested that Budge, a young man with a good education, could have a great future in his company—and offered him a job. Budge thought it would be a good move, especially when H.R. told him it was not necessary to work in a mill. On October 1st, 1934, Budge became an employee of the H.R. MacMillan Export Company at its Head Office in the Metropolitan Building on Vancouver's West Hastings Street.

He began a thorough grounding in the administrative side of the lumber business, starting in the Document Department. He told Nancy, "It is the best place to learn, and the orderly maze of a huge and successful lumber firm is very interesting to me and a great contrast to the Alberta Pacific Timber Company." His starting wage with MacMillan was $50 a month with a promise of a $5 increase each three months for nine months. He felt confident that he had a much better chance than ever before of 'making the grade.' His dedication to learning about the lumber industry was such that his twice a week rugby practice was forsaken in preference to taking night school classes on the subject.

When Budge joined the company, it was already a major exporter of B.C. forest products to markets throughout the world, but it had not yet achieved its eventual status as a major producer. H.R. had quite a reputation in Vancouver for being something of a slave driver—demanding that much midnight oil be burned for the company. Looking back, Budge said, "It would have been far more accurate to recognize that H.R., at the top, was personally largely responsible for the fact that we juniors worked hard, and sometimes late because we wished to."

When the independent mills reached the conclusion that the H.R. MacMillan Export Co. Ltd. was getting too powerful they formed the Seaboard Company to collect a major portion of the sales and shipping profits for themselves. H.R.'s reaction was to invite all his Vancouver Head Office staff to a dinner party at the Hotel Vancouver. He told them what the mills were doing and then advised them not to worry because, he said: "We will have another dinner in a year's time and this room will not be large enough for our extended staff."

In the following months virtually all the inquiries from Europe were promptly sold by MacMillan. There was, of course, sometimes a scramble to fill the orders with much of the normal supply cut off. The company's plants; Canadian White Pine, plus another mill on Burrard Inlet and a Port Alberni operation, were all pushed to maximum performance. The recalcitrant mills were virtually starving for lack of business and in the course of time the MacMillan Company filled its ever growing needs with aggressive acquisition of other forest product companies.

Budge was mostly involved in the United Kingdom department and he became familiar with a number of major timber importers there who were regular customers of MacMillans. There were light moments in the office. Tony, a young executive of a major British importer worked briefly in MacMillan's Vancouver office while on a tour of the west coast. Budge was asked to look after him and show him what was going on—but to withhold certain information not intended for him. All went well, both in the office and on some skiing trips to nearby Grouse Mountain—until Budge saw that whenever he approached his desk, Tony would spread his arms over the desk rather obviously to cover the papers on it. What does one do with a V.I.P. spy? In due course Budge learned that the paper was the beginning of a sonnet to a girl in Tacoma, Washington—"Our visitor was a budding poet, with no ambitions to be a spy."

While preparing the documentation for a full cargo of airplane grade spruce for the Italian Air Force, Budge noticed that the contract called for "Airplane grade, P.L.I.B. (Pacific Lumber Inspection Bureau) certificate final"—which of course meant that the validity of the P.L.I.B. certificate could not be contested. These certificates were normally accepted as proof of the various lumber grades. The normal top grade was "No. 2 clear and better." The one higher grade, airplane grade was "No. 2 clear and better—NO PREVIOUS SELECTION FOR AIRPLANE GRADE."

After considerable thought, Budge concluded that the required endorsement was not possible and cleared the shipment to go without it. H.R. found out about it very quickly and Budge was summoned immediately to get a fierce dressing down, ending with the inarguable instruction: "Never forget, young man, nothing is impossible!" Budge remembered that once or twice in the coming war—and, as the senior Bell-Irving in Canada he has a Canadian grant of arms registered in Ottawa with his own motto, "Rein Impossible." It is partly in token of Budge's lasting respect for H.R., and is in place of the old Scottish Bell-Irving motto "Sub sole sub umbra virens."

While Budge continued his routine existence, claiming that he was leading a 'very sober life', Nancy looked forward to the end of Michaelmas Term and the prospect of skiing in both the Bavarian and Swiss Alps. Her life at Cambridge was still enjoyable but as 1934 drew to a close there was one topic of conversation at parties that presented a discordant note. There was talk of another war over the fate of the region called the Saar and it disturbed Nancy. This was in late 1934 and yet events in Europe were sufficiently worrying that prescient people sensed they could lead the Continent into another conflict. The Saar had been a part of Germany before the first war and it was claimed by France as payment for war damages. It contained coalmines and heavy industry and the Treaty of Versailles gave France their output for 15 years. In the mid-1930's there was unrest because the vast majority of the inhabitants, who were Germans, wished to be re-united with that country. The situation was ugly enough that an international military force was sent to keep control, but early in 1935 a plebiscite was arranged and 90.8% of the population voted for reunification with Germany. Germany paid France approximately $60,000,000 Cdn compensation in 1934 dollars and briefly the fear of another conflict between the two countries subsided.

All this was not enough to deter Nancy from making plans for a winter holiday in Germany. It was at the invitation of German friends in Dresden to join a small house party at the family's chalet in the Bavarian Alps for some Christmas skiing. The party met in Munich before taking a train into the mountains and before leaving they were taken on a walking tour to see some of the city's old landmarks.

Nazi soldiers were everywhere and at one particular location, the Fellehern Halle, there was a permanent guard on duty. Passer's by were expected to give the Nazi salute. Unhappily, but for the sake of her friends, Nancy complied. Despite this the house party was a success, the skiing was excellent, but underneath there was a strange, suppressed fanaticism, especially on the part of one young male member of the party, inducing a foreboding amongst the visitors. She never saw or heard from any of them again, despite attempts at contact after WW II.

CHAPTER FOUR

WHILE NANCY ENJOYED HER SKIING IN EUROPE, the winter of 1934-35, brought excessively cold weather to Vancouver. It lasted well into February and was the worst since the early part of the century. As a prelude to the cold, there was a spell of intense fog. The presence of coal and sawdust furnaces throughout the Lower Mainland was a contributory factor, but the fog of 1934 was the worst that Budge could recall and a foretaste of a most unusual winter. Setting out with a group of friends to ski on Mount Baker, it took forty minutes to drive the first eight blocks. Budge's father was known to be one of the best drivers in fog, yet Henry got out of his car to check an intersection and spent fifteen minutes locating his vehicle, even though the headlights were on.

When the fog ceased the snow came. It was a white Christmas, which gave an added pleasure to the usual family gatherings among the several Bell-Irving households. Budge was disappointed that a heavy snowfall on Christmas Day caused a scheduled afternoon rugby game to be cancelled. The snow lay on the ground for several weeks and the city looked particularly attractive with its heavy snow mantle and above it all, on Grouse Mountain the skiing was exceptional. As well as the main chalet, the Vancouver Winter Sports Club had premises on the mountain. A small group of good friends had rented a cabin once owned by Don Munday, a noted Vancouver mountaineer. Seeking an appropriate name, for some inexplicable reason they called themselves the Guppy Club. The guppy is a very small fish that produces a very large number of offspring at frequent intervals. As an active member, Budge said, "It would be very difficult to find any remote connection between the intent and behaviour of the well brought-up young persons of the club to that fish—but the name stuck."

Budge's recollections of getting up Grouse Mountain is of taking the street car to the top of Lonsdale Avenue and then a climb following Mosquito Creek right up to the plateau where the cabins were. He does not remember any other way and it was frequently done in the dark, inevitably guided by a "bug"—an empty jam jar minus the lid, with a short candle stuck on the inside in its own wax. A looped cord held the bug and kept it stable. He does not recall ordinary flash-lights being used to light the way.

Other memories are varied. At one time there was a dog-sled team which, if not a financial success, was at least an attractive adornment on the mountain. When Budge was president of the Guppy Club he arrived at the cabin late one Sunday morning to find a young lady member, Isabel, lying with a broken leg. Her greeting was bright enough and she told him, "They're going to take me down after skiing." Another member turned up and soon volunteered to help. They obtained a toboggan from the chalet, and Isabel, with splints in place was put into a sleeping bag and strapped on to begin the journey down the road, pulling in unison. In deep snow it was very hard work indeed and almost immediately they felt the sweat freezing on their faces and necks. Later, it seemed a long time later, the down-slope became steep enough that it was possible to get the toboggan up on top and running.

Despite their best efforts they lost control and the toboggan slid down the bank and, fortunately, was soon stuck in some bushes. First the stoic Isabel and then the toboggan were carried back up to the road, strapped together again, and the rescue continued. Eventually, a long way down, the snow getting shallower all the time, they came to a telephone booth beside the road. A call to Isabel's brother produced, remarkably quickly, the brother, a car and, by special request, a bottle of whiskey.

The final memory of Don Munday's cabin was when, from the West End of Vancouver, a fire was seen on Grouse Mountain. While cleaning up after a weekend at the cabin someone had placed too much rubbish in the stove and the cabin burned to the ground. In its place a chalet was rented in the Mount Baker area in the U.S. Washington

State. They hired a local woman who produced a great dinner for the members on Saturdays and looked after the place in their absence.

During that 1934/35 winter, trains and buses were unable to get through the Fraser Canyon and Vancouver was cut off from the rest of the country. Budge enjoyed himself immensely, using cross-country skis to get around. On several days the temperature suddenly went up making the deep snow very wet and heavy, causing damage to some public buildings including the Exhibition Forum at Hastings Park. Getting to work became an ordeal for most people when streetcar service stopped and many were forced to use their initiative in getting to work. A videotape of some of these Vancouver scenes would now be priceless and Budge described them very amusingly in a letter at the time to Nancy:

> "Streetcars are stuck all over the place and pedestrians flounder about in a semi-drowned condition. Ruth and I walked into town this morning via the inter-urban tracks which had been gone over shortly before by a snowplough.
>
> I had on fishing waders and an antiquated cape, and revelled in it. I looked like nothing on earth, but finally arrived stone dry, while most of the others arrived nearly all soaked.
>
> Broadway was a very funny picture. There were dozens of clusters of people wandering up and down and wondering how they could get downtown. We finally got over to Granville Street, through which a traffic lane had been made. Several flat-decked motor trucks passed us, loaded with respectable looking business men in bowler hats and women in fur coats, all solemnly standing in a solid mass. Everyone seemed glad of any kind of lift. One of our directors arrived in plus-fours and field-boots, after a ride on the back of a milk truck!"

In Britain the weather remained mild compared to Vancouver. Nancy had returned to Cambridge in mid-January for the Lent Term and soon realized that some serious studying had to be faced in preparation for June examinations. Ronald Murray sailed to New York to attend a family wedding and lent Nancy his car, so she drove to London and rented a room in a quiet area to get down to work. It was fortunate that she did so because the Summer Term brought even more distractions; punting on the River Cam; picnics on the 'Backs'; tea in the orchard at Granchester, still alive with memories of poet Rupert Brooke;

the May Week Ball. Above all there were early evening drives into the lovely Fen country with Ronald, in search of dinner at some old country inn.

With examinations over at the end of June, 1935 Nancy prepared to return to Vancouver for the summer holidays with deep gratitude for all the experiences of the past year and the satisfaction of knowing that she had been successful in passing the first part of the Tripos examinations in Modern History.

In a letter before she departed from Cambridge Budge described some events at home caused by the depression, which was still affecting the city. Because of his weekly contact with some of the militiamen he showed considerable understanding for the plight of the unemployed, who were struggling to make ends meet. On April 23, several thousand unemployed men had marched into Vancouver from the relief camps to demonstrate outside the Hudson Bay store on Georgia Street and the Riot Act was read to them. On May 1st, 15,000 men women and children marched down the same street singing "The Red Flag." Budge wrote: "You can't really criticize the government for the present situation, because surely they would do something if they knew how. On the other hand I don't blame the unemployed for not seeing it in that light."

More labour unrest followed especially on the waterfront when the Union Steamship Co. seamen went out on May 23, causing havoc for the mills and canneries along the coast. Budge anticipated a quiet summer in the lumber industry and was concerned that he too might be let go temporarily.

At that time the regimental strength of the Seaforth Highlanders of Canada was at its lowest point, with 31 officers and 215 other ranks, compared to 333 other ranks when the depression began. From the summer of 1935 the numbers gradually picked-up. This was brought about by a slow improvement in the economy coupled with the government's growing awareness that there should be greater military preparedness.

Despite all these troubles, on Monday May 6, 1935 the Royal Jubilee was celebrated in glorious weather and no less than 2000 militiamen, representing all the militia regiments in the city, were on parade. The crowds were enormous and roared their applause, which Budge thought was very gratifying in view of the country's labour troubles. It was a stirring sight as each regiment marched behind their band.

Nancy returned to Canada on the *Duchess of Bedford* and to Budge's delight arrived back in Vancouver on July 4. He was less delighted to learn that Ronald Murray, accompanied by another school friend, James Cadzow was coming too—and not far behind. Arriving at Montreal they bought a second-hand Packard Roadster and made their way across Canada to the west coast.

In Vancouver they proceeded to make their mark on the festive activities of a Vancouver summer—tennis parties, dances at the Royal Vancouver Yacht Club, where Cadzow stunned the members by shinning to the top of the club's very tall flagpole. Later he and Ronald drove into the B.C. interior to join in celebrations marking the founding of the town of Wells. Cadzow had won his 'blue' in boxing at Cambridge and accepted an invitation to take on the boxing champion of the Pacific Coast for a three round exhibition match. The crowd ended up very disappointed in the outcome for their local hero.

A visit to Pasley with Budge and his family ended the holiday and the two visitors returned to England where Ronald Murray was to pursue his medical studies at London's St. Thomas's Hospital. To Budge's relief there were still a few weeks of summer left to spend with Nancy before she returned to Cambridge. Once alone they realized there were questions that remained unanswered. Both Budge and Ronald were in love with Nancy and she in turn had become very fond of both of them. A choice would have to be made, but in the flurry of activities before her departure there had been no time for serious thought.

It was not easy for Budge as he saw Nancy off on the train to Montreal. However, two days alone on the train provided her with the needed opportunity and after much emotional turmoil and several phone calls to her parents Nancy made her decision. In a ten minute stop at Broadview, Saskatchewan, the half-way point to Montreal, she crossed the rail-tracks to the other side and joined a train bound for Vancouver. On learning that Nancy was on her way home, a joyful Budge went out to meet her train at Mission and accompany her for the last fifty miles.

Nancy's decision to return to Vancouver instead of going back to Cambridge was a major turning point in her life. She was fully aware of Ronald Murray's love and his desire for marriage. She was very fond of him, in addition to recognizing him as an exceptionally fine person, with a promising medical career ahead of him. She had given considerable thought to the prospect of making her home in Britain, where she still had relatives, many friends and many happy memories.

On the other hand, Nancy's devoted parents were in Vancouver, the city where she had grown up and had formed many attachments. Her U.B.C. Players Club provincial tours had made her very much a British Columbian. She had been good friends with Budge for some time with several interests in common, in particular Pasley. Returning home was not yet a commitment to anything, though it was a bitter disappointment for Ronald Murray and a pretty definite indication that she wished to remain a Canadian.

Up to this point, Budge had no definite intentions for the future. Nancy's relationship with Ronald Murray had, of course inflicted him with a strong attack of jealousy. The pain, however, had been much mitigated by his genuine pleasure in Nancy's Cambridge happiness. With her sudden return to Vancouver Budge changed gears. He realized, perhaps for the first time, that marriage to Nancy might be a reality and from that moment on, he would do his utmost to win her love.

At about this time Nancy's father had indicated that a dowry of $100 a month would be forthcoming if and when Budge could provide an income of not less than that figure. Budge's immediate target was to achieve this. He had been assured by H.R. that he had a good future with the MacMillan Export Company and he wanted to stay, but felt that he could not wait. So he went to H.R. to ask if he might have a raise from $75 to $100 per month to get married. The reply was short and to the point: "No, you're not worth it." Not even an encouraging "Not yet." There was not even room for discussion, so with regret Budge said good-bye to the company. He was neither downcast by this assertion of his ineptitude, neither did he have any feeling that H.R. had lost a potentially valuable employee.

Had Budge some inkling at the time of H.R.'s habit of once in a while bating his junior employees and had he been a bit more mature, he might well have responded with: "I'll do my best, Sir, to be worth it—in time for my wedding day." It might have been worth waiting a week or so for a possible response. As it turned out, Budge's career was to unfold with much satisfaction both to himself and his bride to be.

The next obvious possibility was a return to H. Bell-Irving & Co. Uncle Dick was kind enough to take him on and he now had his $100 per month. It was not till many years later that he learned the extra $25 was paid by Uncle Dick.

To begin with, he was to go north to Knight Inlet for six months, from April to September to assist the manager, Bill Matthews, at the Glendale Cannery. He sailed north on the S.S. *Chelohsin* on the evening of April 23rd. The ship arrived at Glendale with the usual bustle of unloading supplies and Budge was shown his room at the end of a row of similar rooms facing onto a verandah. At first glance he thought it was 'rather terrible' but over a few weeks, in his spare time he made it quite comfortable.

A few days after arriving Budge accompanied Matthews on the seine boat *Adelle M* with two Italian crew members down Knight Inlet to Alert bay. He felt completely happy and very much at home, pitying the poor devils "slaving in dirty old towns" as he said in a letter home. "This is really God's Country and the life is healthy. It couldn't possibly be better and I am in bed by 9.30 every night and up at 6.30 a.m. The food is perfectly marvellous and I am eating like a horse and feel like a million dollars."

At the Alert Bay cannery Budge met Ed Whonnock, the Indian boss, who had been a friend of H.O.'s. Ed's wife was an Indian princess in her own right. One thing that intrigued Budge was to see the little parsonage where, as an infant he had stayed with his parents during the 'A.B.C. Navy' interlude at the start of the First World War. The three packers that were under his father's command were still in company service. As the evening progressed he and Matthews fell in with a crowd of local 'weird characters' at the hotel bar and stayed long beyond their normal bedtime.

Back at the cannery Budge got his introduction to the office routine. When, a few days later the *Chelohsin* returned from the more northerly ports of call he supervised the loading of 4000 cases of salmon into her hold.

Next, Budge was placed in charge of a seine boat to visit a sawmill a couple of hours away and tow back some pilings for the wharves. It had been pre-arranged but when he arrived nothing was prepared. The mill hands set to in booming the piles ready for the tow. The mill manager tried to persuade Budge to accept some that had been in the water for three years, but he was not happy with their condition and firmly declined the offer. He was rather pleased at winning the argument, especially when at the cannery he was congratulated by Matthews for his firmness in refusing the suspect logs.

The salmon season had not yet started and any spare time was devoted to repairing the dock and equipment, hence several trips of this type were taken to pick up lumber and other supplies including a pile-driver and operator. Budge was there to learn the cannery business and at the same time act as understudy to the manager. To keep busy he took over some of the book-keeping and then temporarily left the office to do some physical work by assisting with the pile-driver operations. They were cutting out some sections of the wharf and replacing them with new pieces. It was hard work which Budge revelled in and he was so useful that he was offered a job by the equipment operator.

On several evenings he went trout fishing with Matthews and they had long chats about many things. This pleased Budge as he was able to win the manager's confidence and at the same time learn some aspects of cannery management. The fishing up to this time had not been very encouraging until Budge found that heavy rain had sent the trout down river to the salt chuck around the cannery. He was able to catch several from there and one evening caught enough to feed the whole bunkhouse.

At this juncture Budge got leave to return to Vancouver for a week before the salmon season opened on June 15. On the trip back to Knight Inlet he spent a night at Alert Bay and came across a scene along the beach which must have been common before the second world war but has now disappeared along the coast. In a shack built on pilings a missionary woman sang in full zeal 'at the top of her lungs' to an ancient harmonium while a native Indian congregation listened with varying degrees of attention. There were men, women and children wrapped in blankets with, what Budge described as looks of mute apathy on their faces and in the doorway two children played noisily and boisterously. Budge judged the missionary's efforts to be a good example of preaching strange doctrines to the native Indian population at the expense of their own culture.

Upon his return to the cannery he found the season in full swing. With the mixture of crews in the company boats, native Indian, Japanese, Italian, Czechs and others it kept Budge and Matthews busy, as he described in a letter:

"As this is a tremendous fishing area and the temperament of the many crews are so varied, they really need constant attention from a member of the company. We have arranged that Mr. Matthews and I will alternate in going out to the grounds, so that while one of us is at the cannery the other will be with the fish boats. This will go on for about a month until the humpbacks begin running when we will both travel together to different districts.

While ashore one of my chief duties will be testing samples from each day's pack. That is an interesting job and I hope to develop a useful knowledge of the finer points of the canned product."

In early July the seine boat fishermen went on strike. Most of the fishermen were not in favour of striking but a few agitators put enough fear into the others that they obeyed. The strike continued into mid-July and for Budge it was the most interesting week that he had ever experienced. He accompanied Matthews on the *Fir Leaf* and they headed for Alert Bay. En route they picked up the manager of the Canadian Fishing Company's Bones Bay Cannery, who within five minutes of landing at the Alert Bay dock was in a fight with one of the strikers. The striker was no match and suffered a cut eye that required seven stitches, though both went to the local cottage hospital.

There was a meeting of managers that night and Budge did not on the whole think much of them compared to Bill Matthews and the way he conducted himself. The meetings went on through Sunday and many of the strikers from the forty-five or more seiners were interviewed. Most of the trouble came from one very tough-looking group who appeared very threatening. Other than the incident on the dock when they arrived, there had been no trouble as any violence would have led to arrest. The ones that Budge knew personally were very polite to him, despite a general disposition to use foul language to any of the bosses who came along.

The meetings continued and finally the Native fisherman split from the Caucasians and went out under police protection. Their catch was good, which rather weakened the strikers' position. An ultimatum was issued to the remaining strikers that all boats not fishing by noon on Tuesday, July 14 would be towed back to the cannery and the crews fired. After more talk Budge was asked to draw up a document which the men signed and the strike ended. The entire fleet put out that night.

The strike continued at Rivers Inlet and finally at the end of July the cannery there was closed. Budge went up to bring back the seine boats and most of the nets. He made the journey in the dependable *Fir*

Leaf, which was powerful enough to tow seven seine boats back to Knight Inlet, but off Cape Caution one of them broke free in the open Pacific swell. Budge ended up getting a ducking while trying to get on board to secure another line.

With the addition of the Rivers Inlet boats there was a large fleet operating out of Knight Inlet. The fish showed up in large numbers and the canneries operated twelve hours a day on sockeye, followed quickly by the cheaper and more populous humpbacks. With all the boats working flat-out, Budge found it a very animated scene yet, despite his performance during the strike and the assurances from Matthews about his more than adequate help, Budge thought he was simply being kind. Despite this, there were moments when he felt immensely pleased to be back in the family business again and expressed his feelings to his parents:

> "Though I have a lot to learn, every minute is interesting and enjoyable. I find the whole experience of being here is thrilling. The constant sight of the old boats that I have heard discussed by name in the family ever since I can recall, gives me a queer feeling of belonging, as it was during dad's time in the 'twenties'."

With the strike behind them everyone was pulling their weight. The Knight Inlet catches were significantly higher than in any previous year, the record having been 8,000 cases in a season for sockeye. In 1936 by August 2nd they had put up 9,000 cases and there were several weeks left. The cannery operated late into the night to keep up with the catch deliveries. The *Fir Leaf* began with a delivery of 15,000 fish on July 30 and the other boats kept coming with equally good loads.

On several nights Budge turned in exhausted and had barely got into bed when he was called out again to tally a fresh load. It was not unusual to turn in finally long after 2 a.m. The fish, to that time had been processed into 1 pound cans (talls) but the order came to change to 1/2 pound cans (half-flats), meaning more processing and a twenty-four hour per day operation. Many of the fisherman were making $100 a day, an extraordinary wage for 1936. The women filling cans worked up to 19 hours a day with only two twenty-minute breaks. Each time they ceased operation the plant had to be thoroughly washed down and Budge was full of admiration for the way they kept going. There were eighty-five women, only two of whom were white, and about one hundred Chinamen. The fillers' wages were only 25 cents an hour, which he thought was inadequate.

There was a temporary lull in the excessive numbers of the run and he took an opportunity to join the seine boat *Adelle M* for a week. The Italian crew treated Budge well but he had trouble with the food, especially the sight of a very large pot of boiling spaghetti laced with garlic on the galley stove inside the open door. A live rock fish spilled onto the deck while brailing the pursed-up seine net and was thrown through the galley door straight into the pot. At least death would be sudden, but the eyes in death turned bright blue and looked out accusingly at the assembled company. In anticipation of this feast the crew members sat on the gunwale facing the galley door with a bowl in one hand and half a loaf of bread in the other. Whenever the *Fir Leaf* came alongside to pick up the fish, Budge would disappear into her galley for a more wholesome feed.

His first day's fishing on the new vessel began at 3.20 a.m. with a mug of strong coffee. It was still dark when they reached the fishing grounds, but as the dawn broke, Budge looked upon a remarkable scene. As the sun arose over the mountains, shining across the placid waters of the strait, it was one of the most beautiful scenes he had ever witnessed. The other seine boats, all hauling in their nets, were silhouetted against the rising sun. They fished all day until dusk and then anchored for the night.

By August 10 the fish had returned again in great numbers. 27,000 salmon were taken in to the cannery to find the workers there had been going at full speed from 6 a.m.—and they worked twenty-six and a half hours straight. For two nights running the totally exhausted cannery women left several thousand fish unprocessed, to be cleaned the next morning.

The runs continued well into August with Budge receiving more compliments from Matthews, but incredibly he was still dogged by a feeling that, not only was he not being of help but that he was 'just a parasite and a mere spectator.' It stemmed in part from a desire to be an immediate success in the cannery business. Many of the managers he met with told him that they felt there was no one at head-office who understood the practical side of the business. Whether true or not, it was quite obvious that these men were of the opinion that no attempt had been made to find a replacement who possessed Henry Bell-Irving's knowledge, even though seven or eight years had passed since his departure. Budge hoped eventually to work in the sales end of the business, but wished to maintain an interest in the practical side too. His Uncle Dick had cautioned him "not to go too fast" but that was not easy advice for a young man of twenty-three.

(Nancy was not too concerned about Budge's mental state and she commented in a letter to him that "a little inferiority complex might be a good thing!")

In mid-August the cannery began to wind down and several workers were paid off. The wives and children of the manager and bookkeeper were sent back to Vancouver and the plant became an 'all stag' location. A date of September 18th was proposed to close down entirely. Budge was invited to share the manager's house, where there was a soft bed for him and a Chinese servant to bring him shaving water each morning.

Every week more seine boats were paid off and the main effort now was to clear all the cases before shutting down. Budge was up all night on several occasions loading them onto the Union boats. The last two weeks were busy with final preparations to close the cannery, but when the Mission Ship *Columbia* called into Knight Inlet, Budge, Matthews and the book-keeper were glad to entertain those on board. The minister had been dropped at a remote Indian village and the ship's party consisted of the captain, a couple who were guests of the minister and two provincial policemen. In the course of the evening they consumed two bottles of Scotch and a dozen beer, which Budge thought was not bad for a mission ship.

By the end of September he was once more in the Vancouver office and quickly became aware of the downside of the salmon packing industry. His uncle began preparing figures for the November, 1936 Annual General Meeting in London. Along with the advice "not to go too fast" Dick also cautioned Budge not to think that the firm was on the brink of destruction.

Reading the reports of the Annual General Meetings through the 1930's it was difficult to think otherwise at times. The high profits that were familiar in the days of H.O. Bell-Irving were gone because of changes in world markets, expanded competition from the Japanese and much reduced prices. Profits and dividends had been small or non-existent between 1930 and 1934. In 1935 the U.S. subsidiary, Fidalgo Island Packing Company, had made a profit, against losses for the parent company, resulting in an overall gain of £7,700. In 1936 Fidalgo

Island made a profit of £76,450 which enabled A.B.C. to pay a dividend for the first time since 1930.

Budge had indeed been lucky to go up the coast in 1936 because it was a successful year in terms of numbers of fish caught and canned. The total combined pack for A.B.C., including Fidalgo Island was 353,325 cases. The combined world total that year was 12.5 million cases.

Addressing the 1936 A.B.C. Annual General Meeting in London, Richard Bell-Irving summed up the whole situation very clearly:

> "The American market, with its population of 130 million people is capable of absorbing the bulk of their enormous pack.
>
> Unfortunately, world consumption has not kept pace with world production and as the Japanese, unlike the Americans, still depend upon the world market for the sale of their product, they come into direct competition with the Canadian production, of which between 65 and 70% requires to be exported. It must be borne in mind that Japan's production began in 1910 with a mere 10,000 cases but has exceeded 2.5 million cases in the past three years.
>
> Cheaper labour costs plus a currency depreciation of 40% have enabled the Japanese to capture all but the British Empire markets, though even in sales to the United Kingdom, which was for many years our most important market, they are able to absorb the 10% preferential duty and still be 30% better off than Canada.
>
> The loss to Canada of these markets for Pinks and Chums is an exceedingly serious matter as, unless through cooperation, the production of these varieties is controlled to a figure that can be more readily consumed in the remaining Empire markets, then ruinous prices are inevitable."

Even more disturbing was his news of Japan's operations outside Alaska's territorial limit, as well as rapidly increasing production in their own waters. With a two and a quarter million overall decline in world production, the Japanese managed to increase their share by 100,000 cases.

After a summer of comparative freedom, Budge was soon caught up in the humdrum of office routine, though the return to Vancouver also meant that after a six month's absence from the Seaforths he could resume regimental duties. It continued to be an important part of his life, especially so when, as junior subaltern one of Budge's duties at the annual Officers' Mess Passchendaele Dinner was to propose a toast to fallen comrades, and to read out the names of the officers killed in action in the Great War. First on the list was his uncle, Major Roderick Bell-Irving D.S.O., M.C. The list always ended with the name of H.O. Bell-Irving as "a very good friend of the regiment." It served to bring home to Budge that he had inherited a duty to the Regiment.

Before the opening of the Seaforth Armoury at the south end of the Burrard Street Bridge the regiment paraded in the Beatty Street drill hall of the B.C. Regiment (Duke of Connaught's Own). The Seaforth officers maintained their own mess in a rented house on Seaton Street (now W. Hastings Street). This was, at best, a 'make-do' arrangement and a group of prominent citizens gathered together to further the cause for a Seaforth Armoury.

The Honorary Colonel, Brigadier-General J.A. Clark, C.M.G., D.S.O., Q.C., M.P. was not one to take a back seat with anything that affected his regiment. In this he was aided by the Hon. Donald Sutherland, D.S.O., P.C., M.P., Minister of National Defence, who assured Parliament that no militia unit in Canada was more deserving than the Seaforths. Between them, the government was persuaded to build the armoury and tenders were called for construction within the approved budget of $240,000. In May, 1935 the firm of Smith Brothers and Wilson was awarded the contract. In charge of construction was Walter Douglas, who had been a pipe-major with the Cameron Highlanders. He later became R.S.M. of the 2nd (Reserve) Battalion of the Canadian Seaforths and one advantage of his affiliation with the regiment was that many of the militiamen were given employment in the project. On a visit to Vancouver shortly after completion, Field Marshal Ironside remarked, "This is the finest single-unit armoury in the British Empire!"

On March 30, 1936 the regiment and its cadets marched south across the Burrard Street Bridge and into the new armoury. On August 29 of that year the Battalion trooped the colours on the occasion of the dedication and formal opening of the armoury by His Excellency, the Lord Tweedsmuir, Governor General of Canada (who, as a prolific author, still used his own name, John Buchan). Everyone in the Regiment was delighted with the finished product, and considered it an ideal facility for all activities.

Designed by McCarter and Nairn, the building contains many features found in Scottish architecture, such as conical-topped rounded turrets and end walls stepped to the peak. Over the large fireplace in the officers' mess is a Highland red deer stag's head with a magnificent 'Royal' rack of horns. Opposite is a portrait of the Lord Seaforth. On taking over, 2nd Lieut. Bell-Irving was named chairman of a committee to raise money for the required large carpet designed with the Seaforth stag's head crest woven into its centre.

The sergeants' mess has a cougar head above the fireplace and a large bust of Robbie Burns on the mantle-shelf, doing justice to a Mess that has always been outstanding in peace and war, especially its annual Burn's Supper. The long-serving Regimental Sergeant-Major Tom Anderson (1926-1939) was, in Budge's opinion, outstanding—and Budge had learned a thing or two about R.S.M.s at Loretto where the O.T.C. Sergeant-Major, formerly R.S.M. of the Scots Guards had, in typical fashion once addressed him with that special bark only R.S.M.s possess, exclaiming: "You low-down, worse than useless thing, SIR!"

In the smaller Vancouver of the 1930s, most of the officers knew each other in civilian life, as did many of their families. There was a warm feeling of camaraderie among the officers, always with due respect to the C.O. who, in 1936 was Lt.-Col. J.R.S. Lough, CBE, DSO, MC, VD (Volunteer Diploma). Like many other senior officers he was a veteran of WW I. Apart from that Budge has a vague memory of having been 'beaten up' in the mess by the substantial football player, Captain Cecil Merritt—for being "insubordinate to captains." (It was noted that a high proportion of Junior Bar members were battalion officers.)

Hogan's Alley, an association of subalterns for getting away with rough-housing in the mess, was in full sway then. After-dinner games were sometimes hard on the expensive mess kits, but it was always good fun (besides which, such activity was a tradition in all Militia or Territorial Army officers' messes throughout the Dominions). One other memory is of a mess night when Lieut. Bell-Irving stood on his hands, back and feet to the wall, with a glass of whiskey in his mouth, clamped between his teeth. The object was to drink the glass dry with no help from his hands. Some years later the same, now Brigadier (Retired) H.P. Bell-Irving was asked by Colonel Cecil Merritt, V.C. to do it again with the purpose of teaching the modern entries to Hogan's Alley how it was done. The result was broken glass in a puddle of blood-coloured whiskey on the floor!

In those years between WW I and WW II there was more emphasis on drill and the Seaforth Armoury was excellent for that.

During Lt.-Col. Lough's tenure as C.O. a Military Tournament was staged in the new armoury to encourage recruiting, although it did not bring the numbers up to full strength. There was almost a full complement of officers and senior N.C.O.s but there were never enough other ranks. When company and occasional battalion drills were carried out, there was a simple expedient to give the appearance of a full parade; two soldiers holding a light wooden pole of appropriate length between them would represent a section. When mobilization came in 1939 it quickly brought in the required number of other ranks.

Officers initially learned about tactics on a sand-table, though battle exercises on the ground took place both on the mainland and Vancouver Island. The camps were enjoyed by all ranks but again from a tactical aspect they bore little relationship to those actually used when war came. Those who survived WW II now realize the futility of those activities. Even now, as an active octogenarian, Budge is still defending the need for a strong, well trained Militia. He recently wrote:

"In two wars against foreign enemies, the Non Permanent Active Militia (N.P.A.M.) has performed with distinction. Regrettably, both between and since those wars, the seemingly incurable problem has been the failure of the Regular Force to understand the full potential of the Reserve Force and the Federal Government's too low priority for needed National Defence costs."

Until 1936, Canada could not claim to have a defence policy. On the contrary many of its politicians and people of influence were inclined to favour an isolationist stand. There were rumblings against the mother country, suggesting that the only wars Canada had taken part in resulted from her connection to Great Britain. Furthermore, since Canada had no voice in British foreign policy these people asked why she should contribute towards Imperial Defence. One writer even claimed that "Military isolation from Europe is, under such conditions, a policy not of cowardice, but of common sense."

As a natural result of these powerful opinions in the mid-thirties, the Canadian reserve army had no access to, and virtually no knowledge of, modern arms, armour and military equipment. Despite the Seaforths being looked upon as one of the most efficient Canadian units, throughout the country in 1936 there was not a single tank, anti-aircraft gun, anti-tank gun, or Bren-gun available. Considering the unrest in Europe this state of affairs was unforgivable, but it served to show the influence of the isolationists. Needless to say, these views were not held by the

Bell-Irving family, nor by many others who shared an ongoing respect for the British Empire.

Towards the end of 1936, defence estimates were increased from $25 million to $35 million. The Government also released a plan to reorganize the militia, disbanding those units with a low ratio of commissioned officers to other ranks. This freed up funds for the keener units who were able to hold their numbers. Infantry regiments were reduced from 135 to 91 and six were converted to armoured units—though it would be some time before they might be introduced to armoured vehicles of any kind. The B.C. Regiment D.C.O.R. (Duke of Connaughts Own) attested to their new role by collecting a number of small English open roadsters each with a flag staff and pennant—a preparation for their switch to a reconnaissance role.

The Seaforth strength in December 1936 was twenty-eight officers and 271 other ranks, a slight improvement in the overall numbers from a year before. Under the command of Lt.-Col. Lough some reorganization took place to make them more responsive to the perceived changing role of infantry. More time was allotted to the officer training and weekend exercises were laid on in addition to annual camps at Sydney or Vernon. In previous years much of the training activities had been curtailed through lack of funds. Among the Seaforths officers, five had graduated from the Royal Military College, Kingston: Captains A.V. Creighton and C.C.I. Merritt, plus Lieuts. M.J. Griffin, I.L. Brock and D.M. Clark.

There is no doubt that much of the push to increase Canadian defence spending came from the British government, whether the isolationists liked it or not. Under Leslie Hore-Belisha, the British Secretary of State for War, the territorial army units (militia) were being expanded as a back-up to the regular army. The British cabinet held no doubt that in the event of war it could depend once again on the Dominions to provide men and women and as events turned out they were proven correct.

Throughout this period, as well as continuing his duties with the regiment, Budge began to learn about the activities and office routines of H. Bell-Irving & Co. He sat opposite Jimmy Lord, one of the more experienced staff members but, more importantly, he was encouraged by the wise counsel of company director Peter Traill, his constant mentor, who had emigrated from Fife, Scotland to be quickly hired as a bookkeeper by H.O. about the time that Budge was born. Over time he had become a valuable member of the company and a senior director.

A wedding date was arranged for Budge and Nancy and the banns were published in St. Paul's Church on Jervis Street. Miss Nancy Isobel Symes and Mr. Henry Pybus Bell-Irving were to be married on April 8, 1937. A good friend and neighbour of the Symes family offered to rent them a small but comfortable house on Marine Crescent on the southern fringe of Vancouver for as long as they required it. Among the major benefits were a view of the Fraser River, a tennis court in the sizable garden and a short walk through the McLeary Farm orchard to Nancy's parents. They stayed in the house right through to September 1939 and paid $30 a month for the entire time they were there. It was an older house which needed some fixing up and Budge spent several happy weekends there doing carpentry and painting. Nancy came over on Sunday mornings to cook breakfast for him and help where she was able.

While Budge and Nancy were "playing house" there was trouble at home and abroad and a great deal more brewing. Canada, like many other countries was still suffering from the depression. Despite the additional $10 million in defence spending, individual units did not always see the money. An illustration of this was the case of an old tactical training sand table which had been moved to the new armoury. It required the necessary modest quantity of sand. When the C.O. requested this he was informed that if it were to cost more than $3.50 he must first seek approval from higher authority. It was, as Budge put it, "a case of when tragedy is awful enough, it may become simply funny."

In Europe the threat of war was becoming more serious. In March 1936 Hitler had repudiated the Treaty of Locarno, marched his troops into the Rhineland, thus confronting the League of Nations with a supreme test, leaving open the question of its ability to survive. The rearming of Britain under Winston Churchill's constant urging was finally gaining speed but it was a very late start and Germany was far ahead in preparedness, except in sea power. The German threat would have to become more obvious to put a stop to the inevitable British pacifists, represented by those young 'gentlemen' of the Oxford Union who had no doubt impressed Hitler greatly with their declaration that they would not go to war again for 'King and Country.'

However, putting aside events in Europe, Budge and Nancy were intent on finalizing their wedding plans. It was a shock to Budge when he discovered almost at the eleventh hour that it was the responsibility of the groom to provide the transport to and from the church, as well as bouquets for the bride and her four bridesmaids. It was a trifling sum compared to the munificent outlay of the very generous father of the bride but—while the income for a starting basis was in place, when the bridegroom's costs were deducted from the bridegroom's present cash position, the balance remaining was only 75c! Alarmingly close to the deadline several senior relatives came to the rescue most generously, allowing the young couple to honeymoon in Carmel, California.

Marriage at St. Paul's Church had been a Bell-Irving family tradition for two generations. On this day, as the Rev. Harold G. King officiated, somewhere in meteorological records is the fact that April 8, 1937 was the only day in the month with no rainfall in Vancouver. Four hundred relatives and friends, including Seaforth officers in uniform, gathered in the oval room of the old Vancouver Hotel. The large oval table in the centre of this great room was almost covered with gardenias with the tiered wedding cake in the centre.

Budge and Nancy drove off in her open Silver-Streak Pontiac Roadster to Carmel, with its spectacular ocean-side setting. Two weeks later, upon arriving back at the cottage they set about completing the job of furnishing it. A large van was rented from 'Moonlight U-Drive Company' to begin a tour of relatives and a surprising quantity of usable furniture turned out to be surplus. The cottage was soon furnished attractively and became an invaluable part of Budge and Nancy's furnishings.

Nancy's first dinner party was given at a time when old social customs had not been eroded. Dinner parties were the first order of the evening and if a Ball followed it began much later and was usually finished off with a midnight supper. This dinner was to be followed by Budge and Nancy and their guests going on to the Hotel Vancouver for a Military Ball. It was important that everyone, especially well-trained young officers, be present for the arrival of the Lieutenant-Governor.

The dinner guests were Seaforth officers and their ladies. There was a strict proviso that they must all be on their way in time to meet the ball deadline. As was always her custom Nancy, with no help, produced an excellent dinner and a Seaforth sergeant had been hired to look after the drinks. The front door was too far from the road so everyone entered through the kitchen door, which was much closer to the road and on a level with the parking space. The backdoor bell and the front hall telephone rang at the same moment, which was too much for the sergeant who, at that very moment was carrying a large tray loaded with a variety of pre-dinner drinks. He was unused to the uneven floor and in the commotion the sergeant and his tray went flying. Replacement glasses were found to permit a refill of drinks. It was rather hard on Nancy and very difficult to do justice to a carefully prepared meal in the shorter time remaining after order had been restored. In their sixty years of marriage, Nancy never had to go through a situation quite so disastrous.

In that same summer, Budge's young brother, Roderick (Rog), left Vancouver's Prince of Wales school after completing Grade 12 and joined a school tour of the British Isles. The tour leader was their sister Wendy. It would prove to be a decisive point in Roderick's life. At the end of the tour instead of returning to Vancouver he chose to remain in Britain and applied for a three year short-service commission in the Royal Air Force. His application was successful, helped by having served as a cadet in the Army Cooperation Squadron of the R.C.A.F. as well as in the Seaforth cadets.

In August 1937 he presented himself to the Civil Flying School at Ayr, Scotland and after completing basic flying training was granted the rank of probationary Pilot-Officer. Looking to the future Roderick chose to go into Bomber Command rather than Fighter Command because he felt it might eventually lead more readily to a job with an airline. Within a few months he had received his wings, taken courses in navigation, aerial gunnery and bombing and had his appointment as an R.A.F. officer confirmed. Roderick fitted easily into life in an R.A.F. mess. He was easy going and popular, with a ready sense of fun and would prove to have exceptional leadership qualities.

By 1938 Hitler had introduced conscription and had increased his army to thirty-six infantry divisions and three armoured (Panzer) divisions. Within a year the total was 103 divisions. In March of that year he annexed Austria and began preparations to invade Czechoslovakia to reclaim Sudetenland and its predominantly German speaking citizens. Several diplomatic missions took place throughout the summer in the hope of resolving Hitler's demands peacefully.

This was the situation in Europe as the territorial and militia units in Britain and the Dominions left for their summer camps. The British Columbia Area militia camp took place on Vancouver Island's Saanich Peninsular, between Victoria and Sydney. In camp the Seaforths were in one straight line of bell tents with the C.O.'s field-officers' tent at the end. Another Vancouver unit was in a similar straight line parallel to the Seaforths with their C.O.'s tent across from the Seaforth C.O. This neighbouring C.O. had a chair and a table outside his tent with a guidon (pennant) stuck in the ground to identify his presence. He was also seen occasionally to dictate to a secretary sitting close by. All of this was noted with great interest within the Seaforth's "Hogan's Alley."

One evening there was an officers' dance in Sydney. Initially Budge was disinclined to go, but in a short time he and another officer and an R.M.C. Gentleman Cadet found themselves together and there didn't seem to be any reason why they should not, after all attend. A quick drive into Esquimalt's Naval dockyard produced the admiral's daughter and one of her friends. It was then back to Sydney—and larceny! The pole was taken from the bell-tent of the neighbouring regiment's second-in-command and a square white cloth with 'Men at Work' painted in red was attached to the top of the pole.

Budge claims, "We Scottish peasants couldn't say guidon so we called our pole a gudgeon. We marched into the dance behind two pipers and a drummer playing and with the pole held high as we circled the dance floor with our ladies. As the pipers played *Scotland the Brave* we dipped our 'gudgeon' respectfully in front of each C.O. The colonel of the other regiment shouted 'Throw those drunken Seaforths out!' Having completed the circuit we marched out in good order and spent the rest of the evening parked in the open car being regaled with a succession of outlandish stories by a certain artillery officer. As we entered the dockyard very early in the morning to deliver the ladies safely home, my memory has it that the guards on the gate presented arms—no doubt to the magnificent gudgeon."

Budge thought this would be the end of his military career, but the Colonel, Tom Leslie, a big jovial Scot, was amused by the whole thing and in the morning took the 'gudgeon' unto himself and had it marched behind him, later to be displayed outside his tent with a guard on it so that a changing of the guard ceremony would be in order.

It would seem that Budge's military career so far, was largely given to making a fool of himself. The only, and admittedly vague memory Budge has of an actual training exercise was the sight of a sizable force of infantry advancing to make contact with the enemy, led by a large officer with a stout walking-stick, a pipe in his mouth, a 'sola-topi' on his head and a monocle in his eye. To Budge, this image was reminiscent of a quotation from then Major Douglas Haig (later Field-Marshal Haig) in 1896:

"We shall always win by reason of pluck, and if it is not the only cause of victory, it is always the most essential factor and the one without which we cannot hope to succeed." Years later Budge looked back on this as perhaps the one lesson learned from the Sydney training exercise.

In those two weeks at camp the situation in Europe had become so tense that the French and British had mobilized most of their armed forces, though an initiative was taken by British Prime Minister Neville Chamberlain that many thought would lessen the tension and ensure a lasting peace. On September 30, 1938 he signed the Munich Agreement with Hitler. Its aim was to prevent the invasion of Czechoslovakia which, to that moment Hitler had shown every intention of doing. In the agreement Sudetenland and its 3.2 million people was to be ceded to Germany.

To many people it was appeasement of the worst kind, but to the majority it was like having a great weight lifted off them. As he stepped from the plane on his return he waved the agreement and told the assembled crowd, "Peace in our time." The feeling of relief in Britain was palpable and Roderick wrote home, "Mr. Chamberlain has done a wonderful thing by showing that settlements can be made in peace. People have taken on a new lease of life and are more cheerful than they have been for some time."

The general public could not be blamed for clutching at straws and failing to realize that it would ultimately lead to disaster, as Hitler had no intention of honouring the agreement.

At this time Budge was a subaltern in "D" Company and remembers well that Corporal Cross taught him the intricacies of the Vickers machine gun. In the interests of "further training" it was arranged that "D" Company, with pipers attached should go to Pasley for a weekend, crossing on the late H.O.'s faithful yacht *Emoh*. On safe arrival the base was established in the Henry B-I house at North Bay where adequate food and, in good time, some sleep were enjoyed.

But first a late night swim at the South Bay beach was arranged. Corporal Cross with one crewman was ordered to row a dinghy around from North Bay with several cases of beer on board. The rest marched in single file on the island's centre trail, with a local guide in the lead holding a storm-lantern, while behind him was a piper. All went well, the tide was high and the water hospitable—but then it was discovered that there had been a shipwreck. The beer dinghy had capsized and though righted quickly the beer was lost. The boat's crew had, however, misjudged the Beach-master. They were invited forthwith to return to the scene of the shipwreck, retrieve the beer from the water, now nicely cooled and bring it back to the party. The beer was duly salvaged and a memorable evening was enjoyed.

The last camp before war was declared, took place at the end of June, 1939. The location was at Vernon in B.C.'s Okanagan Valley. Events in Europe led almost conclusively to another war, although many people still did not believe it would come. Despite his promises to the contrary, Hitler invaded Czechoslovakia in midMarch. Only three weeks later Italy placed substantial forces in Albania which was read as a sign that Mussolini was aligning himself with German ambitions. Although there were many high-level meetings and a flurry of diplomatic activity Hitler never wavered in his determination to invade Poland next. Chamberlain felt obliged to issue a clear message that if Hitler followed through with his threat "His Majesty's Government would feel bound once and for all to lend all possible support to the Polish Government."

As the Battalion entrained for Vernon the junior officers quickly congregated in the smoking room of the officers' Pullman car and had an hilarious evening, with no shortage of Scotch whiskey. The fact that Budge had several cans of salmon for distribution to the officers did not go amiss and the Colonel presented him with a double scotch for his generosity.

By ten a.m. next morning they pulled into this attractive north Okanagan town in Central British Columbia. Vernon sits between Okanagan Lake and Kalamalka Lake and is surrounded by indented irregularly shaped hills covered in grass and scrub pine. It is altogether a very attractive setting. A large crowd turned out to see the battalion arrive, to be piped to a permanent military camp overlooking Kalamalka Lake, about a mile to the south of the town. In the first week there were tactical exercises on the surrounding hills in both attack and defence. In the second week the Seaforths were ordered to plan and execute a demonstration attack by an infantry company to be watched by all infantry units in camp. The company was under the command of Captain Cecil Merrit and he was judged to have done very well indeed by the senior officers present.

Though there was no artillery, little or no modern equipment to be seen and demonstrated, the total number and variety of units massed together possibly gave the impression of an army, at least in contrast to the small numbers the soldiers were accustomed to in their own units. The Seaforth official history comment on this camp states:

"... if one were to examine the scene more closely and attempted to compare this force with a similar reserve force training in Europe, the difference [would be] enough to dismay a professional soldier."

In challenging this statement Budge commented:

"On the basis of experience later gained in WW II, one is reminded that in the U.K. in 1940, soldiers of the Canadian Active Service Force were being trained in obsolete trench warfare with 1917 pamphlets. At that time a very senior British general who had just returned from visiting the French Maginot Line addressed officers of the 1st Canadian Division. He told them, 'The Maginot Line is impregnable. From the north end of the line to the sea is a zig-zag of anti-tank ditch with a two-pounder anti-tank gun in each zig-zag corner—totally impassable. Gentlemen, you will not again see tanks in battle.' This was said while the Nazi Panzer divisions were already lining up to invade France. It was utter nonsense from the highest level. One hopes that Canada's 'professional soldiers' may yet learn to appreciate that adequately supported militia units can still offer an invaluable regimental 'esprit de corps', discipline and the vital qualities of leadership. Given the right support they will be more than ready to take on the final up-to-date modern military experience. To deny that required support, will be to destroy a most valuable Canadian heritage."

The camp was judged a 'good show' as the battalion returned to Vancouver. It was now July and the fate of Europe was being sealed as it was slowly, inexorably, dragged into another major war. Those of the battalion that had jobs returned to them, though not for long. In July and August meetings continued in various European capitals in the hope of a last-minute reprieve.

While the eleventh hour approached Budge and Nancy embarked on a memorable sailing holiday. Setting off from Pasley in their 16 foot International class dinghy, they sailed northward up the Straight of Georgia. Before them were many safe anchorages and camping spots on the islets, bays and inlets. Their first stop was Buccaneer Bay where they anchored for the night, with a Coleman stove to provide the evening meal. Next morning they set off again heading for Point Upwood on Texada Island. After a day's sailing they came to rest by a small beach on Lasqueti Island.

The weather remained sunny as they set out to cross the Strait to Denman Island, then sailing up into Baynes Sound, between Denman and Vancouver Island. In Comox harbour they found a "veritable review" of vessels in the anchorage: an R.C.N. destroyer; a steam yacht owned by the Duke of Sutherland; George Kidd's motor yacht *Meander* —and Budge and Nancy's sailing dinghy which they anchored in line with their impressive neighbours and in due time went to bed, one each side of the centreboard. Early in the morning they were awoken by a strange noise, which turned out to be the laughter from a line of Naval ratings looking down on them from the destroyer's deck. Feeling the need for privacy they sailed outside the harbour until opposite a deserted beach to complete their ablutions and get dressed. Halfway through they realized the new anchorage was opposite a sea-cadet camp firing range. Back in harbour, later that day they called to see some old friends, the Oslers, who were kind enough to invite them to stay for a few days in their comfortable private hotel. Budge said, "As a somewhat symbolic gesture to the joys of nature, I had thrown my razor overboard in the middle of the Strait of Georgia. Now seemed to be a proper time to buy another one."

Returning to Pasley in deteriorating weather was the most exciting part of the holiday. As they headed south-east from Comox to pass outside Denman and Hornby Islands, the sea was rough, so they put into False Bay on Lasqueti Island to bail out the boat. Sailing across the Strait to Merry Island running before a strong south-easterly it was not possible to bring the boat around into the wind to reef down the sail to a workable size. Budge said of their predicament:

> "The sail had to remain blown out more like a spinnaker, with the boom up in the air. The jib had not been shipped and Nancy, with remarkable pluck crawled forward to bring both ends of the jib halyard aft to make them fast astern as a back-stay, to prevent the mast from breaking over the bow. It was an experience rather like surfing on the forward slope of a wave. I am sure that we reached 12 knots.
>
> I was in my element, but Nancy later admitted to hoping that some big boat might appear in time to pull us out of the water before we drowned. The run down the coast on a broad reach was exciting and we put into Roberts Creek on the Sechelt Peninsula where we went over the bar on a wave into very calm water. We had a restful night, though punctuated with news on our radio that war was now

imminent. A pleasant sail to Pasley completed the holiday. We were saddened to think it might be a long time before we would see those waters, or even Pasley again."

The news was all too accurate. In late August Hitler issued an ultimatum to Poland to accept his demands, but he was thirsty for war, just as the Kaiser had been in 1914. Receiving no response, on September 1 he hurled his forces into Poland. On the same date the 1st Canadian Division, including the Seaforth Highlanders of Canada were ordered to mobilize. On September 3 Britain and France declared war on Germany and Canada followed on the 10th. The Second World War had begun.

CHAPTER FIVE

WHEN THE MOBILIZATION ORDER CAME on September 1, the C.O. called a battalion parade for that evening. B.H.Q. and the sub-unit commanders were notified and Budge telephoned each member of his platoon to give them the order. At the appointed hour, thirty officers and 260 other ranks, almost a full turn-out, were on parade. The C.O. took over and gave a single order: "All those willing to serve overseas with the Seaforths—take one pace forward!"

There were very few, possibly three or four who, for one or another good reason were unable to volunteer. Budge still recalls one much respected senior N.C.O. with tears in his eyes because ill-health prevented him from volunteering along with the others. Next morning Budge obtained leave from H. Bell-Irving & Co. Ltd. which, in keeping with family tradition was readily granted. He and Nancy moved to a monthly tenancy in a West End apartment and the house was turned over to new tenants.

Recruiting improved and by the end of September the battalion was up to war establishment strength, plus enough men to fill first-line reinforcements. Recruits had answered the call of duty, no doubt also the call to adventure. Some sought escape from poverty and gained weight rapidly with regular meals. A small number came up from the U.S.A.

On October 1, the officers' active service list was published and Budge was appointed to command the No. 4 (Carrier) platoon, though the carriers were not received until the unit had been in the U.K. for some time. The Seaforths became part of the 2nd Canadian Infantry Brigade, 1st Canadian Division, along with the Princess Patricia's Canadian Light Infantry (P.P.C.L.I), and the Edmonton Regiment, which was raised in April 1908 as the 101st Regiment (Edmonton Fusiliers). It has gone through a number of changes in designation, twice as a battalion of the PPCLI, but in July 1943 the unit received the title, Loyal Edmonton Regiment. In 1970 it was re-designated the 4th Battalion PPCLI.

The brigade was commanded by Brigadier George Pearkes VC, DSO, MC, Croix de Guerre, a professional soldier commissioned from the ranks in WW I. He had remained in the Canadian army to help steer it through the peace-time years. He was an efficient soldier and a man of great personal charm who would precede Budge by several years as a Lieutenant-Governor of British Columbia.

On about October 10, Budge reported once more at Work Point Barracks with four NCO's, to take a course in the new Bren Light Machine Gun. The Bren gun on which they trained was at the time the only one in B.C. and the P.P.C.L.I. corporal instructor had not seen one before either. There was a keenness to understand its workings and this was accomplished by a good team effort. The final session was to fire the gun out at Heals Range and it was judged to be a very satisfactory weapon.

Budge had a problem in getting his NCOs to turn out at 06:30 each morning for physical training because they thought the NCOs in the "Pats" would laugh at them. However, with a bit of cajoling he showed his leadership capabilities and, along with himself they began to enjoy the exercise and felt better for the effort.

During this time he again became introspective and attempted to analyse his thoughts on paper. He wrote:

> "Before the war I had a succession of jobs, ending up as a clerk in H. Bell-Irving & Co., which would seem to be a logical place for me to remain. Now war has finally arrived and, of course, has forced a complete readjustment to the mode of living of most of us. When very busy I am able to produce a good deal of work. When not busy though, I rapidly become an excellent 'blotter artist.'
>
> At the moment I am not very busy, so all the forces which used to make me work have disappeared. Something will have to be done

soon to dig up new forces to make me worthy of the 'King's shilling.'"

On the evening of November 9, Budge and Nancy attended a dance at the Commodore Ballroom along with other officers and their wives. Colonel J.B. Stevenson, had taken over command from Tom Leslie and during the evening he told Budge that the next course at the Small-Arms School in Hythe, England would begin December 1 and his name, together with three N.C.O.'s had been put forward to attend. Budge told Nancy that same evening and it was confirmed the next day, to be accompanied by Platoon Sergeant-Major Vance, Sergeant McNutt and Corporal Biddlecombe, who was promoted to sergeant with immediate effect.

On the morning of November 11th, Armistice Day, Budge was placed on six hours notice to leave. Nancy, ever practical, prepared Budge's clothes, washing some in the basement tub then hanging them on lines across the basement to dry. At 4 p.m. Budge was advised that he was to be on the 7:15 p.m. train. Nancy's first thought was, "Well I'm going too." As all the banks were by then closed she phoned her father and told him she needed money for a train fare to Montreal.

She recalled: "We had bought a puppy a few weeks earlier and I found a home for that and found a friend to take the apartment, all between 4 and 7 p.m. My father met me with my ticket. It was a normal scheduled passenger train with coaches at the rear for the army. As there was no other female travelling in that section I took over the ladies room and hung up the washing again to finish drying!"

Nancy needed her passport renewed but at three hours notice she hadn't time to arrange it before leaving Vancouver. Her father was able to acquire the forms, which she signed and he gave them to Colonel Foster, the Vancouver police chief, who by a fortunate coincidence was flying to Ottawa to attend a meeting. There were no passenger planes through the Rockies at that time and he first took the train to Calgary and flew from there. On arrival at Montreal Nancy's renewed passport was waiting for her.

Before leaving, Budge visited the Seaforth Armoury, where he found a very jolly Armistice Day party going on in the officers' mess, with Uncle Duncan present and in very good form. Budge's father Henry, once more in uniform as an R.C.N.V.R. Lieutenant-Commander arrived from the Esquimalt base and was just in time to pick up Nan and drive to the station. There was quite a crowd to see them off; both sets of parents, Budge's sister Wendy and husband 'Corney' Burke, who would soon be in Britain in the navy; the Colonel and Mrs Stevenson, General and Mrs Clark and other regimental officers, including Bert Hoffmeister. Considering the super-secretiveness of the move and the last-minute notice, it was quite a good send-off.

All units that were to be included in the 1st Canadian Division sent one officer and three N.C.O.s to attend the small-arms course. As the train travelled across Canada they were joined by their representatives designated for the course. When they arrived in Montreal Budge went to the CPR and said to the booking clerk "I would like a ticket to Liverpool and when does the ship sail?" He was told, "We can't tell you that, there is a war on!" Budge replied, "Don't be a damn fool, I'm part of this war and I want a ticket for my wife." The amusing answer was, "We can't tell you when the ship will sail, but if your wife is down here by Friday noon, she won't miss it!"

Cousin Robin Bell-Irving, who was in Montreal on Powell River Company business obtained and paid for a suite for Budge and Nancy at his hotel, the Windsor. The sergeants were billeted at the Queen's Hotel along with all the other N.C.Os from the train. Budge reported to the docks on Friday morning to find a furious transport officer who asked "Where in God's name have you been? We've been looking for you everywhere for the past three days."

The ship was the *Duchess of Richmond*, the last passenger ship to leave before the freeze-up. In the military group were approximately thirty officers and after talking to the purser it was arranged that Nancy, who had a third-class ticket would move into Budge's 1st class cabin, which he would normally have shared with another junior officer. Although her steerage class ticket precluded her from meals in First or Cabin class dining saloons there was no apparent objection to having meals delivered to the cabin.

As they steamed across the Atlantic a strict black-out prevailed, but the bar was bright and everyone soon congregated there. The liner, being fast, had no escort and her only protection was one small gun mounted on the bow. The German warship *Bismark* was at that time running amok in the North Atlantic. A large proportion of the *Duchess of Richmond's* passengers were to be seen at all hours wearing life-jackets, especially after she passed through the wreckage of a ship that had been torpedoed by a U-boat.

Budge and Nancy showed considerable amusement at their recollections of the early days in U.K.: "We docked at Liverpool and went from there in a blacked-out train to London. We were met by people from the War Office and were put on busses. We first went around billeting the N.C.O.'s, then all the officers were taken to the Regent Palace Hotel. Piccadilly Circus was absolutely black, and suddenly as we went through the revolving door of the hotel there was a blaze of lights and in the foyer were twenty-nine good-looking, well dressed young women to serve as hostesses to these overseas officers—and Nancy was the 30th! Thirty officers and thirty women. The newcomers might well have wondered if this degree of hospitality was to be expected everywhere in the U.K."

It was time to get down to work. The small-arms course had been moved from Hythe to Aldershot and the officers were billeted in the officers' quarters at Malplaquet Barracks. Budge's first impressions were, of course, based on the novelty and excitement at the outset of a great new experience. On his first opportunity to fire a Boyes anti-tank rifle Budge inadvertently pressed the trigger too soon, with this monstrous weapon pointing about thirty-five degrees above horizontal. He wasn't sure where the bullet landed, but there were no reports of damage. Later, when he learned something about tanks, he had cause to wonder why this heavy rifle was named "anti-tank" and what it might actually be useful for.

Budge recently commented on some of the other weapons of World War II:

> "The two-inch mortar was received with considerable interest as a beautifully made little weapon, enhanced by a smaller version of the aiming device designed for the three and four inch mortars. Sometime later I found myself carrying a 2" mortar at the double on a battle-drill exercise. It wasn't that heavy but it occurred to me that to fire the weapon in a typical battle situation would not provide the time necessary for twiddling wheels in order to achieve accurate range-finding and aiming. I designed a very much simpler, lighter one. General McNaughton was always keen on weapons of any sort and gave great support to the idea. Enthused by this I approached Walter Lines, Chairman of Lines Brothers Ltd., the well-known toy manufacturers with whom I was then billeted in Limpsfield, Surrey. A proto-type was made and passed onto the British War Office. After some time I was told, in so many words, "Thank you,

but it is not necessary." I heard later, though it was not verified, that the refinement was adapted for an air-borne force.

The hand-held P.I.A.T. (Projector, Infantry Anti-Tank) was a particularly interesting weapon in that it introduced the idea of a considerable explosive force concentrated on a single minute point—the contact fuse at front, geometric centre of the bomb. The P.I.A.T.'s maximum range was given at 300 yards. At or close to that range the weapon would no doubt be very destructive, though on the face of it perhaps unlikely to be lethal to a heavy tank. It was over three years later, in Northern Italy before the actual great tank killing capacity of the weapon was identified and made good use of thereafter."

The winter of 1939/40 was the coldest one that Britain had experienced for sixty years. In Budge's Malplaquet Barracks 'dormitory' the officers had a Welsh batman who couldn't, or wouldn't speak English. Attempts to keep a fire going in the inevitable coal-burning open fireplace were negated daily by the batman who insisted on removing the ashes—and the coal to clean out and black-polish the surround. An inquiry to the British Army major in charge invoked the prompt reply, "Young man—I've been cold for forty years and I intend to remain so!"

The course candidates were given leave every weekend. Nancy was staying in a friend's London flat and Budge joined her there on Saturday mornings. For the Christmas 1939 holiday, they were invited to Stagenhoe Park, the Hertfordshire country estate of the Dewars (Timpkins Bearings—not whisky). It was Budge's brother Roderick who met them first. When he received his wings in February 1938 he was given two weeks leave and a list of people who offered hospitality to young officers from the Dominions. It was arranged that he would divide his leave between three of them and the Dewars, whose son John was also in the R.A.F. made it clear that he was welcome any time he had leave.

He became a frequent visitor to Stagenhoe. John was also a pilot and tragically, was killed early in the war. The Dewars invited other Dominion officers to their home to enjoy outstanding hospitality. Fortunately Roderick was able to get Christmas leave and the house-party provided a rare opportunity for he and Budge to spend time together. In a letter to their mother he told her: "I have really got to know Budge much better than I ever did before and we have had some grand times together. I feel I have a real brother now, which was rather hard before at times."

The H.Q. of a British armoured brigade was established at Stagenhoe. The Brigadier and senior staff officers were billeted in the house. In the park were Matilda tanks with their two-pounder anti-tank guns and Budge wondered whether the tank crews were aware of the existence of the German Mark 5 Panther and the larger Tiger tank with its superior armament that would confront them soon.

The Dewars had enough cars to obtain sufficient petrol coupons to run one Bentley—in which a group of the younger guests drove down to London one evening to see the much acclaimed comedy, *Black Velvet*. The London theatres were a popular pastime, especially during the 'phony' war, before the air-raids began. Budge remembers the play well and chuckled at his recollection of Act I: "An elderly gentleman lying in a four-poster bed in a centre-stage bedroom was contemplating with apparent pleasure a pointed 'mound' in the middle of the bed immediately in front of him. He stretched across and pulled the embroidered bell-pull. A bell rang in the distance and his man-servant came into the room and peering at the bed exclaimed, 'Oh, my Lord, shall I call her Ladyship?' The reply was, 'No Simpson, I think we'll smuggle this one up to London!' Curtain comes down—end of scene!"

Meanwhile, back in Vancouver the battalion made preparations to leave for the U.K. One month after Budge and his small entourage had left, Colonel Stevenson, Captain W.S. Murdoch, the Adjutant, with Lieut. D.W. Davidson as baggage officer, were ordered to leave for Halifax at once to make arrangements for departure. They found that a new Royal Mail Line ship, the *Andes*, had been commandeered for troopship service and were able to procure it for the battalion. Members of the battalion were to be denied sharing Christmas with their families; on December 15, two special trains were made ready and by 07:30 hours there was a bustle of activity both inside and outside the armoury. Inside the final preparations were taking place for the march to the station while outside family members, sweethearts, friends and well-wishers were already gathering in the Vancouver rain to see them depart.

There is a poignancy when men (now women as well) go off to war. It was so in the huge numbers in 1914 at the start of the Great War and now it was being repeated. Even in Britain, while several men may leave from the same town or village, it is not the same as a regiment whose members are largely from one location who march off together. On this morning, by 09:00 hours the crowds were thick along the route, over the Burrard Street Bridge, along Pacific Street and north on Granville Street. Lining the streets were men of the 15th Coast Brigade, the 1st Searchlight Regiment and the 11th Royal Canadian Corps of Signals. At the crest of Burrard Street Bridge, Brigadier J.C. Stewart stood ready to take the salute.

Although most of the men were in uniform, it was only from the dress of the officers and the pipe band that the battalion could be identified as a Highland regiment. As a wartime measure, their kilts had been handed in, even those belonging to long-standing members and the new khaki battledress uniform was issued. Even the Balmoral bonnets had been replaced with 'fore and aft' caps, though once in Britain, the bonnets were re-issued. However, when the main armoury doors were opened onto Burrard Street and the battalion appeared, led by the pipes and drums playing *Scotland the Brave*, its morale was high. Major C.C. Ferrie had assumed temporary command in the absence of the Colonel and he led the parade. After passing the saluting stand, on reaching Granville Street, the stirring march *Blue Bonnets over the Border* was played.

As Dr. Reginald Roy, who in 1969 wrote the regiment's official history (*The Seaforth Highlanders of Canada, 1919-1965*) stated: "The shrill defiant cry of the pipes brought surges of emotion to the thousands who cheered the battalion on its way."

It was to be an empty Christmas for those left behind and this knowledge added to the sorrow of parting. The men boarded the trains to begin the 3,000 mile, five day journey across Canada. Hurried goodbyes were said, notes and souvenirs exchanged, to be looked at longingly in the years ahead. It was not then known what plans had been made for the battalion, but it was obvious that sooner or later it would face the enemy in some theatre of war. They could not know that this encounter was over three years away.

At Halifax no time was wasted in getting everyone on board the *Andes*. So good was the accommodation that out of 1500 officers and men, only 200 slept in hammocks. The convoy moved out of Halifax Harbour on December 22, along with seven other troopships protected by destroyers of the Royal Canadian Navy. In mid-ocean the Canadian destroyers departed, to be replaced by ships of the Royal Navy. On December 30 the Mull of Kintyre was rounded and in the early dawn the ship sailed past the Isle of Arran towards the mouth of the Clyde. Those who came on deck early saw the smaller island of Millport and the towns of Largs and Dunoon, with Gouroch framed by the Agyllshire hills to the north.

What were the thoughts of these men from a Canadian Highland regiment as many, for the first time saw the land from whence their history and tradition, the very tunes their pipes played, had sprung? For some, even though their names might not be of Scottish origin their roots were, such as Major Bert Hoffmeister, whose grandmother was born in the small Central Highland town of Pitlochry and was a Gaelic speaker. He had entered the Seaforths as a cadet and, like Budge was commissioned long before the war. By September 1939 he had become sales manager for the MacMillan Export Company's White Pine Division. H.R.'s plans for him were unfolding. He was also married and had a young daughter. Like other militiamen who were in business he was given half a day to wind up his affairs and take leave from his company. He returned five years later a highly decorated Major-General.

Now, on December 30, 1939 he was one of those gazing at the Highland hills beyond the north bank of the River Clyde. It was a stirring sight, made more so by the reception they received, which was recalled by one of the men:

> "... As the sun rose, small white-washed cottages appeared on either bank, becoming more numerous as we reached the boom-ships near Gouroch. Now all the convoy ships were in line astern, our escort destroyers were lined up at the boom opening and their crews had dressed ship. They stood to attention clad in duffel coats against the cold and as each ship passed through, they gave three cheers which were heartily returned. When it came to the *Andes* turn the Canadian Seaforth pipes played *Rule Britannia*, a salute they had practised all the way over."

When the ship made fast to the dock, many on board were surprised at the smallness of the railway engines and rolling stock compared to those in North America. It was time to begin the most uncomfortable part of the whole move from Vancouver. As they disembarked onto the quay and moved towards the railway platform the men felt the blast of the icy wind. The coldest winter in years was continuing and snow covered much of the landscape. They were once more on a train, this time heading south for Delville Barracks, in the town of Farnborough, close to Aldershot. When the train arrived at Farnborough's North Camp station they faced a two mile march to Delville East Barracks. It was a far cry from their march in Vancouver from the armoury to the station, but now at last their travelling was over for several weeks. Within two days of arriving the battalion was granted a week's leave, except for a minimum number for camp duties.

All Dominion and U.S. Forces soon learned to cope with Britain's very efficient black-out. To ignore it was to receive a bellow from a 'bobby' or an air-raid warden. For those who might have come originally from the British Isles, the transition was minimal. For others it was overwhelming. Dr. Roy describes these surprises very amusingly:

> "Possibly the first impact the Seaforth men had of Britain was its comparative smallness in relation to Canada. The trains were smaller, the cars—such as were still on the road—were smaller and freight cars, or 'goods wagons' seemed ridiculously small. At the same time they would be impressed by the speed and efficiency of the railway system. The trains into London not only rattled along at good clip, but they ran with the frequency of tram cars. Language, though odd at first, was soon both understood and adopted; petrol for gasoline, pavement for sidewalk, a wrench was a spanner and a truck was a lorry. 'One and six' meant one shilling and sixpence, a toilet was a W.C. (water closet), and a 'boot' was the trunk of a car. To have a 'mug up' was a cup of tea and to be 'knocked up' was to be awakened!"

There was wartime slang to be learned, such as a "blitzed area", meaning a bombed area; to "prang" was to crash. A "flap" indicated a disorganized state and "SNAFU" was a situation best described by the letters which formed the word—'situation normal, all fouled up.' Dr. Roy dryly pointed out, "There were of course, variations on this."

They became used to the severe rationing—and the generosity of the populace in sharing what little they had with others. Canadian and American servicemen were lucky in that they had their own clubs where food was more plentiful and they could also rely on food packages from home. As the air-raids increased the sight of thousands of Londoners sleeping on the underground system's platforms became commonplace.

Dr. Roy summed all this up succinctly:

"The Seaforths were quick to adapt themselves to their new home, and the local pub became as dear a social centre as it was for the local residents...

The blackout, which first was the object of language that would peel paint off the wall as the men stumbled or groped their way through unfamiliar streets, was ultimately accepted and coped with. Week by week they merged more completely into the British scene—all was to become so familiar and so accepted that years later, when the Seaforth managed to get leave from the continent, arriving in Britain he felt as though he had come home."

Soon after arriving the battalion was re-issued with Balmoral bonnets and this gave a boost to morale. Also as a result of a visit by Col. Stevenson to the Imperial Seaforth Highlanders depot in Scotland, the Canadians received a gift of MacKenzie tartan squares to go behind the cap-badge. There was an offer to share facilities with the Canadians when they were in Scotland. Socks and scarves knitted by women members of the British Seaforths Association were issued to the Canadians.

Things changed for Budge and Nancy when the regiment moved into Delville East Barracks and he resumed regimental duties. Budge felt the full impact of the blackout when he moved to Aldershot. On one occasion while endeavoring to find lodgings for Nancy he walked for five miles in the dark only to find that he had been given wrong directions and the house was actually only half-a-mile from the barracks. It was further complicated by the fact that few people were on the telephone. Eventually he found temporary lodgings in the nearby village of Cove and Nancy moved down from London. Aldershot was in a restricted area and access was only granted because she was an officer's wife. Budge joined her at the cottage whenever he could get time off.

One evening when Nancy was alone there was a knock on the front door and she opened it to find a Canadian soldier from another unit standing there. He assumed she was a local and asked the way to the barracks. Being conscious of the blackout Nancy said, "You had better come in," which he did and promptly produced an opened bottle of rye, from which he offered her a drink. She did not wish to hurt the feelings of a fellow Canadian and reluctantly agreed to take a sip with him. After giving him the required directions he went on his way. A few nights later Budge was home and there was another knock at the door so he went this time to find that there were several soldiers outside. A voice out of the darkness said, "Aw ——, the officer got here first!"

Nancy wished to make better use of her time and upon learning that No. 15 Canadian Military Hospital was soon to open at Bramshott, in Surrey she volunteered to work there, helping to set up a library and assist with handicrafts. She continued to attend daily even as the Battle of Britain began. The staff was almost entirely from the Toronto General Hospital, both doctors and nurses. The hospital was a few miles south of Aldershot and Nancy was able to rent a farmhouse at Great Bramshott for two or three months.

In early 1940 the battalion became part of the Home Forces reserve whose role was to defend the British Isles against invasion. Exercises were frequent and Budge was getting to know the southern counties well, from Kent to Wiltshire. The biggest single exercise took place in the third week of May when the entire brigade joined manœuvres on Salisbury Plain. Training was continuous and in view of the disturbing news from the continent it was a way to ease frustration at not being part of the action.

In early April the Germans began their invasion of Norway and Denmark and for several days all indications were that the Edmonton Regiment and the Princess Patricias might be going to fight there. This did not sit well with the Seaforths who considered themselves the best trained of the three units. Despite the issue of sheepskin coats to the Edmontons and the Pats, indicating transfer to a cold climate, it came to nothing and training continued. Within six weeks Norway was totally in German hands. Despite pockets of strong resistance, Denmark also fell in a matter of days.

Brigadier Pearkes took a great interest in the units under his command and appeared frequently at exercises and lectures. He did not merely offer advice and was not above giving a practical demonstration. Once in a wet and muddy training area he watched a group under instruction practicing grenade throwing in a trench raid and, on an impulse he handed his greatcoat to his driver and got down into the mud and crawled through it to give a practical demonstrate. Needless to say it made a great impression.

The British countryside, with its hedgerows, streams, woods and twisting lanes was ideal for exercises in deployment and map reading. When invasion became a possibility, the famous black and white cast-iron direction signs were removed all over the country and anyone who did not have an intimate knowledge of the area or, in the case of the military, anyone who could not map-read was in trouble.

As spring progressed, with the intensive greening of fields and meadows the warmth increased and by early May it turned hot. On the 6th an order came for two Seaforth companies to meet the 2nd Battalion Welsh Guards for a field exercise. The Seaforth companies were led by Majors J.D. Forin and Bert Hoffmeister. The 'battle' took place around Frensham Ponds, an area of heath land south of Aldershot and the company commanders were most anxious that their men measured up to the Guards. The battle raged from early morning until midnight on May 7, with the Seaforths aggressively harassing the 'enemy.' The British umpires were impressed and in their report wrote:

> "The morale and spirit of the Seaforths was remarkable. Their fieldcraft was excellent as they moved constantly about the area, their positions in cover and were well concealed. When they occupied a defensive position it could not be seen with the naked eye, and discipline in such positions and on the march was extremely high. Each individual Seaforth appeared to be a trained scout and prepared to remain perfectly still at any moment and for any length of time."

Just three days later, Hitler moved his Western Front divisions into Holland and Belgium in an all-out attack with such momentum it swept the German Army Groups A and B across these two countries with devastating speed. Troop-carrying gliders were used for the first time, with great effect. Below them the Panzer divisions pushed through the Ardennes Forest. Taking a leading part in the campaign was an, as yet unknown German officer, who would one day become a thorn in the flesh of the Allies in the desert campaign and yet win their lasting respect. He was General Erwin Rommel.

The British generals in France were, with few exceptions, still mentally fighting the first war, as indeed were many of the French generals. The Germans out-manœuvred them every step of the way. The French generals were concerned about Paris, but the thrust of the Germans was a sickle movement towards the coast. The 'impregnable' Maginot Line fell quickly and the allied armies were cut off. General Lord Gort, VC, DSO and 2 bars, MC, commanded the British Expeditionary Force. On May 19 he learned that his army was surrounded on three sides. He formed defence lines and initiated a small counter-attack with the 51st Highland Division, in which the 4th (Territorial) Battalion, Cameron Highlanders played a major role. The Camerons lost 250 men in this action, some when a dressing station received a direct hit.

It was now imperative for Gort to save what he could of his army and the one avenue still open led to the beaches of Dunkirk. On May 21 the retreat to Dunkirk began. Much has been written of this miraculous escape in which 338,226 men were evacuated from the beaches in nine days beginning about May 27 and ending on June 5, though still with a terrible toll of men and equipment. With the army in disarray and the enemy on its heels, invasion was very much on the minds of the British Government. Steps were taken to deploy the troops who had remained in Britain. All leave was cancelled and the battalion was put on 24 hours notice to move. Ammunition was issued and all the Bren guns were deployed to guard against enemy aircraft or airborne troops.

On May 29 the Seaforths were moved to Kettering in the Midland county of Northamptonshire, with the role of reinforcing the troops that were deployed on the east coast between the River Thames and the River Humber. Nancy gave up the farmhouse and moved up to Kettering—briefly. There was a party in a local pub which she attended. Brigadier Pearkes was there too and the next morning Brigade Major Rod Cellar ordered Budge to appear before the Brigadier, with Colonel Stephenson present as well. Pearkes asked, "I understand your wife is in Kettering, is that correct?" Budge replied, "Yes sir", to which the senior officer reminded him that it was a breach of security—then promptly asked if Nancy had anywhere to stay. The next day Budge was sentenced—his wife was to stay with Brigadier and Mrs Pearkes (Blytha) at their house in Camberly, Surrey!

The next move was to Boughton Park, home of the Duke of Buccleugh, an idyllic setting with its 5000 acres of land. There were sheep, cows and deer that browsed in the oak woods. At the time the house contained for safe keeping the coin collection from the British Museum. Here slit trenches were dug and all ranks had to be prepared to move at very short notice. They were required to 'stand-to' between 03:30 and 04:30 hours in case of an attack by parachutists, plus another 'stand-to' at dusk. A reconnaissance was made to the coast to ensure that the routes would be familiar to all personnel. At Brigade H.Q. the priority was to ensure that in the event of an air-borne attack or sea-borne invasion the Brigade would operate smoothly whatever its role.

Several days passed before tents were available and they slept under the trees. Budge swam in the large lake which was part of the estate. The life suited him and he was in his element as a soldier. In a letter to Nancy he wrote:

> "I look upon this war as a grand championship rugger match. I'm afraid I still don't feel very much hatred. Kicks on the shin will be lethal in this match but none of us mind. We're playing for a good team and the best one will win before we go home. We can't help licking the Hun, just because we're us!"

On June 7 the battalion was ordered to move south once more and were soon back in Aldershot. Barely settled in, the order came to prepare for a visit from Their Majesties the King and Queen. It was seen as a prelude to being sent to France, even though it was only days since the British Expeditionary Force had returned. There was no doubt that this was the intention. Maps of France were issued to all officers, distinguishing marks on all vehicles were painted over. Even a small advance party made its way to the embarkation port of Falmouth. On June 13 all the unit's motor transport and carriers followed and the men were eagerly awaiting the word to move.

The next day it was announced on the radio that Paris had fallen and two days later the advance party and the motor transport returned. The advance party, under Captain Roaf, did in fact get as far as Brest, but it became obvious to him that any thought of an invasion at that time was impossible. This small detachment of the 1st Canadian Infantry Division were ordered to run their vehicles over the dockside or into ditches, slash the tyres and then ignite them with gasoline to prevent capture by the enemy. Hitler now controlled three-fifths of France and was alleged to have pranced with delight at his successes, but to the people in Britain whose only hope lay in a particularly stirring speech of Winston Churchill*, it was a desperate time. If ever there was a threat of invasion it was most likely to be in the next two or three months while the home defences were at their weakest.

---

* *We shall defend our island whatever the cost may be, we shall fight on the beaches, we shall fight on the landing grounds, we shall fight in the fields and in the streets, we shall fight in the hills. We shall never surrender...*

All this frustration was bound to have an effect on the morale of the battalion and following the disappointment of so nearly going to France, some did indeed lose their cool. Worst of all were the snide remarks from civilians as to why the Canadians were still in Britain when the 'Tommies' were fighting overseas. They could not know that it was not the fault of the Canadians. In the unit any anger was taken out on the N.A.A.F.I.* canteen, resulting in broken windows, doors, chairs and the piano, which ended up on the centre of the parade square with what was left of it 'being played like a harp by some music-loving soldier!' (Professor Roy)

The battalion continued the role of an anti-invasion group, to be used as a "hard-hitting mobile force." Mobile they were. Next came a move to Wootton Park, to the north-east of Oxford. It was another country estate, not unlike Boughton Park and again they dug in, this time with a little more urgency after an air-raid in which some bombs landed only a mile away. They had barely completed the slit-trenches when the order came to move again. The reason was a comprehensive plan that had been drawn up for the defence of the United Kingdom in which the 1st Canadian Division had a major role. It was now part of the 7th Corps commanded by General McNaughton which was comprised of mixed units and had in it the 1st (British) Armoured Division and a New Zealand brigade. Pearkes was promoted to Major General and became G.O.C. of the 1st Canadian Division. The brigade was under the temporary command of Brigadier A.E. Potts until Brigadier C. Vokes took over and stayed in command until well into the Italian Campaign.

In this capacity the battalion moved south of London to the Kent-Surrey border where they remained for several months. The main concentrations were around Edenbridge in Kent and Limpsfield in Surrey. Slit trenches were dug and in case of action they prepared all-round defence positions. There was once more a shortage of tents and none were available for the regiment. It might not have mattered as it was early July, but despite the time of year there were several days of rain and conditions were miserable.

Fortunately training was stepped up, which to some extent kept their minds off the discomfort. The battalion became expert at moving on short notice, especially when the tide and weather favoured invasion,

---

* Navy, Army and Air Force Institute

yet good camouflage still had to be maintained to avoid being seen from the air. Close to the centre of the brigade's deployment area was Chartwell, the private country home of Prime Minister Winston Churchill. It was inevitable that he would want to inspect the troops protecting this area, especially to witness an example of the brigade's mobility. He came at one hour's notice on July 6, 1940, the visit spoiled by a sudden downpour and a "snafu" when the inspection party did not make the correct rendezvous. However, a platoon under the command of Lieut. J.W. Blair provided the guard for Chartwell for several days during that summer.

The weather finally improved and the men at last began to enjoy their surroundings and the benefits of fitness that came with constant training. The war diary read: "The battalion is at strength, all misfits have been weeded out and we were well armed, mobile—and spoiling for action."

In July Budge was offered a job as an instructor at a new school established to train Canadian officers promoted from the ranks. He turned it down even though it would have meant a promotion to captain. He considered that it was far too 'cushy' and might have prevented him from moving with the regiment in the event that they were sent overseas suddenly. It was, he said, part of his loyalty to his 'fighting family' and he did not wish to take a job of this type until he had been tried in battle.

Despite turning down the instructor position Budge was soon promoted to Captain and joined "A" Company under Major Doug Forin. The battalion continued to train hard, with frequent and increasingly long route marches. They became popular with the boys of the area as the soldiers marched in column with a piper at the head, an unusual sight in the lanes of Kent and Surrey. The only thing that spoiled this otherwise enjoyable existence was the regular presence of enemy planes overhead as the Battle of Britain continued. There were both night-time and daylight raids and the members of the battalion frequently had a grandstand view of dog-fights overhead and of planes crashing nearby, both friend and foe.

The highest category of alert came on September 7, when all leave was cancelled and all ranks were on one hours notice to move. The codeword "CROMWELL" had been sent out and in some locations the church bells were wrung to warn that the invasion had begun. Fortunately it turned out to be a false alarm but over the next two weeks the raids intensified, though the invasion did not come. Budge was in hospital when this occurred, having badly damaged a finger, which required attention and the fitting of a cast.

Because of the increased air-raids there were times when Budge expressed reservations about having Nancy in Britain. It was fine in the early days of the war, but now he wished to concentrate 100% on soldiering. As the raids intensified and the threat of invasion grew more likely he became concerned for her safety and suggested that she should return to Canada. He told her the U.K. "would very quickly become a damned unpleasant place for civilians to live in. They will be at the mercy of all the horrors of the enemy and completely subjected to all the requirements of our own forces."

At the same time he knew that Nancy would not be happy returning to Canada when she could in her own way make a contribution to the war-effort. He finally conceded, telling her that he had always treated her as his equal and on that basis he would agree to her staying.

The battalion officers were billeted at various country homes in Kent and Surrey, some requisitioned and others where the family remained. Budge's billet was with the Lines family on their large estate near the village of Limpsfield, Surrey. Walter Lines was Managing Director of the family firm, Lines Bros., one of the largest toy manufacturers in Britain. After the war it provided an interesting business opportunity for Budge. Nancy moved to Limpsfield Chart, the country home of Lady Worthington-Evans, who lived on her own apart from a daughter who came down from London at weekends. While living there Nancy recalls:

> "The Battle of Britain was still going on and we had an amusing routine. My hostess insisted that I slept under the stairs on a mattress and her daughter slept under the billiard table when she was home. The maids, whose rooms were over the stables, would bring us morning tea and I always felt very embarrassed having my tea in this bolt-hole under the stairs!
>
> I moved several times during this period. Later I went to a house run by a Mrs Duvene, the family of the fine arts auction company. She was a striking blonde and naturally attracted many Canadian officers who enjoyed the hospitality she offered them. It was an advantage to her having a Canadian women there, especially an officer's wife."

The stay in Limpsfield was long remembered by all ranks because it provided the best billets in all their moves to that time. Aside from the attractiveness of both the village and its surrounding country, there was a profusion of vegetables grown by the locals, which were shared with the battalion. The houses were comfortable and there was a direct train service to London. The lower ranks did not take their luck for granted and there is an amusing description in the regimental history of them in their billets dusting, mopping floors and cleaning sinks and baths. Although no houses in the village received a direct hit there was enough damage from falling shrapnel to keep everyone on their toes. Broken glass and fallen roof tiles was a very common sight on most days following the passage of enemy planes overhead and the attempt to shoot them down by nearby Bofors guns.

In the midst of the raids Budge had a surprise when he learned that his father Henry, had arrived in England on September 27 on H.M.C.S. "Stadacona", and was now in London. Budge motorcycled up to see him. They had a wonderful celebration, but while they were meeting there had been another raid and with his dimmed headlight Budge failed to see a new crater in the road and ploughed into it, fortunately with minimal damage to the motorcycle or himself. Shortly after this he was appointed 2 i/c of "B" Company, under Major Bert Hoffmeister, for whom he developed a great respect and admiration that has lasted a lifetime.

Budge had earlier referred to his 'fighting family.' This was no idle boast, as there were as many Bell-Irvings in the second world war as in the first. Budge's father, with the rank of Lieutenant-Commander (soon to be Commander) R.C.N.V.R. was now in Britain, attached to the Royal Navy. He was to have a variety of jobs and remain active until June 1945, by which time he was fifty-eight years old. It was his constant boast that he was fitter than many of the younger officers that served under him and he was certainly fitter than any who remotely approached his age. During Henry's time in Britain he had a variety of jobs: During the winter of 1940/41 he was based at Milford Haven in Wales with the title Mine Sweeping Officer. From February 1941 until March 1943 he was shore based, first in Liverpool, then in Portland, Dorset and later in London in charge of communications and signals at the office of the Rear Admiral, Coastal Forces. (see Appendix 6)

Duncan Bell-Irving had remained active in the Royal Canadian Air Force and reached the rank of Air Commodore by the end of the war. Aeneas was in Britain commanding the 2nd Heavy A.A. Regt, Royal Canadian Artillery. Roderick was back in Canada as an instructor where he remained until December 1942, when he resumed operational flying. Cousin Ian Bell-Irving, Dick's son, was serving with the Canadian Seaforths, as was another cousin, Duncan Manson. Dick's other son Richard, later joined the navy and was killed in action in 1945. Budge's sister Wendy was in Britain, married to Cornelius 'Corney' Burke of Vancouver who had obtained a commission in the Royal Canadian Navy and was also attached to the Royal Navy. Isabel's son, Sedley Sweeney was in the Royal Engineers. Budge's Aunt Mary had married Hugh Robb and they had lived in Britain for some years. Hugh was an officer in the R.A.F. in administrative duties. His sons, John and David were in the British Army, one in the Seaforth Highlanders and one in the Coldstream Guards. Duncan's son Gordon had joined the R.C.A.F. and after pilot training was transferred to Britain. Gordon's sister Elizabeth had joined the Women's Division of the R.C.A.F.

Early in November, with the threat of invasion still uppermost, the battalion was moved to Brighton. The distance between Brighton and Limpsfield was little more than thirty miles, but in comfort it was a world away. The new location was on the English Channel with its frequent gales and almost constant high winds. On either side of the town are low cliffs that intersperse with other small towns and behind are the Sussex 'downs', high rolling pasture land on which are dotted small villages. There was little protection from the weather in the newly dug weapon pits, which needed constant attention to avoid collapse. The wind-driven rain came slanting in from the sea, finding its way through the khaki greatcoats. The raw damp cold was quite unlike anything the Canadians had met in previous locations. Their billets were not like the cosier homes in Limpsfield, but were empty hotels, boarding houses and golf course clubhouses, where keeping warm was much more difficult.

It was with great relief when, in mid-December the battalion was detailed to return to Limpsfield in time to celebrate their first Christmas in Britain. They returned with a new commanding officer, Major C.C. Ferrie who had also served in the regiment as a militia officer. He took over from Colonel Stevenson who had been promoted to Brigadier and returned to Canada to take up a command on the Pacific Coast.

It says much for the behaviour of the Seaforth Highlanders of Canada that they were welcomed back to Limpsfield very warmly by the local people and there were many invitations to share the sparse wartime fare in village homes. There was, as well, the regimental festivities, with the officers having their dinner on Christmas Eve so that on Christmas Day they could join with the senior N.C.O.s in serving the men.

Budge was in an even worse predicament physically than in September as the result of a fall while on duty on the coast. He was on the roof of a building in which some of his men were billeted to inspect a leak, when a piece of railing gave way and he fell about twenty feet onto a concrete pad. It was only after an alert British soldier saw him and knocked at the door to inform the Seaforth men, "One of your blokes is lying down there unconscious" that action was taken. Budge had severe concussion which kept him unconscious for a week, a broken arm, broken collar bone and general severe bruising. He was in hospital for several weeks, followed by convalescence in Torquay, where some of his grandmother's relatives still lived. He and Nancy spent Christmas with them.

When he returned to regimental duties he was appointed acting Company Commander of "B" Company, as Bert Hoffmeister had gone down with a mysterious ailment that had paralyzed his left leg. It was serious enough that he was taken to a neurological hospital but made a complete recovery and had no re-occurrence. Budge was also appointed president of a Standing Court of Inquiry, convened to examine all equipment losses, accidents and desertions. He was then given command of "C" Company when Major Jim Creighton was made acting C.O. Once again he had cause to write how much he enjoyed soldiering, particularly with command of his own company: "Being completely responsible for absolutely everything in the lives of one hundred and twenty fine men is not only a great honour, but a fascinating life."

There was an improvement in Budge and Nancy's domestic life when they rented a cottage in Limpsfield, with the rustic name of "Oast Cottage." In January 1941, Nancy began driving a YMCA canteen truck provided by the Women's Canadian Club of Vancouver, from which to offer tea, coffee and food to the troops, helped initially by Marci Davidson, wife of Captain Dave Davidson. The truck was very welcome after a route-march or on a cold day at the rifle range and Nancy's warmth and friendliness quickly won a special place in the hearts of all ranks in the battalion.

That same month the 2nd Canadian Infantry Brigade celebrated its first anniversary in the U.K. There had been a considerable turnover of officers and other ranks due to postings or, in some cases, repatriation to Canada as the pace of training was stepped up. The average age of the battalion members decreased as the older ones, including senior officers, were deemed unfit for active service through age.

In mid-January Major-General Pearkes informed all units under his command that there was to be a 60 mile route-march. This was the longest single march the Seaforths had ever attempted and despite a few falling out, the men acquitted themselves well. There were, to quote the official history, 'blisters on blisters' and many swollen feet. A popular form of relief when Limpsfield was again reached was "Ditchburn's Painkiller", a wicked concoction of whisky and cider which was guaranteed to deaden any pain from the effects of dentistry to swollen feet. Despite his still not being completely 100% from the effects of the fall, Budge took part in it and a large-scale Corps exercise a few days later. He wrote to his mother: "It's true that I had a narrow shave when I got hurt, but like Uncle Duncan I have at least nine lives and they are not all used up yet!"

The emphasis was on training and more training to bring about a high degree of battle-readiness. One exercise, "Bulldog" is worthy of note because of an amusing incident involving Budge. It was wide-ranging and took the battalion through London and into the Epping Forest. It was also intensive with very little sleep for at least three days. In the forced marches, there was a ten minute rest period per hour. Many soldiers went into such a deep sleep that it was difficult to wake them. During one march Budge, leading his column, suddenly began lifting his knees higher and higher and then fell flat on his face. When asked what happened he said, "I thought I was going upstairs to bed!" It was some time before he lived it down.

Other exercises took place with the Home Guard battalions. These were civilians holding down full-time occupations who were as yet either too young for military service or too old. Some were in reserved occupations. They wore full army uniforms, had rifles, machine guns and were provided with ammunition. The Home Guard was the last line of defence from an invasion and they took their part-time task very seriously, working well with the army and Royal Air Force and several lost their lives in the line of duty. At one point Budge was responsible for providing the local Home Guard with up-to-date military training and where necessary, improving defences in the area. He found them to be mostly retired senior officers, covered with ribbons, but they did not seem to mind taking orders from a young Canadian captain.

There was another category of defence which neither the army or the Home Guard knew about, unless they were in on the secret. It only became known in 1994, fifty years after the war. Known as the British Resistance Organization it had 3000 especially trained men and women who, if an invasion was successful were to act as guerrillas. They were to all intents and purposes ordinary members of the Home Guard or Women's Auxiliary units but there were secret hideouts filled with the equipment needed to become underground resistance fighters. They were especially trained to overpower and kill German soldiers and to carry out acts of sabotage. The existence of this group was a well-kept secret and it was revealed at a reunion of the surviving members in November 1994 that their activities were kept from even immediate family members.

1942 came with still no sign of the battalion going overseas. It moved a few miles to Redhill Airport, but within a short time was once more sent to the coast, this time to guard a twelve mile stretch of the South Downs. Battalion H.Q. was at Danny Park, near Hurstpierpoint, Sussex where they took over a Tudor period mansion. Budge's officers were billeted in a local pub, but he and Nancy were able to rent one of the smaller houses on the estate.

Throughout this time Nancy had been far from idle. As well as driving the canteen truck she still visited patients at the Canadian Military Hospital once a week. Her efforts with the canteen truck were particularly appreciated in the Spring of 1942 when the Seaforths took part in the biggest exercise to date, code-named "Tiger."

Before the exercise began there was another change of command and several new company commanders were named. Lieut.-Colonel Ferrie left the unit and his place was taken by Lieut.-Colonel Tait. He had also served with the unit between the wars but his tenure as C.O. was, unfortunately short and he was invalided home through ill-health within a few months. Budge was given command of "A" Company, remaining a captain until May 1942 when his majority was confirmed. Major J.D. Forin, became acting C.O. Now the senior officer strength was: Company Commanders—Captain H.P. Bell-Irving, 'A' Company; Captain the Lord Tweedsmuir, 'B' Company; Captain D.M. Clark, 'C' Company and Captain A.S. Campbell, 'D' Company. Lord Tweedsmuir was the son of the late Lord Tweedsmuir (novelist John

Buchan), Canada's 35th Governor-General, who had died in office on February 11, 1940. Major Bert Hoffmeister had returned to Canada for a course lasting several months at the Canadian Junior War Staff College.

Exercise "Tiger" involved six divisions, encompassed several hundred square miles of country and lasted eleven days. It was designed to test everyone from senior officers down. Their task was to manœuvre the units under their command efficiently and effectively as the eleven day exercise went through its phases. It was the culmination of a new type of training learned from actual fighting in both Europe and North Africa and was called 'Battle Drill.' Far removed from the previous concept of trench warfare or drawn battle-lines, the emphasis was on swift movement. A degree of toughness not previously encountered was called for and was essentially the same training given to Commando units. The objective was to harden men to withstand the worst conditions of warfare. It duplicated the sights and sounds of battle, using a variety of ingenious means devised to test the soldier. Orders were carried out at the 'double', whether loaded down with a Bren gun or two inch mortar. 'Sweat saves blood' was the war-cry. Weather conditions were not allowed to hamper the pace and neither was the terrain. All ranks were taught to scale a cliff with ropes, wriggle in cold, oozing mud or wade waist deep through rivers holding their weapons over their heads.

Barbed wire, slippery logs and water-laden pits formed part of the obstacle course, with live ammunition and explosive charges adding a dose of reality. Weapons were fired on the move and live ammunition from mortars and field guns were provided by gunners of a Royal Artillery unit. There were casualties; cracked ribs, sprained ankles and broken legs or arms, but this 'wastage' was accepted for the realism that it provided. The company commanders were put through their paces along with the men and after a particularly hard assault led by Captain Lord Tweedsmuir and Budge, one soldier was heard to say to another, "God, and I thought they said these f—g lords were dissolute!"

Budge had his own succinct comments on the course. He told his father: "I went through it in the ranks and thoroughly enjoyed my two carefree weeks as a private. The most noticeable part of the course was that we ran everywhere, all the time—never walking. It is an amazing fact to me that after a bit of practice and teeth-gritting one can run five miles with both equipment and a weapon then still put in an attack with real punch. We move through rivers, ditches, mud, hedges, fences with real bullets and bombs aimed at us as near as dammit."

The battalion was now in fine shape, which was just as well because 'Exercise Tiger's' Director was a stickler for discipline and good order but, like Rommel, an as yet unknown officer. His name was Lieut.-General B. L. Montgomery and he was to meet the Seaforths again in Sicily. On this exercise he showed the traits that were to make him popular with the men, marching alongside each company for a few miles before breaking off to appear somewhere else. It was "Monty" who had created the battle drill concept of training. 'Tiger' was the greatest test so far of the men's stamina and the Seaforths ended up 130 miles from their starting point, all of it on foot with minimum ration allowance.

At the end of the exercise, the battalion was again deployed on the coast, this time along the Eastbourne section, a few miles east of their previous position at Brighton. The war had entered a different phase and there was much more enemy aircraft activity, especially low-level daylight 'hit and run' raids by small numbers of aircraft. There was one night-time raid on August 10, 1942 which destroyed some of the Edmonton Regiment's vehicles and killed nine men of the No. 9 Field Ambulance Unit. The Pipe Band had a narrow escape as they left Eastbourne railway station having returned from an engagement. They had just left the station when it was hit by several incendiary bombs. (Part of the Seaforths popularity was the entertainment they could offer wherever they were stationed. The ceremony of "Beating Retreat" by the pipe-band was performed several times, along with men adapt at Highland dancing and performing the sword-dance)

A wonderful opportunity for retaliation came on the 26th during an early morning raid. Two German Focke-Wolfe 190 fighter planes came in at low level at about 09:00 hours. Private E.G. Johnstone was stationed on a nearby factory roof with his Bren gun at the ready, as was Private F.L. Wood in another strategic location. Both were in a good position to fire and they saw their bullets hitting home. Although both planes dropped their bombs, one zoomed erratically, flipped over and crashed close by the town's gas plant. Not to be outdone, Sgt N.C. Forsbeck and Corporal Brammer heard the noise from their billets and raced out with loaded Bren guns. They let off several rounds at the other fighter and strikes were witnessed by several soldiers watching close by. Whether it limped back to base is not known but they were satisfied that it was well and truly shot-up and would need considerable repairs to the fuselage. Budge had a grandstand view of the action from the town and remarked, "I was tickled to see the old black crosses again after several months." He was amazed at how calm the civilian population remained, going about their business as though nothing was going on. (Private Wood and Major H.P. Bell-Irving were destined to meet in the heat of battle in Sicily.)

This daylight raid came exactly one week after the Dieppe landing and it was a bitter-sweet retaliation just hours after the fate became known of the Canadian units who took part. Especially close to home for the Seaforths was the news that Cecil Merritt, who had been promoted to Lieutenant-Colonel and given command of the South Saskatchewan Regiment, was reported missing in the action. It was several weeks before it was learned that he was not only alive and a prisoner of war, but had been awarded the Victoria Cross for gallantry in action. The citation describes his actions during the raid:

> "Col. Merritt calmly led his men across a bridge that was under intense fire, waving his helmet in encouragement. He destroyed a machine gun position with a grenade and when forced to withdraw organized it coolly and stalked a sniper with his Bren gun, at the same time covering the withdraw to the beach. He was taken prisoner, but by his efforts helped others to escape."

On October 11, Bert Hoffmeister was welcomed back. He had been promoted to Lieutenant-Colonel and took over as Commanding Officer. This was not just another temporary command, but a long-standing one and he was to lead them into action. He was known as a 'hardworking, business-like, no-nonsense' officer whose popularity would increase during his tenure.

Budge came very close to leaving the battalion at about that time. He had gone to Scotland to umpire an exercise between British infantry units and upon returning south he found that he had been recommended to command the 1st Canadian Paratroop Battalion. Despite the Brigade Commander's input it fell through when Canadian G.H.Q. learned that Budge was married. Nancy, ever alert to the next situation was already packing for him.

He was, however, away from his company for a month running a brigade school for junior N.C.O.'s. He told his father he was glad it was for no longer than that as he did not wish to play 'schoolmaster' in the event of something more exciting coming along. Soon after there were some changes within the regiment, both tactical and administrative. The H.Q. Company was split into two sections, with the Anti-aircraft

Platoon and Signals Platoon joining up with the Administration Platoon under Captain C.C. Tarbuck. The other section became a Support Company, composed of the Carrier Platoon, Mortar Platoon, Anti-tank Platoon and Pioneer Platoon under Budge's command. He had begun the war as I/C of the Carrier Platoon and now had charge of a Company whose role was very much an offensive one, which he would relish. The Pioneer Platoon was no longer a labouring section but consisted of many tradesmen, highly trained as assault engineers and with skills in handling explosives, booby-trapping and mine-laying. They were also responsible for anti-gas precaution and decontamination.

Rumour and counter rumour persisted about possible overseas destinations for the battalion, especially with a growing call for a 'second front', even graffiti demands to: "Open Second Front Now" from many citizens who were equally frustrated with the progress of the war. Fortunately during this time equipment was updated, with improved rifles, respirators, steel helmets, and motorcycles. The Thompson sub-machine gun was added to the weaponry and also, of more importance to Budge and his Anti-tank Platoon, a 6 pounder anti-tank gun of greater penetrating power. This was followed soon after with the previously referred to P.I.A.T. anti-tank gun.

Finally, after one rumour that the battalion might be used to attack Sardinia, it was confirmed in January 1943 that Scotland was the next destination. By this time General Montgomery had made a name for himself in the Desert Campaign as commander of the 8th Army. With his successes, attention was slowly turning towards the next stage, that of invading Italy from the south.

Over Christmas 1942 Budge and Nancy hosted a real 'Bell-Irving' Christmas, reminiscent of those get-togethers in the previous war. Fourteen sat down to dinner cooked by Nancy and marvelled at the quantity and variety of food and drink assembled considering the austere rationing. Roderick had returned from Canada just days before and was now an acting Squadron-Leader. He was waiting for a posting to an operational squadron and had a £5 bet on with Budge that he would be a Wing-Commander before Budge became a Lieutenant-Colonel.

In early January Budge was one of two officers, accompanied by several senior N.C.O.s who left as an advance group to Inverary, on the west coast of Scotland. There was constant troop movement by rail at this time and it was common for special coaches to be attached to regular express trains to accompany the overflow of military personnel. After an uncomfortable night of disturbed sleep they woke as the train pulled into Stirling at 06:00, met by W.V.S. (Women's Voluntary Service) women who served a welcome cup of tea to the troops. The army coaches were attached to another engine and the final haul to Inverary began, a tortuous route which ended at Dalmally on the Oban line. After de-training, there was a seventeen mile drive to Castle Camp, Inverary where the battalion would be based for the next two months.

On February 14 the battalion followed the advance party. St. Valentine's Day was an unfortunate choice for some because by this time several members of the unit had British wives and children who were to be left behind in the south. Nancy remained at Jevington, in Sussex. Budge would now be occupied almost non-stop with exercises until going overseas and within hours of arriving at Castle Camp training began in earnest, part of which was the use of landing-craft. Only two days into training Budge earned himself a place in the unit's war diary when a rope fouled a landing-craft's propeller. One of the naval officers went over the side to unravel it and was overcome by the cold. Budge finished the job.

Inverary is on the west shore of Loch Fyne, approximately seventy miles south of Arnisdale, on Loch Hourn, where Budge had spent time as a boy with the Scottish Bell-Irvings. Nearby is Inverary Castle, ancestral home of the Dukes of Argyll, chiefs of Clan Campbell. As an amusing aside, a note in the official history shows that Pipe-Major Esson was cognisant of Clan Campbell's place in Scottish history—which was frequently on the side of the English Crown! Anxious to be diplomatic while deep in 'Campbell country' he drew up a list of pipe-tunes which would be inappropriate for the band to play.

Budge was not averse to the pipe tune *The Campbells are Coming*. This, however, was not the case with all soldiers of Highland descent. Budge was amused to hear of an incident during a similar Combined Operations course whose participants were invited to the castle. When someone called for "three cheers for His Grace the Duke of Argyll" a solitary but loud voice shouted from the rear rank—"Standfast the MacDonalds!" (See Appendix 7).

The reason for choosing the west of Scotland for Combined-Operations training was the variety of terrain and the wild, rocky coastline. It would satisfy all of the training needs from cliff scaling, moving across hills containing good ground-cover but interspersed with boggy ground which was not easy to traverse.

(Just a few miles up the coast at Inverailort Castle, Commando training was taking place in very similar terrain. One of the leaders was Lord Lovat, 24th Chief of Clan Fraser. He led No. 4 Commando Battalion at Dieppe and, promoted to brigadier, led a Commando Brigade on "D" Day. Many of the newer ideas on aggressive fighting techniques came from activities at Inverailort.)

The weather in the Seaforth's first few weeks at Inverary was not conducive to the activities in which the battalion was engaged and it is a shame that many men formed an uncharitable, though understandable view of the country that gave it dress, music and traditions. However, as the season slowly turned to spring this feeling was replaced by admiration, especially on days when the surrounding hills and moors were visible in the clear northern light.

Although everyone was housed in Nissen huts the ground around them, when not hard with frost was muddy from the alternating rain and there was no hot water for bathing or even shaving. Budge shared a Nissen hut with seven other officers, some from support units such as Artillery, Engineers and the Royal Navy. Attached to the unit was a 'mad' Norwegian officer whose company Budge enjoyed enough to consume a bottle of Drambuie with him one evening, followed by a visit to the traditional 'Robbie Burns' night hosted by the Sergeants' Mess.

These were mere diversions from the most intense training the battalion had experienced to that time. This included a very realistic coastal landing from H.M.S. *St. Hilaire* a ship that was large enough to carry several landing craft. It was a night-time exercise and once the landing craft were lowered the men clambered down scrambling-nets into them. Each company was given a beach sector to land on and an objective to capture.

Budge was very pleased with the work of his Support Company and arranged a dance for them in the N.A.A.F.I. He told Nancy, "Fifty WRENS, fifty Womens' Voluntary Service members and fifty gallons of beer should do them fairly well! It is the only troop's function that has been arranged up here. There have been a couple of officers' parties but I was on an exercise both times."

On March 4, with the training behind them, the battalion headed south again. After the intensive training and the build-up of morale it was a disappointment to take up defensive positions on the south coast once more—but it was not for long.

CHAPTER SIX

ON APRIL 23 1943, GENERAL MACNAUGHTON had discussed the possibility of overseas service for one of the Canadian divisions with General Sir Alan Brooke, Chief of the Imperial General Staff (C.I.G.S.). This request received his blessing, subject to Ottawa's approval for the inclusion of Canadian forces in any proposed landing. No time was wasted in sending an affirmative and on the 26th the Seaforths were told that all leave was cancelled. A few days before, Major Douglas Forin left the unit for a short tour of duty with Canadian Military Headquarters and Budge assumed the duties of second-in-command until his return.

In Henry Bell-Irving's letters home at this time he mentioned that news from his sons was often scarce. He knew that Budge was on the move and that Roderick frequently flew on operations over Europe. His own war had to this time been somewhat erratic though no less important and he had endured many air-raids in London.

Budge was indeed on the move and by May 9 the Canadian Seaforths were back at Castle Camp, Inverary. The first reaction of the men was the change in the weather. May and June are traditionally the best months to be in the West Highlands and May and June of 1943 were no exception. Dr. Roy, in his regimental history waxed poetically: "Nowhere did the pipes sound sweeter and to see the battalion march along past the heather-covered hills with the pipes and drums skirling at its head made the blood tingle. In this setting, to hear *Scotland the Brave* or *Heilan Laddie* sounding across the hills brought home to every

Seaforth more than ever a sense of pride in his regiment and its alliance to Scotland."

At this time it was learned that the German offensive in North Africa had collapsed, leading to more speculation about their final destination, of which even the C.O. had no knowledge. A few days later a strange ship was seen to be easing up Loch Fyne towards Inverary. She was named the *Circassia*, converted from an armed merchant cruiser to a troopship and then to an L.S.I.(L), Landing Ship Infantry (Large). It had accommodation for fourteen landing-craft as well as the men and equipment of the 2nd Canadian Infantry Brigade.

The ship, under Master Mariner Captain David W. Bone, had a combined Merchant Navy and Royal Navy crew, the latter being mainly junior officers responsible for the landing craft. Most had come from civilian occupations and had little previous contact with boats. Knowing that his father would do an admirable job of teaching them, and did not particularly like his job at Warrington, Budge began making suggestions to this effect in the right quarters. It was not in time to help the immediate situation, but did have some influence on Henry's next job. In early June he was given a command at Burnham on Crouch, Essex, and his role was directly concerned with landing-craft training. His personal quarters and office were in the Royal Burnham Yacht Club and with many 'old salts' coming to the club each day he was in his element. He also had a small open boat with an inboard motor at his disposal which he christened "Nan." He remained there until November when he was transferred to Rosemarkie on the Black Isle, where he did a similar job, but in less comfortable accommodation and climate.

In June 1943 Roderick had his Squadron-Leader rank confirmed and was with 226 Squadron at Foulsham, Norfolk, a medium bomber squadron which had just converted from Bostons to Mitchells. Its role was to take part in daylight raids on enemy airfields and communications targets. Roderick's letters to Henry were very guarded but were full of optimism.

In the meantime under Captain Bone's efficient command, by the time the *Circassia* sailed the mixed Merchant and Royal Navy crew was working well. After the war he was knighted and he also took up writing, with six books to his credit. In one of them, *Merchantman Rearmed* (Chatto & Windus, 1949), he wrote of the day that he picked up the Canadians: "It was no token force that we picked up, but the 'shock-troops' of the Canadian First Division, whom we were to transport overseas. They had been in training for many arduous months in the rugged mountains and on the rocky shores of Argyllshire. It is perhaps invidious for a sailor to comment on the relative merits of the soldiers that he embarks, but he surely may express his liking. As I watched them come aboard I thought there was something very special in their bearing and action. At Inverary it was no simple dockside movement of marching up broad gangways. The desire for space in fitting out the vessel had necessitated in discarding these. Instead, steel scaling ladders had been placed at intervals along the ship's side. Towards these the miscellaneous barges from the loch-side converged and with incredible swiftness the sun-bronzed men raced up them. They were self-contained too, every man being burdened by his own personal kit and weapons.

There was no confusion, no running back for mislaid items. With the Canadians we engaged in many exercises and for the last practice landing on the Ayreshire coast we put them ashore at 2 a.m. on a rainy morning to face a thirty-five mile march to the temporary barracks in which they stayed until picked up again."

There were many practise landings before this final one. A key landing took place in Brodick Bay on the Isle of Arran. With weapons, ammunition and only absolute necessities, the platoons were assembled below, led onto the deck, boarded their respective L.C.A.'s which were winched down to the water, and headed for shore. Again, the official history states: "If they were fortunate, the assault craft would land them on the right beach in a minimum of water. If they were unfortunate, as happened on the first run-in, they might be landed a mile or so from the assigned beach in several feet of water, giving a drenching in bitterly cold water before setting off to find the correct rendezvous. Quite a few men were to remark on the similarity between these exercises and the actual assault on Sicily, even to the errors made."

It only remained now for the final preparations and for these they were billeted at the Hamilton Race Course, southeast of Glasgow. Worn equipment was replaced, tropical kit issued, the number of Thompson sub-machine guns was increased. Mepacrine (anti-malaria) pills were issued and a recollection many years later by General Hoffmeister showed that as Commanding Officer he could indulge in a bit of leg-pull. After the unit was issued with these pills, it became a popular sport in which the C.O. played his part to convince new arrivals that they must be chewed carefully in order to be effective. The result was temporary paralysis of the jaw.

Knowing that a move overseas was imminent, Budge renewed his suggestions that Nancy should return to Vancouver. She was pregnant again for the second time, having had a miscarriage a year or so before. Nancy moved to Edinburgh for the baby's birth and was attended by a doctor recommended by Dr. Greenlees, Headmaster still of Loretto. A nursing home was selected for the birth and from that point Budge could do little else but wait for news. By the time it came he was well into the Sicilian Campaign.

The final landing drill referred to by Captain Bone took place on June 17, and this time the Seaforths were told that it should be thought of as a dress rehearsal for the real thing. These landings had taken place under the watchful eyes of Brigadier Vokes, newly appointed to command the 2nd Canadian Infantry Brigade, who was determined that it would be among the most ready when the *Circassia* put out to sea for the real thing, wherever the action might be. The wait was not long; on June 27, he came on board and remained. One of his first actions was to call a meeting of unit C.O.s in his brigade.

Among the visitors was Major Ronald Murray, R.A.M.C., commanding a field ambulance unit. By chance Budge met Ronald as he came on board. A decision was almost instantaneous between the two old school friends (and onetime competitors). The doctor would not really be essential to the Brigadier's meeting. As the Seaforth C.O., Bert Hoffmeister must of course go, so his cabin was empty. The issue rum stock was in his cabin. There were many reminiscences to share and—of course—the rum should be tasted before issuing to the troops, so Budge and Ronald Murray settled down and in the Loretto tradition filled their pipes with John Cotton brand tobacco.

When the non-smoking Bert Hoffmeister returned from his meeting to the smoke-filled cabin he was extraordinarily good about it. Ronald had missed the boat back to his own ship, and it was late. Budge, ever hospitable gave up his own bed to his old friend. He remembered that Dick Malone, the Brigade-Major had a cabin all to himself. He did not think this was fair so, finding his way to the cabin to join the sleeping B.M. he climbed onto a table and went to sleep.

Budge awoke early in the morning, crept out, returned to his own cabin, found his bed had been slept in and came to the weighty conclusion that obviously he had been in bed there. All was well. Later in the morning Budge saw the Brigadier walking towards him and as they approached, Chris Vokes raised his arms forward and closed his eyes.

Budge could not fail to conclude that he had been caught at something—but what? It was later revealed that the 'table' he had slept on in Dick Malone's cabin was the super-secret model of the brigade's beach landing area!

During the morning, preparations for sailing were begun and by evening all was ready. At 21:00 hours the ship weighed anchor. It was the moment for which the Seaforth Highlanders of Canada, its sister regiments, the PPCLI and Edmonton Regiment had waited three and a half years. Dr. Roy paints a very moving picture of the event:

> "With signal flags flying and Morse lamps clacking, the *Circassia* began to ease its way down the Clyde. It had been a beautifully warm, sunny day and the men crowded onto the deck to have a last look at the shores of Scotland; the fields, the small stone houses—everything that had been so foreign to them three and a half years earlier and now was so familiar that it was almost like leaving home. Many Seaforths had married British girls and some had small youngsters. For these men it was the hardest as the long, grey file of transports moved slowly through the anti-submarine nets guarding this great port.
>
> A blazing sunset lit up the heather-clad hills while, on deck, each man seemed wrapped in his own thoughts; not the least of which was a fervent hope to see these same hills again. As the land gave up its rosy hue and changed to grey-blue before turning into the long June twilight, the decks slowly cleared. The open sea was reached and the blacked-out ship began to rise and fall gently with the increasing swell."

There were approximately 250 men in the Second Canadian Infantry Brigade, a part of the largest invasion fleet ever assembled to that time. The next day an announcement was made over the ship's tannoy system: " A signal has been received from the Admiralty which reads 'You are going to the Mediterranean to take part in the biggest Combined Operations the world has ever seen!'"

It was called "Operation Husky" and Brigadier Vokes instructed his C.O.s to open their sealed orders and to learn for the first time what Captain Bone already knew; the landing was to take place on the island of Sicily where the Division was to join forces with General Montgomery's famed 8th Army (the Desert Rats).

At the Casablanca Conference in January 1943 this invasion was seen as a pre-requisite to an invasion of Northern Europe. It would keep the Germans fighting in the Mediterranean and at the same time almost certainly assist in toppling Mussolini. Sicily was chosen because it would provide a base of operation from which to invade the Italian mainland. Planning was begun immediately, though there was opposition from the Americans who could not see what possible help it could be to a later invasion across the English Channel. Churchill used his powers of persuasion and managed to convince the Americans of its wisdom.

That it was the largest invasion to that time was no idle boast. No less than 2,600 ships took part, coming from all directions, some from the British Isles and others from North Africa. As evidence of the American agreement to take part, the U.S. 7th Army would land to the left of the British 8th Army. A brief outline of the Battle Plan is as follows:

1) Landing in the area between Syracuse and Cape Passero on the east side of the island, the Eighth Army would assault with two corps, comprising a total of six infantry divisions, one independent infantry brigade (the 231st Malta Brigade) and one airborne division. The immediate objective would be to capture the airfield at Pachino, just inland from Cape Passero, then swing north to take Augusta and Catania with all speed.
2) The U.S. Seventh Army, with four infantry divisions, one armoured division and one airborne division was to land on the south shore between Cape Passero and Licata. When the two armies had firmly established themselves in the south-east corner on a line from Licata to Catania, operations would then be developed to complete the conquest of the rest of the island.
3) The 1st Canadian Division was on the western flank of the 8th Army and its objective was to capture the ground between Pachino and Pazzallo on the south-east section of the island. On their immediate right was the restructured famed 51st Highland Division.

"D" Day was set for July 10 at 02:45 hours. The convoy passed through the Straits of Gibraltar and into the Mediterranean on July 5. Despite the occasional dropping of depth charges by a destroyer escort, the convoy suffered no damage from U-boats, although the slower convoy carrying supplies lost several ships including one that carried some Seaforth equipment. There were frequent 'dummy runs' to practise getting into the landing craft at night, right from assembling below deck with full equipment, to finding their way in semi-darkness to the boat-station and then boarding. The battalion's padre, the Rev. Major Roy Durnford, also took part in these practices. He wrote:

> "... one by one the men would file past the leader and into the landing craft as it swung from its davits at the ships side. Here they would kneel on one knee with their rifles vertical until the craft had its full compliment aboard in three rows, the officer being the last in as he was first out on landing.
>
> There was always a slight hesitancy about taking the step from the ship into the swinging craft, as the gap between revealed a long drop into the watery depths below."

(Padre Durnford would make an outstanding contribution to the battalion and be always in the thick of things, from Sicily to Northern Europe. He was born in 1902 in the small English town of Fromme, Somerset and was almost forty when he offered his services to the Canadian Army in 1940. He had emigrated in 1930 because he wished to take Holy Orders and could not afford to do so in England. He arrived in Saskatchewan where he began studies at Emmanuel College, University of Saskatoon, no doubt working part-time as well. He was a deacon in 1931 and then curate at the North Park Anglican Church at Meadow Lake. After ordination he moved to Rollo for four years, then in 1938 moved to Seal Cove, near Prince Rupert. He remained minister there until joining the army. In 1941 he was sent to the U.K. where he joined the Seaforth Highlanders of Canada as Padre. He met his future wife, Mary, who came from Devizes, Wiltshire which was no great distance from his home town of Fromme and they were married in 1942. His sense of duty and devotion to the men of the battalion soon became evident and he was revered by all the ranks.)

On the morning of the 9th the good weather changed and a gale blew up. It was a moderate Force 7, but the seas ran high and Captain Bone was not alone in wondering if the invasion might be postponed. By evening the wind began to moderate, though the sea remained restless long after the wind had died. Despite the possibility of complications, postponement was not contemplated. The worst that could happen was broken surf on some beaches, making a landing tricky.

The ships performed well in keeping station, even when assembled in close proximity to each other to release the multitude of landing-craft. Budge wrote a personal narrative on the landing, dated July 17, 1943:

> "The greatest fleet of ships ever seen was spread out to the horizon all around us. The scene was indescribably magnificent; tiny little R.N. motor launches fought their way through huge waves, between battleships and stately liners, now converted to troop carriers.
>
> Every type of ship was on display, all heading the same way. It was a thrilling sight. Preparations for landing were completed fairly early in the day, topped with the waterproofing of all our documents, maps etc. The spirit of the regiment was terrific; morale was staggeringly high, with every man raring to go. I tried to get in a bit of sleep, but eventually found enough to do without it.
>
> As darkness fell we began to close on the coast and the sea slackened off. It was a brilliant night with a bright quarter moon until midnight."

The RAF were at that moment bombing the Paccino airfield to soften it up for the invasion. No searchlights were directed out to sea and it was apparent that neither the Italian or German defence forces were aware of the armada laying off the coast. By the time the raid finished the glow of flames was visible far out to sea yet still the enemy shore batteries gave no indication that they had seen anything untoward.

The *Circassia* dropped anchor and the men of the 2nd Canadian Infantry Brigade were braced to go. After months of preparation they were about to find out if their training had made them battle-ready. There was a sense of unreality—a feeling intensified by the silent ship, the dimmed lights and the subdued voices as they stood waiting to get into the landing-craft. Orders came over the tannoy system and the men of "A" and "C" Companies began to move up and scramble aboard.

Although the wind had abated considerably, the sea had taken on a heavy swell and many of the men were seasick as the landing craft made for the beach. However, those that were not affected kept up the high spirits that Budge had reported previously. One soldier was heard to sing *Heading for the last Roundup* at the top of his lungs. There were some casualties in the landing, including one sailor killed and several soldiers wounded as the ramp was lowered on one of the first landing crafts to hit the beach.

In the Seaforth assault plan, the first wave to go ashore consisted of "A" Coy, Captain Syd Thomson, on the right and "C" Coy, Major Jim Blair on the left. Attached to each company were members of the pioneer platoon and also sappers with bangalore torpedoes to cut gaps in the barbed wire. Following a success flare from Major Blair, two L.C.A.s of Battalion H.Q. would be the next to go in. In one was the C.O. with the first echelon of his Tactical H.Q. and on his right, within sight and running parallel the second L.C.A. carried Budge, in his capacity as Acting 2 i/c. With him was a workable remainder of the Tac H.Q., in case the C.O.'s boat was lost on the way in. Captain Freddie Middleton's "B" Company and Captain E.W. Thomas's "D" Company were to follow Battalion H.Q.

(One note of interest is that of the entire group of officers who left Vancouver in 1939 only Col. Bert Hoffmeister, Major Doug Forin, Major Jim Blair and Budge were left. All the others had either retired through age or had been transferred. Several had been promoted and were commanding other battalions or brigades.)

Budge's narrative continued:

"No one could understand why such a mighty fleet, streaming on its course all day, was not met with the most powerful attack the enemy could deliver against us.

The moon had gone down now and it was very dark when we manned our craft and waited for the order to lower away. The dim rows of men, just visible in each craft were a very grim reality. In spirit we were like a football team going onto the field to win the biggest game of the season. Our months of preparation were complete. The command came, 'Lower away'.

The sea was still fairly rough, but we slid silently over each wave with the dim outline of other craft both ahead and astern of us. A searchlight stabbed the darkness towards us, then paused before spluttering out. A few odd things went over the top of us, but caused no inconvenience whatsoever.

Suddenly a stream of red dots issued from our left announced the beaching of the first wave. No great amount of firing developed and a few minutes later we received Jim Blair's success signal and we went into land. A grate, a bump, then down went the door and I was in the water, wading ashore. About 15 yards, and there it was—Sicily, the land of the Wop and the Hun. I could hardly believe it." (See Appendix 8)

Budge's first impression was of a peculiar, though not unpleasant smell which he remembers as his introduction to the beaches of Sicily. An uninterrupted double up the broad sandy beach found a string of barbed wire much less formidable than those on the beaches of Britain and with ease they hacked a few holes in it. Budge joined the C.O. and they assembled the full complement of Tac H.Q. Dawn was breaking and in the increasing light the C.O. asked Budge to go straight inland, away from the beach to see whether, as the map indicated, the small lake named Puntana Cuba was close by, just to the right of the larger Puntana Longarina. Having progressed a couple of hundred yards, he reached a rather shabby looking small cottage. He banged sharply on the door with the butt of his Tommy gun and an old woman came out with her hands up and in an obvious state of terror. Budge wasn't sure what to do next, but he pointed his gun downwards, successfully indicating her hands might come down.

At this moment from around the corner of the cottage came, in Budge's words, "A veritable model of an 'Eyetye' peasant, hands in pockets and an ancient black homburg on his head. His greeting was very matter of fact: 'Hi Joe, about time you guys showed up!' Like so many Italian peasants, Mafia or otherwise, he had spent a good part of his life in Chicago."

Finding no lake, large or small, Budge decided to return to the beach and on approaching it he was met by fire from a group of Patricias. Thankfully they were either bad shots—or feeling charitable. He recalls at that moment finding a bullet-proof obstacle, perhaps a big log and opening his issue self-heating can of soup.

Not knowing whether Major Doug Forin, the Battalion 2 i/c had arrived on the S.S. *Alcinous* which, with the slower convoy was bringing vehicles and stores, Budge decided that for the moment he would carry on as Acting 2 i/c. His immediate concern was the discovery of numerous weapons and other articles. It was as well that the invasion was met with little opposition because sand very quickly found its way into the firing mechanism of both rifles and machine guns, making many inoperative. He found a cart of some sort and began collecting the equipment for later cleaning and repair.

He learned that the *Alcinous* had arrived, when confronted by a tank with the usual main armament projecting from the turret. Usual —until he realized that the 'gun' was a painted wooden pole. It was in fact a mobile naval post for the F.O.O. (Forward Observation Officer) for a warship off shore. Heading west to rejoin the C.O. and Tac H.Q., Budge got a lift on this vehicle.

When they came close to a sizable body of Italian cavalry on horseback drawing mortars behind them, Budge was very amused to see the horsemen gallop away, obviously scared of the big wooden gun. Back at Tac H.Q., Lt.-Col. Hoffmeister informed Budge that the naval officer whose job it was to direct assault craft to the beach had inadvertently given the Tac H.Q. plus "B" and "D" Companies craft the bearing to the Patricia's sector, hence the absence of a lake—and the unfriendly fire when Budge appeared from the wrong direction. The C.O. used great restraint when he later said, "There was a scene of great confusion."

The situation caused him considerable concern. There was no sign of the two leading assault companies, it was still dark and there were no landmarks which coincided with the aerial photographs they had studied so hard on board the *Circassia*. It would have made no sense to begin moving off without knowing where he was going, with half of the battalion behind him. It was fortunate that although the C.O. did not recognize the area in the dark, neither did the defenders spot the Seaforths, though once it began to get light, enemy fire began to come into the area. So intent was the Colonel on finding his location that, as he stood to peer forward through his binoculars he did not realize he was in danger until Budge hauled him back to the ground with the information: "You're under fire—you are being shot at!" It was now fully light and Tac H.Q. along with the two companies began to move westward to rejoin the rest of the battalion.

Soon after, Major Forin arrived in a Seaforth carrier and regained his proper role as 2 i/c, leaving Budge as an 'odd job' major, which he would learn was an interesting role. In the meantime Budge continued to write his immediate thoughts on the battalion's progress:

> "The causeway that we expected to fight hard for was undefended when we actually got there. Signs of a most hasty departure were evident everywhere; the machine guns were all in position and loaded and stacks of grenades were laid out around each post. The first fifty or so Italian prisoners were rounded up and they seemed

resigned for anything in store for them. Daylight showed us well established, with very few casualties and everyone in grand form. The advance continued according to plan and we found ourselves in a vineyard on a hill overlooking the beach area. We moved by night to a high position further inland and by daylight on Sunday we were well established in Sicily. Towards evening an ineffectual counter attack put in an appearance and mortar-fire smartened up our enthusiasm for digging in! Our guns soon put a stop to it."

This mortar fire was from the Italian cavalry that Budge had seen while with the naval F.O.O., who had spotted them again some hours later as they set up their mortars behind a high cemetery wall. It was from here they lobbed a few bombs towards the Seaforths. The F.O.O. was able to give the coordinates of their location to his warship and her guns found the unfortunate cavalry unit.

Budge continued a few days later:

"Our advance has been very rapid. We passed through deserted Ispica in the moonlight, the first southern town I had seen. It was all very beautiful, but too hot and dry to be perfect. The people are indescribably poor; they have no clothes, no shoes and haven't eaten for days, but they seemed glad to see us and they cheered and clapped and made a great fuss. It is, I think, partly relief at losing the Germans, who had used up everything for their army, but chiefly an eagerness to cadge cigarettes and a sound instinct as to the side on which their bread is buttered.

We dug into a farm in the mountains, where I managed to get some riding on a beautiful charger which I borrowed from an Italian cavalry officer. We have collected quite a string of pack horses and mules from the countryside, but as our vehicles arrive we gradually become too fast for them.

Looking back on it, it would seem that either we achieved total surprise (almost unimaginable) or, the Germans didn't want to help and the Italians didn't want to (or couldn't) do the job without help."

Despite the limited resistance there were still casualties. The first Seaforths to lose their lives in the campaign were Privates Fieldhouse and Hunter. A hospital was set up in a large house which had belonged to a local landowner, but as the wounded came in it soon became too small, though there was no alternative available. The flies were a problem and it was necessary to use mosquito netting to prevent them from reaching the blood-soaked bandages of the wounded.

Ispica had been taken by the Edmonton Regiment and daylight revealed it to be more damaged by shelling than had seemed to be the case when Budge saw it in the moonlight. Following this came a gruelling forced march, with many blistered, bleeding feet to reach the town of Modica. Here the battalion found a confused situation, with some reports that the town had been cleared of Germans, another that a delegation of town officials had asked to surrender to a despatch rider who had simply lost his way.

The truth was a little more disconcerting, as Transport Officer Captain A.W. Mercer discovered when he attempted to bring up the first 'square meal' to be enjoyed by the battalion since the landing. Besides the driver he had with him a Sergeant-Major of the P.P.C.L.I. and as they entered the town an Italian anti-tank gun opened fire at point-blank range. The truck was damaged and the Sergeant-Major received a severe leg wound. A Patricia mortar platoon was nearby and they fired at the gun. Soon the Italian commander surrendered and in a second truck Captain Mercer continued on his way. He found the main body of Seaforths just beyond the town, where they received the long awaited food.

Another forced march of 60 miles brought the battalion to the deserted town of Ragusa, again passed in moonlight. The march continued in intense heat on switchback roads. The towns of Grammichele, Caltigirone, Piazza Armerina and Valguarnera were passed, each one having been cleared of Italian and German troops, though occasionally the Seaforths came under fire from pockets of resistance. On the way through there was some doubt about the situation in Piazza Armerina and wishing to confirm whether the town was in fact clear, the C.O. asked Budge to take out a patrol to check it out.

The official Seaforth history states on page 171: "Major Bell-Irving led a small patrol composed mainly of men of the Pioneer Platoon to appraise the situation. They found the town to be vacated, so the battalion, instead of having to attack it, was able pass through and onto the high ground beyond."

This bare statement is perfectly true, but Budge feels that posterity requires a bit more detail to do it justice. The battalion was halted, still several miles short of the town and Budge went forward. Whether it was

Budge's idea (he hopes not), members of the patrol were dressed in fatigue clothes, with all badges removed, rubber gym shoes, blackened faces, no hats and probably no weapons. They proceeded forward in the dark, becoming even more stealthy as they approached the first buildings, anticipating a well-armed body of German troops waiting for them. Entering the town without incident, Budge spied in the square a small Italian tank with its top hatch open. With no possible good reason he climbed into the hatch, at best wanting to ensure that no enemy lurked inside. Finding it empty he amused himself pressing levers and buttons and, about 3 a.m.—the gun went off with a very loud bang.

The first person to arrive, from a wine shop on the edge of the square was a little man with a head of fuzzy hair who to Budge looked exactly like Groucho Marx. Querulous to begin with, he broke into an enormous smile, shouting for joy, "Amichi, amichi, bueno o Canadese, amiche." These repeated 'kiss me's' to a Canadian officer made frontpage headlines in the Vancouver Sun newspaper a few days later!

Budge was most anxious, but not immediately successful in trying to discover the Italian word for bicycle. The battalion was a fair distance back and the news that the Germans had left must get back as soon as possible. Because of the nature of the patrol they had no radio. Finally an acting job produced a bicycle and the news got back, "Come on in."

The first determined German resistance came on July 19, on the road between Valguarnera and Leonforte. Two miles north of the former, in open country the Seaforths came under heavy fire. As they were about to enter a wide valley with the highest rim to the east, the C.O. became suspicious because the north rim was a perfect spot for the enemy to wait, with a view down the length of the valley. He ordered "A" Company, commanded by Captain F.W.I. (Bill) Merritt to deploy towards the east rim, to the right and they had scarcely begun to move when the Germans opened up with mortars and machine guns, backed by artillery.

It was assumed that the enemy had originally intended to hold fire until the entire battalion was in the valley, which would have made a 'killing ground.' Lt.-Col. Hoffmeister's decision prevented this, though "A" Company, and Lieut. E.G. Begg's No. 7 Platoon in particular suffered several casualties, including the platoon commander. In the meantime "B", "C" and "D" Companies were led behind a reverse slope ready to resume the advance once supporting artillery and armour were in place. Medical Officer, Captain Ken MacDonald, was awarded the

M.C. for his part in tending the wounded in the open and two orderlies, L/Cpl Story and Private McBride were awarded the M.M. (a few days later Captain MacDonald delivered a baby to an Italian woman in a farmhouse).

The next morning both "B" and "C" Companies were pinned down for several hours by an enemy rearguard action. In his recently published book, *A Narrative of War – From the Beaches of Sicily to the Hitler Line with the Seaforth Highlanders of Canada, 1943-1944*, (The Golden Dog Press, 1996), Dr. Robert McDougall said, "The two occasions, as was certainly intended, imposed caution on the battalion. It was also taught the rudiments of discipline under fire." (Dr. McDougall served in the battalion throughout the Italian and European campaigns.)

Ahead lay Leonforte and as they approached the town the battalion came under more fire, pinning down some of the platoons as they made their way across the craggy landscape. Leonforte, which was defended by the crack 104th Panzer Grenadier Regiment, sat on a high escarpment and provided the Germans with a clear view of the Seaforth's movements. Robert MacDougall, at the time commanding No. 13 Platoon, took his men up the escarpment right under the walls of the town, but they came under fire from Allied guns that had begun another phase of the attack. Some soldiers were wounded but none were killed.

A much more sombre act of friendly fire was soon to unfold. The C.O. had his Tac H.Q. in a farmyard just off the winding road to Leonforte but not visible to the town's ramparts. Intelligence reports suggested that Leonforte was by now only lightly held or even possibly vacated by the Germans. To the west an open slope was plainly visible to anyone observing from there and Budge volunteered to take out a small patrol in full view to draw the enemy's fire if they were still there, thus avoiding the whole battalion being caught unaware.

The answer came quickly. The patrol immediately drew heavy fire from across the exposed front of the town. Budge, followed only by Corporal Gordy Tupper ran straight down the hill to get underneath the enemy field of fire. The remainder went instinctively to ground in such minimal cover as they could find and were machine-gunned and then mortared, with serious results. Corporal Jim Cromb, was wounded in the action, but his brother, Private Charlie Cromb, was killed. It was a high price to pay, especially as the information they so bravely obtained was not able to be put to good use.

Next day, July 21, Brigadier Vokes informed Bert Hoffmeister that the Seaforths would launch a frontal attack on Leonforte under a barrage, with covering fire from the Edmonton Regiment. The C.O. called an "O" group of his company commanders at 15:30 hours in a farmyard which he was using as battalion H.Q. What happened next is best described in Dr. McDougall's words:

> "Company commanders, commanders of supporting arms and signals personnel gathered at Battalion H.Q. for orders. These they received, but not carried out; as the group dispersed they were faced with a sudden and perverse disaster when a salvo of shells fired short by Allied guns burst in a tight pattern around the H.Q. position. Four persons were killed; the Adjutant, Captain D.H. Strain; the Pioneer Platoon Officer, Lieut. J.H. Budd and two signallers. Half a dozen others were wounded, including Captain F.W.I. Merritt and Lieut. J.M. Scott. With the C.O. himself suffering shock from the concussion of the blasts, the nerve centre of the battalion was badly damaged."

Major Forin, the second-in-command, was also unharmed, though shocked, and his first reaction was to role off the concrete pad on which they had been standing into a sunken cart-track. His next action was to stop the various companies that were coming down to form up for the assault and get them to return to safer ground. The firing was, fortunately, stopped immediately.

When the wounded had been taken care of and some order restored, Lt.-Colonel Hoffmeister signalled the Brigade Commander to express his willingness to carry on the attack, but he was told to stand down and the Edmonton Regiment was ordered to prepare to take over, while the Seaforths took on the support role. All this time "D" Company, commanded by Captain E.W. Thomas had been pinned down on high ground, named "Bloody Hill", where they suffered many casualties.

While the other companies were in preparation to advance in their support roles, the Seaforths were also asked to supply a composite company of 100 men to circle behind Leonforte and act in a cut-off capacity if the main attack resulted in the Panzer Grenadiers evacuating the town. They were to be led by Budge, who had once more taken over command of "A" Company, replacing the wounded Bill Merritt. It was a dark night as they set out and as Robert McDougall wrote of this action in *A Narrative of War*:

> "This patrol, because of the darkness and the distance travelled over strange and difficult country, was not exactly a textbook success... but it aroused confusion in the enemy, who showed signs of alarm at having a hostile force in his midst and another at the rear."

Budge recounted his memories of the Leonforte episode for Robert McDougall in July 1960 and it was included in his book:

> "There was a single exit road behind Leonforte and a volunteer composite company of Seaforths based on "B" Company, but under my command, was sent around to block the road exit of the Germans while the Edmontons attacked the town. Some of the company got split up from the main group partly because it was a very black night. We reached the back of Leonforte with fewer troops than we had set out with. Many were so tired that arriving at the top they lay down and went to sleep.
>
> We skirted the town to the left and came to a large wall, but by this time I had not much more than a good-sized platoon with me. I remember [cousin] Lieut. Dunc Manson was my only officer. We took a position astride the road and the noise of battle came closer to us. Though the German tanks close to us were facing north, there was no sign of an evacuation and, as yet, no sign of the Eddies.
>
> We were at the town's north-east corner on the road leading out and my idea at the time was 'Well, we're here and we'd better stay put.' I thought we might find something relatively strong that we could hold and stay there until somebody caught up. We could see German tanks in the street and I remember lying in the ditch with one right alongside me, and another firing along the ditch with tracer; there was tracer all over the place. I tried to throw a grenade into the tank beside me but it didn't go in and I was lucky not to be killed by my own grenade. We evacuated along the road and found a big farmhouse that I thought we might hold. I left my troops with Dunc Manson in charge and entered the house, which was clear, but as I came out, a tank right in the road in front of me, fired. I ran, the tank chased me and I dived over the cliff.
>
> Eventually I made my way back to the battalion with one corporal of the Edmontons that I'd picked up on the way. I had taken a composite company of Seaforths into my first battle and came out

with one Edmonton. I wished to God I'd been killed I was so ashamed. I thought that those I'd left behind had been killed, but when I got back and found them all safely returned I felt better about it. I credit Dunc Manson with doing a splendid job."

Manson had attended the "O" Group earlier in the day and the force of the explosion had thrown him several feet into a ditch followed by a wounded signaller who landed on top of him. A piece of shrapnel punched a hole in Manson's "baggy British tropical shorts." As part of Budge's Leonforte group, he was in a shed attached to the farmhouse when Budge made his dash in—and out of the house. At the moment Budge took off chased by the tank Manson saw him completely encircled with tracer bullets and thought "My God, he's had it."

So confused was the situation that on the way back to re-join the battalion, Manson and his platoon walked into a group of Germans just sitting cleaning their rifles. Some shots were exchanged, but both sides quickly took off. The platoon leader was pleased to find cousin Budge very much alive even if embarrassed at the outcome of the raid.

One man who volunteered to go with Budge was Private G.A. Reid, who was part of the group that became split up. He recalls the long walk before the rear of the town was reached and he was so tired that he couldn't feel his knees in the end. There was a sergeant in charge of his section, but when they reached the top, Budge was there, having fired a Verey pistol. He recalled the tanks shooting all around them, but there was a further split up and he found himself with about 16 others with a lance-corporal in charge. They went through an orchard and found a flat-topped hill to set up their guns—when there was a 'click' nearby. He realized that some enemy troops were very close. Reid yelled 'down' just seconds before they were fired upon. He had one of the Bren guns and yelled again "Come on, let's go", only to find as he looked around that he was on his own. Such is the suddenness with which this can happen, over strange terrain in the dark. He told Robert McDougall:

"So here was my chance to win the M.M. I yelled and fired at the Germans, who seemed to be behind some trees and they began to throw 'potato mashers' [stick grenades] at me and I was rolled over with the concussion. I figured they would get me sooner or later so I fired up the hill and made a run behind the first trees that I could find. I changed the magazine and let go another burst, emptying it, and took off. The hills are all terraced, but I was running so fast I took only two steps for each one until I reached the bottom of the hill and actually got burnt on the inside of my arm from a Jerry bullet."

Reid made his way back to the battalion and found most of his patrol there. Amazingly there had been no casualties amongst the composite company, though the overall casualty rate in taking Leonforte was high. The Seaforths, even in support, had the highest numbers even though the official army history had little to say about their involvement because the earlier tragedy stopped their direct attack. They suffered 28 killed and 48 wounded, while the Edmontons had 7 killed and 17 wounded. The Patricias lost 21, with 40 wounded. After the taking of Leonforte the Seaforths were pulled out for a 48 hour rest period.

During this time reinforcements arrived to replace casualties. There was a re-shuffle of officers and Captain J.H. Gowan took over as Adjutant. The rest period ended and the action now swung eastward towards the towns of Nissoria and Agira. As Dunc Manson said later, "Budge's reputation as an enthusiastic, very active and fearless leader was building quickly." He was to prove it again soon in going to the aid of Private Frank Wood who, with Bill Metcalf were snipers in "A" Company. Metcalfe had been a sergeant but had taken a demotion in order to become a sniper. Since landing in Sicily the two had remained together and had acted as scouts, often ahead of the battalion to reconnoitre.

Wood had already earned a place in the regimental history for shooting down the Folke-Wolfe 190 fighter at Eastbourne. He was an individualist, and prior to coming to Italy had given many officers and sergeants a headache with his ability to get away with incidents that would have landed less fortunate soldiers in deep trouble. An avid card player he most often won. On one occasion playing with some local businessmen when the battalion was in Limpsfield, he was caught returning after lights-out and when marched in front of Company Commander Major Cecil Meritt he calmly stated that he thought it would be impolite to break up the game even though he knew it was getting late. Returning to the billet he got a flat tire on his bike, which made him even later. Major Merritt said it was the best story he had heard and let him off! Frank was also a mandolin player and song writer, whose songs were played over the air by several Vancouver radio stations after they were recorded in London during the war.

Early in the Sicilian Campaign he and Metcalfe had captured a young Italian soldier who led them to a cave filled with medical supplies. A few yards along they rounded a bend in the road and came upon a large group of civilians, among them the Mayor and Police Chief of a small local town. One of the men in the group had driven a taxi cab in New York and his English was quite good. Woods and Metcalfe ended up eating with the local dignitaries.

Between Leonforte and Agira, the battalion's next objective, lay the town of Nissoria. As they moved off, the two snipers were instructed by Budge to go ahead, but to remain within hearing distance. A little later he caught up with them and asked them to cover himself and a small group while they went forward to investigate the cause of a commotion towards the enemy. What happened next is best told from Wood's own privately published auto-biography:

> "The major told Bill and me to 'right and left flank' him and the others. They disappeared down a slope to the left and I decided to cross the road to the right and circle round to see what was going on and what had caused this commotion. As I took my first step I heard someone from that direction giving a command, then right in front of me the flashes from a string of tracer bullets went zooming by.
>
> I threw myself to the left and crawled a few feet to a low spot in the ground. As I looked for something to shoot at some of our tanks began a return fire, causing the German machine guns to change the direction of their fire towards our fire. There I was directly underneath the cross-fire. I heard one of the fellows in the Major's party cry out and concluded he was hit.
>
> I decided that I had better crawl further down the slope to seek safer shelter. At that precise moment a mortar shell landed a few feet from me from the direction of the enemy. The blast threw me a few feet and I was shocked by a terrific pain between my legs. Although I was hit in many places, my main recollection was this pain. I found myself hollering, 'Oh my balls, oh my balls.'
>
> Major Bell-Irving was taking shelter in a foxhole with some of his patrol and asked, 'Who is that hollering?' Someone told him that it sounded like Frank Wood and the major promptly asked him to go out and give me a hand."

The man allegedly said that he would not go out there 'for the King of England.' In the meantime Wood was kicking and crawling his way as best he could, with his right leg completely immobile. At this point, Frank Wood's journal continues:

> "Major Bell-Irving suddenly appeared and asked if I had been hit. It seems he was not very observant, but he said to climb on his back and I told him that I was not able to do so. He took hold of me and dragged me some distance to the shelter of one of our tanks. The firing was still coming thick and fast and how we were not hit is far beyond me.
>
> A medic corporal gave me a shot of morphine. I could still see the tracer hitting the other side of the tank and I shouted to the crew not to move it, which they assured me they wouldn't."

The bearers came for him eventually and he was taken to a forward dressing station in Nissoria. Frank Wood was out of the war. He had lost a testicle and much of the skin of his inside right thigh. By a miracle although his 'private parts' suffered damage from a piece of shrapnel, his injuries were not permanent and his wife boasts that he still has 'lead in his pencil!' He lost a lot of blood and was saved by plasma. When, after he recovered following many painful months in hospitals in England, he returned to Vancouver and became a spokesman for the Red Cross, giving many talks to factory workers and office personnel. On an official advertisement with a cut-out donor pledge he told the whole story of his wounding, including Budge's part in his rescue. He succeeded in recruiting many donors. Bill Metcalfe was wounded three days after Wood, but was able to return to active duty. He was wounded twice more, in January 1944 and in December of that year also.

Following the battle of Leonforte the Seaforths continued northwards towards Nissoria. Up ahead the 1st Brigade had been having a very bad time in their attempts to approach Agira. The 231 (Malta) Brigade, advancing from the south with intent to block the road eastward from Agira to Adrano and the coast, had been unable to break through the Agira southern defence. In the meantime a captured German report contained information that the entire 1st Battalion, 15th Panzer Grenadier Regiment of the 29th Division had been hastily moved in to replace the decimated battalions of the 104th Panzer Grenadier Regiment.

Early on July 26, Brigadier Vokes held an "O" Group at which Lt.-Col. Hoffmeister was informed:

> "The 1st Canadian Infantry Brigade has now been withdrawn from their incursions towards Agira and the 2nd Canadian Infantry Brigade will relieve them in area Nissoria this evening.
>
> The North-South ridge east of and close to Nissoria is code-named "Lion". The next, parallel ridge about a mile and a half beyond it, where the road crosses over a small plateau is code-named "Tiger." The third ridge rises to an oval-shaped plateau named Monte Fronte about one thousand feet west of Agira and will be code-named "Grizzly." This hill provides complete visual domination over the town of Agira."

The Nissoria-Agira road runs along the north side of "Grizzly," which has steep sides on its east and west flanks. The south side though, is almost sheer; a fact which became significant in its capture. The battle plan was for the Patricias to go ahead of the Seaforths, ensure that "Lion" was clear and then take and hold "Tiger." The Edmontons were to make a left flanking movement and take the ridge north of the road, which is virtually an extension of "Grizzly." The Seaforths were to go through the Patricias and continue on, with "C" Company flanking well to the south, "D" Company flanking to the north of "Lion" and "A" Company pushing on to "Grizzly."

The Seaforths received some much needed reinforcements, and having had a hot meal plus an issue of haversack rations they closed up to the Nissoria position and were put on half-hour's notice to begin the advance on the Brigadier's order. The battalion was to pass through the Patricias' position and then to continue forward with artillery and tank support. Soon after they began, the Patricias ran into a strong defence on the right (south) flank of "Lion." It became immediately obvious to the Brigade Commander that the position had not been silenced. If that were the case he surmised that "Tiger" had also not yet been captured and decided that it was time to put in the Seaforths.

Lt.-Col. Hoffmeister committed his battalion at midnight with "C" Company on the right of the road, "A" Company on its left, with "B" and "D" in close reserve for deployment when needed. "C" Company, moved off at a tangent towards the south, with No. 13 Platoon leading, and soon came under heavy hostile fire from machine-guns located just beyond the wooded crest of the hill. They did their best to advance in the darkness but dawn found them well short of "Tiger."

"A" Company proceeded for a very short distance along the road when they came upon a German tank close in under a hedge by the side of the road—facing them but not firing. Attempts to throw grenades into the hatch proved unsuccessful. Budge did not yet recognize this 'God given' opportunity for a PIAT. The tank was finally left to Major 'Tiger' Welsh's 90th Anti-Tank Battery of the R.C.A. and the Seaforth company continued on.

In *A Narrative of War* Dr. McDougall wrote: "The success which opened up the way to Agira lay with 'A' Company and, more especially, it seems fair to say, with its commander, Major H.P. Bell-Irving who was to be at his venturesome best that day and well and truly earn the first D.S.O. awarded to the battalion in WW II. 'C' Company's No. 13 Platoon, committed to the right flank of 'Lion' on the south side of the road, ran immediately into stiff opposition. 'A' Company on the left was also opposed on 'Lion', but pressed on and, by doing so, saved the day."

Budge led "A" company across country on what appeared to be a donkey track. The single file column plodded on a very long time it seemed, quiet and very much alone. Dawn appeared slowly in front of them and he felt that they must by now be somewhere behind enemy lines and he fervently hoped that his self-doubts were not infectious to the troops behind. Recollecting that moment, Budge described his next action:

> "There was a rather steep hill rising on the right and as higher ground might provide a relatively more defensible position, and in any event it would be in the general position of the axis, I thought it would be better to climb the hill and wait for full daylight.
>
> If I had been half asleep at the time, I woke up rather suddenly when all five barrels of a Nebelwerfer, one after the other, went off almost in my face. The rockets, going right over our heads made a hell of a scream.*
>
> 'The Company will advance, right turn, take the hill.' This order was unspoken but, following the leader, was instinctively carried out. There was a certain amount of indiscriminate firing on the

---

* A five barrelled enemy rocket projectile known as a 'moaning minnie' because of the noise it made.

way up, but nothing serious. On top of the hill was open ground and—lo and behold the road was running across it. Purely by good luck the top of the hill was in fact the middle of the objective, 'Tiger.' We had arrived right where we should be."

There was only token resistance and one officer, Lieut. Frank Bonnell was wounded but was able to carry on. However, on the road about 75 yards away was a German Mk5 Panther tank. Lieut. Jim Harling, who was shortly to prove his capability and courage on "Grizzly", was told to take the PIAT and clobber the tank. Only then was it discovered, in one of the few comedies of war, that the donkey carrying the PIAT bombs had gone home and was probably by now back at Battalion H.Q. The tank crew hastily manœuvred their vehicle into a retreat, but a shell from "Lion" dispatched it.

"A" Company had collected, and were using some German weapons. In the quiet of the night march the company had done nothing to advertise its Canadian presence on Tiger. It would have been understandable for the Patricias and their supporting arms, somewhere in the Lion vicinity to believe that Tiger was still a German stronghold. Though there was no visual contact at all, a 'stonk'* of Canadian shells landed on Tiger. The German tank was hit once but moved away to the south. Unfortunately Lieut. Marriot Wilson, a young "A" Company Platoon Commander was killed and others were wounded. The wireless set was inactive so there was no way to communicate with the units responsible. After this episode Budge banned the use of all German weapons within the company, and with some regret presented his very efficient Mannlicher sniper's rifle to Brigadier Vokes.

The Tiger plateau was more or less level. On the eastern edge was a gentle downward slope toward the, as yet unseen, 'Grizzly Hill', with the town of Agira behind it. Facing to the north was the steep hill which "A" Company had just climbed. Further to the north, about twice the distance of the recent climb, was another road on which could be seen a considerable German force moving eastward in the direction of Agira. This column presented a clear target to the Canadian artillery, with one or two Forward Observation Officers to create havoc on it.

Captain Gordon Money of the Anti-Tank platoon arrived almost immediately on his motor-cycle. The C.O. was looking down the

---

* A concentration of shells in a small area.

eastern slope in the direction of 'Grizzly'. An "O" Group was summoned, orders for the advance were quickly given. "H" hour was to be 14:00 hrs. The objective would be the capture of 'Grizzly Hill', which would quickly bring ownership of Agira.

(The day before, July 25, Mussolini was deposed and the Italians were, to all intents and purposes out of the war. This event had little or no impact on the day-to-day operations, but it meant that the German forces were now left to fight on Italian soil while its populace was apathetic to the outcome of the fighting.)

"A" Company left "Tiger" at 14:00 hrs and advanced rapidly under cover of orchards. "Grizzly" came into view over a crest and with No. 8 Platoon in the lead, the bottom of the hill was reached. At this moment the enemy brought their fire to bear on No. 8 Platoon. Budge and his H.Q. personnel were immediately behind them, followed by Nos. 7 and 9 Platoons. He recalled:

> "No orders were given or needed. While No. 8 Platoon engaged the enemy I wheeled right and led the remaining platoons on a wide flanking movement towards the rear of the objective. We were not detected by the enemy until the actual top was reached after scrambling up the very steep, almost perpendicular southern slope. In the meantime No. 8 Platoon continued to engage the attention of the enemy, working its way forward under such cover as was available (one section actually scaled the face and captured a German machine gun).
>
> The Germans were badly outflanked and had to move their machine guns quickly to face the south, releasing No. 8 Platoon who worked their way around following the same route and rejoined the main company. Before they had reached us we managed to occupy a small area bounded by a rough stone wall about three feet high. Having gained this small patch, Corporal Terry led a charge which captured a machine-gun and he turned this on the enemy. They in turn quickly shifted their main attention to this hostile enclave and the situation became, to put it mildly, somewhat precarious. There was a good deal of small-arms fire and a few mortar bombs, but not as many as there should have been. We managed to take a few prisoners.
>
> With my radio set I requested artillery fire to be directed on the main part of "Grizzly" with particular emphasis to exclude the south end. The radio batteries were getting low and the message was not clearly understood, with the result that the concentration

was ON the south end. It was extraordinary that there were no casualties, but it was quite an experience. There were no slit trenches and most of the ground was solid rock but it was sufficiently irregular to allow quite a bit of protection. The radio batteries were too low to allow us to re-confirm our original instructions.

We got some satisfaction from the abject terror of our prisoners. The company itself was very low in numbers until rejoined by No. 8 Platoon, but more importantly we were low on ammunition. It was very hot and the most urgent requirement was for water. There was a well in sight but it would have been suicidal at that stage to make any attempt to approach it.

Towards evening I was seriously concerned that the Germans might send a detachment down the hill and around to the south to come on the back of the Company. Accompanied by Corporal Terry I went partially down the hill and around into the valley between 'Grizzly' and Agira. We climbed to the top to have a look at what was going on in the centre of the German position. Unfortunately Corporal Terry was shot and killed at that instant. He was later awarded a posthumous M.M. for his gallantry in the capture of 'Grizzly.' I returned later with another soldier and this time got myself a tracer bullet between the legs which burnt the crotch seam in my shorts."

It was now 40 hours since they had any sleep and their hunger and thirst was increasing. Budge was very concerned about going to sleep—and of course did so—walking in his sleep as well. He had an extraordinary dream until woken suddenly by the bolt action of a rifle held by a nearby soldier. One other incident was recorded; Sergeant Penman ordered a junior N.C.O. to check out a cave on the "Grizzly" hillside and to his surprise out came an elderly couple followed by several women and children.

Budge continued his recollection:

"At midnight the Germans attacked in strength, an attack that was concentrated and heavily supported by point blank small-arms fire. There was a great deal of noise and a lot of metal flying around, but for some unimaginable reason they failed to destroy the small force perched precariously at the top of the cliff right in front of them.

The star on this occasion was Lieut. Jim Harling—a huge man with red hair, singing *Uke-aluka-a luska* at the top of his lungs while throwing hand-grenades one after the other straight at the enemy.

He was standing behind the stone wall, which came up to just above his knees. He, more than anyone was responsible for the successful holding of 'Grizzly' hill.

There could never have been an incident in military history where a man displayed less regard for his own life. His survival untouched was nothing short of a miracle."

This was not the end of Jim Harling's action. Lieut. John McLean arrived with his No. 14 Platoon from "C" Company, relatively fresh, with a fair quantity of ammunition, but also lacking water. The only well on the hill was still covered by enemy fire, so a plan was devised whereby Lieut. McLean and three volunteers would crawl towards the enemy occupied house where the well was located, under cover of smoke grenades and fire-cover from his and Harlings platoons. When close in they would all rush the house together. The plan worked well, with Harling again lobbing grenades "as though they were softballs." So successful was the charge that they cleared the enemy beyond the objective.

By 09:00 hours "Grizzly" was totally in the hands of the Seaforths after one last attack by the Germans had been beaten back. Budge was able to relay this fact back to the battalion H.Q. thanks to one persistent signaller, Corporal Meade, who had placed himself in a position where, in order to improve failing communications, he was in the full line of enemy fire. He was awarded the M.M. that day along with several other N.C.O.s and privates, including Frederick Webster, a B.C. native Indian. He was with No. 8 platoon and, according to the citation "... in the face of heavy enemy fire he brought his Bren gun to bear so effectively that his section was able to wipe out the opposition and permit the platoon to advance."

Incredibly, despite Budge's best efforts, Lieut. Jim Harling did not receive an M.C. Sergeant (later R.S.M.) David Penman said of Harling's actions that it was like "handing guts out on a platter to his men." Jim Harling was later transferred to another unit and was killed in action on July 9, 1944. Budge was awarded his first D.S.O., as was Lt.-Col. Hoffmeister for his skill in directing the battalion during the battle. In the total action "A" Company lost two killed, Lieut. Wilson and Corporal Terry, and five wounded. The enemy lost 75 killed, 15 captured and an unknown number of wounded.

Within hours the fall of Agira was completed and was announced on the B.B.C. (British Broadcasting Corporation) that same day. So was the "Beating Retreat" ceremony, performed in the town square by the pipe-band of the Seaforth Highlanders of Canada under the direction of Pipe-Major Esson.

The Battalion was given a few day's well-earned rest to receive a batch of much needed recruits, for 'make and mend', to receive and send letters and, best of all—make use of the mobile baths.

In an August 1943 letter to his father, Budge wrote:

> "As advance guard to the battalion, 'A' Company has been privileged to meet and soundly defeat the Hun on two memorable occasions recently. The success has been due to a spirit in every man which is simply unconquerable. Everything the Hun can throw at them is so much wasted iron. If I should catch it, it can be remembered that I have already had the greatest honour a man can have; to have had command of this bunch of fighting devils has been far more than I deserve.
>
> ... I get scared as hell once in a while but manage to survive on it. I think actually the life agrees with me."

The remaining German forces were now contained in Sicily's north-east section. The Canadian thrust lay eastward towards the town of Adrano at the foot of Mt. Etna. Between Agira and Adrano lay Regalbuto, the immediate objective of the 1st Canadian Infantry Brigade, while the 2nd was to be deployed in the hilly country to the north between the Salso and Troina Rivers, all but dried up at that time of the year. This area had some of the most difficult terrain encountered so far. Dr. McDougall refers to it as "a succession of steep crags stretching eastward like the knuckles of gnarled fingers."

Within this terrain lay the immediate German positions that would have to be taken by the Loyal Edmonton Regiment and the Canadian Seaforths. Leaving the rest area under cover of darkness on August 3, they moved into position on Troop Carrying Vehicles. Daylight gave them a look at the barren, parched hills they would fight to capture in the next three or four days, sometimes held down by enemy mortar fire, before taking another few yards. Among these were Hill 736 and another crest simply known as a 'rocky crag.' The Germans held on tenaciously to both. While the Edmontons were detailed to take Hill 736, the Seaforths slowly advanced towards the nameless crag. It was tough going against the machine guns perched on it, but with some cover on the right flank, some supporting fire from the tanks via a radio link through B.H.Q.—and with "A" Company's 'disinclination to be pinned down', they eventually took and held the crag.

Lt.-Col. Hoffmeister came forward to join Budge for an appraisal of the situation and it was well past midnight when he returned to B.H.Q. to be called to an "O" Group. Here, Brigadier Vokes unfolded the next move. It was an imaginative plan that would involve both infantry and tanks; in this instance those of the Three Rivers (12th Armoured) Regiment. The reason for this move was that the ground for the proposed advance suited such a combination, with a less craggy terrain. This would take them well towards Adrano on the slopes of Mount Etna and shrink the only remaining wedge of land left to the Germans.

The orders given to Brigadier Vokes by General Simonds (G.O.C. 1st Canadian Division) was to "strike a quick blow in the undulating country north of the River Salso, which will carry your brigade right up to the western bank of the River Simeto."

This armoured and infantry combination was named the "Booth Force", after Lt.-Col. E.L. Booth, C.O. of the Three Rivers Regiment, who was given overall command of the operation. The Seaforths were selected to provide ground troops for this thrust and Lt.-Col. Hoffmeister rode in Booth's Sherman tank. From it he controlled his companies with the aid of a wireless network.

When called to bring "A" Company down from the crag to join the Booth Force, Budge was concerned about the likelihood of a counterattack and left No. 7 Platoon there under the temporary command of Corporal Chris McCardle. They spent an uncomfortable and very busy 48 hours without food and water and the war diary records their 'extreme devotion to duty.'

By 06:00 hours on August 5, the Seaforths were at the start line by the dry river bed of the Salso. Here they endured two hours being eaten alive by mosquitoes while awaiting the arrival of the tanks, which were held up by an unexpected difficulty with a railway bridge. Despite the hitch, things went well from the start of the operation. It was an impressive force as the tank squadrons moved off across the parched, dusty ground with the troops of "A" and "C" Companies riding precariously on them. "B" and "D" Companies were held in reserve to follow upon the C.O.'s orders to move. In support were the 90th Anti-Tank Battery, a self-propelled Battery of the 11th Royal Horse Artillery, the 165th and

3rd Canadian Field Artillery Regiments and the 7th Medium Artillery Regiment.

The Seaforths dismounted and began to move up the slope towards the first objective, a long spur of the hill upon which the German 3rd Parachute Regiment was dug in. The tanks provided supporting fire as the battalion advanced. Just before starting the climb, crouching behind a cactus hedge, Budge was very narrowly missed by a burst of machine gun fire. Although no bullets got him, his face was full of barbed cactus needles. Fortunately his eyes were spared.

"A" Company was committed to support "C" Company, which had gained a foothold on the southern tip of the objective. "A" Company began an attack on the right flank of the spur, while "D" Company was brought up to perform a matching movement to the left. Although the whole length of the slope was being shelled and mortared by enemy fire from machine gun posts on the ridge, one by one the paratrooper positions were mopped up. Most of the NCOs losses, eleven killed, were from one sniper who shot at least six men including the gallant battalion Medical Officer, Captain W.K. MacDonald, hit while tending some wounded in an exposed position on the slope.

Two officers were taken prisoner, Captain G.N. Money, i/c the Anti-Tank Platoon who, on his motor-cycle turned left instead of right when crossing the Troina, and Major J.W. Blair, captured in a daring move by some German paratroopers who dashed into the farm building he was using to direct his platoons. It was at first assumed that he was killed, but later confirmed that he was a prisoner. Budge's "A" company, reduced in numbers by the absence of No. 7 Platoon and a second platoon that had missed the orders to storm the hill, pushed forward and reached the top of the spur. The regimental history says of him: "Major Bell-Irving is not a man to wait about to count his chickens and with good use of their basic equipment, rifles, grenades and Bren guns he and his men pressed on. In doing so they captured enroute four enemy machine gun posts."

In a letter to Dr. Roy dated July 6, 1967 Private C.A. Rivers recounted his recollection of events that day, including an action of Budge's at the end of the battle which could be described as typical. The letter recounts how they reached the top and found on a ledge about 50 feet below on the reverse side a small building which was the 3rd Paratroop unit's H.Q.:

"... in the roof of this building and in the corner facing the crest were holes cut so that they could fire at us as we came over the top and down to them. These holes proved just as valuable to us, as our Bren gunner emptied a magazine into each of them. You can imagine what it must have been like in a stone house with all those .303 bullets bouncing off the walls. There were badly wounded paratroopers in there as a result. The uninjured surrendered to us. Major Bell-Irving put a note on one of the wounded prisoners asking for the best medical attention for him as he considered him a very brave man."

Shortly after 4 p.m. the Seaforths were able to report the objective taken and secured. Aside from the 11 Seaforths killed there were 32 wounded, one of them Budge's batman, Private C. Neilson*. Corporal D. Hadden won the Distinguished Conduct Medal for outstanding bravery in advancing with a Bren gun over 700 yards, lobbing five grenades into an enemy post and then using his section in a bayonet charge. The prisoners were at first fearful that they might be shot, but were surprised when the Seaforths began sharing cigarettes and water with them and soon they were looking at each other's family pictures.

By the evening of August 6, the 2nd Canadian Brigade had taken all its planned objectives and on the 7th Adrano was captured by the British 78th Division. The "Booth Force" operation was considered to be a classic in tank/infantry cooperation and Lt.-Col. Booth was awarded the D.S.O. for his leadership. Regrettably he was killed in France while commanding the 4th Canadian Armoured Brigade.

(One interesting aspect of this last Sicilian battle for the Seaforths is that it was watched by Prime Minister Winston Churchill from the heights above the town of Centuripe due south of the battle area. Many years later, in London, General Hoffmeister (Retired) had the opportunity to discuss the battle with Churchill over lunch as guests of the Hon. George Drew, High Commissioner for Canada.)

The Seaforths received the welcome news that they were being withdrawn for a rest and were pulled back to Militello where, surrounded by orchards of orange, lemon and almond trees it was likened to the Garden of Eden and immediately given the name "Happy Valley."

---

* In this battle, Private Neilson had his arm almost severed and apologised to Budge for being so 'stupid' as to allow it to happen, thus preventing him from firing his weapon.

There were three highlights during this well deserved rest period. The first was a visit by General B.L. Montgomery, (Monty) G.O.C. in C. of the 8th Army, who addressed the Brigade on August 20, when a general inspection was held in the Edmonton's area. This was located 1000 feet above the Seaforth's lines. The climb in single file with Lt.-Col. Bert Hoffmeister leading the battalion to the inspection has been captured in a painting, seen on the dust cover of the official history.

Although fighting was winding down, the Luftwaffe still made themselves felt occasionally and having reached the assembly area the C.O. ordered dispersal under such cover as was available. However, when 'Monty' arrived he gave instructions for the whole assembly to gather round his jeep. The Colonel thought what an incredible sitting target the 2nd Canadian Infantry Brigade—and a top British general—would make if German aircraft came over at that moment. Monty told the assembly that they had fought magnificently and ended with the compliment, "I now consider you one of my veteran divisions." It was during a rest in the early stages of the Italian Campaign while on a visit to Divisional H.Q. that 'Monty' pinned the D.S.O. ribbon on Budge in recognition of his leadership during the attack on "Grizzly."

The second memorable occasion was an unusual sermon preached at 'Happy Valley' at Budge's request by Padre Durnford. Months before in England the Seaforths had taken part in an exercise with a certain British infantry unit whose other ranks had, in their chatter liberally used one very ugly four letter swear-word as adjective, adverb and verb. It was infectious and had been taken up by the Seaforths to still be heard long afterwards in Sicily. At rest in this veritable Sicilian 'Garden of Eden' Padre Durnford gave a sermon on a text combining, as Budge put it "the name of the Lord with the sin of Adam." Those in attendance most certainly got the message. Among the memories of surviving veterans is that sermon by their much loved Padre.

The third highlight took place five days later when the Canadian Seaforths met the 2nd, 5th and 6th Battalions of the Imperial Seaforth Highlanders at Catania, on the east coast of the island. Their presence had been known for some time but it was not possible to arrange a meeting until the fighting had died down. The Officers' and Sergeants' Messes of the 6th Battalion were located on the estate of an Italian baron, above the town on the slopes of Mt. Etna, with a huge garden for entertaining. The first event was a 'Beating Retreat' by the massed pipes and drums of the joint battalions for which the Catania Stadium was appropriated. With only one brief rehearsal the bands put on an impressive ceremony after which a feast was laid on at the 6th's location. There was a good supply of whisky and into the small hours there was piping, singing and much blethering. There were Japanese lanterns after dark which added to the festivities and it was with a few sore heads that the officers and senior N.C.O.'s made their way back to the respective units. The fighting would resume soon enough.

Someone who missed the party, as a 'new boy' was Robert Bonner, later a Q.C., Attorney General of British Columbia and Chairman of B.C. Hydro. He had just joined the battalion along with several other replacement officers. He joined Budge's "A" Company and took over No. 7 Platoon to replace Lieut. Eric Begg who had been wounded on July 19 in the advance on Leonforte. While his brother officers were enjoying the Seaforth reunion, Lieut. Bonner and his men looked after security at Happy Valley. It was to be almost a month before he saw action.

Aside from the opportunity to socialize with sister regiments, the rest provided time for letter writing. Looking back at the intense action that he had experienced, his letters became reflective. He told Nancy:

> "Old Etna continues to smoke imperturbably above us, a reminder that greater things than puny man inhabit the universe. The country is really very picturesque and the colouring of the mountains, particularly at dawn is simply an artists dream. Most of the inland towns are built on the steep slopes of rounded hills surmounted by very old ruined castles. The light effects at sunset are really glorious.
>
> When perched on a hill beyond range of the receding battle one gets an increased sense of the futility of war. Day and night we watch people throwing things at each other with loud bangs and it all seems very silly. I can assure you, however, that when personally engaged in the pastime, a mixture of both exultation and panic makes it anything but dull.
>
> ... Of course, I hate war but when actually in a scrap there is an undoubted feeling of exhilaration. The sense of achievement with each little success is simply enormous. I think it could be likened to a cold bath—trepidation, plunge, vigorous puffing and blowing—then the tingling of well-being."

Among letters received in the rest camp was one from Roderick. Echoing Budge's thoughts on engagement with the enemy he said:

"As you can probably guess I am very envious of your recent experiences as well as being damn proud that you were there. From various people I have heard that you have done extremely well and would not be surprised if next time I saw you, you were bedecked with gongs! Since I last saw you I have had the odd crack at the Hun, which pastime I find very interesting even though a bit scaring."

In a touching reference to Budge in a letter to their mother, he said: "We are very thrilled at the news of Budge's D.S.O. and if I am ever as good as he is I won't have much to worry about. I wish that we were in the same theatre of operations as I miss him very much. In the last few years Budge has become my greatest friend and my only regret is that we don't see enough of each other."

(During the stay at Happy Valley there was also a surprise visit from brother-in-law 'Corney' Burke—accompanied by a much welcome bottle of gin. Corney, together with Doug Maitland and Tom Ladner, all of the Royal Vancouver Yacht Club were to become well-known and much respected as the "three musketeers" by Royal Navy gun-boat crews in the Mediterranean and Adriatic Seas)

Budge received an intimation that all was not well with Nancy's pregnancy, but it was not until September 2 that he received confirmation from her that the baby, christened Aileen Ann, had lived only three days. She was born on July 13 while Budge was in the thick of fighting in the early days of the campaign. He wrote to tell Nancy that she had been very brave and tried to minimise this setback. Budge wrote of his "robust self-confidence for their future together and his sense of well-being." He claimed to be the fittest man in the battalion and was unaffected by the heat, the dirt and the flies.

While they rested at Happy Valley, the Sicilian Campaign ended. With the defeat of the occupying army by 'Operation Husky' in just 38 days from the beach landings it may seem odd that the balance of the German forces were able to make a planned withdrawal across the Strait of Messina. There were two reasons for this. One was that the terrain in the final north-east wedge of the island, the enemy's escape route, was in their favour. This is best described by Lt. Colonel G.W.L. Nicholson in his Volume II of *The Canadians in Italy—1943-1945*:

"After the capture of Adrano... the track of the advance lay between the high trackless slopes of Mt. Etna and the deep gorge of the upper Simento, along a route which gave the enemy full scope for delaying tactics.

On the 8th Army's right flank progress was equally slow, for in the narrow defile of the coastal strip the German engineers had blocked the roads with every conceivable obstacle."

These tactics delayed the allied final advance right to the end so that when they finally entered Messina on August 17th the enemy rearguard had successfully crossed the Strait to the mainland. The other reason was the effectiveness of their air and sea defences over the Strait with both flak and coastal artillery. Despite this, the bravery of the Allied airmen was never in dispute, especially the crews of three Canadian Wellington bomber squadrons. There were several fighter squadrons based on Sicily flying supporting patrols, but only one was Canadian, the 417 (City of Windsor), flying spitfires from their base at Lentini. The battalion enjoyed social visits and sports events with them.

The squadron had a narrow escape when, on August 11, in a moonlight raid some fifty German bombers raided the airfield and destroyed it. Ammunition, fuel supplies, fighter aircraft of several squadrons—all were destroyed along with dozens of personnel killed. By a fluke most of the 417 Squadron planes along with its pilots and ground crew were saved, but ground defences were caught by surprise.

The evacuation of German troops and equipment had gone as planned by General Hube, Commander of the 14th Panzer Corps and his Chief of Staff, Colonel von Bonin. Both were realists who knew that the German forces were losing ground daily and had set August 10 as "X Day"—the date on which the general evacuation of the island would commence. The overall responsibility for the rearguard action and evacuation rested with Field Marshal Kesselring and there was a division within the German hierarchy as to the wisdom of leaving Sicily, versus fighting on to delay the invasion of the Italian mainland by the Allies. Predictably, Field Marshal Erwin Rommel was for holding on at all costs. The evacuation argument won and took place over six nights, transferring over 50,000 troops and an impressive amount of equipment to the mainland. The allied objective in Sicily was not just to drive the enemy out, but to destroy them. Therefore this substantial evacuation by the Germans from Sicily was their success and an Allied loss.

Budge at one year old outside his parent's Vancouver home.

Budge (extreme left, 2nd row seated) in about 1921, Lord Roberts Elementary in Vancouver's West End.

At croydon Airport en-route to Switzerland via Paris with H.O. Bell-Irving and aunt Beatrice, December 1927.

Budge at Pontresina, Switzerland, December 1927.

The Lance-Caporal, Loretto School Officer's Training Corps, Scotland, 1929.

A fully loaded 'Glendale II', Glendale Cannery, Knight Inlet, mid 1930's.

At Arrandale cannery, on the Nass River, a typical northern B.C. cannery scene in the 1930's as the fishermen prepare to be towed out to their positions.

Salmon cans ready for loading, bound for Vancouver.

Budge and Nancy off Pasley Island, late 1930's.

November 1939, Budge and Nancy bound for the U.K. with Sergeant-Major Vance and Sergeants McNutt and Biddlecombe.

Nancy driving the Women's Canadian Club canteen truck in Surrey, England.

Nancy, 'somewhere in England' 1940.

A Bell-Irving gathering, London, England, 1942.

Rest camp, Sicily, August 1943, Budge front row, 3rd from right.
Lt. Col. Bert Hoffmeister 5th from right. Padre Roy Durnford extreme left back row.

Budge and brother Roderick the night before he was shot down and killed over France, May 7, 1944.

L. Col. Budge Bell-Irving, C.O. Loyal Edmonton Regiment and 'Lady Bell-Irving', the donkey-Derby winner, Piedmonte d'Alife, Italy, June 1944.

Brigadier Budge Bell-Irving and his father, Commander Henry Bell-Irving outside Buckingham Palace, where Budge was invested with a bar to his D.S.O., July 1945.

'The Brigadier who sold toys' – Budge demonstrating a toy selection made by Lines Bros. of Londgon, Enland.

Lieutenant-Governor the Hon. H.P. Bell-Irving, poses at Government House, May 1978.

Budge and Nancy with the Aga Khan and Begum Aga Khan at the Ismali Centre dedication, Burnaby, B.C., July 1982.

An unrehearsed moment! With the Aga Khan unveiling a plaque at the Ismali Centre in Burnaby, B.C., July 26, 1982.

A touch of humour at a U.B.C. convocation; Budge wearing a Cowichan toque as he receives Peter Webster, an elder of Vancouver Island's Ahousaht Fist Nation people.

Speeches in Dam Square, Amsterdam. On the left: May 1945 the day after the city was liberated and on the right: the 35th anniversery in May 1980.

Naming the General Bell-Irving tulip, Kukenhof Gardens, Holland, May 1980.

Budge with the children of Waglisla, northern B.C., spring 1981.

Budge and Nancy with newly installed Lieutenant-Governor Robert (Bob) Rogers and his wife Jane, July 15, 1983.

CHAPTER SEVEN

WHEN OPERATION "HUSKY" WAS in the planning stage, the question of how to proceed following the capture of Sicily was hotly debated by the Allied leaders and their senior military advisers. It was not a foregone conclusion that an invasion of Italy would simply follow. What was agreed was that an invasion of Northern Europe was vital, but it would be premature until the spring of 1944 at the earliest. The Americans wanted only limited offensive operations in the Mediterranean area, enough to destroy Italy's war potential by continuing air attacks from Mediterranean bases. They also stressed the need to continue support of Russia to divert Axis forces, which would eventually facilitate a cross-Channel invasion.

Winston Churchill, on the other hand, posed the question of what to do with several thousand well-trained troops between the end of the Sicilian Campaign and the launch of a 'Second Front' in Northern Europe. To have them stand idle would, in his opinion, be out of the question. Eventually a compromise was reached: The British agreed on the need to select target areas and the size of the forces needed for a cross-channel invasion. The Americans then withdrew their opposition to further operations in the Mediterranean provided they were limited in scope. This was how the situation stood at the beginning of Operation "Husky."

Once the invasion was into its second week it became so obvious that this would not be a long campaign, the planners began to look more seriously at the next stage. They realized that if most of the enemy were to escape across the Strait of Messina it would need, in author Nicholson's words, "much bolder strokes than they had previously considered." The invasion of mainland Italy became that bolder stroke.

The Seaforths enjoyed their well earned rest at Happy Valley until September 1 when the 2nd Brigade made preparations to cross the Strait of Messina to continue the offensive until surrender. Early on September 4 the Strait was crossed without incident and by late afternoon the advance into Italy began. The German high command purposely offered little resistance in the southern portion of Italy, thus drawing the allied units into a series of forced marches during most of September. They are etched in the memories of the veterans. Dr. MacDougall refers to them as "the gruelling test of those September days, most them lived in a haze of weariness and hunger."

Climbing through the mountainous terrain of the Calabrian Peninsula still in tropical shirts and shorts, Budge recalled:

> "It was cold, it was raining—and the rain was cold! The C.O. was off in front somewhere in his jeep. I was in front of the column when we passed a large building to our left with wide-open doors through which we saw a fireplace with a fire blazing. It was extremely inviting and with a simple 'left wheel' we marched into gorgeous, heavenly warmth. When the Colonel came back looking for his battalion following an 'O' group he was somewhat cross.
>
> The next time we were warm was after descending to Catanzano Marina. We swam in the Ionian Sea in lovely clear, tepid water. It was just the thing. The Seaforths, having been indoctrinated into the dangers of mined beaches invited the local stationmaster—a facist official, who would know where the mines were—to lead the parade sitting on the bonnet of a jeep. We got into the water safely and it was heavenly—for a very brief time. Another enemy in large numbers, a very small sea creature with a taste for 'private parts' caused a somewhat hasty retreat to dry land!"

The soldiers were fast learning to live off the land. They procured meat, vegetables, eggs, and fruit. The meat was with the approval of the animal's owner—mostly. After killing the animal they would proffer a receipt for it signed in the name of General Montgomery or even Winston Churchill! Budge wrote in the early days of the Italian Campaign, "It's a glorified walking tour. It has been tough marching, particularly for the reinforcements, who are not really hardened yet." Robert Bonner said that after several days he could no longer feel the underside of his feet and it was months before any feeling came back. The main complaint was fleas, which seemed very persistent.

As the Seaforths progressed northward, virtually all bridges had been destroyed in their path by German engineers. Battalion transport was, inevitably, far behind. One night the C.O. ordered Budge to lead a recce, taking a couple of soldiers with Bren guns some miles ahead to a certain cross-road and to remain there if it was not occupied, or to return to meet the advancing battalion if the enemy were still holding it. The position appeared to be unattended and they settled in for a while, covering the cross-road to wait for whatever might develop.

After Italy's official capitulation on September 8, what little resistance its few remaining fighting regiments had offered was now no more. Following surrender the Italian army wasted no time in getting out of uniform, though some still wore odd bits of it. As a result an amusing incident happened at the cross-road. A rumble of wheels suggested the approach of some Italian horse artillery. Instead a large farm wagon pulled by two huge white cow oxen came into sight. Two Italians rode on the wagon seat and the spokesman of the two, Budge took to be at least a generalissimo, whom he described:

> "He was a dirty little guy wearing a once white tunic, with gold epaulettes and medals—everything but a general's hat with feathers on it. Instead he had a mop of black curly hair, immediately reminding me of Harpo Marx [Budge had already met 'Groucho' at Piazza Armerina]. With no common language conversation was difficult, but I tried to induce them to return to their village and bring back some groceries. The message seemed to be getting through alright and soon they got to the 'amiche, amiche bono Inglese—cigarette stage' and General Harpo repeated a word sounding like 'lartie.' I couldn't make out what they meant until the driver grabbed my mess tin and in the middle of the cross-roads sat down and milked one of these huge oxen into it, a first installment of the requested groceries."

Budge then remembered the Italian word for milk (larti) and, as he observed this picture of an Italian 'general' milking into his mess tin, he fervently wished he'd had a camera handy. With all seemingly well at the scene he decided to leave his two soldiers with their Bren guns and return to meet the oncoming battalion. Walking across a broad open plain he carried a Biretta Italian rifle, merely because it was half the weight of his own Lee-Enfield. The fact that he had no bullets didn't bother him. In due time he noticed an Italian soldier with a similar rifle walking in the same direction off to one side; then several others on the opposite side—then more joining the lone soldier—all converging on him. Budge climbed onto a large rock, waved his rifle and shouted at them, gesticulating to them to lay down their arms, which they all did.

Soon the column appeared and continued the march north. For some time the only sound of war was the noise of hand-grenades left behind by the Italian army which the populace were letting off in celebration at being out of the war. Major Doug Forin wrote that they could be heard at night—"reverberating through the hills, accompanied by the reflection of flashes from the explosions and from Very pistols, which went up into the sky in their hundreds. It was truly a Mardi Gras throughout the whole of southern Italy."

In the meantime an assault was taking place on Salerno, just south of Naples, by a combined U.S./British force under the command of U.S. General Mark Clark. His Fifth Army and two divisions of the British 10th Corps met strong resistance, though Salerno fell to the 10th Corps on September 10. A crucial part of the bridgehead, around Battipaglia on the Salerno plain, was almost lost again but massive air support, aided by weak enemy air defences, saved the day and slowly the bridgehead was expanded.

Montgomery's 8th Army, including the Canadian Seaforths continued advancing north. By September 15 when the British 5th Division and the 11th Canadian Armoured Regiment reached Sapri, only forty miles separated the two allied armies. On September 21 the battalion reached Potenza and five miles beyond it took up defensive positions. From here, with 400 miles of Italian mainland behind them they could finally hear the sound of enemy guns. A large section of southern Italy was secured by the allies, from Salerno in the west to the Foggia Plain in the east.

Budge commented on the obvious relief of the peasants now they were under the allies. Fresh white bread was a change from hard-tack and it came along with fresh eggs. Passing through one town in his jeep, through the joyous mob came in quick succession, a plate of hot scrambled eggs and bacon, a few feet further along cheese and bread, followed by a tray of neatly sliced melons. This food supplemented army rations, especially as the speed of the advance made it necessary for the 8th Army to pause and bring up much-needed supplies.

Potenza was the last rest before going into action again and time was made for a Division sports meet at a large new stadium just outside Potenza. While attending an event there Colonel Hoffmeister was informed that he would take over as acting Brigadier of the 2nd Brigade, while Brigadier Vokes took command of the Division due to the illness of Major-General Simonds. Major Forin became acting C.O. of the battalion and Budge became acting second-in-command. Captain Tom Vance took command of "A" Company. Approximately two weeks later these changes were confirmed as permanent.

During the lull at Potenza, in a September 26 letter to Nancy, Budge broached an idea that would have a far-reaching impact on their future. He wrote: "I have thought several times recently that an agency for Lines Bros. toys in Western Canada might be mutually beneficial and very profitable. It might be either separate or within the framework of HBI & Co. If you are ever staying with the Lines perhaps you might broach the subject. I have lots of ideas for the future. I expect one of them will develop." He also talked about the 'infinitesimal' chance of getting killed or wounded and was obviously becoming surer of his chances of surviving, even though heavy fighting still lay ahead.

With Budge as 2 i/c, on October 1, the battalion went into action again and during the month were in two major engagements. He complained bitterly of being 'L.O.B.' (left out of battle), though realizing the importance of his support role. The first objective was Hill 1007 (Mount San Marco), from which German artillery were able to shell a crucial crossroads at Decorata. In this new phase of the battle the British and Canadian forces were hampered by successful demolition work of the retreating Germans, who had made just about every road impassable. It was extremely difficult for the supporting transport to bring up supplies for the troops. There were craters, blown bridges, mines and felled trees to contend with, keeping the Allied engineers working twenty-four hours a day and contending with shell-fire to discourage their activities. Budge and his batman, Nash, who had replaced Private Neilson, spent most of the night of October 2 manœuvering his jeep across a deep ravine because of a blown-up bridge.

Several patrols were sent out to learn what conditions prevailed before launching the next attack. One was led by Lieut. Robert Bonner and though no direct contact was made with the enemy, he learned from an Italian farmer that some tanks and self-propelled guns had been seen. As there were, however, no direct sightings from any of the patrols the reliability of this information was held in question by both the battalion and brigade commanders.

By the morning of the 5th it seemed certain that the Germans had been cleared from a large section of terrain and a strike towards the next crucial objective, the Decorata road junction was ordered. This intelligence proved inaccurate and from a pocket of resistance the enemy began to shell the 2nd Brigade area. Some shells fell around Hill 910 where "A" Company had dug in. A favourite of the battalion, 'Curly' MacLeod, the oldest serving private at 45 years old, was killed and several were wounded. One of these was Lieut. Bonner, who received a head wound, a fractured shoulder and an arm broken in two places. He was removed to a field dressing station but his injuries were serious enough that he was sent to a military hospital in N. Africa where his arm was reset twice. He took with him his .45 revolver given to him by his father, courtesy of a Detective Copeland of the Vancouver Police. It had not been fired in action. He was sent back to U.K., eventually becoming a training officer—and had much to say to senior officers about the need to improve the quality of training before sending men to front-line areas.

Bonner's six weeks with the battalion were spent entirely with "A" Company. Even in this short time he formed the opinion that Budge was an outstanding company commander and tactically would come up with ideas that showed great originality of thought. He said "It was kind of mind stretching, and Bert Hoffmeister was like that too. After the war I told them 'You provided more terror than the enemy!'"

Concentrated enemy fire came from Hill 1007 and its capture became vital before any advance on the Decorata cross-road could be achieved. "C" Company's commander, Acting Major Syd Thomson, called for return fire and so intense was the combined shelling that the war diarist noted that it was the fiercest ever experienced by the battalion since landing in Sicily. In the final 600 yard dash four enemy self-propelled guns appeared and fired at the "C" Company troops but under Thomson's leadership the objective was secured by 20:00 hrs on October 6. Nine men were killed and 23 wounded. For his "cheery confidence which had already become his mark in battle," Syd Thomson was awarded an M.C.

With Hill 1007 taken it was possible to concentrate on the Decorata cross-road in a night attack helped by a full moon and only light cloud. The Scout Platoon led the way followed by "D", "C" and "B" Companies, all in single file. Increasing cloud hid the moon, then fog descended, so thick in places that it blotted out one platoon from another, and sometimes one man from another.

The fog was, in the main, a curse, but it had the effect of surprising the enemy and a few machine gun posts were captured. Unfortunately, tanks and self-propelled guns appeared between the patrol and the cross-road, the very weapons that assurance had been made were nowhere near. Firing randomly they managed to inflict several fatalities including "D" Comp. Commander, Capt. Jim McMullen, Sergeant George Fairweather and two privates, all killed together by a shell from one of these vehicles. When, the next day two men of the Scout Platoon returned to the area, the enemy had departed leaving the Decorata cross-roads to the Seaforths. This was the last battle fought in tropical dress. The weather was turning wet and cold and it was with great relief that battle dress and great-coats were re-issued.

(George Fairweather's brother David, was also a sergeant, but had returned to B.C. to attend officer training at Gordonhead, Victoria, where he was commissioned. Returning to the battalion just in time for Ortona he saw action right through to the end of the war. David Fairweather commanded the regiment from 1961 to 1963 and later became both Honorary Lieutenant-Colonel and Honorary Colonel, following Budge's terms.)

During the following week heavy rain slowed progress once again for the transports, making life generally miserable for all. Budge wrote that his jeep, his blankets, his clothes and himself were all covered in mud from ground that was so sticky it was almost impossible to walk through it. Dry river beds were now torrents, making the job of crossing them much more difficult and requiring more ingenuity. It was not hard to understand his discontent. From the rear, more concerned with day to day administration and distribution of supplies by mule trains with Tunisian Arab drivers, Budge could hear the sounds of battle, where other members of the battalion were engaged in what he did best; using initiative and constantly prodding to find the enemy's weaknesses.

Baranello was taken, then re-captured by the enemy. After a struggle it was again in allied hands and it was here on October 24, while enjoying a respite that the officers held their annual Passchendaele dinner. Budge drove up to Campobasso to buy a suckling pig for the dinner. This journey was not without incident. Coming across a temporary diversion around a destroyed bridge he politely gave way to a larger vehicle. As it moved through, the truck hit a mine but fared much better than his jeep would have done. In Campobasso he got his pig and a gift of two miniature pistols from the mayor. One went to Bert Hoffmeister and the other to Nancy.

On October 22 a message from the 1st Cdn Div H.Q. brought the news that Budge was promoted to Lt.-Col., with orders to return immediately to the U.K. on high priority. He was to assume command of the Canadian O.C.T.U. (Officer Cadet Training Unit). Budge asked Orderly Room Sergeant E.H. Squarebriggs to send a message around the battalion, offering to take up to sixty letters per company back to the U.K. when he left the following morning. Budge recalls with amusement:

> "With the usual Squarebriggs efficiency the message was promptly circulated—'Major B.I. has been caught in bed with the Contessa by her husband (who is recovering) and is returning to London tomorrow morning for Court Martial. He is willing to take 60 duly franked letters from each company back to England.' Included among the hastily written letters were one from a major-general and one from the squadron-commander of another unit."

While promotion was to be looked upon with pleasure, saying good-bye to one's regiment and the friends made in years of peace and war was not. Budge's departure was made easier by the rousing send-off dinner he was given, with the officers wearing their kilts, brought up especially from the rear. With his departure, Douglas Forin was the only one remaining of the original battalion officers who had paraded in the armoury on September 1, 1939.

By the time he arrived in Bari, on Italy's Adriatic coast, Budge began to realize his good fortune. He could look forward to at least several months in U.K., with new possibilities beyond that. He would be able to spend time with Nancy and help her to overcome the loss of their baby. He would also be able to see his father and Roderick occasionally. An Air Transport Command DC3 (Dakota) was on the tarmac and, waiting to board was a full compliment of servicemen; British, American and Commonwealth forces. Budge became aware of his new-found importance when he took the seat of a U.S. Army sergeant, who was bumped from the passenger list. During a stopover at Gibraltar, happily anticipating his reunion with Nancy, Budge removed most of the items from his travel bag and replaced them with a variety of items purchased for her. A batman promised to forward the left-behind items to one of the London clubs frequented by Henry Bell-Irving.

The plane's destination was Croydon Airport, once upon a time the main international airfield in Britain. Because of fog they were diverted to South-West England, where a quieter reception awaited them. To the request "Have you anything to declare" from a young officer, Budge replied, "No, just a batch of personal letters, all properly franked by officers." It wouldn't wash. "No letters may be carried from one theatre of war to another," was the reply.

A bargain was struck. Budge gave up the letters, which were taken to London for checking and mailing, with one exception, the one from the general, which Budge had promised to deliver personally when he arrived in London. First he visited Canadian Military H.Q., where a brigadier asked that oft repeated wartime question, "What are you doing here?" To the reply that he had returned on high priority to take command of a Canadian Officer Cadet Training Unit, came, "No, we are expecting an officer from the R.C.R.—and the O.C.T.U. term doesn't begin for another two weeks, anyway."

Budge's ready response was that he could use a week's leave and as he had agreed to deliver a letter for the general he would appreciate a car. He got both and the letter was duly delivered. The week's leave with Nancy was wonderful—but there was one difficult moment though. It was when she had to tell him that the expensive stockings he had purchased in Gibraltar were utility grade, produced by the British Ministry of Supply for the female labour force!

With his leave over, Budge reported once more to C.M.H.Q. where he was promptly 'on the mat', confronted by a large file containing all the letters, minus the General's, all openly displayed. Heading the list was the letter from the squadron commander to his English womanfriend. The letter began with a statement to the effect that it wouldn't have been possible to send it except that it was being brought by a friend returning to England to take command of a brigade. The 'friend' had remained in Italy and Budge had unwittingly inherited the letter—which contained a simple code enabling the lady-love to be continually informed of her hero's whereabouts. He had the bad grace to think it was funny and asked the brigadier to lend him a C.W.A.C. (Canadian Womens' Army Corps) secretary so that he could dictate a confession.

Budge returned to Aldershot, where the O.C.T.U. was established. He has little recollection of the day-to-day details of running the school, other than what he considered an over-emphasis on table manners, presumed to be lacking in first-class N.C.O.s who were about to become 'officers and gentlemen.' His graduates were required to go to another level before gaining their commissions so he was, in effect, running a pre-O.C.T.U. He did not merely request a posting to a more challenging job—but instead persuaded C.M.H.Q. that the course was a waste of time and money and it was discontinued after his one term of command.

Budge was then successful in obtaining a place in the 25th War Course of the Senior Officers' School, held at Brasenose College, Oxford, from mid-February to mid-April, 1944. The course was by no means simply the usual 'staff college' for staff officers; it was a preliminary to unit command and beyond. The approximately one hundred candidates were mainly of major rank but there were, like Budge, a few lieutenant-colonels.

As well as lectures there were exercises on the ground in the form of T.E.W.TS. (Tactical Exercises Without Troops). The two months of intensive work at the school was interesting, very demanding and occasionally good fun. There were runs around Christ Church meadows by way of fitness training, but it was not only the outdoor activities that toughened the candidates. His room was an 'ice-box'; damp, totally unheated and on an open stairway. Budge survived at night by wearing his sweater and placing his greatcoat over the bed.

A fellow War Course officer was Major Robertson-McIsaac of the Imperial Seaforth Highlanders. He was one of the officers who had entertained the Canadians so warmly at Catania after the fighting in Sicily was over. Also at the school were Budge's fellow Canadian Seaforth, Syd Thomson and the Patricias' Reg (Slug) Clark. Thomson had by this time won both a D.S.O. and an M.C. but had returned to the U.K. to take the Senior Officers' course in preparation for further promotion. The fact that he and Budge were at Brasenose, both battle hardened and decorated, is an indication of the course's value and it gave Budge exactly what he needed to know for higher command.

An inevitable night on the town was planned, led by Robertson-McIsaac. Driving into the city it was realized they would be there long before the 6 p.m. pub opening time so he suggested they call in on his girlfriend, but not before extracting a promise of good behaviour from the 'colonials', telling them, "I know you Canadians can't be trusted around a pretty girl." Promises were given and in due course they arrived at her flat where, upon opening the door the girl immediately gave Budge a kiss and said "Oh, Budge Darling, how wonderful to see you!" One advantage of his Scottish education was that some of his Loretto friends had sisters. Budge had sometimes attended Sunday tea at the Edinburgh home of his friend Craig, and the passage of fourteen years had done wonders for the boy's little sister. She was now grown-up, extremely pretty and bright enough to quickly play a joke on Robertson-McIsaac. He recovered from the shock and a very good evening in town was enjoyed.

When the course was over Budge was able to take a few days leave while waiting for his next posting. He again raised the question of Nancy returning to Canada, but up to this point was wise enough not to make too big an issue of it. Budge does not recall any actual documentation at the end of the course, but as he maintained his rank he presumes the War Office was happy with the results. When his posting came through it was a step up from the now defunct pre-O.C.T.U. It was to command the No. 5 (Tactical) Wing, Canadian Training School, in effect a battle school, near Steyning, Sussex on the south coast. Its purpose was to give a taste of reality under battle conditions.

Budge took time to study the district, the facilities and the prepared syllabus. He was soon convinced that the course offered a valuable opportunity to give a taste of realism for those destined to go into battle for the first time and he quickly put his own stamp on it. When the first intake arrived he told them, and all subsequent intakes:

> "You will be tired out most of the time and very frequently scared to death. When you finally go into battle the Germans will be a 'piece of cake' compared to what I have in store for you. You will learn to master any situation that you may face and by the time you leave here you will be physically indefatigable."

The simulation of battle was very real. Platoons advancing over open ground were quietly followed closely by directing staff with electronic controls to detonate mortar bombs previously buried at appropriate distances from the line of advance. The machine gun fire from other unseen directing staff was accurate and close enough to be very frightening. Perhaps the most terrifying aspect of the training was the requirement to crawl through a long tunnel just big enough to squeeze into, with no possibility of turning around. There were one or two forks along it, one of which led to the end and the others to dead ends, necessitating a crawl backwards to the fork to try again. There were two towers about thirty feet high made of poles lashed together, about fifty yards apart. Between was a narrow, rickety bridge with no railings, over a muddy pond.

Budge has an unhappy memory of a man standing on the top of tower one, not able to face the crossing. Looking up at the man he said rather cruelly, "Are you going across or are you going back to Canada?" The poor man came down and then, of course, Budge had to do it. Halfway across he lost his balance and fell head-first into the pond with his feet waggling in the air—and a good intake of muddy water! Fortunately it wasn't very deep and after being extricated he thanked God for a sense of humour. At the end of the first course the whole school was in great form and ready for the real thing. The C.O. was aware that they would lose some of their 'warrior vigour' in the pubs of London, but he hoped not too much.

While he was at the Battle School, Nancy stayed in nearby Jevington. Roderick's 98 Squadron was also close by, and Henry had moved down from Rosemarkie to Portsmouth to take part in preparations for the upcoming "D" Day landing. They were able to get together once in a while. In mid April Roderick was promoted to Wing-Commander and, on one memorable night, May 7, he and Henry dined with Budge at the battle school mess.

The next morning Roderick led several wings of Mitchell bombers on a mission to a V1 site at Abbeville in northern France, but heavy fog hid the target and the raid was aborted. That same evening a second attempt was made, this time with good visibility. It was Roderick's 37th. mission. Take-off was at 17:05 hrs, flying at 13,000 ft. The official report described the enemy anti-aircraft fire as very heavy.

Flying-Officer Gordon Grellman, an Australian flying in the R.A.F. was No. 2 to Roderick. They had completed the bombing run and were just turning away when a bracket of shells scored a direct hit on the leader. Writing to Budge many years later, F/O Grellman told him:

> "My aircraft was in station on the leader's right, within a 100 feet. I witnessed a direct hit under the cockpit. It was obvious the damage was catastrophic and W/C Bell-Irving was seen to slump forward

in his straps as the aircraft, trailing smoke and flames nosed down sharply and was soon lost to sight."

(Grellman's own aircraft was so badly damaged that the next day it was scrapped for spare parts. Even the tubes supporting his seat were riddled with shell fragments.)

An agreement with the Air Ministry to inform Henry if Roderick should be wounded, reported missing, or his death confirmed was not followed and instead a telegram was despatched to Nan in Victoria. In the meantime Henry was sending his usual cheery, newsy letters home and assuming the reason he had not heard from Roderick was that he was too busy to make contact. The first news that Henry and Budge received was from Victoria by way of a cable from Nan saying that her thoughts were with them.

On May 19, Henry finally talked on the telephone to the Station Commander, Group-Captain Dunlap, who informed Henry that he had been trying to make contact ever since the 8th, without success. Budge and Henry went immediately to the airfield just in time to see Roderick's squadron depart on a bombing mission and thankfully, all 36 aircraft returned safely. They were invited to the bar when the aircrew members had been debriefed and a toast was drunk in Roderick's memory. Budge reminded his father the essential fact was that Roderick's job was still being done by the men he had led. It was not until September that a communiqué arrived via International Red Cross confirming the crash, and the burial of all four crew members at Abbeville cemetery.

By the end of May, preparations were completed for the Allied invasion of Europe. The whole of south-central England presented the appearance of a massive military camp of men, equipment and supplies, as they converged on the main ports from where the invasion would set sail.

On June 1, Budge was informed that he was to return to Italy to take command of the Loyal Edmonton Regiment. He was replacing Lt.-Col. Rowan Coleman, who had been wounded while leading the battalion in the battle to penetrate the well-defended Hitler Line.

CHAPTER EIGHT

BUDGE LEFT THE U.K. ON JUNE 2, flying again in one of the 'workhorse' Dakotas. He landed in Naples, where he obtained a jeep and drove north to find his new regiment. In the months he had been in England the Allied advance had been slow but steady. Rome had fallen even as Budge was returning to Italy. The war was entering a new phrase, with the "D" Day landing about to begin on June 6.

Budge's father, despite his age, was directly involved in the Normandy landing and only one day later, Henry revealed in a letter to Nan that he had played a part in overseeing the loading of this large 'armada'—"Thousands of vehicles; tanks, guns, trucks and all sorts of weird instruments of war and thousands and thousands of personnel into hundreds and hundreds of craft of all shapes and sizes. Everything had to be exact, every person in the right craft, but it is quite beyond description in a mere letter."

Now wearing a khaki uniform, though still with naval insignia, on "D" Day plus three Henry moved to the French coast to join the staff of the Senior Naval Officer in charge of the landing. His job was to supervise the unloading of stores into amphibious vehicles that would take them as close to the front as possible and Henry went ashore with them a couple of times to within a few hundred yards of the fighting. Parts of the beach were shelled by enemy guns, but the unloading continued without a pause.

When he returned to England, Henry tried his hardest to persuade Nancy to return to Canada, especially as he had applied for Canadian leave and was awaiting word on a sailing date. His plan was to try to get her passage on the same ship. However, she felt it would be letting Budge down to return, even though he was in full agreement with his father and had again tried to persuade her before returning to Italy. He thought that it was dangerous to remain in the U.K. She was staying with the Lines and the area was now in the line of flight of the V1 'buzz bombs'.

(These pilotless aircraft were powered by an engine designed to cut out at a pre-set time, usually over, or just short of London. There was an exhaust flame from the engine and once the flame ceased, watchers knew that the engine was about to cut and within a few seconds it would crash and explode. On one or two occasions British fighter pilots nudged them off course, to crash without harm in open countryside, or even turned them around to crash harmlessly in the sea. These were followed by the much more dangerous V2 rockets that were fired on a trajectory and came without warning to explode with some accuracy anywhere within greater London. In one letter home Henry told a joke that the author had not heard, even though he was brought up in the blitz: "The buzz bombs are also called 'knicker bombs'—because when the light goes out they come down!)

Back in Italy Budge was quickly briefed on the war situation. In his absence the capture of Ortona and crossing the Hitler Line were the two bitterest Canadian battles in the whole course of the Italian Campaign. The Hitler Line battle had ended only two weeks before Budge landed back in Italy and he was aware that in missing it he had dodged more than "D" Day! (See Appendix 9)

Acting C.O. Syd Thomson was awarded the D.S.O. for his leadership in remaining with his forward troops almost the whole duration of the battle for Ortona. Once again his unflappable cheerfulness was noted in the citation. When, in January 1944 he returned to England to attend the Senior Officers School, command of the battalion was temporarily in the hands of Lt.-Col. Creighton. In mid-May Syd Thomson returned with his command now confirmed, just in time for the Hitler Line battle.

In Budge's absence, other people had also been promoted. His former company commander and former C.O., Bert Hoffmeister had been promoted to Major-General and was in command of the 5th Canadian

Armoured Division. Brigadier Chris Vokes had also been promoted to Major-General to command the 1st Canadian Infantry Division. Brigadier T.G. Gibson commanded the 2nd Infantry Brigade.

Budge began a long drive to find his new regiment, at the end of which he met Major Jim Stone, acting C.O. It was already late evening and the night ahead was to be a very unhappy one for both of them. Within the regiment Jim Stone was already recognized as a first-class leader, much respected and popular with all ranks—in every possible way an excellent candidate for command of the battalion. He must certainly have been expecting the job at this time and was understandably very disappointed to be by-passed in favour of an import. Budge, on the other hand, had not asked for the job. He would have preferred to go back to his own unit had there been a vacancy, though having fought side by side with the Eddy's through the hills of Sicily, he was proud to be given this command.

After a long and bitter session, Jim Stone's superb military good sense came to the fore. He saw that this was an order from higher authority and it would be in the interests of both, and more importantly the regiment, to obey the order. They must support each other as a team. The pact was made and both agreed to get on with the job. In the four months they remained together, Budge became convinced that Major James Riley Stone was most likely the best all-round fighting second-in-command the Canadian Army would ever know—and he was obviously destined for higher command.

Before they saw further action the 1st Canadian Corps was pulled out for a rest and on the evening of June 7, the battalion proceeded in convoy back down the Liri Valley, south of Rome where they eventually arrived at a little village in peaceful countryside named Piedmonte d'Alife. This was to be a much appreciated location for the Canadians to forget the carnage of war for a while. There were sports and parties at all levels with happy participation from the local people. Leaves to Rome and Naples were granted.

On July 5 came the second Donkey Derby of the "Eddy's" campaign. The official history states: "The winner was a moke named Lady Bell-Irving and the only animal according to our observer, to realize that a straight line was the shortest distance between two points." Budge had nothing to do with naming it and was amused by the thought that had this donkey been a male, no doubt it might have been named Lord B-I, to denote its relationship to their new "stuck-up" C.O. As the straight-line moke won, all was forgiven.

Training began again throughout the division and Budge organized his with a view to getting to know his officers and how they handled their companies and platoons. He had some well-tested thoughts on leading a company and he was anxious that this should be readily understood by his company commanders.

At the rest area, parties were in full swing and Budge was determined that his Loyal Edmonton officers would have the biggest and best party, with guests from other officers' messes. In a local vineyard a wooden dance floor was laid and decorations were created among the overhead vines. A military band would play at one end and an Italian orchestra at the other, each taking turns. A large brick oven was to be built with a sufficient capacity to roast or bake a large quantity of small chickens, together with pommeadori and other vegetables required to complete the first course. A substantial quantity of vino—enough to float a ship, as someone suggested, plus plates, cutlery, glasses—all would have to be procured. While these arrangements were put in hand, invitations were sent out to the C.R.A.M.C. nursing sisters from the nearby Canadian General Hospital.

On July 24, while the sergeants were enjoying a similar party, the officers and their guests dined at small tables around the dance-floor, lighted by the coloured bulbs strung among the vines. All went according to plan, with the military band and the twelve-piece Italian orchestra in place to provide soft Italian dinner music, followed in turn by the dance band. The big brick oven was going full blast, with enough small chickens to go round and more. The whole setting was enhanced by the presence of their lady guests.

The Corps commander, Lt.-General E.L.M. Burns, had 'regretted', but getting a hint of what was planned, had turned up after all, all fired up for the party. Syd Thomson was there as was Lt.-Col. R.P. (Slug) Clark, C.O. of the Patricias. He was sitting close to Budge, who realized for the first time that the party had expanded somewhat when a soldier waiter appeared, grasped Col. Clark around the shoulder with "Hi, Slug old boy, have another chicken!" The original eight soldier waiters had expanded to several times that number. As dawn broke, a very senior officer stood alone at the edge of the dance-floor singing quietly to himself a rude song about a misbehaving fly. Someone had temporarily borrowed his car.

On August 5 the rest ended and the brigade prepared to go back to war. The advance north of Rome continued at a rapid pace, though there were pockets of resistance. The Three Rivers Regiment (12th Cdn Armoured Regt.) who had worked so well with the 2nd Canadian Infantry Brigade in Sicily was, at this stage engaged in support of the British 10th Infantry Brigade. The nineteen German Divisions that had attempted to defend Rome were battered and disorganized and according to their C-in-C., Field Marshal Kesselring, their fighting strength was reduced by 50%. Losses were 38,000 dead, wounded or missing. Captured documents and transcripts of the Field-Marshal's phone conversations with his field commanders showed confusion and an inability to begin preparation for the next move by General Alexander (Allied Deputy Supreme Commander, Mediterranean).

The Loyal Edmonton Regiment took a long, circuitous route to the south bank of the Arno River, where they relieved the 28th Maori Battalion of the 2nd New Zealand Division. As the line of Edmontons marched in, they passed a long line of huge Maoris marching out. The Canadians were amazed by the extra-ordinary collection of fancy hats, clothing and various musical instruments in possession of the Maoris. Across the Arno lay the ancient city of Florence, still occupied by the Germans. Budge established his H.Q. in an unoccupied fire-hall. He called a battalion "O" Group and in his orders made it clear that there was to be absolutely no looting, reminding everyone that soldiers who took time out to loot would be quite useless. A very short time later, an officer came across a Leica camera in the Fire Chief's upstairs office. He offered to sell it to Budge for $10. In recalling the incident, Budge had cause to reflect on what he may have done had he found it first.

There were gaps between some of the river-front buildings and they were covered by German machine guns across the river. These inflicted a number of casualties among the Edmontons in spite of constant extreme caution. Eighth Army orders forbade shelling or bombing into Florence in deference to the presence of so many priceless art treasures within the city. The famous old bridge, the Ponte Veccio was a short distance upstream from the battalion position and it was in an easily fordable part of the river. On the night following their arrival a patrol was sent over the ford to find out whether the Germans were preparing anything untoward, such as a crossing in some strength over the bridge. To ensure the safe return of the patrol, a tank was placed to cover their withdrawal, which turned out to be necessary as the patrol suffered several casualties.

Before leaving the Arno front, Budge succumbed to his curiosity by going up river past the Ponti Veccio to have a look at a small but interesting castle, or palazzo, perched on top of a steep little hill. He climbed up to the door and was admitted to find a lady, who appeared to be of some consequence and was in fact an American-born baroness and was very friendly to this Canadian officer. Budge recounted the gist of his conversation with her: "She told me that the German army commander had been sharing her home, but the 'nasty Nazi man' had up and left her. She professed great hatred for the Germans and brightened when she produced a pair of German 'donkey ears' binoculars, rather like twin telescopes. Through them she pointed out a large house on a hill some distance beyond the city, in which her recently departed guest was now living. She asked 'Could the brave Canadesi do something about it?' A medium artillery regiment F.O.O. was found, invited to use the donkey ears—and quickly did the deed. The big house was no longer and hopefully the 'nasty Nazi' had gone with it. The lady was very happy and I was free to go back to work."

At about this time Nancy returned to Canada. She had remained with the Lines family where she was very happy, but knowing the perils of remaining in the London area, Henry was still trying to persuade her that it was time to return home. His leave had been confirmed from mid-July to early October and he had arranged a cabin for her. He knew the only thing that would convince her was to hear it directly from Budge and he placed a telephone call through to Italy. Budge was intercepted by a dispatch rider as he was leading his regiment up to the Arno and in a short time spoke to both his father and Nancy. He was able to finally convince her that she would not be letting him down by returning to Canada.

Budge was still writing to Walter Lines about employment possibilities in his toy manufacturing company and outlining ideas for North American representation. He realized that he was perhaps being audacious, but in part it was precipitated by the thought that he did not wish to return to a $125 a month job 'pen pushing' as a glorified office boy at H. Bell-Irving & Co. His audacity paid off—a few weeks later he had a positive response from Walter Lines himself, who told Budge:

"I would like to tell you that we have had a talk with a world renowned sporting goods company, whose views are on similar lines to ours in regard to the U.S. and Canada. As far as you are concerned we would have the utmost confidence in your energy and trustworthiness. In any case, after further consideration I can say that Lines Bros. would be prepared to give you a run for a year on a guaranteed salary."

Budge admitted that it seemed strange to be thinking of the future again after living from day to day for so long, but the news of Nancy's return to Vancouver gave him a wonderful boost which added to a job that he was enjoying immensely. He frequently told Nancy that she must not worry on his account. Now he no longer had to worry about the dangers she had faced in England. He felt a sense of relief and implored her likewise to relax and enjoy herself.

His battalion, relieved from the Florence Line, moved eastwards to the Adriatic coast from where there was a continuous move northwards. The enemy were intent on holding the Gothic line, which they had begun to construct as early as the fall of 1943 from just north of Pesaro on the Adriatic, to south of Spezia on the Ligurian coast. An area 12 miles in depth was prepared with minefields, bridge and road demolitions and the installation of obstacles such as anti-tank ditches. Completion was delayed as other priorities came and went and even as the Allies took Florence there were gaps in the line's progress.

General Alexander next carried out a feinting move in the western sector, with ostentatious preparations by the Fifth Army. He had lost seven divisions to the forces amassing in the Mediterranean for the invasion of southern France in early August and yet was still able to outwit the German 10th Army's senior commanders at the Adriatic end of the Gothic line. Some had taken leave and those remaining behind blithely assured Field Marshal Kesselring that there were no new developments.

The first phase of the attack was to cross the Metauro River at midnight on August 25, beginning with an artillery barrage in support of the first wave of troops. They were unopposed in their first objectives and in fact the artillery barrage caught several German units on the move. Budge's immediate objective was Mount San Giovanni which his unit took at about midnight on the 26th, then pressed on to the next summit, Mount Marino. He sent one company around Mount San Giovanni to come from the rear while two other companies pressed on to take the defenders of Mount Marino at bayonet point. According to the unit war diarist they found seven horses and eight Germans alive to be taken prisoner.

Pressing on towards the Gothic Line, the Loyal Edmontons next objective was the hill town of Monteciccardo. Resistance was stiffening by August 27 along the entire Canadian front as the enemy set up a defensive line that included Monteciccardo and the neighbouring town of Ginestreto. Colonel Nicholson wrote at some length on Budge's actions and eventual capture of the town in Volume II of *The Canadians in Italy*:

> "The bombing of Monteciccardo on its perch 1200 feet above sea-level by the Desert Air Force that afternoon, and an assault by the Edmontons that night seemed likely at first to give early possession of the town, but the overlong interval between the air and ground attacks gave the Germans time to re-occupy the village in force, as the Canadians learned to their cost through some twenty heated hours. When the Edmonton C.O., Lt.-Col. H.P. Bell-Irving, sent his first company in from the right flank at 01:30 hrs on the 28th, they found Monteciccardo apparently empty. About ten minutes later, however, they ambushed a company of Germans marching in to set up defences in the town. Fire from the quickly sited Bren guns of an Edmonton platoon accounted for an estimated 60 to 70 Germans and drove the rest of the shattered column to cover. This sudden rout down the narrow street seemed to have settled ownership, but only for a few minutes. The appearance of a tank which had followed the marching enemy changed the aspect of things. More Germans arrived and the Canadians, finding themselves engaged from several points, and in the face of the oncoming tank, withdrew to the ridge just outside the town.
>
> An attack put in during the afternoon aided by tanks of the 145th Regt, Royal Armoured Corps, drove the enemy back to the western edge of the town where a ruined monastery made a stubborn fortress and resisted a violent artillery bombardment. Not until late evening did a third attack succeed."

(The action cost Budge 64 casualties and he remembers it as 'not a happy show'—though determination won the day.)

The Edmonton's main battle of the Gothic Line was the capture of Monte Luro on September 1 with support from the 12th Royal Tank Regiment. Budge has two particular memories, the first was the demonstration of Major Jim Stone's constant practice of taking over control of all supporting fire, making sure that it all functioned as planned. In the case of Monte Luro the support was tremendous. As well as an artillery barrage, provided by both New Zealand and British Field Artillery regiments, a squadron of rocket firing Typhoon fighters responded immediately to indicated targets.

Budge was sitting on the tank of the 12th Regiment's C.O., Lt.-Col. Van Straubenzee. They had an unimpeded view across the valley to the summit of Monte Luro. This extraordinary picture as seen by the two C.O.s on the hill-top tank, showed the Loyal Edmonton companies spread out one behind the other, "A" Company in V formation in front, marching towards the summit. The enemy guns in concrete emplacements were spotted, fired upon and usually silenced in turn, to make way for the advancing troops. The C.O.'s tank was hit by a shell, which fortunately failed to penetrate though Col. Van Straubenzee was rendered unconscious. He was moved out and Budge took over his command radio. He made a quick recovery and was soon back in command. As soon as the Edmontons gained the summit, Budge took off in a jeep to join them—and drove into a hidden gun-pit. From there he made it to the top on foot. There was an intricate system of deep trenches with several machine-gun positions, but it did not save the defenders and only four prisoners were taken. Budge was amazed to find in a house at the summit a springer spaniel who seemed none the worse for wear despite the ordeal of battle. He immediately adopted the dog and christened him 'Monte.'

On September 3rd came the Loyal Edmonton's last engagement before a brief rest; the capture of Fanano with help again from the 12th Royal Tank Regiment. By now the Gothic Line had been firmly breached and the enemy pushed several miles beyond to the Conca River. Here Field Marshal Kesselring ordered his 10th Army to form another defence line. His 4th Parachute Regiment had taken the brunt of the Allies' push and reported casualties of more than 70%.

In due course Cattolica, a coastal fishing village was captured. It was an ideal location with a sandy beach and was very quickly designated as a rest area for the battle-weary troops. As Budge put it: "Cattolica by the Sea; first-class food and lodging for all ranks. A well-earned rest." Monte the spaniel enjoyed the rest and followed Budge everywhere, including church parades.

While at Cattolica Budge had a caravan custom-built for himself. A bed was placed across the end nearest the cab, to double as a couch. Along the starboard side was a long desk with drawers and a small liquor cupboard. On the port side was a long sofa with a space for a big map above it. The caravan was built onto a Canadian truck chassis and immediately behind the cab was a generator providing power for the lights, radio and telephone communication to Brigade H.Q. and the companies. Total blacking-out of doors and windows allowed good lighting inside; there was adequate space and comfort for up to ten visitors, making it an excellent place for an "O" Group. The caravan was quite often far forward, but almost always tucked behind a stone building or other good protection.

Meetings with the other brigade C.O.'s took place in it and on one occasion included Lt.-Col. Ross of the Gunners. Here they completed the final details of a 'language' between the infantry and the F.O.O.'s, down to platoon commanders and back, or directly to the guns. A map was created to be distributed to all concerned to show area targets in colour, as well as with numbers. This meant that if a company, or platoon advancing in an attack was under fire from enemy guns or mortars in a discernible position, the message might go back to the guns: "Target 16 at 3 o'clock engage mortars. Will report shot." Under other circumstances the message might be "Target Yellow—cease firing."

A 'rolling barrage' has its place in an attack but it also had serious deficiencies. Unless it stayed accurately ahead of the advance it could have disastrous results for the troops it was meant to support. Budge suspects that the concept has been better developed—or perhaps thrown out all together in the half century or so since that meeting in the caravan.

The Commander-in-Chief, General Sir Oliver Leese, was very pleased with the overall progress of the campaign, particularly the part played by the Canadians. He told them: "It would have been a difficult and expensive task to capture the line if the enemy had had the time to occupy it properly. It is therefore very much to the credit of the leading divisions that by aggressive patrolling and quick follow-up they 'gate-crashed' the enemy." He also singled out Major-General Hoffmeister for praise: "A great deal of our success was due to the energy and daring of this commander and his Division."

There was no reason why the momentum of the campaign should not see the Allies sweeping onto the Lombardy Plain, which would take them well into Northern Italy. A breakthrough over the last foot-hills of the Apennines would bring them to Rimini, which General Leese saw as the hinge on which the German withdrawal from Italy would swing.

Perhaps he under-estimated the desperation of Field-Marshal Kesselring, who hastily brought in the 26th Panzer Division and the 29th Panzer Grenadier Division from other parts of the front, along with units of the 100th Mountain Division. They formed the next line of defence—the Rimini Line.

Kesselring used these units to his advantage on the last remaining spurs and ridges separating the Allies from the flat ground so tantalizingly close. It slowed their momentum and delayed the capture of Rimini, which took eighteen days, from September 3rd to the 22nd.

A crucial objective was the Coriano Ridge, involving several units of the 1st Canadian Corps. It displayed the desperate tenacity of the German defenders but despite their efforts the ridge fell on September 13. The Canadians were joined by the 3rd Greek Mountain Brigade which ironically, in view of their training, were kept to the coastal approach to Rimini.

(Throughout the Italian campaign the composition of the 1st Canadian Infantry Division under Major-General Vokes was as follows:
— 1st BRIGADE: The Royal Canadian Regiment: The Hastings and Prince Edward Regiment: 48th Highlanders of Canada.
— 2nd BRIGADE: The Seaforth Highlanders of Canada: The Princess Patricia's Canadian Light Infantry: The Loyal Edmonton Regiment.
— 3rd BRIGADE: Royal 22e Regiment: The Carleton and York Regiment: The West Nova Scotia Regiment.
Over the next stage of the Campaign these units fought so closely together that there was often little separation between them, especially at San Martino and on the San Fortunato ridge.)

On a low, elongated rise on the coastal plain, four miles south of Rimini was Lorenzo-in-Correggiano, another tenaciously held position. In the pre-dawn of the 15th it was attacked by the West Nova Scotia Regiment supported by the 12th Royal Tank Regiment. The attack failed and a second one with tank reinforcements took until 18:30 hours to secure the badly battered village. Throughout the day, from their positions on the higher San Fortunato Ridge to the north, the Germans took a heavy toll, killing all the officers of one West Nova Scotia company.

The final objective at the north end of this rise was the very small village of San Martino (code-named "Kestrel"). It was cleared except for a small group of enemy dug in on a spur who held on so tenaciously that several units were engaged in trying to remove them. The situation was more precarious than was realized, for through faulty liaison, the Royal 22e Company (the Vandoos) was withdrawn before a relieving Seaforth company had taken over. Quick to seize the opportunity, a German parachute unit, assisted by artillery from the San Fortunato Ridge soon regained the village.

To retake San Martino, occupied companies of both the Seaforths and the Patricias. Open ground surrounding the village aided in pinning down these units so successfully that several planned attacks were delayed by agreement between the C.O.s and the brigade commander. Shelling and mortar bombing was still coming from San Fortunato Ridge, which gave the Germans full surveillance to the south and east. Its early capture was essential. Between the steep sides of "Kestrel" and San Fortunato were the nearly dry Ausa River, a road and a railway.

Moving forward from Cattolica, Budge received the following order: "The Seaforths fighting on the 'Kestrel' ridge will have taken it. You are to take the Edmontons through the Seaforths, down and across the Ausa River, then up to capture and hold a strong position across the flat top of the San Fortunato Ridge."

As the Edmontons approached "Kestrel" it became evident that the Seaforths had not taken it and were in fact still heavily engaged with the enemy paratroopers and at the same time under heavy fire from the San Fortunato Ridge. Budge made a decision that under these circumstances it would not be practical to mount the attack by going through the current heavy fighting on San Martino. He changed the plan to bypass "Kestrel" on the left, into the 3rd Brigade area, thence down to the Ausa and upwards to attack the crest of San Fortunato.

When General Vokes heard about Budge's change of plan, displaying some anger he ordered an immediate stop, but somehow or other the order got lost and this vital ridge was secured from San Fortunato village to San Lorenzo in Monte. Budge credits this success to the initiative displayed by his regiment:

> "With no further orders from their 'temporary' C.O., imbued with their regiment's fighting spirit, motivated by gallantry and an exceptional performance by every man, the 'Eddys' took and held their objective across the top of the San Fortunato Ridge. In the fight for this ridge the Loyal Edmonton Regiment added a well deserved second Battle Honour in the Italian Campaign."

Among the C.O.'s memories of that battle were:

"First of all, in a position by the Aussa River, from which could be seen some German tanks at the top of the hill, was the never to be forgotten sight of Major Frank MacDougall, the senior major, leading his company in single file, straight up the ridge. The Regimental History tells us that this gallant major captured the first German he met by unarmed combat.

Captain John Duggan won a well-deserved M.C. that day for taking one of the positions on the ridge under difficult circumstances and much needed tenacity.

Where some Nebelwerfer (moaning minnies) shells fell at this river-side position they set fire to a barn and a few other buildings, but there were no casualties.

A British Tank Corps officer, no doubt supporting the 3rd Brigade, not unreasonably declined an invitation to take a tank or two up the hill to meet the enemy Tigers visible at the top. Seen from his point of view, after surviving the fierce battle with Rommel in North Africa not many months before, a likely suicide at this juncture did not sit well. Very sadly, just a few minutes later this no doubt fine officer was seriously wounded by a nearby shell-burst.

Then the 'one and only' Big Jim Stone seeing a job to be done, on his own initiative hitched a 6 pounder anti-tank gun behind a soft skinned 15 cwt truck and drove it up the hill himself—'dam the Tigers.' As he made his way up, 'Stoney's' first D.S.O. was in the making."

Budge's other recollection covered an incident that would have far-reaching consequences. He had just established his Tactical H.Q. in a house at the top of the ridge when a Tiger tank went past the window. Following the tank was a column of enemy infantry. When they were out of sight some Hawkins grenades and anti-tank mines were laid out on the road and made as unobtrusive as possible. Soon the tank returned, the new occupants of the house as yet unnoticed. One of the Hawkins grenades blew a track off, right in front of the window. Sergeant Powell's section fired a PIAT bomb at close range, hitting something attached to the tank's exterior, with little damage. A second bomb scored a direct hit on the heavy frontal armour, exploded and penetrated the metal, killing all inside the tank. While rifle fire scattered the enemy infantry, with this newly-found knowledge the 'dead' Tiger was, for a few minutes, used for further target practice for the PIAT.

Yard by yard the San Fortunato Ridge was taken. The Seaforths, relieved from their "Kestrel" engagement when the paratroopers were finally dislodged, were now moving to the right of the Edmontons to clear the top towards Rimini. The Patricias then came though and carried down the north-western slopes forward to the Marecchia river. The capture of San Fortunato was a decisive point in the Northern Italian Campaign. The enemy were seen streaming north towards the Marecchia and were now the recipients of deadly fire made accurate by the uninterrupted views from the ridge, from which it was possible to see far into the Romagna Plain.

On the afternoon of September 20, a limited resistance mounted by the 29th Panzer Grenadier Division in the village of Monticello enabled the withdrawal to continue. It was aided by an unusually early deluge of the expected autumn rains. Despite the worsening weather, by late on the 21st the Patricias had secured a bridge-head well north of the Marecchia.

Rimini fell to the Greek Brigade, fighting with New Zealanders placed under the command of Colonel Tsakalotos. It was another example of the tremendous goodwill between the diverse groups making up the various brigades and divisions of the 8th Army. They had suffered together and the casualty figures bore this out. In the weeks from August 25 to September 22, the 1st Canadian Infantry Division lost 626 officers and men, killed or wounded.

On September 23, the 2nd Canadian Infantry Brigade were pulled out for a rest, once more to Cattolica. Within the Edmonton's objective some fine looking horses had been discovered, along with some fist-class tack of appropriate quality for officers' chargers. This was an opportunity for Budge and his 2i/c to acquire two fine mounts. Arrangements were made with one of the supporting services to feed and groom the 'conscripted' horses.

When the Edmontons were relieved from the battlefield they were to march down the coastal highway back to Catollica. It was perhaps an unusual sight in WW II to see the C.O. mounted on a bay mare, renamed Molly, riding at the head of his marching column. A number of empty 8th Army trucks were travelling south along the road and the well-trained Molly stopped each one in turn to be fully loaded with 'Eddy' soldiers. After they were safely in camp, the C.O. arrived, now leading from the rear, 'like the famed Duke of Platzitoro!'

This second visit to Cattolica did much to rehabilitate and rejuvenate—a valuable contributor to the continued high morale of the Loyal Edmonton Regiment. Jim Stone's horse was a big chestnut and he and Budge frequently rode along the sands, enjoying an early morning gallop. The Adriatic was still not too cold for a swim and away up the coast, on another beach a large number of figures similarly undressed could likewise be seen swimming; German soldiers enjoying a brief rest from battle too.

By October 6, a change of command had taken place. Brigadier Gibson called Lieut.-Col. Bell-Irving for a private meeting. The present Seaforth C.O., Syd Thomson, was returning to the U.K. to a staff job as a full colonel (He eventually became C.O. of the Black Watch—the Royal Highland Regiment of Canada). Major D.M. Clark, the Seaforth 2 i/c was in hospital with jaundice and a new C.O. was imperative at that point in the campaign. Would Budge be willing to return to the Seaforth Highlanders of Canada as C.O.? The response was an immediate "Yes," especially with the added good news that Major James Riley Stone was at last to be given command of the Loyal Edmonton Regiment.

As soon as possible after that meeting Budge went to 5 Division H.Q. where he had a private discussion with General Hoffmeister—both with their 'metaphorical' Seaforth bonnets on. Soon there was a change of command at Brigade level. Brigadier Gibson also returned to England to be succeeded by Lieut.-Col. M.P. (Pat) Bogert, D.S.O., a first-class officer from the West Nova Scotia Regiment. In the opinion of all 2nd Brigade commanding officers, his promotion was well deserved.

In a letter to Nancy, Budge told her, "Stoney, though he doesn't know it yet, assumes command of this regiment when he returns from leave in Rome tonight. My three months with the unit have been a wonderful experience. As the character of the regiment differed so greatly from my own, I have learned a great deal. I like to think that perhaps the regiment may also have profitted in a small way from my tour of command. I cannot disguise my great pleasure in once more putting on the tartan, in command of the regiment which has been so much a part of my life for so many years. It's like going home after a wonderful trip abroad..."

Jim Stone returned from his short leave to be warmly greeted by Budge with, "James Riley Stone, this first-class battalion is all yours now, at long last, and so well deserved. I leave it to you to break the good news to your soldiers, who I am sure will be filled with joy at the news. Thank you for your magnificent support. I am now returning to my Seaforths, but in the hope that we can remain life-long friends."

Budge removed the pips from his epaulettes and placed them under Major Stone's crowns. He commented to Nancy "From private to colonel in one war is no mean effort. One can imagine the exultation of every man in the regiment when they learned that they were to get their own 'Big Jim' in command at long last."

There had been a turnover of officers and other ranks in the Seaforths in Budge's absence and men who joined the battalion at Ortona were now considered old-timers. He remembered one or two, especially Bob Peebles. Sergeant Peebles was a splendid man, always at his best in close contact with the enemy. As soon as he came out of the line he became bored and usually had too much to drink. Paraded in front of Budge he inevitably lost one or two of his stripes, until such time as he made good on his "Please sir, I'll never do it again." Twice wounded, Bob came home safely at war's end and remained an active member of the Seaforth Association for many years.

One of Budge's first actions on rejoining the Seaforths was to give prompt attention to the PIAT, after the successful target practice on the San Fortunato Tiger. It has already been mentioned that the PIAT bomb was designed to concentrate almost all its explosive power exactly on the percussion fuse protruding from the front-centre of the bomb, so that a direct hit squarely on a tank's armoured casing would penetrate with lethal effect. A hit on any of the exterior attachments would dissipate this power, so obtaining a sight on the bare armour was vital even though it presented a small target area at best. The engagement on San Fortunato proved to Budge that the range of a PIAT was not the 300 hundred yards claimed in the manual, but about 20 feet—a range in which the necessary accuracy could be achieved. The PIAT man had to know his weapon and be well trained in its use. He had also to be imbued with the knowledge that aggressive infantrymen are a tank's worst enemy.

The danger of metal pieces flying back from a direct hit required an armoured steel shield. Budge designed a light steel band approximately 24 inches by 2" wide to be attached at the top of the PIAT, with both sides curved to form a narrow shield. A minimum aiming gap of about half an inch was provided between the shield and the firer's helmet. This attachment was made in a workshop, tested, proved satisfactory and adopted.

The infantry 6 pounder anti-tank guns were too frequently useless because of the difficulties of getting them into suitable firing positions. It was soon evident that an independent tank-hunting platoon armed with Hawkins anti-tank grenades to blow the track off, PIATs to destroy it at point blank range and the Thompson sub-machine gun to combat the enemy infantry could, in combination, be of great value.

The Seaforths put such a platoon together and after some initial training its value became so self-evident that the brigadier instructed the other two battalions to do likewise. Soon all three tank-hunting platoons were ready to be tested in action. The three 2nd Brigade C.O.s came to an agreement that the first Tank-Hunting Platoon to kill a Panther or Tiger tank would get a week's leave in Rome with their own platoon truck for transport.

While the 2nd Brigade had been resting, Sir Oliver Leese was replaced by Lieut.-General Sir Richard McCreery as 8th Army C-in-C. He was just as seasoned, having commanded the 10th British Corps from the time of the Salerno landing. The 1st Canadian Division resumed action on October 14. Following a move north to Riccione it took over from the 56th British Division. The rains had begun in earnest and there was considerable flooding on the flatter ground now being fought over, requiring much bridging by Engineer units. Several times major offensives were cancelled and replaced by limited 'wet weather' objectives. The weather gave the enemy time to regroup and stiffen their rearguard, though they lost some of this opportunity when the new British C-in-C moved his advance onto their more vulnerable left flank.

Orders came to Budge on the 16th to advance to the banks of the Pisciatello River (the Rubicon of Caesar's time). Here, hidden by trees the battalion waited. While Budge was holding an "O" Group the new battalion Medical Officer arrived. Captain J.C. Portnuff introduced himself and sat down. To end the orders, as was normal, the C.O. defined a location for the regimental aid post (R.A.P.). The doctor went off to find it and came back soon afterwards to tell Budge that he had found what he considered a better location—an early indication of an independent mind.

The enemy were obviously aware of the Seaforth's presence, as they were shelling the area from time to time. While one company was having a meal in an empty building it received a direct hit and there were several casualties. Budge went to the house to ascertain the situation and found the new M.O. on one end of a stretcher removing a wounded man. Following them to the R.A.P. he was very pleased to find it well organized. The reason for the shelling was a supporting British tank on the road close by and every time it moved, more shells were fired at the location.

On the 20th, Budge received further orders from Brigade H.Q. to cross the Pisciatello and proceed towards the Savio, a river whose winding course followed a route more north and south than most rivers so far encountered. The thrust of the advance would veer westward to cross the river. Arriving within sight of the river, Budge went forward to recce the lay of the land and found at San Martorano, within 500 yards of the river a church in which he set up his Tac H.Q. He hoped the cellar would offer reasonable protection. The location provided easy access to the river while the tower provided a wide view across it to the land beyond. A disadvantage was the fact that it was a most obvious artillery target.

In the ensuing battle the church tower was, regrettably, destroyed and with it the opportunity to observe enemy activity. The movements of H.Q. staff were extremely precarious during its occupation, but by a miracle there were no casualties. Both the Tac H.Q. and the R.A.P. managed to carry on in spite of the horrendous experience of being a desirable target for enemy guns.

A reconnaissance party of Engineers left Tac H.Q. to check the route to the crossing. As they neared the bank three members of the party were wounded by Schu (anti-personnel) mines. Shortly afterwards a shell killed the officer in charge. The two survivors made their way back to the church for help, and warned Budge that the mines were so thickly sown and so well concealed in the mud that it was almost impossible to locate them.

M.O. Captain Portnuff volunteered to go and render what aid he could. He gave aid to one engineer before a second mine exploded nearby. Mud and fragments struck him in the face, temporarily blinding him. He groped his way out of the minefield, his face bloody, got back to the R.A.P. where his medical sergeant treated him and helped clean his eyes. Dr. Portnuff refused to be evacuated until a relief M.O. arrived.

During this time Budge wrote out a citation for a Military Cross for the doctor, who was to survive the war to become Professor J.C. Portnuff, M.C., M.D., at a famous university in California. To this day, in the Seaforth regimental family he is, and always will be, affectionately known as "Joe the Mo."

The Savio crossing commenced with "B" and "D" companies first, one on each side of the toehold still held by the Patricias on the far bank. At that point the river depth was about waist high. The steep, muddy banks were a considerable obstacle to soaking wet soldiers with their weapons, but they got ashore and pressed on to their objective.

By 23:30 hours the two forward companies had made sufficient progress to permit "A" and "C" companies to cross the river, which they did at about 01:00 hrs on the 22nd. As they crossed over, the October rain fell incessantly, causing the river to rapidly reach flood proportions. Despite the appalling conditions, all four companies were now engaged, each in its own battle. The regimental signallers wrestled with their sodden equipment to keep in touch with Tac H.Q. One of them, Private Carrington, was awarded the M.M. for repairing a No. 18 set while lying exposed to enemy fire in an open field to get the best reception. Budge said of that day's achievements: "The complete success in widening the battalion's bridgehead, with a large number of enemy killed or captured was a tribute to the skill, determination and guts of the company, platoon and section commanders, plus every single one of their men. This especially applied to 'C' Company's tank hunting platoon, which became involved in one of the finest little battles of the campaign."

By close to 04:00 hrs, "C" Company, led by Major Stu Lynch had reached Pieve Sestina, a very small village at a road junction. Because of the foul weather and the supporting artillery, the enemy occupants kept their heads down and were captured with very little resistance. A defensive position was set up, with a total company strength of barely fifty men including the tank-hunting platoon, under Sergeant K.P. Thompson. There were as yet no tanks, guns, or any vehicles across the river, as the floodwater had prevented them crossing. The only defence against a tank attack was the tank-hunting platoon. Thompson deployed his men so as to trap and destroy any approaching armour. Setting a string of Hawkins grenades across the road junction he deployed the PIAT groups to cover the most likely approaches.

Half an hour later a counter-attack began with a force consisting of four Panther tanks, two self-propelled guns and about thirty infantrymen. The first Germans to arrive were an officer and his driver in a Volkswagen staff car. They were quickly killed, though the officer managed to shout to the driver immediately behind him.

One of the self-propelled guns appeared, to be stopped when its tracks hit a Hawkins grenade. It was finished off by PIAT bombs and hand grenades tossed into the open hatch. As Sgt Thompson moved about encouraging his men and re-siting weapons as needed, a Panther tank appeared. Private E.A. (Smoky) Smith of the tank-hunting platoon had taken one of the PIATS and two men to a position in a nearby field where it could best be deployed. He left one man there and returned for a second weapon to take on the approaching tank from a ditch, when it opened fire with a machine gun, wounding Smith's comrade.

Smith's next action, as confirmed later, destroyed the tank with the PIAT and killed or wounded many of the dozen infantrymen who were riding on it, moving into the road immediately in front of the tank to do so. The remaining enemy soldiers finally withdrew. The tank-hunting platoon lost five men and several were wounded including Sgt Thompson, but he was able to carry on. The combined initiative displayed by the PIAT platoon resulted in the destruction of both self-propelled guns and two of the tanks. The third was abandoned in a deep ditch from which it could not get out and the fourth was captured intact.

By now all the companies were low on ammunition, including PIAT bombs and it became urgent to establish a river crossing to replenish much needed stores. Budge's 2 i/c, Major "Ollie" Mace ensured that these were made ready to transport across at the earliest possible moment. At midnight on the 22/23 a raft was made available and Mace guided it across, then personally directed distribution. The raft also carried a jeep and two anti-tank guns. On the 24th a pontoon bridge was put in place and larger items were taken across and the wounded brought out.

Budge received the following message from General McCreery:

"My best congratulations on your gallant and successful action in the night crossing of the Savio River under most difficult conditions. Stop. The maintenance and enlargement of your bridgehead in the face of armoured counter-attack shows determination and skill of the highest degree. Stop. Your part in this attack has made a decisive contribution to the army plan. Stop."

Budge recognized the last sentence in that signal as a quotation from King's Regulations and Orders as a qualification for the awarding of a Victoria Cross. Budge went forward without delay to Major Lynch's area to find the appropriate recipient for a V.C. citation. As he approached Pieve Sestina it was only just getting daylight and there was still a little desultory small-arms fire. Once again his immediate reaction was, "Oh, why don't I have a camera?" The church appeared to be intact together with the building behind it. In front was a modest sized lawn largely covered by neat rows of German crosses from an earlier engagement. A tank was still burning, the ditched one was obviously beyond easy recovery, the self-propelled guns were twisted wrecks—only the one Panther was intact and awaited its new owners.

After offering hearty congratulations to Major Lynch and having a lengthy talk with Sgt Thompson, Budge privately decided that among this collection of undoubted heroes, 'Smoky' Smith would be his choice. He entered the barn building attached to the church. Inside were the men of the tank-hunting platoon, the battle forgotten. They had been three days without proper food, but at least were warm and dry. One man was distilling alcohol from a barrel and transferring it into bottles. It was Private John Stagliano, the platoon's bomb carrier. Barely twenty years old, up to this point in his army carcer he had been a self-confessed rebel.

This resentment came from his early treatment by the Canadian army because of his Italian background. Although born in Italy he was only three years old when brought to Canada. When the war came he was a mere sixteen year old but was classed as an alien and had to report monthly to the R.C.M.P. Despite this, in 1941 he joined the Duke of Connaught's Own Rifles militia, but was still not acceptable to the Canadian Army until 1943, when he was conscripted. He was immediately placed into the 'Zombie' (conscript) army. After this, John became a radical:

> "At that age I didn't care. I never did anything criminal but was thought a smart-arse. I was finally interviewed by the C.O. and I told him I wished to go on active service. He saw that I meant it and set the wheels in motion for me. I was finally sent overseas when Italy capitulated."

Stagliano joined the Seaforths on June 11, 1944 immediately after the Hitler Line when Syd Thomson was C.O. After a couple of months he was pulled out of the line when a group of partisans were to be interrogated and he was asked to interpret. When Budge took over as C.O. he wished to return to action, especially to join the tank-hunting platoon. Told he couldn't, his answer was, "Yes I can. You asked for volunteers and you can't refuse me." At barely twenty he became a member of the platoon, carrying the heavy PIAT bombs and thirty-year old 'Smoky' became like a father to him. Now they had achieved the colonel's objective of knocking out a tank in accordance with the inter-battalion bet.

Entering the barn, Stagliano had spotted the still and immediately set it up. They all knew that distilling was strictly illegal and there were frequent reminders of the dire consequences if anyone was caught making wine or spirits. When Budge appeared, without batting an eyelid 'Smoky' said,

> "Hey Junior, get the colonel a drink." Stagliano recalled "There was I stripped to the waist by the fire making the alcohol and I poured a glass then offered it to the C.O.
>
> He never put us on orders for making it and he drank it along with us. The stuff was not refined or diluted and was almost 100% alcohol. I had produced just about enough to make about a 26 oz bottle. You could actually put some in a saucer and stick a match to it and see a little blue flame—that's how potent it was. It would burn all the way down your throat!
>
> I handed this drink to Budge and he downed it without flinching. How he got it straight down, I don't know. It took a lot of guts to not show any reaction. I must say he is the one man who I ever saw do that.
>
> He just said, 'So this is where you are Stagliagno, how come you're no longer interpreting?' I told him I wanted to be with the boys. He asked, 'Would you like to come to B.H.Q. and carry on interpreting.' I told him as best I could my feelings on that and he said, 'Well, I need a batman, why don't you come back to B.H.Q.'
>
> He told us that we were going on leave to Rome so to think about it. We loaded the truck with anything we could beg borrow or steal to sell in Rome, because that was our pocket money. 'Smoky' convinced me to take up Budge's offer and I took the job."

Years later Budge reflected: "How could such a gang of splendid ruffians ever possibly lose a war? Stagliano became my batman and in due time 'Lord High Everything Else' of the caravan. He had more time to devote to his many other talents, especially his proficiency in Italian, a purposely kept secret that went well with his job. He accompanied me to the occasional Italian event and it was of some interest to me to know what they were really talking about. Whatever else, 'Smokey' had earned a spell away from the sharp end and I made him driver of my caravan until he was whisked away to England, bound for Buckingham Palace."

The Volkswagen was still intact and Budge drove it back over the new river crossing to return to Tac H.Q. to write up the citation for 'Smoky' with careful thought. Without delay, Budge took it to 8th Army H.Q. where he talked to Lt.-Col. The Lord Tweedsmuir, former "B" Company Commander of the Canadian Seaforths and, after a brilliant performance as C.O. of the Hastings and Prince Edward Regiment (the "Hasty P's") in Sicily, was now Canadian Liaison Officer to the C-in-C. The citation, with 8th Army approval, was taken back to Brigade H.Q. to go up through the proper channels. It confirmed 'Smoky's' "Dogged determination, outstanding devotion to duty and superb gallantry." Sergeant Thompson was awarded the Distinguished Conduct Medal (D.C.M.).

('Smoky' was born and raised in the City of New Westminster (the Royal Borough) and the reason he joined the Seaforth Highlanders of Canada instead of the Royal Westminster Regiment was that some of the latter's senior officers had been his school teachers! He joined the Seaforths in January 1941 and caught up with the battalion in southern England. Following the Sicily landing he had been twice wounded, in August 1943, just before crossing over the Strait of Messina and again in February 1944. When Budge had made his decision to recommend 'Smoky' for the V.C. he took him aside for a serious talk to remind him that this high award was in a sense for the battalion and, for the rest of his life he would have to be mindful of the honour bestowed and conduct himself accordingly. Over the years he has done just that and has represented Canada proudly many times at occasions worldwide, commemorating the 1st and 2nd World Wars.

In early 1945 he returned to Canada and assisted in the War Bond programme. During the Korean War, 'Smoky' was a recruiting sergeant as a member of the Black Watch (Royal Highland Regiment of Canada), although he rejoined with the intention of going to Korea as an active soldier. As owner of a travel business he has since travelled widely.)

By the time the battalion was withdrawn for a rest in the first few days of November, hundreds of German soldiers had been taken prisoner, once in an amusing incident. Fifty-six infantrymen, deciding it was time for breakfast converged on their H.Q. complete with mess-tins, only to find it had been over-run and was now the Seaforth "D" Company H.Q. They were given breakfast.

The Seaforths returned to the Riccione rest-camp. At the same time there was an announcement of thirty days leave back to Canada for a certain number among those who had been longest away from home. The Seaforth share was three 'winners', one of them Corporal Greig, a veteran of WW I. He was the sanitation corporal, an important and demanding job which he had always done with efficiency since the early training days in England. Not content with this responsibility, he could often be found with the stretcher-bearers collecting wounded, and worked tirelessly in the battalion R.A.P. Now, as a bachelor and a totally unselfish man, he gave this opportunity to another soldier who had a wife in Canada to return to. The British Empire Medal (B.E.M.) later given Corporal Greig was very well earned.

Budge always thought of him as one of a very special group of three. The other two were M.O. Captain Portnuff, M.C. and Honorary Major, the Rev. Roy Durnford. 'Joe the Mo' continued his unremitting care of the wounded long after his episode with the mine on the bank of the Pisciatello. Budge was soon to make sure that Padre Durnford's unique contribution to the battalion was properly recognized. These three outstanding men became known affectionately as the "Holy Trinity."

On November 4 the Seaforth Officers once again held their annual Passchendaele dinner. With the battalion's record of action to date in the Italian Campaign, there was an added significance in remembering the event that it honoured. It was the capture of Crest Farm by the 72nd Seaforths in the Battle of Passchendaele in November 1917. The C.O.'s of the 2nd Brigade and senior commander were all there to join in the commemoration. General Chris Vokes, sitting beside Budge, and knowing his man, told him of a very important corps operation in the planning stage—then asked him if he would be interested in leading it. Within a few days Budge was summoned to Corps H.Q. for a secret briefing and given the basic plan to study. A force of about 500 infantry of which the Seaforths might form a major part was to move up the coast by sea, and then move inland to a town to the north of Comacchio

Lakes, to seize and hold it. The town was astride the only escape road north through the lakes for the German forces. The final task of the special force would be to close off the escape route.

After a brief study of the plan Budge requested a sufficient number of DUKWS (amphibious troop carrying trucks) and landing-craft to carry them. His thoughts were: Plan "A"—DUKWS's swim off LC's and drive straight inland to take the town by surprise before daylight. Plan "B"—fight their way through if necessary (and if possible). Plan "C"—if passage by road became impossible, abandon vehicles and scatter, make for the target town and do best to hold it.

His force would have a small detachment of engineers and plenty of mines, but no field guns. They would be out of range of friendly guns from both land and sea. Air was probable, but not yet factored in. To assist in preparation and planning, Budge had Captain Robert MacDougall and one other officer join him, where they were 'wired' into a house in the Seaforth area to ensure privacy. Budge arranged for Major Scott Murdoch, now 2 i/c of the battalion to remain L.O.B. (left out of battle) to take over command of the battalion if necessary.

The proposed operation was given the code-name Operation "Chuckle"—a name that in itself might have suggested something untoward. Just one day before going south to Ancona to load the landing craft, with no steps yet taken to assemble the required components of the strike force, a signal came to cancel. It was said that the Navy was unable to land the force because of the mines in place off the landing beach. Budge's small planning group decided that two or three days in Rome might be a suitable way to celebrate the welcome prospect of a "future life".

A rumour later circulated that someone, sometime, found a young lady in Rome who knew about Operation "Chuckle." She doubtless had a friend at Corps H.Q., but Budge had several thoughts in quick succession. Number one was, "What a terrible breach of security." His second thought was that perhaps Corps H.Q. had deliberately invented "Chuckle" to be leaked for the sole purpose of scaring the Germans into an early withdrawal. His third thought, reluctantly was, "Am I the biggest sucker in the 8th Army?" He did not think of this one soon enough to tackle Chris Vokes on this possibility.

From December 1 until almost Christmas, the Seaforths were engaged in some fierce fighting in the Battle of the Rivers; pushing the German forces across the Naviglio Canal, the Fosso Vecchio and, finally the Senio River. It was noted that Padre Durnford did outstanding work, not only in succouring the wounded and dying, but under intensive fire organized several stretcher parties, even using prisoners to help bring in men. In one instance "B" Company Commander, Stu Lynch advised him (backed up as an order from Budge) not to go forward. The Padre's reply was, "My orders come vertically, not horizontally." At a crucial collection point he found the ambulance broken down and organized a shuttle with the remaining vehicles while under fire, remaining until the last of the wounded was taken away.

On December 15 Budge was evacuated from the front with malaria and 2i/c Major Howarth Glendinning took temporary command. As Budge lay in his caravan bed, sweating profusely a shell landed almost under the vehicle, but failed to go off. He was taken to a field dressing station, tested for malaria, pronounced clear and told to return to his unit. Then an orderly asked if his temperature had been taken. The answer was no. It was done—and read 106 degrees! He was evacuated to the general hospital at, by coincidence Loreto on the Adriatic coast, from which his old school was named. He took one or two pipers with him and some whisky for the benefit of Seaforths already hospitalized there.

By the time he returned to the unit it was Christmas and Captain Borden Cameron, the battalion Quartermaster had been making preparations for some time. Geese, turkeys and pigs were collected, sometimes by bartering, sometimes when they 'followed' a platoon member back to his dugout or, where necessary by outright purchase from a farmer. It was not until the 27th that Christmas was celebrated, after they had been pulled from the front-line to the town of Russi. (See Appendix 10)

It was a clear, cold day and the decorated townhall was large enough to take one company at a time to sit down to a full dinner with all the trimmings followed by Christmas pudding with rum sauce and mince pies. The pipe-band performed and the officers and sergeants were kept busy from noon until eight with serving their troops. One of Budge's more pleasant duties was to pin an MBE ribbon on Borden Cameron.

The battalion rested until early in the new year when, at a Brigade "O" Group Budge learned that they were to attack a German pocket on the east side of the Senio, which included the towns of Cotignola and Granarola. The Patricias were to attack over the Naviglio Canal with a supporting artillery barrage to set up a bridgehead south of Granarola. The Seaforths orders were to cross the canal to the right of the bridgehead in four successive phases, with precision timing, to swing behind the town and move towards the next canal, the Fosso Vecchio. Budge ordered "D" Company forward, under A/Major Don Duncan, followed by "Ollie" Mace's "A" Company. Both ran into resistance, but "D" Company managed to capture intact a self-propelled gun and its crew.

"B" Company commander, Major Tony Staples, headed for their farmhouse objective just as an outbuilding was hit by shellfire. He reported that in the confusion it was difficult to tell friend from foe. Reaching the farmhouse he went upstairs to see if it would do as an observation post. Standing near a blown-out window was a huge German signalling across the canal. Staples later reported: "In true wild-west style I yanked out my pistol and let fly—missing him by a yard. Fortunately for me he was so surprised he fell from the opening and broke his leg."

Soon Staples was hit and saved by the action of one of his corporals. At the R.A.P. he was visited by the Assistant Adjutant, Captain John Bassett, who relayed the situation to Budge. John Bassett, who later became an important figure as a Canadian media tycoon was a captain on the junior staff at Corps H.Q. and had been sent to the battalion for some regimental experience at the sharp end. Budge made him assistant adjutant, but when the situation with "B" Company was learned, he ordered Bassett to go forward and take command. Recalling the final few yards endured by the new company commander, he commented:

> "The last crawl to reach the company H.Q. was no doubt a useful contribution to his military education. C.S.M. McKim greeted him warmly, gave him a slug of rum and they were in business. A short time later John was on the 'blower' to me to report that several German tanks were approaching and what should he do? My response, 'For Heaven's sake don't let any of them escape!' He followed my orders so well that they beat the hell out of the Germans. Some time later I went forward to visit "B" Company and was moved to take off my crowns from my epaulettes and pin them onto John's, with the comment, 'A good start MAJOR Bassett. "B" Company is yours now. Do well with them—I am sure you will.' One could get away with that in those days."

By the evening of January 4, the Seaforths had successfully completed their action, had taken seventy-five prisoners with over sixty known killed or wounded and had captured five guns. One of the crews had been surprised in the course of a 'brew up.' From the end of this action the winter offensive was brought to a close, though not the end of the fighting. The main thrust was now towards the Senio River, several miles north of Ravenna. The weather had improved, with some frost and the ground was slightly harder, though still easily churned to mud. On the 19th the battalion met strong resistance while being supported by tanks of the B.C. Dragoons "A" Squadron. Resistance continued throughout the next day, but on the evening of the 20th the Germans were ordered to fall back to the Senio and take position on the north side of the dyked river.

The battalion reached the Senio and spread out over a 3000 yard front from which patrols were sent out towards the twenty foot-wide river dike that stretched across the farmland. The enemy were very much in evidence on the far side and occasionally sent patrols across the river, sometimes trying to re-occupy buildings. They were easily captured and yielded some useful information. Budge's instructions to his platoons were that they must patrol aggressively and with the enemy sometimes only thirty feet away on the other side of the dike, the contact became more personal. The Brigade Commander held an "O" Group and explained that the idea was to inflict as many casualties on the enemy as possible without employing extensive raiding.

Upstream on the left flank were the Loyal Edmontons. Downstream on the right flank was one troop belonging to a Royal Tank Corps unit. Just to the right on the other side of the dike was the village of Fusignano where just back from the river a tall building overlooked the Seaforth position. The battalion was deployed with two companies forward, in spaced slit trenches in a bank of the dike, connected by a footpath about 6'6" below the rim. Any head protruding above it (on either side) would be shot at immediately.

The remaining Seaforth companies, with the Tac H.Q. between them, were just far enough back for the supporting field artillery unit to be able to fire (in case the necessity arose) a predicted defensive fire plan with reasonable safety, between the forward and rear companies. This was feasible because Budge and Colonel Ross, the gunner C.O., trusted each other. With the Germans in such close proximity Budge was determined to have fun with this situation. He recalled:

"This period was more often hilarious than frightening—for our side. With frequent loud laughter the morale of the Canadians continued to rise, while that of the Germans was so obviously declining."

One day Budge was walking along the road towards "B" Company's position, opposite Fusignano, with John Bassett and the tank troop commander. He was giving Bassett a bit of a lecture on the constant need to dominate the enemy, when suddenly a burst of machine-gun fire was much too close for comfort. The tank officer's comment—from the bottom of a ditch—was memorable:

"D-do you thu-think they c-can see the sm-smoke f-from my p-pipe?"

Budge's next action was to send a message tied to a stone to be thrown, addressed to the German commander, saying that unless the tall building in Fusignano was vacated entirely, within twenty-four hours it would be destroyed by gunfire. The reply stated that it was used as a hospital with most patients unable to be moved. Above the signature was the salutation, "Heil Hitler." Budge's next communication to the German commander finished with "God save the King."

A very powerful sling shot was made from the fork of a tree and a piece of inner tube. A grenade with a seven second fuse was placed in the contraption, then it was stretched and released with the pin pulled. With a range of a hundred yards it would sail over into the enemy lines. Another device was named the 'Dagwood sandwich.' It consisted of one or two Hawkins anti-tank grenades tied to a Mills hand-grenade as the detonator and placed into a sandbag, which was then whirled around like a throwing hammer. It required a strong arm. Once there was a more comprehensive operation; a metal garbage can with a stack of mines in the centre was packed with a liberal volume from the contents of a latrine. With a detonator placed at the top, the lid was then wired shut. The garbage can was rolled up the bank, assisted by liberal use of the inevitable four letter adjective and let go down the other side where it went off with an enormous bang. A short silence then 'slosh-slosh', the sounds of a disgusting rainfall on the German side and hoots of laughter on the Seaforth side. There was reliable evidence that all these incidents led to a serious deterioration in enemy morale, causing their officers to apply force in restraining the troops from deserting.

There were several footbridges across the canal and the Seaforths had only been successful in destroying one of them, after three attempts, by means of floating a barrel of grenades under it. On the second attempt a too short fuse caused a huge cascade of water to pour over the pioneer platoon as they tried to float it in place. The remaining bridges needed extra vigil to guard them.

The Seaforths responded with great good humour to another of their C.O.'s and the Padre's capers. Budge explained:

> "To complete the picture it must be noted that soon after we took up position on the Senio, Padre Durnford added to his collection a large umbrella made of heavy silk with tassels around it, used by priests on certain formal occasions. With a small No. 16 wireless set under the umbrella he and I went out to the dyke rather audibly and ostentatiously for the sake of the 'audience', netting in to God. We would cover the whole front from one end to the other, saying good morning to the soldiers on duty in the slit trenches. Sometimes, when the top of the holy umbrella was seen above the rim of the dyke a 'potato-masher' grenade came over, bouncing off it to burst down below. I would take a Mills bomb off my belt, pull the pin and throw it over to the enemy's side. Amazingly, no one, at least on the Seaforth side, was ever hurt during this enjoyable morning caper.
>
> Roy Durnford was a deeply religious man, entirely capable of his personal motto 'Working to beat Hell', though he was not averse to the odd opportunity to even things up a bit in favour of the Protestants. He had acquired a rather heavy bell and when dared to ring it on the dyke, he of course immediately did so. It was worth at least two 'potato mashers.' That bell is still in the Seaforth Officers' Mess in Vancouver."

There was a brief respite from February 4 to the 10th when the battalion was pulled back once again, offering a well deserved rest. Just before they left the front, Budge learned through Division H.Q. that he had been awarded the Order of the British Empire. The citation read, in part:

> "Lieutenant-Colonel Bell-Irving has made a most outstanding contribution to the fighting success of the 1st Canadian Division in

his organization of a tank-hunting company within his battalion. It is trained to operate with assault companies, and to seek out and destroy enemy tanks in the area of the objective...

Throughout his long tour of active operations, Lieutenant-Colonel Bell-Irving has always displayed the same high qualities of leadership and initiative. The battalions he has commanded have reflected his efficiency and organizing ability. The successes achieved by the tank-hunting groups formed as a result of his forethought and tactical ability, have been a most outstanding contribution to the war effort."

On Valentine's day, the 14th, at the front once more, Budge paid a visit to the forward platoons and despite some mortaring back and forth there were only two minor casualties. His next offering to the Germans was a valentine card with a picture of a pretty girl on it, tied to a can of M&V (army meat and vegetables). The response, tied to a hammer, was three-fold: "We gave the M&V to our dog, who wouldn't eat it. Come on over; the girls here are better looking." And finally, "Why is that you are fighting against us and letting the Russians come into our old Europe?"

Suddenly, on February 24th, with a new battalion especially trained for the job, the Germans attacked. The Seaforths were shelled from the rear—because bends in the river actually put some of them behind the 2nd Brigade front. During the day, nearly all the buildings on the Seaforth's right flank were destroyed. In addition to radio communication, Budge always had phone wire laid throughout the battalion area. By noon all the phone-lines had been cut out. The first news of a renewed enemy attack came from the Edmonton's position. Budge was in a forward company H.Q. and called the platoon on the dyke by radio to ask if any Germans had come across there. The reply, in a true Scots brogue was: "Nae one comes thrroo herre wi'oot a pass." A few minutes later the voice added: "Wad ye send us up some passes noo Sirr!"

From across the span of fifty years the ferocity of the attack is still clear in Budge's mind: "And then they came—how well they had been trained for it. The first lot rolled fused anti-tank mines down over the dyke, virtually all of them missing the slit-trenched defenders. Next came the back-packed flammen werfers, the flame-throwers. The sight was truly horrendous but the Padre's great faith must have helped us as hardly anyone was burned. Then came the mob, the 'Poor Bloody

Infantry.' When the area between the four companies was sufficiently filled with Germans, our well prepared artillery defensive fire plan pretty well put an end to them. As well—just to make sure—our battalion's 3" mortars had been firing almost straight up in the air. Because we were in slit trenches while the Germans were standing up—or running, we got away with it. By morning there were no live Germans on the Seaforth side of the river and our casualties had been remarkably light, only about a dozen. The Seaforths had won their first truly defensive battle."

Unknown to them at the time, it was to be the battalion's last fight on Italian soil. They were relieved by the Mahratta Battalion of the Indian Army who were disappointed that the comfortable billets they had anticipated were now mainly rubble. A long drive back down the coast ended a few miles inland at the attractive small town of Offida, a great place for a well deserved, peaceful rest and providing even better billets than Cattolica. On February 28, the day after arriving, Budge was at the 2nd Brigade H.Q. and learned that it was to move to Northern Europe to aid in the fighting there. The 'rumour mill' had been working for some time and he could now put it to rest, but first he had another task.

Budge also learned at Brigade H.Q. that his citation for a D.S.O. for the Padre had been approved and he wished to make it a surprise. It was not just for the work he had done since landing in Sicily, with the exemplary conduct on the Senio bridgehead, or the 'capers' on the dyke that Budge had very special words for him. It was his entire devotion to his calling and to the men of the battalion. Budge explained: "The Padre was a man of God and a very dear friend to every man in the regiment. He was in a very real way the man of God most needed by a young man in the last minutes of his life, or a man about to go back into the attack with a letter in his pocket from his wife announcing that she is tired of waiting and has taken up with someone else. Roy Durnford never found it necessary to misbehave in any way to be one with the soldiers. He was always the model of goodness and understanding, adored by them all."

Budge phoned Battalion H.Q. and called for a parade later in the day that would include ALL ranks, with no exception. The 'rumour mill' was abuzz once more, but the surprise was complete. The diary of Honorary Major, the Rev. Roy Durnford, for that day read:

"Feb 28, Wed. Rise early as usual. Interviews and writing till noon. A big parade called. Whole battalion called out. Something secret they say. Burma? Curses, I hate big parades and have a lot to do anyhow. All arrive at the football ground—form a hollow square. What a church parade this would be.

The C.O. takes over after much ceremony. He begins to tell of Smokey Smith and his V.C. then says 'I have called you together to help me in presenting what constitutes a Padre's V.C.' [the award of a D.S.O. to Roy Durnford] My God! ME? Surely a mistake. He goes on talking. I hear none of it. I am dazed. My heart flutters like a bird pounding against the bars. Budge says 'I now call upon Major Durnford to come forward.' I heard it. I drop my gloves (thank heavens I left my stick on the wall just before). I march forward. God knows I felt every step was going to be the last. I salute. Budge grins and I advance still closer and he pins the ribbon on. 'Good work, Roy, it's a great honour for me to present this award and I am proud of you.'

I respond, 'Budge, am I dreaming this? I can't believe it's real.' I step back. He shakes my hand. I step back and salute (unnecessarily) again and return to my place, which seems an age away. 'Three cheers for the Padre' says the C.O. The roar was instantaneous. The parade falls out. This was what it was called for. THE WHOLE BATTALION FOR ME! What an honour. How undeserved too. Everyone shakes my hand and congratulates me. I am overwhelmed. I go back with the C.O. in jeep. The boys meet me at the Sally Ann and congrats are hearty and very sincere and universal.

I reach my cabin and weep there. Tonight I put on my kilt and after dinner the M.O., the C.O. and myself visit all companies at their parties. What a welcome I got—and what parties they were! This has been the greatest day of my life in or out of the army. The salute of brave men. I shall by God's help endeavour to be worthy of so great an honour. I wear it on behalf of all fallen heroes..."

Within the next few days Padre Durnford had an unwelcome visitor he was not to meet. All the adornments and memorabilia he had collected were stolen from his modest chapel-caravan. Budge said of this act:

"Knowing Roy, he quite possibly believed the 'Supreme Court in the Sky' thought the theft was justified, considering where many of the items had come from. I asked him to take my own rather more comfortable caravan, by land and sea to Belgium."

By this time the battalion knew about its next destination, to Northern Europe, via Leghorn to Marseilles in an assortment of craft. On March 6 they began the long drive across Italy to the embarkation point. As they passed over ground fought so hard for, Italian farmers were already ploughing the fields and tending to neglected vines.

CHAPTER NINE

ON MARCH 13, ALMOST 20 MONTHS after landing in Sicily the battalion loaded men and equipment onto American LCI. (L) and crossed the Mediterranean to Marseilles. Budge recalls a large Negro seaman practice firing his Oerlikon gun. When it jammed or misfired, one twist of his powerful wrist removed the barrel, which he threw overboard without a pause and replaced it with another. Another memory was the ward room. U.S. Navy ships being dry, 'wet' visitors were very welcome. Canadian soldiers were busy skinning their sailors with dice and a whole variety of card games.

The drive up through France, particularly in the south, was past an almost continuous line of assorted wrecked German vehicles, following the allied invasion from the Mediterranean. The convoy eventually came to rest in very pleasant Belgian countryside where billets were found in three small villages, Westmeerbeek, Houvenne and Ramsel. After a cold, wet miserable winter in Italy the billets in these towns were unbelievably comfortable and the villagers extremely hospitable. Roughly one in ten were given U.K. leave, fitted out smartly in the kilt. Others were given short leaves to Brussels or Paris.

Budge reclaimed his caravan which was parked in the driveway of an attractive country house, and also 'acquired' a large German open staff car, once the property of a senior officer. He had the cross of Lorraine painted boldly on one of the front fenders. On March 25 he took three of his officers, Majors Bassett and Thirwell and Captain

Roberts on a trip across Belgium to the bank of the Rhine, from which the allies had crossed a few days before. The H.Q. and some fighting elements of the 51st Highland Division were still in the area and gave a warm welcome to the Canadian Seaforths. Remnants of gliders were scattered over the German side of the river.

The battalion crossed into Germany on April 3. It revealed a stark change from the reasonably intact rural Belgium, to scenes of almost total destruction. Budge remembers being in a small log cabin built by the Canadian Forestry Corps right on the Siegfried Line, Germany's fortified western defence line. There was a clothes-line from the cabin to a tall tree from which hung some washing. A large sign in the centre of it declared: "THIS IS THE SIEGFRIED LINE." Another sign said: "AND THIS IS THE WASHING!"* They stopped in the Reichswald Forest until the morning of the 7th. Moving on again they passed through the city of Cleve, where the destruction was worse than anything they had seen in Italy.

The Seaforth's first battle in Northwest Europe took place on April 12, after they crossed the Ijssel River, from Germany into Holland. It was to be Budge's last and saddest battle. As they entered this final stage of the war, reinforcements had brought the battalion up to full strength. Equipment had been overhauled or replaced, especially the Thompson sub-machine gun, which were replaced by the British Sten gun. Although much lighter, they were not as well liked.

At 16:30 hours the battalion crossed the river in buffaloes (armoured amphibious vehicles capable of carrying 28 men), fast, efficient vehicles that made the crossing safe and easy, a new experience after crossing the many Italian rivers on foot. 2 i/c, Major Howarth Glendinning, had just returned from a brief leave to get married in London. Budge, crossing in the first wave of Buffaloes told him to stay behind to oversee the loading and dispatch of the fighting echelon, then to come across last of all. Not long after his own crossing, Budge turned, to find Glen beside him. To the question why? Glen's jocular answer was, "You know very well that I wouldn't trust you out here alone." Within a very short time Glen was killed. His bride of one week was a widow.

---

* Many readers will remember the British ribald wartime song "We're going to hang out the washing on the Siegfried Line, have you any dirty washing mother dear?"

Once across the Ijssel the first objective was the village of Wilp, but first the German troops along the river dyke had to be dealt with. Budge had deployed all his companies, less "A", which was held in reserve. The others were to attack on a wide front, but "D" Company's leading platoon came under heavy machine gun fire from the dyke. Budge called for tank support from a British armoured unit , but when they failed to achieve the desired effect he ordered up 'Wasp' flame-throwers. Mounted on carriers, they were brought forward to be used in action for the first time by the Seaforths. The sheer sight of these long squirts of liquid flame was enough to break the enemy's morale and soon they were surrendering in great numbers. In the approaching dawn of April 12, a total of six enemy officers and 214 other ranks were rounded up, along with numerous weapons. It was discovered that many of the soldiers were Hitler Youth members. They had dug into the dyke and at first were utterly determined not to surrender. For Budge, it was an abhorrent thought to have to kill them, particularly because the war was now obviously so nearly over, though the large number of prisoners taken was a good indication of the modest number of casualties. As well as Hitler Youth there were several older men who had been pressed into service as the German military became more and more desperate. Some Seaforths were seen to be taking personal effects from the lined-up Germans. Budge, once more very angry, lined up his own men and made them give everything back.

Budge recollected:

> "When leaving Scotland for Sicily, a senior commander had made an absurd, frothing speech which attempted to imbue the Canadian soldiers with a ferocious hatred, a fervour to kill every living thing. Of course that didn't happen. Throughout all the action I saw, both sides fought hard and generally tended to abide by the laws and usages of war."

Unfortunately, in the midst of the battle, Budge lost a second officer who was at his side. Moving forward across the flat expanse of open land bordering the river, to appraise "D" Company's situation, he was accompanied by Lieut. Douglas Nageleisen. When half-way across, this promising young officer, who had been wounded at Ortona in December 1944, was killed beside him by allied shellfire. Furious and perhaps a bit shaken up himself, he called on the radio for an immediate ceasefire of all supporting artillery.

Budge was awarded a bar to his D.S.O. in the Ijssel River action. The citation read:

> "Though exposed to heavy shelling and small-arms fire his presence and coolness were a great influence... and under his firm direction the bridgehead was soon secure. He visited all his companies to encourage and supervise their actions.
>
> The battalion's success, during which a large quantity of enemy equipment was destroyed, some two hundred prisoners taken and eighty enemy killed, was due largely to the fearlessness and leadership of Lt.-Colonel Bell-Irving. His bearing and conduct in battle and his handling of the battalion ensured success and are worthy of the highest praise."

Soon after the Ijssel action, Budge developed a serious second bout of malaria and was evacuated to hospital in Nijmegen. From there he had a spell of sick leave in London before returning to the battalion on May 7, just in time to lead it into the liberation of Amsterdam on V.E. Day, May 8, 1945. In his absence Major 'Ollie' Mace had been in temporary command.

The last three weeks of the European war saw the Seaforths moving west past Appeldoorn. It was a strange time; village by village and town by town, Holland was being liberated, yet there were great contrasts in what the soldiers found. In some places the plight of civilians caught in the fighting was pathetic to see. Dead and dying women and children kept Padre Durnford busy trying to give succour to them and their grieving relatives, while in other locations less affected there were scenes of great joy with people, including nuns, dancing in circles, often putting soldiers in the middle. The Dutch National Anthem was frequently heard being sung by grateful citizens.

By the end of April, German resistance was weakening and on the 28th the first negotiations for a ceasefire were begun. Amsterdam and Rotterdam were still controlled by the enemy and their large populations were starving. There was a concern that if the allies attacked these cities the Germans would put up a strong defence and cause unnecessary destruction and loss of life when, instead, patience would win the day. The Russians were at the gates of Berlin and the Italian front, now well up the Po Valley, was about to collapse. For the Canadian Seaforth's their war ended in the village of Barnevald, west of Appeldoorn on the day negotiations began. Brigadier Bogert ordered an end to offensive fire along his brigade front, because by now it was bordering on the enemy's defensive Grebbe Line. This ran from the south-east corner of the Ijsel Meer (Zuider Zee), south for approximately 30 miles to the Waal River and behind it lay Holland's two largest cities and the largest segment of population.

It was for the safety and welfare of this population that the negotiations took place. Before any fighting could resume, in quick succession came the news of Hitler's death, the occupation of Berlin by the Russians and the German surrender in Italy. On May 4 came the news that all German Forces in Northern Europe had surrendered unconditionally. The ceasefire would go into effect at 08:00 hrs on May 8. The Canadian Seaforths were ordered to go directly to Amsterdam as part of the division's take-over of the German 30th Corps.

Budge had returned to the battalion the day before and left by jeep a couple of hours ahead of the convoy to do a recce, accompanied by Major Dennis Pierce and a driver. It was still very early in the morning when they entered Amsterdam, crossing the Berlagebrug (Berlage Bridge) at Diemen. Their first impression was of large crowds lining both sides of the main thoroughfare, still and silent. Budge felt an air of expectancy, or was it perhaps fear still? He learned that just the day before, nine Dutch people had been lined up against a wall in Amsterdam's Dam Square and shot. Would today bring the hoped for, prayed for liberation? Budge could not stress strongly enough the significance of that day for both himself and his battalion:

> "It's a matter of great moment to British Columbia that in a country which considers itself to be governed by Ontario, the great honour of entering and liberating the historic City of Amsterdam should have been given to the Seaforth Highlanders of Canada, the 'D' Day Dodgers', from Vancouver."

The first contact was an old lady kneeling beside the road who handed up a rose to Budge, in the driver's seat with "Thank God you've come." The next contact was with a smartly uniformed Dutch officer, who requested "May we now hoist the Dutch flag again, Sir?"

The memory of that historic request to a young officer from Vancouver has remained with Budge all his long life. The final contact on that drive was with Mr. Herbie Velthorst, who joined them in the jeep. He was a Dutchman of some consequence, fluent in English following a career in the Netherlands-India Commercial Bank in Bombay, where he was also Consul for the Netherlands. With his wife Lucy Mary, they had returned to Amsterdam on May 6, 1940 for six months leave and were caught in the German occupation. Herbie joined the resistance fighters and was called out on May 4 ready to greet the arriving Canadians. Anxious to help in any way he could, he made the practical suggestion of driving directly through the tall gates into Vondelpark. Budge immediately saw it as an ideal solution for the dispersal of his incoming Seaforth convoy, together with the accompanying Princess Louise's Dragoon Guards' armoured recce vehicles. The convoy would be met and guided to the park.

While Budge was driving around organizing things, Herbie Velthorst spied his wife, Lucy Mary, and introduced her. She was immediately invited to join them in the jeep. Writing to Nancy sometime later she expressed as only a participant could the importance of the day of liberation:

> "The tremendous reception that we gave OUR Canadians you will have, of course, already heard about from your husband, who allowed me to join them. I sat behind in the jeep and felt like the Queen as we drove through the streets of Amsterdam. You, who have never been occupied cannot realize what it felt to see our liberators in our beloved city and to know that the years of oppression had come to an end at last.
>
> I always thought I should throw myself at the first allied soldier I saw and hug and kiss him for joy, but when I did meet him (your husband) I was so overcome by emotion that I couldn't say a word because I wanted to cry!"

When the main Seaforth convoy crossed the Berlage Bridge and entered the city, all doubt disappeared. The silence up to a few minutes before gave way to an outpouring of joy and gratitude which quickly spread to many thousands of happy voices, audible for miles. When the convoy leader approached the Vondelpark gates there appeared to be more young women than soldiers in, or on, every vehicle. To get them off before entering the park was a delicate job, somehow accomplished without any ill-will.

Billets were arranged in four local schools, as well as the Marine barracks. B.H.Q. was established at the Colonial Institute. While all this was going on Budge was approached by an elderly man who, with due ceremony presented him with a cigar which he had saved for a very long time for this moment of liberation. He chose to forego the pleasure himself and offer it to one of the liberators.

With his units settled in the park, Budge gladly accepted the Velthorst's invitation to visit their house. Lucy Mary asked if he would like a bath. She knew that serving soldiers on the move were always grateful for such opportunities. Budge's response was immediate—and affirmative. He was not, however, prepared for what happened next:

> "A short time later, looking out of the window, I saw a woman coming up the street with what appeared to be a kettle in her hand. After an interval there was another woman, also with a kettle; and then another—and then another. I was shortly to learn that the content of each kettle was destined for the Velthorst's bathroom—and my wonderful hot bath!
>
> I was also to learn that in those days of virtually no fuel, a citizen of Amsterdam was just as likely to desire a bath as was a serving soldier. I learned that such heat as they had was, for a long time obtained by (1) a look-out to see that any German sentry who might be nearby was going in the other direction, (2) a quick run into the street, most likely with a hammer and chisel to dislodge a wooden paving block out of the road surface, return to the house before the sentry turned around and (3) to break the block into small chips to put into a small empty food tin placed on top of the stove. With the tin suitably slotted for the purpose this little fire served to do all their cooking and anything else requiring hot water. As for heat, they just didn't have it. I will always remember that bath as something very special from all those grateful women.
>
> Some time later I was able to send a convoy of three ton trucks to Arnheim, where the heavy battle had destroyed a large number of big trees. Brought back to Amsterdam they supplied a large number of families with much needed firewood. It was a relatively small thing, but I have a beautiful Dutch print signed by several grateful Amsterdam people on the back of it."

Another couple Budge came to know well were Henk Hooft Van Woudenberg and his attractive Swedish wife Ebba. As well as their city townhouse, they had an estate in the country where Henk took Budge shooting for pheasant and woodcock. As life began to return to normal and social events increased, Budge would sometimes take Ebba as his partner for an evening, all above board and with the full knowledge of Henk. When Budge took his father to dinner at their townhouse, on the way home Henry castigated his son for being so stupid as to take out a beautiful woman in the evening and then go shooting with her husband in the forest next day!

On May 9 came another great occasion in his military career when Budge was invited by the Dutch Prime Minister to address a crowd of over 100,000 people from a high podium in Dam Square. He said:

> "It has been our good fortune to have the honour of relieving you from your tyrannical invaders, to have been a part of the great allied achievement in giving you back the opportunity to live the decent, civilized lives you have long been famous for. On behalf of the Seaforth Highlanders of Canada and the Princess Louise's Dragoon Guards with us, may I express our warm thanks and deep appreciation for your tremendous display of gratitude and your friendliness and hospitality to all of us."

In his address Budge attempted to explain to the assembled people what this moment meant to the Canadians who had liberated their city. He said: "It is not easy to persuade a Western Canadian soldier to hate anyone, not even Hitler. There are perhaps many reasons why a soldier from Western Canada might join the armed forces rather suddenly and go off to war; but why? After several years away from home, the constant loss of friends in battle and a good deal of personal misery it is natural to ask, 'Why did I do this? Why did I come? You, the good people of Amsterdam, in your demonstration of deep gratitude, have given us the invaluable answer. We may all go home now filled with the knowledge that our journey, every year of it, has indeed been so well worthwhile. Thank you, Amsterdam!"

As Military Commander of Amsterdam his immediate concern was the fact that German forces were still in their billets, with fully armed sentries marching up and down. The fact that their strength was more than double his approximately one thousand soldiers was very much on his mind too. Members of the Dutch resistance had received an air-drop of British Sten-guns only a few weeks before and the possibility of a few pot-shots by some of the younger ones at an armed German seemed a real and very dangerous likelihood—what better way to celebrate their joy of liberation. Budge had orders to disarm the resistance fighters but felt that they might not obey. Another of his concerns was the tempting presence of a dockside warehouse, used by the German occupation forces to store tons of food. He was anxious to arrange a fair and equitable distribution as soon as possible. As a first priority he organized a twenty-four hour patrol of the city, with emphasis on areas still occupied by the Germans, and the dock area, by both Seaforths on foot and scout cars of the Princess Louise's Dragoon Guards.

The rounding up of the German military began, both soldiers and marines who had been guarding the docks. A large Ford factory enclave outside the city was sufficiently isolated as a suitable holding area. Here the process of disarming and preparing them for return to Germany would take place. Having 'lost' the order from higher command to disarm the Dutch resistance, Budge showed his flair for strategy by calling on them to line the streets, complete with arms as the long column of enemy soldiers passed on their way to the Ford compound. Included were numerous, obviously Dutch vehicles and sundry looted property and, perhaps saddest of all, a number of women who had been living with German soldiers. They knew that to begin with their heads would be shaved to mark them and, from that moment on, their lives would be very much at the mercy of the new military authority. In the German ranks were some whose behaviour towards the Dutch had been particularly bad.

They must have presented tempting targets for the resistance fighters lining the streets, but it all worked well. Budge's trust in their behaviour paid off and there was not one single incident. The only escort was one Seaforth Bren-gun carrier with three or four soldiers in it The prisoners arrived intact at the Ford compound to be checked off, disarmed, relieved of their loot and made ready to return to Germany. Sometime later the German commander sent a staff officer to Budge with a request to borrow one or two rifles to shoot some of his soldiers who had earlier been caught trying to escape. Budge remarked; "This was perhaps one of numerous examples of the difference between the German military and Western Canadian militia. I told him to go back to the general and tell him he was a fool because the war was over."

Sometime after he left Amsterdam, Budge was led to believe the rifles were obtained and these recalcitrant soldiers were shot. A few years later he had a call from Ottawa about an Italian film that had been made depicting the brutal conduct of a Canadian general in shooting poor, unarmed German prisoners after the war. The film's principal character was a rather plump, bemedalled character with a large cigar in his mouth being driven around in a fancy car. It was presumed to depict Budge. Though he would have given anything to see the film he 'shamelessly' told Ottawa that he knew absolutely nothing about it.

On May 11 Budge received news that he had been promoted to Brigadier. He learned that the promotion had been proposed well before cessation of hostilities but confirmation was delayed until ratified by Ottawa. Budge remained in Amsterdam until after the Germans had been removed from the city and only then did he leave for his new posting which was to command the 10th Canadian Infantry Brigade. Budge received a brigadier's cap-badge, the Lion and Crown (known derisively as the 'dog and basket'), which he placed on his balmoral rather than wear the correct, but far less dashing peaked cap.

On the evening of May 13, he arrived at the 10th Canadian Infantry Brigade H.Q., near Oldenburg. His excitement far outweighed any trepidation at the prospect of commanding an infantry brigade with its own tanks as part of a fully equipped armoured division. There was a party going on and the new brigadier had a couple of drinks then, glad to call it a day, went to bed early.

Budge, Major Gordon Armstrong, the Brigade Major, and his Staff Captain shared an attractive, and comfortable cottage on the shore of the Bad Zwichenahn. Along with the cottage came the use of a small, fast, racing dinghy, moored nearby. Both belonged to a U-Boat skipper who was still at sea. Budge was very concerned that his wife, their 'hostess' must have been going though hell in her worry over her husband. It was likely that she was already a widow.

Over the next few days he set about introducing himself to his personal staff and then went on to the units and other attachments. As a latecomer, Budge read all he could find on the performance of each unit of the brigade right up to the ceasefire. Observing his units at the end of hostilities, their splendid performance in war was no surprise to him—or the fine reputations of the various commanding officers.

The 29th Canadian Armoured Reconnaissance Regiment (South Alberta Regiment), was commanded by Lt.-Col. G.D. Wotherspoon, D.S.O., known throughout his life as 'Swatty', who had come to them from the Governor-General's Foot Guards, and had led both with great distinction. Budge noted that on several occasions he had made suggestions to Brigade or Divisional H.Q. as to how a proposed operation might profitably be altered to increase the likelihood of success and probably fewer casualties. They were usually accepted and drew positive results.

'Swatty' Wotherspoon, was equally familiar with both infantry and armour—and thoroughly familiar with the attributes of the 10th Canadian Infantry Brigade. Though certainly pleased to have been promoted, Budge felt very strongly that 'Swatty' should have been given this command and, in fact, in a very short time he was promoted to command the 4th Armoured Brigade, to be replaced by Lt.-Col. Darby Nash.

The Lincoln and Welland Regiment was commanded by Lt.-Col. R.C. (Rowan) Coleman, son of the then C.P.R. President. He had landed in Sicily as a Patricia officer. Later, in Italy he was given command of the Loyal Edmonton Regiment but was severely wounded soon afterwards in the fierce battle for the Hitler Line, at which point Budge was appointed to command. He was evacuated to England and after recovering was appointed C.O. of the Lincoln and Welland Regiment.

Lt.-Col. J.F.R. (Jack) Akehurst, D.S.O., commanding officer of the Algonquin Regiment had served in it before the war. In August 1942, while in command of "C" Company he had been stolen away to join the Canadian-American Special Service Force. He served in the Italian Campaign, commanding first a battalion, then a regiment (roughly equivalent to a brigade in British military terminology) before being wounded and awarded his D.S.O. When he returned to his old regiment as C.O., he brought with him a wealth of battle experience to add to a battalion already known for its achievements. The final words in *Warpath*, the official regimental history, are among Budge's favourite lines:

> *Lord grant this gallant company*
> *The rest and peace they have won,*
> *Reward their last Gethsemane*
> *With hope that war is done,*
> *And let their names forever be*
> *Warmed by memory's sun.*

Lt.-Col. A.F. Coffin, commanding the Argyll & Sutherland Highlanders (Canada), had been promoted and transferred from second-in-command of the 29th Canadian Armoured Reconnaissance Regiment (South Alberta Regiment), He was obviously first rate, with a keen understanding of the varying responsibilities of an infantry brigade in an armoured division. As the new Argyll's commanding officer he was perhaps not aware of the significance of the pipes and drums to the regimental pride and morale and had planned to send them back to Canada, based on their high number of points for overseas service. Budge influenced him to retain them at least until there was some indication of his battalion's future moves.

The 10th Canadian Independent Machine Gun Company (New Brunswick Rangers), commanded by Major Les Bastin, was of special interest to Budge. Their weapons, Vickers guns and 4 inch mortars, he had been familiar with before the war in "D" Company of the Seaforths.

There was much more to his new command than these fighting units; there were signallers, engineers, a field ambulance unit and many more. There were times when he regretted not getting to know his brigade much sooner and to have had the opportunity to fight with them. However, he realized that the time was past and for now it was party time—and these officers could certainly set the pace. The highlight of one evening of fun was a jeep race around the airport by two brigadiers, Budge Bell-Irving of the 10th Canadian Infantry Brigade and Bob Moncel, then of the 4th. It was akin to a bull-fight. Both were lucky to make the course in one piece. The next event was somewhat of the same order. The two senior officers were this time at opposite ends of the field, Bren-guns at the ready while between them, centre-field was a plaster bust of the Fuhrer on a pedestal. To Budge's chagrin, Moncel shot the head off first—and happily neither competitor caught any of the bullets, allowing the two youngest brigadiers in the Canadian army to live to get a little older.

Despite the coming of peace, incidents still occurred. Tanks of the 4th Armoured Brigade's B.C. Regiment were deployed close to the small town of Wieffelstede. A trooper had his arm blown off by a booby trap grenade fixed inside the hatch of his tank. The generals were away at the time and Budge, as the senior officer was informed of the incident. Having looked at the tank and the surroundings he informed the town's burgomeister that if he produced the culprit by 08:00 the following morning he would consider what should be done with him. A man was duly produced and with a dependable interpreter Budge interrogated him very thoroughly. He was soon convinced that the man knew nothing about the incident.

Budge then informed the burgomeister that he would not move the tanks but instead would clear a field of fire around them by destroying several large houses close to the tanks. The owners were to have a few hours to remove what they could from them after which the houses would be razed to the ground—which they were—to the satisfaction of a local priest who told Budge that he had done the right thing.

The City of Amsterdam began preparing a massive celebration, to take place over three days, June 26-27-28. On the last day there was to be a large Victory Parade. Because of his original role in the liberation of the city Budge was chosen to lead it, and was also invited to a reception at the Palace following the parade, to meet Queen Wilhelmina. He was able to arrange for his father to come over from London for the event—who was well looked after by everybody up to General Chris Vokes. He went to the races with 'Swatty' Wotherspoon and introduced him to the capabilities of 'French 75s' (a drink of some potency). Henry was assured a good spot to see his son lead the parade.

It was a great honour to the Canadian troops that no other Allied forces were invited. This was appropriate as Queen Wilhelmina had just returned from her war-time sojourn in Canada. There were to be detachments of the Dutch Navy and Air Force, members of the Dutch resistance, and three groups of civilians, one representing those who took part in a protest in February 1941 against the prosecution of the Amsterdam Jewish population; a second group who took part in the May 1, 1943 strike opposing forced transportation of Dutch labourers to Germany and the last to represent those who took part in the September 17, 1944 railway strike ordered by the Dutch Government.

Leading the parade were fourteen pipe bands making it truly the massed pipes and drums of the Canadian Army (until the post-war cuts began there were at least twenty-five Canadian regiments with Scottish affiliations). In addition to the pipes there were six Canadian military bands as well.

The units marching were: The Royal Canadian Regiment; Le Regiment de la Chaudiere; The Calgary Highlanders and The Seaforth Highlanders of Canada; The Royal Canadian Dragoons (in armoured cars, scout cars and half-tracks). There were six Sherman tanks; a Battery of 25 pounder field guns of the Royal Canadian Horse Artillery; a Battery of 17 pounders, 1st Anti-Tank Regiment, Royal Canadian

Artillery; self-propelled guns of the 2nd Light Anti-Aircraft Regiment, R.C.A. and a Valentine Bridge Layer.

The organization took several days and many "O" Groups, but finally all was ready and after a final one with the C.O.s at the start point the parade moved off at five minutes to noon. The order of march was: Massed pipes and drums—flags of the United nations—Budge (wearing his Highland-dress uniform)—Brigade Major Gordon Armstrong followed by the regiments, with the bands at intervals between them. The armoured and artillery units came next, then the Dutch military units and the civilian contingents.

Queen Wilhelmina took the salute from the Palace balcony and she bowed graciously to each contingent. Henry was seated with sundry V.I.P.s on a balcony immediately below the Queen. Budge, arriving at the finish had laid on a jeep plus a provost escort with sirens to get through the crowds. He returned to the Anstel Hotel, which was under Canadian Army supervision, where he and his father had suites. After a quick lunch he left sharply to reach the palace for 2.30 p.m. to join the Queen's reception—the lone foreigner there.

Budge told Nancy: "There were many people of consequence at the Palace. From the street level there was a broad staircase which led up to the main salon. Here the large gathering was facing the top of the stairs with eager anticipation. I was modestly in the rear of the gathering, close to the back door of the salon, where I had my first introduction to Her Majesty because of her quirk of doing the unexpected. Unannounced she came quietly in through this door, straight towards me. I did an immediate about-turn. The Queen was very sweet indeed and spoke to me for several minutes, expressing her gratitude for Canada's kindness to her, and also her gratitude to the Allied liberators of her country."

With barely time to recover from the victory celebrations, Budge was invited to attend an investiture at Buckingham Palace on July 13, to receive from King George VI the Bar to his D.S.O. and the Order of the British Empire. News of his Bar for the Ijssel River battle did not reach Budge until after he had been promoted and it came as a complete surprise to him. Once more he was on his way to London, where he arranged to take his father and also 18 year old Jill Lines along as guests, a major outing for her, especially the celebration that followed.

It was an all-Canadian investiture and many old friends were to be received by the King, including 'Swatty' Wotherspoon. The get-together that evening was one to be long remembered and left a few sore heads in its wake. When Budge returned to his H.Q. it was to find the brigade was moving to Naarden, just south-east of Amsterdam and close to the south shore of the Ijssel Meer. There was no definite news of a return to Canada and Budge had to deal with a lot of speculation as to when this might be. He had applied for an early return home, with a high priority based on the points system, but there was a strict rule that commanders should remain with their brigades and go home with them, unless the formation was broken up. It was, of course, not easy for Nancy, waiting in Vancouver, knowing that hostilities were over, yet not only was Budge still away, he was enjoying himself immensely in his new job.

The brigade officers were enjoying a lot of socializing, with dances, cocktail parties, sporting events, always women to escort to all of them. All of the officers and men within the division were battle-weary and it is perfectly understandable that they would seek one last chance to 'let their hair down' before facing the uncertainties of civilian life. Budge had concluded that the peacetime army was not for him and he gave firm assurances to Nancy that his one aim in life was to return home as soon as possible to begin their post-war life together. One of Nancy's biggest fears was that after the intense action Budge had experienced he would find civilian life drab and dull. He admitted this was a real possibility and wrote:

> "... I will quite possibly be insufferable much of the time and will have fits of extreme and rather uncontrolled energy and a desire to throw my weight about. Afterwards, I will no doubt lapse into periods of utter lassitude—too lazy to do up my boots...
>
> [However] I feel quite confident in my ability to settle down eventually to be a reasonable husband and citizen. The war being over, the thrill of battle and great responsibility has gone anyway. I have decided quite definitely that civilian life will offer more scope than peacetime soldiering could do. I would hate the regular army in peacetime."

His greatest uncertainty at that time was whether Uncle Dick would offer him a position with responsibility in the family business or whether he should concentrate on the promising possibilities with Lines Brothers. The latter began to look more and more interesting when he received nothing but evasion about his prospects in H. Bell-Irving & Co.

In the meantime life was to be lived to the fullest. Budge had met a Dutch couple, Dick and Loekie Lequit, who lived in the Hague. They owned a 65 foot twin-screw motor yacht called "Zilvermieu" (Seagull). They had never been out without a paid captain, or at night. A cruise together seemed a good idea after the enforced tie-up during the war years. Budge persuaded them that he had a good deal of experience in small boats and, of course, he wouldn't hear of being paid as a skipper.

He was also constantly trying to get as much change of pace as possible for all ranks—to try something different before the great change came in returning home. As well as educational lectures and sports activities he offered them adventure and, something he felt to be very important, a chance for the men to make decisions for themselves after four or five years of taking orders and instructions. Budge discovered that there were some sturdy open boats available with outboard motors that had been produced for the Rhine crossing. He distributed a notice around the brigade units inviting any group of six soldiers under a corporal as 'skipper' to take one of the boats for a week to go cruising wherever they wished. His requirements were that they must produce a prepared route plan; keep a detailed daily log to submit to Brigade H.Q. afterwards; and must fend for themselves by acquiring fuel, food and drink. Rain-gear, blankets and clothing they obviously had or could obtain from stores before departing. Only two groups took up the offer, but they had a wonderful time and produced humorous reports. One boat became lost and ended up in the Frisian Islands, which Budge was soon to visit himself.

His offer to the other ranks gave him another idea. Why not take a couple of the C.O.s on a long cruise aboard "Zilvermieu" while their seconds in command organized the move to Naarden. And so it was arranged. "Zilvermieu" was made ready by her owners. Madame Lequit turned out to be an imaginative and capable cook. Starting at Warmond, near the Hague, six people were aboard: Budge; Darby Nash of the South Alberta Regiment; Les Bastin of the New Brunswick Rangers; a Dutch river pilot and the Lequits. With all belongings stowed, the "Zilvermieu" set forth with the Canadian ensign at the stern, the Netherlands flag at the masthead and Budge's brigade car pennant on the bow.

Their route took them through several major cities and past some areas of the recent fighting, especially the Ijssel bridgehead battle. Most of the bridges were intact and the crew soon became accustomed to the method of payment required to have them opened—dropping the money into a wooden clog hanging on a cord. One bridge was still damaged and unable to open. Even with the mast down the top of the wheelhouse was six inches too high and Budge had the bright idea, at first resisted by the owner of inviting on board some of the people who had gathered to watch. Finally he relented and the weighed-down boat cleared by the required few inches. The holiday ended with several days of saltwater sailing around the Frisian Islands which Budge found much more of a challenge.

Once ensconced at Naarden, Budge not only had the benefit of the "Zilvermieu", he also had access to an equally attractive boat, the "Neerlandia", a yawl-rigged large yacht. She was comfortable, with lots of accommodation for guests and was designed for the shallow waters of the Ijssel Meer, with lee-boards on both sides that could be raised or lowered as needed. She was used primarily by senior officers of the 4th Armoured Division's "A" Mess and though Budge was not a member he was frequently invited to sail with them. The "A" Mess members came by her because the owner, for reasons associated with the recent war was not at liberty to use her. The local Dutch community, many of whom were guests from time to time knew very well the reason for the owner's absence and may have had a quiet chuckle over their liberators' rather bold 'ownership' of this beautiful yacht. It was never discussed; the war was over and these Canadian officers had worked long and hard for several years. A Dutch caretaker also served as a barman and in return for paying him and assurances of competent handling, they were free to use her. There were several experienced sailors in the mess and her safety was assured. This free charter was a just reward.

Naarden is a very attractive small town and Budge found a house to his liking, "the Haspel," where he and his Brigade Major and Staff Captain set up. He had spent time in Naarden before his promotion and had met a neighbouring family from which a lasting friendship grew, the Dudok van Heels, a prominent Dutch family.

Stagliano remained as Budge's batman when he took over the 10th Brigade and was promoted to corporal. He had served Budge well and was picking up the business acumen which would become his trademark in Vancouver after the war. One day, after they were installed in "the Haspel" there was a knock on Budge's office door and he described the following conversation that took place:

> "Corporal Stagliano came in and waffled nervously for a moment until I pressed him for what he actually wanted. He then blurted out, 'Can you get drunk on Triple Sec?' My probable response was 'Yes, but why on earth would you want to?' This produced a strong inference that it was really none of my business. There was never any acrimony and I was on the verge of rather enjoying the conversation. Finally Stagliano gave in with a forceful statement 'Who do you think is paying for all this?' It was now my turn to waffle!—'Well, you know I won't stand for any looting or short changing anybody and, come to think of it we have been spending rather a lot on food and drink for so many guests. Frankly, though, I haven't really thought about it.'
>
> Stagliano then, without any shame, played his trump card. With his business acumen to the fore—he had been procuring liquor at a low price of 11 guilders per bottle and re-selling a portion to various battalion messes for 25 guilders. The difference, along with a few other procurement 'deals' was paying a portion of my mess bills."

By the end of October 1945 Budge was counting the weeks to returning to Canada. The fact that the *Queen Mary* and *Queen Elizabeth* were now transporting troops back to the U.S. and Canada made a huge difference because of their sheer carrying capacity. The social whirl that surrounded him was beginning to pall and he would be glad to leave it behind. In the meantime Nancy had been busy looking at property and had nearly purchased a lot at the western end of the District of West Vancouver, an attractive area with spectacular water views. Their immediate financial position looked rosy, with Budge's pay and allowances, plus his gratuity on leaving the army. He joked that with the ideas he had picked up ready for building their home it would be "a magnificent Gothic-Italo-Dutch cottage where we will live happily ever after!" Unfortunately, there was one nagging problem in these rosy prospects; despite requests to his Uncle Dick as to his future in the family business he did not receive any indication as to what his role might be and expressed a concern to Nancy that he might be tied down both mentally and monetarily if he returned to it.

With his remaining time in Europe limited, on October 25 Budge set out to try to locate the grave of his brother Roderick at Abbeville. He took with him the brigade's French Canadian Roman Catholic Padre, who was a great asset as an interpreter, and also Corporal Stagliano. They found the cemetery but despite the provision of grave numbers and locations from London, Budge was not positively able to identify the graves of Roderick and his crew. There were two custodians but they were of no help. A visit to a War Graves Commission Office in Arras was even more frustrating as the staff seemed far more concerned with the graves of WW I.

However, directed to another office in Brussels it produced some results. A file on Roderick included an Air Ministry memo as recent as February 1945 confirming that approval had been given for the erection of a cross on each grave. An undertaking was given that this would be done forthwith and as proof an official photograph would be sent to Budge. This was as much as he could accomplish before leaving. Imprinted on his memory is the sight of miles and miles of crosses on the graves from both wars.

Budge's remaining time in Europe was taken up with two courtmartials. For the first one, in Brussels, he was appointed President of the Court, in which a Canadian N.C.O. was on trial for murder. The circumstances were strange. The soldier was seen running bare-footed up the centre of a busy Brussels street, clad in army issue yellow longjohns. Chasing him some distance behind was an irate civilian, fully clothed. There was a pistol shot and the civilian fell dead.

The fatal bullet was recovered, as was the pistol. It was agreed that the bullet unquestionably came from the pistol, which was proved to be on issue to the accused. This gave the prosecution a very strong case—until the defence produced evidence that the entry wound was in the deceased's back. Witnesses stated that neither the accused nor the deceased turned around at any time. In spite of the evidence of both the gun and the bullet, the soldier could not have fired the shot and therefore could not be guilty as charged. The judgement of the court was that there was no proof whatever of this murder having been carried out by the Canadian N.C.O. and a verdict of "Not Guilty" was returned.

The Court had given its judgement and was dismissed, but Budge still pondered on what could possibly have happened to cause the man's death. The following scenario occurred to him: It was not disputed that arriving home the deceased had found the Canadian soldier in bed with his wife. That is where the chase began. The wife, disturbed from her tryst and noticing the accused's pistol on the table beside the bed, suddenly saw an opportunity to be rid of her husband. She threw on a dress, grabbed the pistol and chased after both men. Catching up on her husband she shot him in the back. From the hindsight of fifty years Budge is sure that some tasty details came out, but are long forgotten.

On the morning of December 7 Budge relinquished command of the 10th Canadian Infantry Brigade. The next day the units embarked for England as the first stage of their return home. One of the last acts of his Brigade H.Q. before leaving was a large party for children to celebrate St. Nicholas on December 5. It was to be a tea party with unlimited supplies of ice-cream, movies, games and presents. For the older children with memories of privation during the war, it was a fine gesture. In procuring the food and toys Budge was assisted by Ebba Van Woudenburg. Between them more than enough was produced to feed several hundred children. A black Canadian soldier admirably played the part of Swarte Piet, Saint Nick's traditional black helper. There was one critical moment when the children became excited and began to scramble over each other, but order was restored in time to avoid injury.

A month after the Brussels trial, on December 10 Budge was a member of another court-martial, of greater significance in terms of the offence. SS Brigadefuhrer (Major-General) Kurt Meyer was accused of committing war-crimes against Canadian soldiers, the highest ranking front-line German officer to be so charged. There were five charges in total, covering events at two locations, though all revolved around similar accusations. The essence was that he committed a War Crime in that "In the Province of Normandy and Republic of France on or about June 7, 1944, as Commander of the 25th SS Panzer Grenadier Regiment, in violation of the laws and usages of war did incite and counsel troops under his command to deny quarter to the enemy." He was allegedly responsible for killing prisoners of war when twenty-three Canadian prisoners were killed at or near the villages of Buron and Authie. Also that on or about June 8, 1944 he gave orders to kill seven prisoners at his H.Q. at Abbaye Ardenne.

The laws governing treatment of prisoners had been written into the 1907 Hague and the 1929 Geneva Conventions. Germany had been a signatory to both. The evidence would clearly prove that Canadian soldiers had been killed by members of his units, without justification. The trial sought to establish what degree of responsibility must rest on the shoulders of Meyer as their commander.

A list of his accomplishments and his decorations for valour indicated a fearless soldier. Aged 35, he had won the Iron Cross, both first and second-class; the Knight's Cross and Oak Leaves to the Knight's Cross. He was known for always being well forward in battle, had been wounded in action and had served on many fronts. Meyer was keen on fitness, even while incarcerated and took every opportunity to jog, handcuffed to an officer—who had to be equally fit to keep up the pace.

This, then was the man who came before Budge and his brother officers on December 10, 1945 in the Naval barracks at Aurich. These were: President of the Court Major-General H.W. Foster, Judge Advocate Lt.-Col. W.B. Bredin; Members of the court—Brigadier Ian S. Johnston, D.S.O.; Brigadier H.S. Sparling, D.S.O.; Brigadier H.P. Bell-Irving, D.S.O., and Brigadier J.A. Roberts, D.S.O.

For the prosecution were: Lt.-Col. C.S. Campbell; Lt.-Col. B.J.S. Macdonald and Lt.-Col. D.G. Dean. For the defence was Lt.-Col. M.W. Andrew, D.S.O., an experienced trial lawyer from Stratford, Ontario. He received some bad press in Canada for his role and it became necessary to remind the public that he was seconded to act as defence (Col. Macdonald subsequently wrote a book on the trial in 1954). The proceedings lasted three weeks, longer than at first allowed, and was extended beyond Christmas.

Key witnesses were a Polish conscript named Sturmann Jan Jesionek, who had been placed in a reconnaissance company of the 25th SS Panzer Grenadiers and two German soldiers from Meyer's own Division. Both swore that many times orders came from Meyer's H.Q. not to take prisoners. Perhaps the most telling order was the edict that S.S soldiers do not surrender and should commit suicide rather than be taken prisoner. In pep talks to his troops Meyer told them he had sworn to his wife that he would not be taken prisoner, but he was in fact captured without resistance when his H.Q. was overtaken.

Meyer insisted that he would be very foolish to expressly order the killing of enemy soldiers and could prove that many had received extremely good treatment at his hands. He also reiterated the capture of the 150 other prisoners, taken in the battles around Caen without incident. One of Meyer's officers claimed to have seen him having supper with three Canadian prisoners. Examples were presented of discipline within the German army itself, especially his own Division. Meyer claimed to have ordered one of his soldiers executed for raping a young French girl.

Evidence from Canadian officers and other ranks, confirmed by several civilian witnesses, proved beyond doubt that the atrocities were conducted by S.S. units. Re-convening after the Christmas break on December 27, Lt.-Col. Andrew, as defence counsel had to demolish the assertions of Jesionek and the two German soldiers; in Jesionek's case that he had misheard Meyer's orders at Abbaye Ardenne and there were inconsistencies in his evidence. Perhaps the strongest defence was that once in battle, Meyer could not exercise direct influence over the behaviour of individual soldiers. There was evidence of further shooting being stopped by the intervention of officers, and most of the approximately 150 prisoners had been safely delivered to prisoner-of-war camps in the rear.

Lt.-Col. Andrew sought to show that while executions were committed, they had not occurred as the result of any order or action on Meyer's part. In his final urging to the Court, he stated that although the regulations might, in these circumstances raise a prima facie case of responsibility on the part of Meyer, having in mind all considerations—"such presumption should not be given effect on this charge."

Summing up, for the prosecution, Lt.-Col. Macdonald concentrated on the words 'denying quarter,' stressing that Kurt Meyer had counselled and incited his troops to take such action. Colonel Bredin, the Judge Advocate then made his summation in which he defined war crimes as opposed to civil criminal offences. He reminded the Court that the broad question—'when may a military commander be held responsible for a war crime committed by men under his command and thus be subject to punishment as a war criminal'—was not easily answered. The fate of the accused rested upon their determination of facts to convict or to find not guilty.

On December 28, after deliberating for three hours, members of the Court found Meyer guilty of inciting and counselling his troops to kill prisoners. Further deliberations of only twenty-five minutes brought General Foster and the four brigadiers back into court. All were tight-lipped and pale as the accused was brought in to face them. This group of senior officers, had all experienced battle conditions and, like the man facing them had faced the responsibility of front-line command. General Foster alone had the difficult task of pronouncing sentence:

"Brigadefuhrer Kurt Meyer, the Court has found you guilty of the First, Fourth and Fifth Charges. The sentence of the Court is that you suffer death by being shot. The findings of Guilty are subject to confirmation. The proceedings are now closed."

Standing stiffly at attention, Meyer showed little emotion other than a tightening of the jaw, as the sentence was translated for him. He bowed to the court and, after saying in perfect English, "Thank you gentlemen for a very fair trial" he was led away.

A firing-party was detailed and the date of January 7 was confirmed as the date of execution. There were those who thought the sentence was appropriate but there was enough questioning in both military and civilian legal circles that after due consideration the final decision fell to Budge's long-time senior officer, General Chris Vokes. As Commander, Canadian Army Occupation Force the trial took place under his jurisdiction. In accordance with his right and duty, General Vokes revued the findings of the court and after due consideration he commuted the sentence to life imprisonment.

When the commutation was announced in Canada it was the turn of the Canadian public to get angry—especially when it was found that Meyer had been secretly brought to Canada to serve his sentence in New Brunswick's Dorchester Penitentiary. He was later returned to Germany and his total prison time was nine years.

Budge had been counting the days to his return to Canada and, but for the trial, he would have been in England with a good possibility of a firm sailing date for New York. However, by the time the sentence was commuted Budge had returned to England to await final instructions to join a ship. It was the Cunard Liner, *Queen Elizabeth*, still painted in wartime camouflage. After seeing as many friends and relatives as possible in the U.K., he sailed on January 27. In the meantime arrangements had been made for Nancy to join him in Montreal, followed by a cross-Canada train journey. It had all been arranged for them by Rowan Coleman's father, then President of Canadian Pacific Railway.

The *Queen Elizabeth* sailed into New York's Hudson River at noon on February 1, after a stormy crossing. Sailing on the same trip was a large contingent of medical officers and padres, due for demobilization. A picture of Budge taken on the dockside looking splendid in his Highland service-dress jacket and kilt was in fact used as an advertisement for a pre-styrofoam type of coffee cup he was holding. One newspaper referred to him as the Canadian general wearing a skirt.

After a few glorious days in Montreal with Nancy they headed home in style on a C.P. Rail inter-continental. A relaxed leave which included skiing in Banff took Budge up to Monday, April 8, when he officially retired from the army. This did not, of course, sever his involvement with the Seaforth Highlanders of Canada, which has continued unbroken.

CHAPTER TEN

ALTHOUGH HE HAD NOT RECEIVED ANY further assurances from Dick Bell-Irving on his future prospects, Budge decided to at least find out if there were any at all for him at H. Bell-Irving & Co. After a few minutes in Dick's office he quickly learned that he could not expect to inherit leadership of the company and it was made clear that this would pass to his younger cousin Ian, Dick's son. Ian had returned to Vancouver several months ahead and was now firmly ensconced in the office. Budge wondered why this outcome had not occurred to him before and he left the office about twenty minutes after entering it.

One belief Budge carried was the certainty that he could always count upon the help and guidance of his mentor Peter Traill, who was still a very important part of the family firm. This belief was to be put to the test sooner than he might have wished—and he was not disappointed.

Walter Lines was fully aware that Budge intended to approach Dick first and was generous enough to suggest that if it did not work out to let him know. Fortunately, before leaving London, Budge had met Walter Lines and came home with an option in his pocket for a trial period of one year to be North American sales agent for his substantial toy manufacturing company, Lines Brothers Ltd. The scope of the U.K. plant included certain other items such as a high quality perambulator. Among its outlets was the world famous toy shop, Hamleys of London, owned by the company.

Lines Bros. Canada quickly became not only an alternative career, but a very exciting prospect. So quickly did things happen that Budge became the Lines' representative with an initial agreement made by wire. He began at once with a confirmation that he would receive a commission of 6 1/4% plus expenses. It was not until the following September that he returned to the U.K. plant for a full discussion of future plans. The job Budge had thought of carving out for himself while in Italy in 1943 was about to become a reality.

With Nancy's initial help he planned an itinerary of sales calls in several major cities in Canada and northern U.S.A. The first request was for a sampling of Lines Bros. products to be shipped urgently to Montreal where display space had been arranged in a hotel. He and Nancy set off to Montreal, checked into the hotel and, armed with a wrench and a screw-driver they found the showroom in which was a large pile of boxes of all sizes from the Merton, England plant. They began assembling the items, including tricycles and other children's toys, large and small, none of which they had seen before. There was a good deal of trial and error but it was all finally assembled. Budge has no recollection of the show itself but it must have gone well because he immediately wired requests for a similar shipment to be sent to New York. The Montreal samples were loaded into a large truck and sent to Toronto for another show held at the Royal York Hotel. Afterwards the samples were sold off on the Toronto market.

New York was quite an experience for both of them. They had to get around by taxi and found that New York cab drivers are unique. They found an adequate hotel, the Prince George on 14th St., just off Broadway, which was particularly suitable because there was an empty beauty parlour in the hotel, fronting onto the street. It quickly proved an adequate showroom.

Contacts with a number of substantial toy buyers in New York failed to produce a single visitor. So Budge reasoned, "If they will not come to us we will go to them so, off we went—in a cab—with one or two others following loaded with samples. We called on the big buyers, one by one." Sitting on benches with other salesmen awaiting his turn to see the buyers it occurred to Budge that it was quite a good way to 'unfrock' a brigadier! Unfrocked or not, in the first two month of business Budge received almost $4000 in commissions. Among early sales, he recalls an order for a gross each of the Minic miniature model cars as a sample order to each of the 1600 J.C. Penney stores. Another one was a sale of tricycles at $18.50 each to Montgomery Ward at the rate of 400 per month.

It became apparent that the substantial United States toy manufacturing industry had not yet completed its re-adjustment from manufacturing the necessities of war. The toy market was hungry and Lines Bros. Ltd. was able to make very good use of this opportunity. After New York Budge made his way to Chicago, San Francisco and Los Angeles. Nancy returned to Vancouver to stay with her parents until the future looked more certain. During this time Nancy's father Reginald became ill with cancer, so she was on hand to be with him and to help her mother.

In September 1946 Budge returned to England for discussions with Walter Lines on the North American market. He was treated much the same as he was in wartime, staying as a guest in the Lines' family home in Surrey, going to the plant in the London suburb of Merton each day in Walter's Rolls. He lunched in the boardroom with both Walter and his brother Arthur—but worked hard, learning as much about the toy business, both manufacturing and sales, as he could in a two month visit.

One thing became quickly evident; Walter Lines showed great confidence in Budge and it was obvious that he was serious about taking on the vast North American market. The export department was re-organized to reflect this and some toys were given immediate priority as export items, especially with Christmas looming. One advantage was that several of the larger retail companies, both Canadian and American, had purchasing offices in London and several orders were secured by visiting them.

After much discussion a decision was made to incorporate a branch company in North America. The Chairman's first suggestion was that the operation should be in the United States, but Budge with his previous experience in the salmon industry, told him that serious impediments could be put in the way of foreign-owned companies. Walter Lines did not have sufficient knowledge of the potential pitfalls of manufacturing there and he finally went along with Budge's suggestion that the plant should be in Canada. The first requirement was relative proximity to major markets. On that basis it was agreed that choice location for the plant would be in the Montreal area.

Captain Bob Swinton, M.C., a fellow wartime Seaforth officer was in England and available, so Budge took him on as his first assistant.

Before returning to Canada they visited the other Lines Bros. plants, in Birmingham and Belfast. After the first night in their Belfast hotel Bob claimed that he had been attacked by bed bugs. His complaint to the manager produced a typically Irish response: "Well now, would this not be an extraordinary coincidence; this is the first time we've ever had a Canadian in the hotel—and its certainly the first time we've ever had bedbugs!"

By the time Budge returned to Canada in mid-November it was with a contract as Managing Director of the Canadian subsidiary, to be known as Lines Bros. Canada Ltd. He had instructions to find premises and establish the plant, and an authorized capital of $500,000 to set it up. His starting salary would be $8,000 per annum and the 6 1/4% commission would remain at least temporarily.

Back in Montreal, Budge made a diligent search, as far away as Quebec City where he looked over an ex-government munitions factory, but eventually settled on a large, empty factory in the Montreal suburb of Lachine. The one-time Scott-Paine factory was exactly what they needed. It was owned by American interests and Budge went to New York to negotiate the purchase. Feeling it appropriate to take a chance on an alleged eager competitor, Budge made his bid. He contacted Walter Lines to request that the $500,000 be placed in his personal account at the Bank of Montreal by the next morning. It was—and by noon Budge had secured the premises.

He learned sometime later that there had indeed been a very hot competitor—the Northern Electric Co. Having secured it there were a great many decisions to be made and work to be done. Some immediate concerns were availability of labour, purchasing raw material such as steel and the purchase of presses to mould it.

From a perspective of fifty years Budge looks back in amazement at his naiveté, but he was once again, to use Robert McDougall's phrase on the Sicily campaign, "at his adventurous best" and with more enthusiasm than expertise he set out to transform the large, empty building into a busy, thriving toy factory. The questions he had to provide answers to were: what basic planning was required; what manufacturing objectives were to be decided upon; what machinery would be needed and, above all, what was the projected gross income, total costs and consequent profit? He had at least proved to himself that he was capable of selling toys—and estimating the North American market better than it could be done from England. In all other respects he was totally without experience.

Budge travelled widely looking for the best equipment; metal presses that cost up to $50,000 a piece, purchase of the most appropriate steel and tin to be moulded into the desired shapes. As well as the mills, he visited toy stores and toy departments of several large stores. More importantly he was also made welcome by more than one toy manufacturing company where, among other things, in one of them he took note of a bicycle-frame painting process on a conveyor system. He sent the details back to Lines Bros. resulting in a very positive improvement of the company's production.

The Lachine plant was soon a going concern, producing a wide variety of goods tuned to the North American market and selling well. There were several toy fairs held each year, notably Toronto and Chicago and the orders which came from them were extremely gratifying for a new company. It was inevitable that the best ideas would be copied by Lines Bros. competitors and this happened with a bicycle model and also a pedal-car which was copied to the nearest detail.

There were many teething troubles, which Budge faced with his usual philosophical demeanour, but always quality was his uppermost concern. The enterprise was still being heavily subsidized, but by October 1947 they were selling toys at the rate of $1000 per day—although to make the plant pay its own way the target had to be that much per hour. It says much that by December production rose to $35,700 per day. Among the numerous very popular items was a pedal driven jeep, gray with a white star on the hood in token of the white stars on the thousands of jeeps used by the allies in the recent war. Another one was a coaster wagon with four wheels and a handle for pulling, an almost inevitable possession of thousands of Canadian and American children, though not then as well known in Britain.

The workforce was almost entirely Francophone. Budge's command of French was minimal but he nevertheless got along with them very well. When union organizers appeared with pamphlets and much talk in aid of persuading them to join a union, there was a great deal of opposition among the workers. When faced with a major problem, such as the paint shop exhaust fans breaking down, they worked cheerfully into the small hours to rectify the problem. The office staff was small and friendly enough that a ski club was formed at Morin Heights in the Laurentians.

Frequently, war veterans dropped by looking for work. One day a young man came into Budge's office and introduced himself as a former R.A.F. wing-commander, recently arrived in Canada. He began by apologising for having taken the liberty of entering and taking a close look around the entire factory, particularly at various functions on the assembly lines. After he complimented Budge on every facet of the business, especially the morale of the workers, he then stated candidly as Budge's memory serves him: "I want a job. I don't suppose you have much use for an ex- fighter pilot, but I would be quite content to sweep the floors and do my best to keep them clean. That would be my main task, though I would hope from time to time to be found some other tasks as needed. My eventual hope however, is that one day I might be able to succeed you in your job. To begin with it would be entirely your decision to pay me whatever you might consider me worth."

Budge concluded that on those terms he couldn't possibly turn the man down. He became a useful addition to the workforce even though at the very bottom of the long ladder of civvy street. In years to come, during his term as B.C.'s Lieutenant-Governor, when talking to high school graduation classes, Budge often told that story, which he introduced as "How to get a job."

For the first six months of 1947 Nancy stayed in Montreal, but as her father's condition worsened it became necessary for her to return to Vancouver to help nurse him. It was a difficult time in the plant and Budge recalled that for every problem solved six more arose. The situation improved when Walter Lines' son Moray (Sandy) came out to stay for a full six months. His knowledge of the business was impressive and—more importantly—he and Budge got along extremely well. Besides working extremely hard Sandy enjoyed his leisure activities to the fullest. Budge has never forgotten the time they had a night out with the senior Eaton's toy buyer. Both were aware of the necessity to get along with this very important customer. The evening began with dinner at one of the major Montreal hotels. After this they were invited into a police car, driven by a policeman friend of the buyer.

The evening quickly developed into a good humoured effort to shock this visiting Englishman as they showed him the seamier side of Montreal life. Having experienced some pretty rough times in his life, in the northern canneries and through the war, Budge was used to strange situations, but Sandy Lines had almost certainly received a more gentle upbringing. It is to his credit that during this very novel evening, part of which was a visit to the city morgue, he kept his cool and his impeccable manners. To Budge it was a commendable performance.

There was one exception to the overall success of the items made, which fortunately Sandy was quick to see. Budge was ordered to initially import and subsequently make, a large English perambulator of the type often seen being pushed by nannies in London's Hyde Park. His objections that they would not sell well in Canada or the U.S. were overruled. It was called the "Park Lane" and Budge jokingly called it the "snob line", describing it as "the glittering chrome job to slay the masses!"

To convince Walter Lines what was needed he sent over from the U.S. a light, folding baby carriage, widely used by young mothers there and in Canada, who had to carry it up to their apartment. A similar design was produced and put into production in Montreal. Budge was informed that Walter Lines was very pleased with it and they were marketed in Britain as 'Nib's Chariot' (nibs was in common usage in Britain where a child would be refereed to as 'his nibs').

When on November 3, 1947 Henry Symes Bell-Irving was born in Vancouver he became the owner of a grey "Park Lane" pram, proudly pushed by his mother. Hal, as he has always been known was born three months early and weighed only 2 lbs 14 ozs. He spent his first few weeks in an incubator but his birth and survival was a great blessing to Budge and Nancy. They had endured disappointments in the past, but now they had a son. In a touching letter Budge wrote: "We have been fairly enterprising in our first ten years of life together. With our God-given son to crown it all, we are both being pretty enterprising now. It is our way of life and we'll go places together—we three."

The Lines Bros. Canada Ltd. sales force was expanded and a branch showroom opened in Vancouver, with Bob Swinton in charge. One of the first large orders was placed by Woodward's downtown Vancouver Store, despatched from Montreal in a full rail car. The T. Eaton Co. was the most important toy buyer across Canada based on the number of stores. The next time Budge met the Eaton's toy buyer after the evening out with Sandy, it was in the new, large Lachine showroom to negotiate a very important order; a constant supply of tricycles, which were to be a special item with the 'Eatonia' label on it. The order included a saddle that looked, felt, and would behave like leather—but wasn't. The deal was almost made, but the buyer insisted that he must have leather. Budge replied that he didn't think it could be managed within the very reasonable price agreed upon.

Immediately the buyer excused himself, went into Budge's office and phoned Walter Lines in London. When he came out he informed Budge "Mr. Lines had agreed to the leather." There was no comment to Budge from the chairman either then or later. Budge was, of course, surprised and unhappy, but his fondness for Walter Lines was such that it did not occur to him that he should at least have had an explanation.

Should he have also concluded that head office's high opinion of him had waned or even disappeared? When Walter Lines came out on April 7, 1948 to visit his Canadian subsidiary, Budge was of course delighted to see him. He had no doubt come to take stock of what was going on and Budge was proud and happy to show him. It would have been obvious that despite the day-to-day problems to be solved, Budge was enjoying his job—and life in Montreal immensely, sometimes walking to work from Westmount, even when winter temperatures were well below zero, just to keep in shape.

To all intents and purposes their relationship was the same. Only a few months before his arrival, Walter Lines had written:

> "Now look here Budge, I want to give you a real pat on the back. I am sure you have worked tremendously hard and the future will be the results of your efforts. I am inclined, as you know, to be very forthright and not say too many words, and perhaps I have wrapped you on the knuckles too hard occasionally, but it was only with the intention of helping you, so do not worry in the least about that."

He went on to say that Budge and Sandy would make a first rate team and it would not be long before results began to come along. He admitted that many mistakes had been made at the parent company and more would probably be made, but the main thing was to put them right as soon as possible. Even so, he was coming out at Budge's request because this third year was a crucial turning point in the Canadian venture. He had made mistakes too, and he expected to be "properly sat-on."

Walter Lines remained in Montreal until the end of June and though there were pleasant social times there were also underlying currents. At one point, in mid-May Budge wrote: "Walter feels the responsibility very deeply, so cannot blame him for being intolerant and outspoken with everybody at times... my own stock is very low at the moment but that doesn't really worry me as I am determined to do my best to make the grade." Here was the decisive, highly decorated soldier sounding much like the defensive boy who had written to his father from Loretto years before. Budge told Nancy he had taken on a huge job and without doubt faced the most difficult period of his life, as he strove to bring success to the venture under circumstances which were not particularly easy.

There is little doubt that if anybody could achieve success, it was Budge. Other circumstances before and after proved his mettle, but were some things in this venture beyond his control? He had become unhappy about the performance of the plant manager. He wrote to Walter Lines expressing his doubts and asking if the man might be replaced with "one of the best toy makers in England." The letter was not acknowledged. Once again, had it not been for Budge's still strong respect for Walter Lines he might have resigned and gone home to Vancouver. The serious consequences of this lack of action only occurred to Budge later. He did not immediately reach the most probable conclusion; that the man may have written a negative report on him to the chairman, and might in fact have been asked to make such a report.

Budge returned to Vancouver at the end of June for a month's holiday during which Hal was christened. Two of his wartime friends were asked to be Godfathers; Jim Stone and Rowan Coleman. It was a great party, in the best Bell-Irving tradition. One sad note was that Reginald Symes had died on June 20, a blow felt deeply by Budge, who had always held a high respect for his father-in-law.

When Budge returned to Montreal he found a house in Dorval which he purchased. He had been longing for the time when Nancy would be able to return there, and though he had a good social life, living a bachelor existence, even in comfortable digs did not please him. Everything went according to plan. By September Nancy and Hal arrived and moved into the house, where they lived as a family through the winter and well into the following spring of 1949.

Production and the orders were growing in volume. It was therefore a surprise when Walter Lines brother, Arthur, arrived from London unexpectedly. The reason for this sudden visit was revealed when, with tears in his eyes he said he was there to ask for Budge's resignation from the company. There was no discussion and no request for reasons, no objection or any thought of compensation. Budge went home to Vancouver with feelings of great sadness, because he had been very proud of Lines Bros. Canada and had gained immense satisfaction from his endeavours.

In retrospect, Budge views the main culprit as a serious lack of communication and possibly a disinclination by Walter Lines to let go of the reins, even partially. His first selling spree in the vast U.S. market must surely have been an excellent start. His visits to the United States produced some tools, material and expertise not available in Canada. He had always believed that the purchase of the Scott-Paine factory in Lachine was a right step. If not, he wasn't told so.

Budge admittedly did not initially have any deep knowledge of the actual manufacturing process of the articles he was to make. In his several business careers, including his later chairmanship of the Canadian Real Estate Association, he has always made sure that his financial help was absolutely first class, because he fully realized its importance and he himself had always preferred the more active side of business. If he had been guilty of poor judgement in any facet of the operation, as he now presumes he must have been, he was never specifically advised or warned at any time that things were 'off track.' After such a long and happy relationship with Walter Lines and his family, Budge feels that there must have been something very wrong for him to have been dismissed so summarily, without explanation.

He will always be proud of the many and varied things he accomplished in the toy business, though sad indeed that he accepted responsibility in matters perhaps beyond his knowledge and experience. If the main culprit was indeed lack of communication Budge sees no reason why he himself should not be satisfied to take all the blame and leave it at that. It is to his and Nancy's credit that they still remained friends with the Lines family and Sandy in particular, who is in contact still. Any regrets have now faded away. So ended Budge's tenure with Lines Bros. Canada Ltd.

Back in Vancouver, Budge escaped for a brief interlude to go fishing on Denman Island with his old school friend, Commander 'Chuggy' Lacon. Very early one morning Budge went down to the beach to go 'skinny dipping.' Somehow a leech bored its way into one of the cheeks of his behind. He returned to Vancouver for a Seaforth Highlander's officers' mess meeting and was rash enough to tell the paymaster about the leech. Within minutes he was lying face down on the billiard table with his kilt up over his waste. A Highland claymore was produced for the operation, possibly frightening the leech to death. The claymore was used to enlarge the hole so that the leech could be extracted. A lighted cigarette cauterized the hole which was then washed off with whisky. It was altogether not untypical of the Hogan's Alley members of the Seaforth Highlanders of Canada, even if their 'patient' was a brigadier!

It was an appropriate time for Budge to ask himself: "Where to go next? Real estate sales might be a possibility." At least in this field he would not be alone in having no previous training. Bell-Irving Insurance Agencies Ltd., a subsidiary of H. Bell-Irving & Co., was managed by Duncan Bell-Irving. It had one real-estate desk and its long-time incumbent was about to retire. He had been paid $200 per month, about equal to his gross commission earnings. Following a few days of indoctrination Budge moved in at the same figure. He now had a desk in a downtown office, with the usual facilities, simple as they were, but he wouldn't live long on $200 per month so any success in this latest venture was going to be up to him. Walking up and down the fashionable streets and avenues of Shaughnessy Heights, ringing doorbells and asking, 'Might you be interested in selling this beautiful house?' was not something Budge enjoyed. He in fact loathed every minute of it. More often than not the door would be opened by the Chinese cook; they at least were mainly polite.

His first listing came from a friendly relative who owned a good, well-used house on Cypress Street. With pen and India ink Budge drew detailed plans of both main and upper floors for inclusion in the first newspaper advertisement he had ever written. The next evening a telephone call came from a woman in the B.C. interior town of Kamloops who asked if he would hold the house until the next day and she would come immediately. She arrived early in the morning and had no objection to waiting until 10 a.m. to see the house because she wished to be driven around to see the immediate neighbourhood. It wasn't long before, inescapably, they saw a 'For Sale' sign in front of another house and, of course, she wished to see it. Budge spent an unhappy two hours keeping his prospect 'hot' and eventually they returned to Cypress Street and had a thorough look over the house. Her comments were mainly favourable other than: "It certainly has been lived in by a boisterous family. There's a lot to be done here."

Budge's response was to emphasise how well the house fitted the requirements of the woman's family and it would be a shame if it was sold to someone else for what she would be 'glad' to pay for it. He said "Let's consider how much it would cost to put it in first-class condition and then make an offer based on what you would be prepared to pay for it." The woman bought the house for the asking price and Budge had sold his first listing.

As business increased, he and Nancy wanted a house for themselves, preferably with a sea view, perhaps in West Vancouver where Nancy had nearly purchased a lot while Budge was still in the Army. House hunting for themselves might produce some listings. Walking on hilly Creery Avenue, overlooking the sea at West Bay, Budge met a little boy and pointing to a house on nearby Hayes Street asked, "Do you think that white house up there might be for sale?" The reply was prompt: "That's my house. It's not for sale!" Budge went up to the door anyway to call on the boy's mother and in due course purchased the house. It became a happy home for their growing family for the next few years. In July 1949 Roderick was born and in August 1951 Donald arrived. To accommodate three boys, Budge built an addition on the house, which served them well until their next move.

As the sole salesman for the real-estate arm, Budge realized that he needed something more to offer his growing clientele. Believing that some further training in real-estate valuation would be a good beginning he took the American Appraisal Institute course in Seattle. He returned to Vancouver as an officially qualified appraiser with the M.A.I. designation, recognized throughout North America. During the course Budge was not afraid to question the instructor if there was some point he did not fully understand. It sometimes bordered on an argument and the instructor finally joked that if Budge agreed on a point it must be correct. Something must have stuck because Budge came out with high marks.

He much enjoyed the appraisal business, liking the challenge of finding the key to apparently unsolvable problems, thriving on the occasional cross-examination by a lawyer who did not understand the problem. Making appraisals in expropriation cases both for and against the federal, provincial and local governments, in time the Bell-Irving appraisal department became one of the best and largest in Greater Vancouver, if not Western Canada. One highly qualified company appraiser, E.W. (Ted) Palmer, later became Senior Vice President and Chief Appraiser, Canada, for A.E. LaPage Ltd.

Though he had learned something of real estate values and general appraising, which was a useful beginning, Budge was well aware of his ignorance in the matter of building and operating a real estate brokerage company. As a competitor, he didn't expect established local real-estate people to teach him. He and Nancy had some good friends in Seattle who introduced him to John L. Scott, owner of one of the best known Seattle real estate firms, which enjoyed a commanding position in the high-end residential field. The company's sales manager was detailed to pass on every conceivable idea to Budge, while John Scott's own contribution was the suggestion that in building quality residential sales staff he should try to find forty-year old, Junior League divorcees. While he did not accept or use all the ideas offered, this one particular suggestion was, he thought, an excellent one. Budge in fact interpreted it as women who, divorced or not, were likely to be asked to the 'right' social functions, yet with some need to earn extra income. The concept was a wise one and Budge recruited several such women, who became very successful.

When H.O. died in 1931 it was stated in his will that his estate would cover the yearly expenses for Pasley for the next fifteen years. After this time the island could be disposed of. In 1950 Budge received instructions from the trustees, Richard and Duncan Bell-Irving, and Peter Traill, to put it on the market. It was priced at $35,000 with favourable terms for the whole island, including the five original Bell-Irving houses and a caretaker's house. Initial local advertising produced little or no interest and eventually an advertisement in the American magazine *Previews*, which displayed exceptional properties produced a Californian couple who came to Pasley and appeared to be delighted with it. They were going to make an offer right away. At this juncture the man asked a small boy standing nearby what he thought of the island. The reply was, "We love it here and come over every summer, however, you have to look out for the snakes." The American couple made immediate arrangements to return to California and the sale disappeared with the snakes (actually harmless small garter snakes).

Budge approached family members, a few local friends, and others he thought might be interested, soon producing enough people to form a syndicate. At a total price of $25,000 he had no difficulty in persuading them to buy into this concept, especially with interest at 4 1/2% and the outstanding balance to be paid off over 15 years. When eighteen names were signed up, the idea was born of a truly wonderful island resort.

When the number reached thirty, Pasley Island Ltd. was incorporated, to have thirty shares, each one representing a lot of as near as possible equal value, plus the site for a caretaker, making a total of thirty-one. The six original houses already in place were included as part of the new lot disbursement.

A substantial part of the island would be retained as common property, including the North Bay former orchard and vegetable garden, the tennis courts and the island's central meadow-land, which would later become the site of the annual island games. Most of the island's surface is in forest, interspersed by a trail network. The highest point of the island, 'summit rock' has stone memorials to the memory of H.O. and his eldest daughter Isabel.

Budge plotted the lots onto a detailed map. The size would, of course vary, but every attempt was made to ensure equal value. Each would have access to the trails and, in varying degrees to the water-front. Numbers were attached to the lots on the map from one to thirty-one, anti-clockwise around the island beginning and ending at North Bay. Tickets for each number were placed in a hat and then drawn for.

Budge commented: "Pasley Island members were soon to realize the benefits; close proximity to the city while retaining the absolute privacy of a private island—a beautiful central meadow, not found on any other island for many miles, plus availability of fresh water from its own wells, adequate for fifty families at city standards. There can be no doubt that Pasley will continue to grow as an exceptionally valuable gem within the beautiful waters of British Columbia."

By the mid 1950's it became necessary for Budge to incorporate an independent real-estate company rather than continue to operate under the Bell-Irving Insurance Agency name. One reason for this was that the insurance agency, and Uncle Duncan in particular, was unhappy with the idea that sales persons should get as much as a 50% commission. The most important reason though, was for Budge to have total control, according to the requirements of the real-estate industry.

Bell-Irving Realty Ltd. was incorporated and a joint move to larger premises on Pender Street meant that Budge could have separate office space. One person who had watched his growing success was Peter Traill, who was not only willing to back him with moral support but also to arrange a draw of $10,000 to get the new company started. Budge never had to draw on this generous start-up offer but he was nevertheless grateful to his old friend.

With the boom in real-estate sales and the increasing number of both companies and sales people there was a need to organize the industry along professional lines and to create standards. The process of interviewing prospective salesmen did not provided a clear answer to the question, 'what was required of candidates?' Budge gave this much thought and came up with some conclusions. At this juncture, lawyer Irwin Davis was persuaded to leave his law practice and to join Budge as secretary of what was to become the Real-Estate Agents' Licensing Board. Together they drafted the first B.C. real-estate licensing examination, including an essay "Why I want to become a real-estate salesman."

With two other principal agents, Budge met with the Attorney General of British Columbia, a position then occupied by Robert Bonner, Budge's one time brother officer who had been wounded in the Italian Campaign. Their discussion focused upon the urgent need for a university course to assist in improving standards. Bob Bonner sent them to U.B.C. President, Dr. Norman MacKenzie. He in turn introduced them to the Dean of Commerce, Dr. Earl MacPhee who was very receptive to the idea and gave his time enthusiastically in setting it up.

In 1958, Budge's first year of four as president of the Vancouver Real-Estate Board, the salesmen's pre-licensing course was established as a first step in what became U.B.C.'s comprehensive real estate program. A wide search was made for a suitably qualified academic and ultimately Professor Philip White, head of the College of Estate Management, University of London, England, was chosen. In that same year the B.C. Real-Estate Act was passed and given Royal Assent. The concept eventually spread across Canada.

The establishment of Bell-Irving Realty's first branch office came about by the arrival at the Pender Street head-office of George Bulhak, a Pole who with his wife Wanda, had crossed China enroute to Vancouver. He said they had been living on University of B.C. Endowment Lands for some time (where there are many streets of expensive homes), knew them well and had no doubt that he could open and run a successful real-estate office there. He was taken on and an office was opened on University Boulevard.

On the day that it was officially opened, present among others for the occasion were George Bulhak, Budge and two 'senior' Bell-Irvings. Recalling the event, Budge noted:

"Senior Bell-Irvings in those days were somewhat guilty of self-importance. When the first guest to arrive, U.B.C. President Dr. Norman MacKenzie, went up to our new manager and greeted him heartily, 'Hello George, who are all these people?', it made the day for me and George!'

He more than earned his keep by producing, or possibly enticing just one high-calibre saleslady. She was well-known and admired by just about every person on University Hill and had no need to spend time on listings. The clients automatically came to her. Isabel (Betty) Iredale was, financially a most valuable contributor and a very great influence in building the mutual respect and friendship in our steadily growing company. George, in his own way also contributed to the pleasant atmosphere of the company. He earned more points by taking the U.B.C. President and me on a successful steelhead fishing trip in the upper Capilano River before the days of the Cleveland dam. He is also remembered walking into the head-office one day in long waders clutching a 6 to 8 pound steelhead. The University Boulevard office did not last too long, but Betty Iredale did."

While all this was going on, Budge and Nancy had decided that the Hayes Street house was no longer big enough for their growing family and built a house on Farmleigh Drive in West Vancouver's British Properties. There were several modifications to the plans, but eventually they were satisfied and the house served their needs for the next eight years until they moved over to Vancouver's Shaughnessy area.

West Vancouver, with its proximity to the ocean is one of the most attractive municipalities in the lower mainland. With its winding lanes reminiscent of Devonshire, it is a desirable location. Despite attracting the fabulously wealthy who build million dollar homes, there are many streets of modest bungalows. It also made good sense that Bell-Irving Realty's next expansion was a West Vancouver office, fronting onto the south side of Marine Drive and conveniently provided with the generous parking space of the Park Royal Shopping Centre. There was plenty of room for a staff of about a dozen or so, many of whom were women.

Continuing with his recollections Budge added:

"Once again, the Park Royal office was fortunate to recruit Audrey Sayle, a most charming addition to the office who was to have a major share of sales in the higher priced West Vancouver bracket.

Unfortunately, for perhaps the first and only time I had hired a manager who simply was not a gentleman. One day he made a most atrocious remark to her and, understandably, she promptly walked out, never to return. Needless to say, that manager was not far behind."

(After leaving Bell-Irving Realty, Audrey worked for another realty company before forming Audrey Sayle Realty, where she maintained her share of some of the highest priced real estate in West Vancouver—a formidable competitor!)

Also in 1958, Budge hired Bert Edwards, president of the Salesmen's Division, Vancouver Real Estate Board. Budge had developed a considerable respect for him which resulted in Bert joining Bell-Irving Realty to manage the residential division. Under his guidance sales increased and another office was opened in the attractive west-side area of Kerrisdale. Budge and his family moved to approximately the same location in 1959 when he purchased a house on W. 40th Avenue. It was their last move before the call to Government House in 1978.

Despite his growing success in business, Budge was not at his best sitting at a desk, managing. He enjoyed being out and about, making deals, serving clients and always learning. Having bought some land on Vancouver's West Hastings Street for a Winnipeg client on which two large high-rise office towers and a hotel were to be built, the developer persuaded Budge that the office structures should be pre-leased to the tenants before construction began, to help off-set construction and operating costs. Budge and his team calculated the operating costs for a building not yet built. It was the beginning of a good friendship and a mutually beneficial business relationship.

Another interesting transaction was the sale of a large property at the north end of Annacis Island, an industrial estate on the Fraser River that was originally developed by Grosvenor Laing, a part of the Duke of Westminster's business holdings. The sales agreement was drawn-up so expertly, it gave the new owner an assured considerable future income through various lease agreements, including riparian rights on the Fraser River for log storage. The new owner-vendor came out from Chicago to pay an un-requested large additional commission to Bell-Irving Realty, as a way to express his thanks.

Investment, Commercial and Industrial business was steadily gaining ground. A bright young man, A.R. (Randy) Symons, arrived from Montreal where he had studied art and design at the College des Beauxarte, majoring in ceramics. With a friend he had set up an interior design business near Boston, but left it to come to Vancouver in December 1954. He then decided there was more money in real-estate, though he knew little about the business. He was offered $200 per month and invited to 'get on with it.' Budge taught him a few things and fed him some opportunities to get started. It was not long, however, before he began to display a singular talent which the boss lacked—a willingness to take personal risks in buying property in the right places for the right price at the right time. He went on to become extremely successful and financially secure. It seemed that the few ventures in which he lost money were the ones in which Budge invested too, ostensibly to help him along!

It must have been a source of pride for Budge's parents to see their son succeed in business, just as he had succeeded in the army. They had moved to Whonnock, in the Fraser valley and had purchased a small farm, where they were very happy and frequently surrounded by young members of the growing Bell-Irving clan. Unfortunately, Budge's father Henry had been declining in health for some time and he died on September 23, 1959. He had lived his life to the full, as his adventures in two world wars clearly showed. He had maintained his naval connections throughout the years since the end of the second world war, and in recognition of his long naval career many serving naval officers came over from the Esquimalt R.C.N. base for his funeral.

Henry wished to be buried at sea and following cremation, Budge waited a while until 'Swatty' Wotherspoon came out to Vancouver on a business trip. Henry and 'Swatty' had remained good friends following their horse-racing escapade in Europe and Budge wished him to be present to join the family at a sea burial off Pasley. Among others, Corney Burke was also present to give Henry a good send off, which was followed by a wake at the Vancouver Club. Aeneas Bell-Irving took the opportunity to proclaim Budge as the new 'chief' of the Bell-Irving clan in Canada.

Although immersed in business, Budge did not neglect community obligations and had for some time been active in the Boy Scout movement. It had begun in West Vancouver when Budge took Hal, Roderick and Donald to join the local cub pack. When Budge came out he had been talked into taking on the job of leader, the Akela. His interest grew and by the time the family moved back to Vancouver he had become District Commissioner for Vancouver Centre. He persuaded a friend in the Fraser Valley to lease a large section of property for $1.00 per year for a scout camp.

In June 1961 Budge earned his Wood Badge, an important step for leaders in Scouting. It confirms a level of commitment to Scouting ideals and requires at least 60 hours of special training in people skills, woodcraft and imparting knowledge to others. Some believe that in modern times much of the initial meaning of scouting has been lost, particularly the simple, outdoor woodsman element. Whether this is so or not, at the bottom of the Wood Badge certificate are evocative words by poet Rudyard Kipling:

"Who hath smelt wood-smoke at twilight? Who hath heard the birch log burning? Who is quick to read the noises of the night? Let him follow with the others, for the young mens' feet are turning to the camps of proved desire and known delight." Budge has maintained his contact with the scout movement and it had a special meaning during his time as Lieutenant-Governor of British Columbia. He still attends council meetings in his capacity as Honorary President of the B.C. and Yukon Provincial Council.

Bell-Irving Realty's appraisal business grew and in 1964 Budge landed a large and unusual federal government contract to evaluate the Rocky Mountain national parks: Banff, Kootenay, Revelstoke, Yoho and Glacier. Included was a complete rent review of developed properties in the town of Banff to bring them up to current market value. This had not been done before and Budge was asked to ascertain their lease potential. University students were recruited to collect the data, among them seventeen year old Hal who proved to be a great asset. There was considerable local opposition and Budge went to Banff several times to make speeches in support of the changes that would result. With no rental comparisons available, it presented a challenge and a fictitious Alberta town was concocted on paper as a model. Budge's assessment confirmed the figures arrived at by the government's assessors. In a later separate contract Budge was asked to appraise the land value only of Jasper national park, excluding improvements. As the park has no income and therefore no profit value, it cannot be developed because its sole purpose is a national treasure. Budge assessed the value as one dollar and this figure was accepted.

By the early 1970's the total strength of the sales force was about fifty. Another useful addition to the company was a young New

Zealander, Mel Newth, who soon showed his talents lay not only in the accounting field, but management as well and he became Budge's right-hand man until he returned to New Zealand with his wife and three daughters. An outstanding feature of Bell-Irving Realty was the 'one family' atmosphere, the genuine liking and respect for each other and pride in the company, which many of the early Bell-Irving Realty group still fondly remember.

Hal obtained his real-estate salesman's license and joined the company after graduating with a B.A. in Geography from Simon Fraser University, where he was a charter student. His natural warmth and ability impressed his father enough that he forecast Hal would make a valuable contribution in a short time. In 1972 Roderick graduated from U.B.C. with a degree in marine biology, eventually joining the federal government's Department of Fisheries and Oceans. Earlier, at Shawnigan Lake School he had taken up rowing and maintained a keen interest in it right through the 1970's, winning a bronze medal at the 1971 Pan American Games. In 1976 he took a crew to the Henley Regatta and won the Steward's Cup. In 1979 he was appointed coach of Canada's Olympic team for the 1980 Olympics, to be held in Moscow, but a big disappointment came when Prime Minister Joe Clark chose to follow the lead of U.S. President Jimmy Carter in boycotting the Games because of Russia's invasion of Afghanistan. Donald was studying Electrical Engineering at U.B.C. and in 1974 graduated with honours, having taken a year out to travel Europe and ski in the Alps.

With a view to investing in real-estate as well as selling it, in May 1969 Bell-Irving Properties Ltd. was incorporated. The company was formed to generate income by investing in selective real estate in Greater Vancouver. The first share issue was sold at $10 each. There were eleven shareholders including his three sons. Budge invited some of his closer associates to purchase shares and those who stayed in until the company was dissolved did quite well.

When Bell-Irving Realty was sold to A.E. LePage, Bell-Irving Investments was incorporated and Bell-Irving Properties Ltd. became its wholly owned subsidiary. The original people remained as shareholders of Bell-Irving Investments Ltd. This investment arm was created on the advice of a tax lawyer to minimize taxation on the sale of properties. During the life of these two companies only two properties were involved and only one was actually purchased, an older commercial building adjacent to the downtown core (the other, in the suburb of

Coquitlam, was managed under a clever lease arrangement for which they took a handsome profit and a management fee). By November 1975 the shares, helped by a rise in real estate prices were valued at $80 each. The downtown building was sold in April 1977 for a handsome profit. Upon completion of the sale an offer was made to shareholders who wished to pull out at that point. The share value of Bell-Irving Investments Ltd. had risen to $114.87. When the two companies were finally wound up in March 1980, the shareholders realized $120.45 per share.

In June 1972, Brian Magee, Chairman and C.E.O. of A.E. LePage, Ltd., the substantial Toronto based real-estate company, visited Vancouver with his President, Gordon Gray. He told Budge that they had purchased Boultbee Sweet Ltd., another well-known Vancouver real-estate company and asked if he would be willing to sell Bell-Irving Realty and manage the two as a new company. On reflection Budge accepted the proposal, with an agreed price of half a million dollars for his company. In the deal he would remain President for five years, and also take a seat on the parent company's board. He concluded that it would make sense to maintain a degree of local independence while enjoying the strength of being part of a successful national company. Magee offered to let the present name remain if Budge so wished, but his choice, which turned out to be a wise one, was to instead name it A.E. LePage (Western) Ltd.

The sale provided an opportunity for Budge to invest in a boat. It was something that, with an eye to eventual retirement he had long dreamed of having. He settled for a 33 foot cabin power-boat which he named "Shieling." With its 4 births and twin inboard diesel engines, capable of producing a speed of 17 knots, the boat was a good investment. Many coastal cruises were enjoyed in her until she was sold in the early 1980's.

The much expanded company was more complex than the relatively small Bell-Irving Realty. The area of operation was larger and included offices beyond Vancouver and West Vancouver into outlying municipalities in the Fraser Valley. This brought in many new salesmen and sales managers and the 'family' feel was lost. Added to this, whereas Budge welcomed having a senior executive from the parent company, indeed he suggested it, Brian Magee saw it more as keeping an eye on his Vancouver venture. He sent out David Crawford, who came with an 'eastern' mentality, not unknown in the competitive spirit between Toronto and Vancouver. It was one more blatant example of the east 'knowing best' resulting in a loss of the old company's identity and, worse still losing long-time, once loyal salesmen.

In December 1974 another New Zealander, Bryan Grover, was sent out by the Toronto office and he took over from the departing Mel Newth as V.P. Finance and Company Secretary. Bryan sensed that he was imposed on A.E. LePage (Western) Ltd. by the eastern company without first checking with Budge. He was to report back to the senior finance V.P. Ken Stephen, but quickly developed a closer affinity with the Vancouver office. He was sure that Budge saw through the 'charade' and admired the way he played along and avoided embarrassment to his new executive.

Budge continued as Chairman of A.E. LePage (Western) Ltd. and remained active in the affairs of the Real-Estate industry, both provincially and nationally, in 1972 serving as the first president of the newly formed Canadian Real Estate Association. In 1974, on January 21 (his 61st birthday) he became President of the Vancouver Board of Trade, seventy-nine years after grandfather H.O. Bell-Irving was appointed to the same office, though H.O. served for two years, from March 1895 to March 1897. In April Budge led a group of members on an official trade tour to several European capitals—Amsterdam, Gothenburg, Copenhagen, Helsinki, Stockholm and Oslo. It was fitting that in Amsterdam he was recognized by the city for his part in its relief from the Nazis. Budge received another surprise—zerox copies of May 1945 press reports from the city archives of the arrival of the Canadian Seaforth's and Budge's part in freeing the city. The tour mostly consisted of meeting each town's boards of trade and commerce, industrialists and bankers, with a few side-trips and much socializing.

Budge's year as President was in the second year of the B.C. New Democratic Party's first mandate as government, under Premier Dave Barrett. As the first socialist government to rule, following defeat of W.A.C. Bennett's Social Credit Party, they were treated with suspicion by the business community and did indeed bring in some legislation which caused concern among members of the Board of Trade.

As a free-enterpriser, Budge had been among these, but was open-minded enough to acknowledge that some of their legislation made sense, particularly over the issue of land-use and housing. In an interview with Vancouver Sun business writer Mike Grenby, he said that as President he wished to use the experience of Board of Trade members to "take a positive step in helping to make the political process a more effective one." From a business perspective, his main concern was the mining industry, on which the New Democrats came down particularly hard. Bill 31 had been introduced, under which royalties would be subject to higher taxation, ultimately eroding exploration and resulting in fewer jobs in the industry. Budge nevertheless gave support in principle to the proposed Land Commission Act.

For several years until the late 1960's, the Lower Mainland Regional Planning Board had regulated planning for all municipalities in the region. Some of the more powerful, *laissez-faire* local politicians saw the board as an attack on their autonomy and the Social Credit government gave in by abolishing it. The effect was to increase the threat of urban sprawl, which continues to this day. In a *Journal of Commerce* interview Budge pointed out that his views were not necessarily those of the Board of Trade, but "... over the years we have become accustomed to the single family dwelling with a garden in front, behind and on both sides. This has been the standard, and one that the population in the main wants to preserve. It is becoming more and more evident that we cannot afford this. We must learn to live closer together in high-rise apartments and terraced housing, with party walls which may be under condominium or corporate ownership with leases."

His views were prophetic in that after initial resistance, townhouses and condominiums have become very popular. He saw an increasing population putting an added strain on transportation and the limited supply of available land. He was an advocate for increased density on the U.B.C. Endowment Lands and Fairview Slopes, above False Creek, south of downtown Vancouver, both of which have been introduced very successfully. Although the Land Commission Act was extremely controversial, it had Budge's firm endorsement as a means of conserving farmland. In a March, 1974 *Globe and Mail* interview he said: "Urban sprawl has been creeping into the Fraser Valley for years. The act was designed to do something about it, and that's commendable."

Budge expressed some reservations over the provincial government's purchase of a private development company, Dunhill Development Corporation Ltd., to boost the number of residential units built annually. This was not public, or rental housing, but homes for private purchase, backed with a $40 million fund to provide first and second mortgages. The first year target was 20,000 additional units extra to those provided by the regular building industry. As a social experiment it had limited success, primarily because the N.D.P. mandate lasted less than a full four year term before being defeated once more by the Social Credit Party.

Restrictions had been imposed both federally and provincially on rental housing, especially the removal of tax deductible expenses for investors. In a critical speech to the Junior Chamber of Commerce Budge stressed that there would be no shortage of affordable accommodation if private investment in rental property were encouraged instead of discouraged, adding "Free competition would do much to keep both costs and rents down to a constant minimum. Historically governments have never done these things as well as private enterprise, anywhere in the world. If the same money were paid to underprivileged tenants as rental supplements it would be much better."

At the end of his term, in January 1975, the many letters of endorsement from both Board of Trade members and staff was a clear indication of Budge's success. He had not held back where his views might have differed from those of the members at large, but his leadership skills were admired by all. He had stressed all through his tenure that whatever ideological differences the Board of Trade may have had with the New Democratic philosophy, though they might oppose some legislation, it was not their job to defeat the government. Instead he had set out to make the organization and its various committees perform the role of an analytical critic to examine each piece of legislation and to maintain good communication. Ministers were invited to luncheons regularly to put forth their ideas on all manner of issues affecting the province and to allow board members to challenge and question them. Budge's other legacy was the speed with which he could get through a committee agenda, yet still cover every point thoroughly.

In December 1975 a provincial election was called and the Dave Barrett government was defeated by William (Bill) Bennett, W.A.C. Bennett's son, who had taken over leadership of the Social Credit Party from his father. The N.D.P. formed a challenging opposition party and Dave Barrett was still its leader when Budge became Lieutenant-Governor three years later.

In April 1977 Budge's mother, Nan, died at the age of eighty-four. Her life had been remarkable, with a 'ringside seat' in Dover during the first world war, a husband active in both wars, and her two sons in the second. Seventeen years earlier she had nursed Henry through a long illness before he died, but harder still to bear was the death of Wendy in

1976 at only fifty-nine. Budge gave an eloquent eulogy at his mother's funeral, held in St. Paul's Church, where so many Bell-Irving weddings, christenings and funerals had taken place. He said, "In the second war, left behind in Canada this time, Nan once again became fearful of the telegraph boy, this time for a husband and two sons. When he did call it read: 'Wing Commander Roderick Bell-Irving missing, believed killed in action.' She contained her terrible grief in a magnificent determination to give strength to the rest of her family. It didn't show very much but she never did get over it."

Budge's five year agreement with A.E. LePage ended in 1978. He was ready for retirement, having reached the age of sixty-five on January 21. On February 16 while returning on a C.P. Air flight from a company meeting in Toronto, Budge was approached by the Hon. Ron Basford, then Federal Minister of Justice, who came and sat beside him. Speaking in confidential tones, the Minister asked Budge if he would allow his name to be put forward as a possible successor to the Hon. Walter Owen, Lieutenant-Governor of British Columbia. Budge agreed to the proposal but an actual invitation seemed so remote that other than briefly discussing it with Nancy he thought little more about it and told no one else.

On April 5, he and Nancy attended a State Dinner in Victoria and the next day while waiting at the Swartz Bay ferry terminal to return to Vancouver, Budge was called by loud-speaker to the terminal office. His immediate concern was that he would hear disturbing news concerning a family member. Instead it was once again the Hon. Ron Basford, calling from the Cabinet Room in Ottawa and asking Budge to provide biographical details for a possible press release—'just in case.'

Nothing more was heard and on April 20 Budge returned to Toronto to attend the A.G.M of A.E. LePage at the Granite Club. His term as president of A.E. LePage Western Ltd. was officially over and he had resigned from the board as required by the company's age policy. The meeting ended at noon and before Budge left the club he was once more called to the telephone. Taking it in the liquor cupboard he recognized the caller as Prime Minister Pierre Trudeau, who asked Budge "Would you like to go and live in Victoria?" The brief reply was "Yes, Sir." The Prime Minister cautioned him, "Don't tell anybody yet because I have not informed the Governor-General."

A call also came from his Vancouver secretary, Mary Law, who asked Budge what he had been up to. She said there was a scrum of reporters in the office—somehow the news had been leaked in Vancouver. Budge pleaded innocence and immediately phoned the Prime Minister's private line to say that the word was out. He was told that Governor-General Jules Leger had now been informed and it was alright to release the information. Budge was able to confirm what had up to then been a rumour and make it official.

Four days later he and Nancy were at Government House in Victoria, as guests of retiring Lieutenant-Governor Walter Owen and his wife Shirley. During a quiet dinner Budge asked if they could discuss expenses for running Government House. Walter Owen told him that if they were 'very careful' they could possibly get by with a cash deficit of no more than $35,000. It was a restless night after this news, with still no idea as to what financial assistance might be forthcoming and assuming they would have to foot much of the expense. They could not possibly refuse the job at the last minute and remain in B.C. Their sleeplessness was compounded by the 80 degree temperature in the Royal Suite, with a window that would not open. Next day at a meeting with Government House private secretary, Commander Gar Dixon, and comptroller Tom Duckitt, they were relieved to find that a salary close to $35,000, plus both personal and entertainment allowances would be paid. Also much of the actual Government House expenses were paid directly by both the federal and provincial governments. Budge and Nancy were not wealthy and they knew it would be hard-going, but they were determined to make it work.

The swearing-in was arranged for May 18, 1978 and in the three weeks leading up to it Budge and Nancy were overwhelmed by the volume of letters, cards and telegrams offering good wishes. They seemed surprised at the outpouring of goodwill and the belief of so many people that it was a wise and well-deserved appointment. With help from secretary Mary Law he answered them all and wrote in his diary: "We gain strength, enthusiasm and resolve from them and we are looking forward to our new career."

Replying to a letter of congratulations from his friend and ex-colleague Audrey Sayle, he told her:

> "In contemplating the obligations of this high office I'm reminded of Winston Churchill's alleged description of Labour Prime

Minister Clement Atlee—'A modest man with a good deal to be modest about!'

Nancy will make a great chatelaine and on that basis we'll make the grade. We're looking forward to it."

On the evening of May 17th, in the Governor's Suite at the Executive House Hotel there was a family dinner in which everyone shared in the preparation. Guest of honor was Aunt Pye. Budge and Nancy returned to one of the guest suites at Government House and this time had a good sleep, with no overwhelming worries about the job ahead. Budge availed himself of the outdoor pool which he would use almost every morning for the next five years when in residence at Government House.

At 11 a.m. on May 18, in front of assembled dignitaries and one hundred guests, Budge was sworn in by Chief Justice John Farris. In his sixty-fifth year Budge had put retirement aside to become British Columbia's 23rd Lieutenant-Governor. The official guests included Premier Bill Bennett and members of the Cabinet as well as four former Lieutenant-Governors: Major-General George Pearkes, V.C.; Clarence Wallace; Jack Nicholson; and retiring Walter Owen. Mrs Phylis Ross, widow of the late Frank Ross, another former Lieutenant Governor, was also there. Budge's A.D.C. for the ceremony, the first of many, was Brigadier Dick Danby.

(Gordon Winter, Budge's contemporary at Loretto was, at this time, Lieutenant-Governor of Newfoundland. Budge received a cable from a group of former Lorettonians with the following message: "Thank God both flanks of Canada are now secure!")

At 5 p.m. Budge attended his first formal engagement; a reception to mark the opening of the R.C.M.P. E Division H.Q. In the next few days there were several sessions with Gar Dixon and Tom Duckitt to go over the budget in greater detail and to plan an engagement schedule. There was a visit from a member of the Protocol Office with instructional papers. There was much to learn about this new job and Budge was determined to do it well.

On May 22 he and Nancy rode in the Victoria Day Parade. It is always a large parade, usually three hours in length with many out of town groups participating; high school bands, drum majorettes, floats of various kinds and smart fire trucks of local fire departments. In a smart

BMW, with his official flag flying and police motor-cycle outriders, Budge thoroughly enjoyed it and admitted to feeling like a little boy again.

The five-year commitment as Lieutenant-Governor of British Columbia had well and truly begun.

CHAPTER ELEVEN

THE FOLLOWING MORNING BUDGE AND NANCY were driven to the Esquimalt Naval Base to join H.M.C.S. *Mackenzie* for the first of their spring cruises. The itinerary was Ahousaht village on Flores Island; Tahsis; Walters Island in Kyuquot Sound; Winter Harbour; Port Hardy; Sointula on Malcolm Island; Gilford Island; Glendale and Good Hope Canneries and lastly, Texada Island.

Two of the calls were to coastal Indian villages, Ahousaht and Walters Island. They were received with great ceremony and generous quantities of native food, much dancing and speeches of welcome. In responding to the welcome speeches Budge was able to draw on his time in the canneries and his memories of the native people he had worked with. From his wartime experience he recalled the contribution of native men (and women) to the war effort. As the visit to Ahousaht ended Budge and Nancy were in procession with most of the villagers and their children, slowly wending their way back to the ship behind the piper, Pipe-Sergeant Donald McInnes. Back on board the generous gifts of the native people were examined, all of them skillfully made or carved; paddles; miniature totem poles, bead-work; cloaks; and necklaces. Similar presents, always appreciated, would accrue over the next five years.

At Tahsis a citizenship court was held on the flag deck of the *MacKenzie*, with Justice of the Peace H.K. Tasker officiating. It was a most unusual and imaginative setting in which to become a Canadian citizen and those participating must still hold special memories. During his tenure Budge attended several citizenship courts, but none in such memorable surroundings as this one.

There was a spring cruise or land tour for each of the five years during Budge's term at Government House. At all stops children were an important part of the festivities and many were invited to go on board the ships used for the cruises. Scouts, cubs, guides and brownies were always featured in the welcoming 'guard of honour.' In the villages children featured in much of the dancing. This first cruise introduced Budge to the reality of what the job would entail—five years of events, sometimes four or five per day; cocktail parties, parades, luncheons, dinners, dances, balls, school visits, university convocations, rodeos, country fairs and a variety of others. Both he and Nancy were very aware that these occasions were important to the people involved.

While Budge could occasionally be introspective in the diaries that he kept daily for the full five years, he frequently came up with self-deprecating humour. One such was shortly after the *MacKenzie* cruise. He attended a U.B.C. Convocation, made all the more pleasurable by the fact that his long-time friend Jack Clyne, past chairman of MacMillan-Bloedel (and a character in his own right) was sworn in as Chancellor. Budge, in gown and mortar-board reflected "Do I look elegant or simply a fool?"

Many of the student graduates acknowledged his presence with a bow or curtsey before kneeling in front of the Chancellor (the outgoing Chancellor was another friend, Donovan Miller, a fishing company executive who had at one time worked for the A.B.C. Company). In return Budge 'doffed' his mortar-board, enjoying himself immensely during the proceedings.

One question that needed resolving early in his tenure was the purchase of a suitably smart car for official functions in Victoria and Vancouver. Outside of these locations a car was almost always provided by a local auto-dealer or prominent citizen. A Vancouver auto sales company offered Budge a maroon Brougham Cadillac but when Nancy examined the lease agreement she found that it would be better to purchase outright and they settled for a black Buick—equally smart looking but less costly.

One of the most important functions of protocol for a Lieutenant-Governor is to give Royal Assent to Bills presented in the Legislature by the Government and approved by a majority of the House. On June 6, Budge was there to give assent to Bill 4—"B.C. Hydro & Power

Authority (1964) Amendment Act" and Bill 15—"Provincial Homeowner Grant Amendment Act." Budge wrote of this first visit to the House:

> "Entered the Chamber with great ceremony—all standing. Some desk thumping from both benches. I stood in front of the Speaker's chair, bowed to the government benches then to the opposition before saying 'Pray be seated.' I then sat down and the Clerk recited the title of the Bills, then someone else said 'His Excellency the Lieutenant-Governor doth give Royal Assent'—and we then trooped out. And that is the principal function of my office. My only speaking part was 'pray be seated' and I might as well have been stuffed and pushed in on wheels!
>
> As a first step I must arrange an opportunity to read and understand all Bills presented for Royal Assent regardless of my very limited powers to affect them in any way."

He did not have long to wait for an opportunity to discuss his concerns with Premier Bennett. A meeting took place at Government House the next day. The air was cleared on a number of points about which Budge had some concerns. The first one stemmed from the previous day's Royal Assent and Budge asked if it was possible for a copy of each bill to be made available beforehand so that he could study it and if necessary have the minister responsible explain it. This was agreed to subject to the limitations of the minister's time. A Lieutenant-Governor has to be available at all times to sign Bills and Orders in Cabinet but since this was not practical, when away his whereabouts must be known so that he can be reached and the papers flown to him or, alternatively, he (or she) could be flown back to Victoria. The House did not have to be sitting, as Cabinet sometimes produced order papers that were deemed an emergency.

Government House is the official location to entertain Royal, 'V.I.P.' or other important guests and therefore the direct responsibility of the Lieutenant-Governor, his chatelaine and his staff. When a function is the direct responsibility of the provincial government, such as entertaining visiting missions, members of other provincial legislatures or meetings between federal and provincial leaders, it is paid for by the province directly, but all the culinary requirements for these were Nancy's responsibility, as chatelaine, with staff help. There were several garden parties each year as well as two state dinners and a state ball. In addition to the Lieutenant-Governor's guest list, the premier was, of course, entitled to provide one.

The first V.I.P. guests during Budge's term arrived at the end of June; Lord and Lady Brabourne. Lady Patricia, Countess Mountbatten of Burma, is the elder daughter of the late Lord Louis Mountbatten, killed by an I.R.A. bomb in August 1979 while enjoying a day's fishing with his family off his summer home near Mullaghmore on the west coast of Ireland. Both Lord and Lady Brabourne were seriously injured when Lord Mountbatten's boat was blown up, and took many months to recover. Their son the Hon. Nicholas Knatchbull, aged 15, was killed in the blast. This act of terrorism which shocked the world was a year away when they arrived as guests at Government House. Lady Patricia was in Victoria in her role as Colonel-in-Chief of the Princess Patricia's Canadian Light Infantry and was there to attend a regimental military show, regimental ball and a formal dinner at Government House. It was Budge and Nancy's first experience in having V.I.P. house guests, but it proved to be one the most pleasurable and a close and lasting friendship developed.

There were many visits from Ambassadors, High Commissioners, and Consuls General throughout each year, an average of three or four a month. There was one combined visit in that first year, however, that was a little out of the ordinary. It was the overlapping stay of His Excellency Sir John Ford, United Kingdom High Commissioner and Sir George Kakobau (Thakobau), Governor-General of Fiji, with their wives. Like the Brabournes, the Fords became life-long friends.

Sir George and his wife were equally delightful and a most relaxed and enjoyable dinner party was held, with Sir George proposing the toast to the Queen. What set him apart though, from the usual run of V.I.P. guests was the gift he gave to Budge before departing—the Tabua—the whales tooth. It is a very significant Fijian honour and would signify a blood brother-hood with Sir George, but—in Budge's words "the price of acceptance is the obligation to kill one's own brother—if the necessity should arise. This having been done for me by the Germans I was able to accept it."

In early August the Commonwealth Games opened in Edmonton and it provided an opportunity for a meeting of Lieutenant-Governors from across the country. Budge was, of course, delighted to see his old Loretto friend Gordon Winter from Newfoundland. It was a revelation to meet the other nine Lieutenant-Governors and see the variety of personalities and backgrounds they represented. He was particularly impressed with Pauline McGibbon from Ontario and found her bright and amusing, fully justifying the high reputation she had earned.

Budge was surprised to find that the official residence for the Lieutenant-Governor of Alberta was no longer used for that purpose but instead used as a conference centre, although the official dinner was held there. The residence of the Lieutenant-Governor, at the time the Hon. Ralph Steinhauer, was a spacious, modern bungalow, ideal for entertaining small groups but not for large scale gatherings or Royal guests. Budge felt that in Alberta the position of Lieutenant-Governor was not accorded the same importance or regard that it was in British Columbia.

The Commonwealth Games provided Budge and Nancy their first opportunity to meet the Queen, who they found to be very warm and friendly. Budge was impressed that after conversing in French with the Quebec Lieutenant-Governor, Her Majesty immediately turned to him and repeated the conversation in English for his benefit. A few days later Prince Philip and Prince Andrew arrived in Victoria, the former to attend a Duke of Edinburgh Awards ceremony at the Legislature where he personally presented the prizes, followed by a garden party in honour of the Princes.

From August 10 to 16 Budge and Nancy toured Central B.C. starting with Kamloops and visiting Salmon Arm, Revelstoke, Armstrong, Merritt and Cache Creek. The tours and spring cruises provided an opportunity for the people in remoter parts of British Columbia to share the reality of his office and created tremendous goodwill, especially in the small northern towns and villages. The facilities were often simple and more than once accommodation was provided by taking over the nurse's private quarters in a local health unit, or sleeping in the bunk beds of a small cabin. As the Queen's representative Budge was constantly on the alert as to how they were received and whether the right impression was being made, especially his speeches. It demonstrated a remarkable sensitivity to the locale and his audience. He was genuinely interested in any problems that the communities might be facing and whether he could facilitate solutions.

Budge's aide-de-camps were either militia regiment or R.C.N. reserve officers, or police inspectors. He developed a warm relationship with them and arranged summer parties for them and their families at

Government House. With his military background he enjoyed any opportunity to meet ex-servicemen, especially if they had belonged to a unit in which he had also served and, he came across them with surprising frequency. He was a welcomed guest at all of the Victoria militia units and the Esquimalt naval base.

Budge set out to form a good working relationship with all members of the provincial cabinet, particularly those whose portfolios brought them into close contact with Government House; the Hon. Grace McCarthy, Deputy Premier; the Hon. Garde Gardom, Attorney General and the Hon. Hugh Curtiss, Provincial Secretary (later Minister of Finance). Unfortunately, after a seemingly good beginning with Premier Bill Bennett, Budge felt that they were not communicating as well as he had hoped. A meeting was arranged and Budge was assured that their line of communication was normal and actually better than with his predecessor. There is no doubt that Budge was determined to put his own stamp on the position of Lieutenant-Governor, to make it meaningful and to avoid being a 'rubber stamp' operator for the convenience of the government.

Budge was still an active Seaforth and was still a strong voice in guiding the peacetime activities of the regiment. After serving as Honorary Lieutenant-Colonel, he was appointed Honorary Colonel in May 1976 and remained so until succeeded by David Fairweather in April 1990. On October 11, 1978 he joined other members of the regiment to fly to Scotland, including a platoon of young militiamen to take part in a special occasion. It was to celebrate the bi-centenary of the raising of the 78th Regiment (Ross-shire Buffs), which in 1881 became the 2nd Battalion, Seaforth Highlanders. The original 78th Regiment was raised in 1777 by Kenneth, Earl of Seaforth, a Chief of Clan MacKenzie.

On October 14 in Elgin, the Vancouver contingent attended the Freedom of the District of Moray parade extended to the Queen's Own Highlanders (formerly the separate regiments of the Seaforth Highlanders and the Cameron Highlanders). Due to cutbacks in military spending the British government had amalgamated several regiments throughout the British Isles. Later cuts reduced the number of regiments even further.

The salute took place outside the Elgin Town Hall, where Budge shared the platform with Lieutenant-General Sir Chandos Blair, Honorary Colonel of the Queen's Own Highlanders, and James Anderson of the Moray District Council. Budge noted the good deportment of the

Seaforth Highlanders of Canada platoon. The final function was a regimental dinner in the venerable Station Hotel in Inverness. Budge and Nancy left by train for London where, on October 20 they had a private audience with the Queen. It is a custom for the Governor-General and newly appointed Lieutenant-Governors to pay their respects to Her Majesty as soon as possible after installation, and this visit to the United Kingdom provided Budge with just such an opportunity.

Instead of returning directly to Victoria they flew to Ottawa for a meeting of Lieutenant-Governors at Rideau Hall. This was the last meeting held there with the Hon. Jules Leger as he was soon to retire to be replaced by Edward Schreyer, formerly N.D.P. Premier of Manitoba. The discussions largely dealt with protocol and agreeing on suitable subjects for their speeches and how best to define what were political and non-political subjects. Relations with the media was another topic discussed. Budge would soon come up against the B.C. media for remarks made in his 1979 New Year's message. The topic of greatest concern to Budge was the role of the Monarchy in Canada and it was the one he spoke on most frequently to both adult and student audiences.

In his effort to explain the role of the Monarchy in Canada Budge talked to many diverse groups, from the pro-Royalist Monarchist League of Canada to service clubs where sometimes American guests were present. There was no shortage of opportunities to speak to students on the subject because schools were scheduled in every town and village visited, often three or four in the same day. Budge enjoyed these talks to students, from kindergarten all the way to Grade 12. His main concern was to keep his talks fresh and meaningful and, above all to ensure that his approach was appropriate for the age group he was addressing. When talking to the younger grades Budge introduced the monarchy by talking about the 'olden days' when kings and queens ruled, made the laws—and cut people's head off if they didn't behave! When knights in armour rode about looking for maidens to save and, of course, hoping to slay any dragons that happened to be about. He then told them how things have changed in the role of the monarchy and its relationship to Canada. He was concerned about the number of schools visited in one day, feeling that there were sometimes too many for him to keep sounding fresh.

The behaviour of students varied immensely from school to school, from those who stood straight and sang *Oh Canada* in both French and English followed by bright, eager questions, to the inevitable lolling louts—the ones he found difficult to reach—who sat at the back and yawned—"both boys and girls, sloppy-looking, chewing gum, playing the fool, with no interest in me or what I had to say. But I must learn, somehow, to disregard them and concentrate on the majority; decent and intelligent kids who ask sensible questions." Much depended upon the teaching staff and Budge invariably noticed that where there were keen, interested teachers, the students responded in a similar manner.

If an example of stamina was needed it took place over December 8/9 of Budge's first year. The Legislature sat all day on the 8th over an emergency bill—Bill 46 "The Kootenay Schools Relief Act." The bill finally passed 3rd reading at 1.20 a.m. on the 9th. Budge was summoned and with a police motor-cycle escort entered the House and gave Assent at 1.35 a.m. He was up at 6.30, had a swim in the dark and after an early breakfast took a government flight to Cranbrook in the East Kootenay region of B.C. to attend a ceremony at historic Fort Steele.

Budge was accompanied by two B.C. Parks officials and they met an assembled group of about sixty volunteers there. Fort Steele played an important part in the early history of British Columbia. Before the fort was built to maintain peace among the local Indian nations, the location was known as Wild Horse Creek. The setting is dramatic, sitting on a bench above the Kootenay River, with the steep wall of the Rocky Mountains rising to the east. The fort was named after Sir Samuel Steele, who rose from constable in the North-West Mounted Police to General in the British army. As well as keeping law and order during the Yukon gold rush, Steele also served at the fort that bears his name and the Indians respected his wise counsel. Budge praised the volunteers for their work in keeping alive a vital part of Canada's history. In Fort Steele's hotel guest book the name of his grand-uncle Duncan appears —May 29, 1898. Budge was asked to sign on the same page.

On December 17 the annual staff Christmas Party was held at Government House, with the band of the Salvation Army present to play carols. Budge and Nancy also invited their neighbours from the immediate area to join them in this Christmas festivity. On the 20th the immediate family made for Pasley where they remained until the 29th. One of their last acts of 1978, with an eye to the future, beyond Government House was to purchase a condominium on Panorama Ridge, high above West Vancouver, which they leased out for four years to 1983, when they looked forward to moving there permanently.

The year ended on a sour note when one of the government ministers, Rafe Mair publicly chastized Budge for what he termed a grossly political statement. One of the Prairie Lieutenant-Governors had circulated a document expressing hope that the people of Quebec would remain a part of Canada. In his 1978 Christmas message broadcast, Budge said, "As we approach the end of another year, let us reaffirm our loyalty to Canada—our Country. I would be happy if you shared my desire to tell the people of Quebec that we really want them to stay with us, by signing the 'People to People' petition soon to be circulated." There was, however, support from other cabinet ministers, and the early January newspapers mainly supported Budge's speech, including the "Globe and Mail." Some of the letters he received were anti-French but the majority were in support and he drew encouragement from this. He was still spending as much time as his schedule would permit on learning his constitutional duties and professed the more he read the more interesting it became. He invited Rafe Mair to lunch and "with mutual cordiality we cleared the air. Though still believing I should not have said what I did, he agrees that members of cabinet should not criticize me in the media."

New Year's Day is always busy for B.C. Lieutenant-Governors. In the morning a levee is held at Government House to which the public is invited. For their first one Budge and Nancy had 697 callers. The levee began at 11 a.m., but at 9 a.m. in his No.1 Seaforth uniform Budge did the rounds of the militia and naval officers' messes, also the Mayor's office. To help at the levee he had nine of his A.D.C.'s on duty.

On January 21 Budge celebrated his 66th birthday. It was not a restful day; he and Nancy made a 6.45 a.m. start for the airport, the destination being Ottawa for the swearing-in of the new Governor-General, Edward Schreyer and the official departure of Jules Leger. Deep snow blanketed the eastern provinces and Budge's plane was fortunate to make Ottawa, as other planes were delayed or forced to turn back to Toronto. Because of this the Leger's farewell ceremony took place in unusual circumstances—in a huge hangar at Rockcliffe Military Airport, with a 100 man guard of the Governor-General's Foot Guards, and a Royal Salute.

The next day to more fanfare Edward Schreyer was sworn in as Canada's 22nd Governor-General. It took place in a small chamber in the Senate building in the presence of the Prime Minister and his Cabinet, the Justices of the Supreme Court and the Lieutenant-Governors and Territorial Commissioners. In replying to Prime Minister Trudeau's introduction, the new Governor-General's speech was given in English, French, German, Ukranian and Polish. It was, in Budge's estimation: "A forthright speech, stressing the benefits of our ethnic differences and the essential need for tolerance and cooperation. It was an historic and very emotional hour in Canada's history. Nancy and I both felt very proud and grateful for the privilege of being there."

In March 1979 there was a change in the position of Government House private secretary, when Gar Dixon retired after 33 years in the post. His place was taken by Michael Roberts of Kelowna. Gar Dixon's last major event was the March 22 opening of the British Columbia Legislature's 3rd Session of the 31st Parliament, followed by a state ball. Both were a first for Budge, but he was very pleased with the way they went off. A gun salute commenced as he approached the Legislature accompanied by two aide-de-camps. A naval guard presented arms as the R.C.N.'s very popular (but now disbanded) H.M.C.S. *Naden* band played. At the ball the band's light orchestra section provided the dance music.

(Recalling his earlier visits to Government House as a young man, Budge regarded the receiving line as a time-wasting necessity. One innovation he introduced was to serve champagne to people in the line, so that by the time they were received they felt happy and ready to enjoy the evening.)

Michael Roberts began to take on increasing responsibility as Gar Dixon prepared to retire, especially during the opening of the Legislature and the state ball. When the next V.I.P. guest, the Prince of Wales, arrived he had fully taken over as Budge's private secretary. It soon proved to be a very satisfactory working relationship and a great mutual respect is still evident today. Looking back to that time Michael Roberts is sure that few Lieutenant-Governors before or since have acquired so much understanding of both the legal and protocol requirements needed to be the Queen's representative. He says of their five years together:

> "Budge makes the generous comment that we taught each other, but in fact I was the student and he was the teacher. He had a particular interest in wanting to understand fully what he might be called upon to do in the event of either a constitutional impasse or crisis. He read all the material he could find that enabled him to better understand the complexities and talked to constitutional

experts to broaden his knowledge of the office. He never opened his mouth until he was sure of what he was saying, to avoid speaking from a position of ignorance on a topic or a situation. He was one of the major mentors in my life."

Budge had at first suspected that Michael was the Premier's choice and he was being 'railroaded' into accepting the new secretary, but he soon had cause to be pleased with the appointment. Any early misunderstanding arose in part because the position of private secretary is filled by Order-in-Council and is not posted for competition. This is not for political reasons, but because of the job's sensitivity. If a secretary caused embarrassment to either the Lieutenant-Governor or the government it would be expedient to dismiss them at once rather than remain to exacerbate the situation. The initial approach was made by Tony Tozer, then the Premier's right-hand man. As fellow officers in the B.C. Dragoons militia unit, in Tozer's view Michael Roberts' background in administration and in the militia made him the ideal candidate. Not wishing to leave Kelowna he rejected the idea several times but in January 1979 he was asked again to visit Budge in Victoria, which he did. Although appointed early in Budge's tenure Michael Roberts served no less than three succeeding office-holders before retiring in September 1998. The job demands hours and days away from home and Michael's wife Sharon has, deservedly, won the respect of all at Government House for her understanding of these demands and her willingness to help out when occasion requires it.

On April 1 came what Budge termed "The Great Occasion"—the arrival of the Prince of Wales at Victoria Airport in an R.A.F. DC10, touching down on schedule at 12.30 a.m. After inspecting a guard of honour from Royal Roads Military Academy and introductions by Senator Ray Perrault to the various dignitaries, the Prince spoke to many of the spectators, then accompanied by Budge they drove to Government House where a crowd had gathered. Throughout the three-day visit the Prince displayed the friendly, natural interest in people and places for which he has become famous. Budge also found it was easy to have a wide-ranging conversation with him on all manner of topics.

After the Prince had visited Pearson College, one of the senior staff members of the United World Colleges, of which Pearson College is a member, was moved to write to Budge, "It is not just by reason of

Royal status that he commends himself to our multi-national student bodies. It is because at each of our colleges he has deeply impressed students and teachers alike with his simplicity, lack of pomposity and his concern for people. We all salute him for his attractive qualities as a human being and for the great contribution he makes to our movement."

On April 3, Premier Bennett came to Budge to request dissolution of the Legislature, which was granted. Election Day was set for May 10. The Premier told Budge privately that he was preparing for a hard fight. Having for the first time given assent to the dissolution of the Legislature, it was fitting that less than two weeks later Budge had an opportunity to describe the framework in which the Queen's representatives fitted, and of Her Majesty's role as Queen of Canada. He was guest speaker at a Rotary International Convention in New Westminster, District 504. As it covered Washington and Oregon there were many Americans there. Budge acknowledged the U.S. visitors and in part directed his remarks to them:

> "The Canadian Monarchy. Why do we have a Queen? What do the Queen, the Governor-General and the ten Lieutenant-Governors do for us which cannot be done by our elected Governments? Our Crown is in no way a ruler; not even a person. It is an institution, embodying centuries of experience. This institution is now a most valuable adjunct to the democratic parliamentary system of government. It provides numerous advantages, particularly by comparison with those republics wherein Head of State and Head of Government are embodied in one single person.
>
> In some other countries heads of government have become much too powerful. In our Canadian system of Monarchy, the executive authority is vested in the Crown, as Head of State. However, except in the most extraordinary and extremely rare circumstances, the representative of the Crown may not use this authority except on Ministerial advice. Executive authority is exercised by way of advice to the Crown.
>
> The Crown does have a constant responsibility to ensure that we have a government at all times. Except in the most unlikely circumstances, the choice of Prime Minister or Premier will have been pre-ordained by an election or, in case the leader might have resigned or died in office, it is then by recommendation of the Party caucus. In case the choice is not clear, the Crown will act as a

referee among the members, who will be expected to choose the leader they will support...

Queen Elizabeth II has inherited many centuries of tradition in the evolution of our Parliamentary system and has been trained since childhood for the Throne. She is personally dedicated to her role as Queen of Canada, quite apart from her similar responsibilities for other countries of the Commonwealth. She does, in fact, represent a connecting link between Commonwealth countries which is of direct benefit to Canada.

The Queen is highly esteemed as a world figure who automatically focuses international attention on any event or place at which she may be present. Her visits to Canada not only provide us with a non-political Head of State to pay our respect to—they are also, frankly, good for business.

Queen Elizabeth has delegated all her Royal prerogatives to the Governor-General of Canada, either exclusively or in the granting of honours and in the performance of international acts, to be held jointly with herself. In every case, however, these powers will be used only on the advice of the Canadian Prime Minister. The Queen reigns—she does not rule. There is no subservience whatever by Canada to Her Majesty, or to any other country.

The Governor-General-in-Council—which is in effect the Prime Minister with the required executive order of the Governor-General—appoints the provincial Lieutenant-Governors, who are as much a representative of the Queen in provincial government as the Governor-General himself is to the national government...

Our Canadian Monarchy, the Queen and her eleven Canadian representatives—provide a Head of State of great benefit both to the political process and to the ceremonial function. This is a valuable adjunct to elected government, never a competitor—yet it does provide a remote safety-valve to protect the people in the unlikely event that a government were to get into serious trouble. At minimal cost, our Canadian Monarchy incorporates the wisdom of the ages. It provides one of the most up-to-date governmental systems in the world. We may—and should be—very proud of it."

On May 22 Budge and Nancy began their second spring tour, this time a northern land tour starting at Smithers, then to Hazelton, Kitimat, Kincolith, New Aiyansh, Canyon City, Terrace, Prince

Rupert, Stewart, Telegraph Creek, Deas Lake, Cassiar and Atlin. Much of the tour was covered by the R.C.M.P. Grumman Goose, with side-trips by helicopter. The Bulkely Valley, where the tour began embraces the town of Smithers and the villages of Telkwa and New Hazelton. With Hudson Bay Mountain and its glacier forming a backdrop to Smithers, the distant peaks of the Babine Range to the east and the Coast Range to the west it is an outstanding area of British Columbia.

The aluminum smelter at Kitimat was built in the 1950's in the wilderness, south of Terrace, along with a new town to accommodate the hundreds of workers and staff. The Douglas Channel provides good access for shipping. Budge was given a tour of the smelter before being helicoptered to the power plant, built inside a mountain and some distance away at Kemano. There are eight turbine generators turned by water delivered through a 16 km tunnel from the Nechako reservoir. The power is fed to the Kitimat smelter overland by a 48 mile long transmission line. Kemano is accessible only by air or by sea, so remote is the location.

One side-trip of special interest to Budge was on May 24 when they were flown by helicopter through the northern mountains to Kincolith. He had not returned since his days at the Nass River cannery. Despite some modern houses there were still reminders of the old village he had known forty-seven years earlier, when nets were strung across the Kinkolith River to catch fish. In answer to a concern about their isolation and the need for a highway to connect them to other Nisga'a communities, Budge reminded them that they should be careful not to lose their own ancient civilization, which he had been privileged to see as a young man.

Returning to Terrace, Budge and Nancy were invited to the Civic Arena to watch a display of First Nations dancing. A large audience of native people were already seated when they arrived, to be seated in the front row, centre dais. Budge did not know it was to be a very special evening for him. He described the scene as it unfolded:

> "Dancers entered in procession, chiefs in their colourful costumes, head-dresses, blanket cloaks with clan symbols, decorated skirts, leggings and buckskin moccasins. Then the women entered followed by the children, also adorned. The young braves were last, with bare tops and carrying spears.

The leading chiefs, James Gosnell, Percy Tate and Rod Robinson beat time with one-sided skin drums. The assemblage, however, made no attempt to march in time; instead they moved, each in his or her own time, giving a most imposing impression of a 'people' on the move—a migration. Having crossed the floor, they all disappeared behind the curtain of an improvised stage at one end of the arena.

The lights were dimmed and the curtains drawn aside. A central figure was faintly illuminated with red light, going through statuesque and solemn dance motions to depict the beginning of time—the creation. The rest of the cast were in darkness except for occasional 'lightning' flashes which accompanied the very realistic taped thunder—and other noises appropriate to the creation of the world. This was all very well done; artistic and very impressive.

Chief Rod Robinson re-appeared to tell us that we were now to see the 'prologue.' The dancers came in costume, the women formed a circle 80 to 100 feet in diameter sitting on chairs facing inwards. A gap in the circle towards the main entrance of the hall permitted entry and exit of the various groups of dancers. Another group on the opposite side was occupied by a phalanx of the children.

The two skin drums were accompanied by a small box-like drum and a bigger one of similar shape. The combination gave a pleasing accompaniment to a melodious and most pleasing chanting by the circle of women. The first dances depicted the origins of man and his habitat. The last was a gathering of the animal symbols of the tribal clans—the wolf, the eagle, raven and killer whale.

Towards the end, two chiefs came out of the circle and escorted me into the centre where, with solemn ceremony I was invested with the ceremonial blanket cloak bearing all the Nisga'a clan symbols; the decorated skirt, leggings, the chief's collar of cedar bark and, finally the circular cedar bark headdress denoting 'unity.'

The story was told of the beginning—the coming of light, the coming of the water (the Nass) and, finally, the rock at the mouth of the river—the 'heart' of the river. Then Chief James Gosnell invested me with the name 'COOV LISIMS', meaning The Rock.

I knelt on one knee and each chief in turn put his hand on my shoulder and repeated my new name in Nisga'a twice. At the end I was politely asked if I would like to say a few words, with the comment that it would be an imposition to expect me to do so.

Much moved, I felt that anything in English would at this moment be out of place. I did my poor best to repeat my new name in Nisga'a, in a loud voice, following the preceding chiefs.

The Rev MacMillan, in his chief's vestments then put his hand on me as I knelt again and blessed the new chief in the name of Jesus Christ. Needless to say I was deeply honoured by this dignified, generous gesture to the Monarchy and, perhaps in some small part to the Bell-Irving name. At the end, instead of being allowed to hand back the chief's rainments I was given a new pigskin bag in which to put them, to keep for future occasions. Within the bounds of office and personally, afterwards, I will, in any event do whatever I am able, to help my Nisga'a people."

The northernmost community visited was Atlin, close to the Yukon border on the east shore of Atlin Lake. It is only accessible from the Yukon by road. In this small, isolated place the Lieutenant-Governor and his party was particularly well-received, with a full programme of events and even a morning's fishing at Canoe Cove, a fishing camp on the Taku River owned and operated by Sylvester Jack, Chief of the Tlinget Indians. They found Atlin had a bright, cheerful atmosphere, aided by the setting; on the shore of a large lake, surrounded by the snow-capped Coast Mountains just before they enter Alaska.

On May 31 they were once again in Vancouver, where they had an unenviable task—moving to new quarters to be used as a base for their trips to Vancouver. With an eye to retirement even though it was still four years away, Budge and Nancy had sold their Vancouver home and their boat, the *Shieling*, which was becoming expensive to run. With the Folkstone condominium rented out they purchased an apartment in Shaughnessy. There were enough events and meetings in Vancouver to make this advisable, though they were always pleased to return to Government House, which they now regarded very much as 'home', perhaps more so than any Lieutenant-Governor and chatelaine since their term of office.

It was soon time to be on the road again. In the British Columbia interior during summer months rodeos and stampedes are frequently held. They are a part of the cowboy heritage of the province's early days. B.C. boasts some of the biggest ranches in North America, such as the Douglas Lake Ranch and the Gang Ranch. Both of these are still operating ranches, the cowboys still wearing Stetsons, with kerchiefs around their necks. It is exciting to drive, or better still ride out on their high, rolling grassy range-lands with jackpine stands and views westward to those same Coast Mountains, to see the branding take place as it has done for a hundred years or more.

One of the best known events is the William's Lake Stampede in the Cariboo country of west-central B.C. Participants come from far and wide but many come from the ranches of the Chilcotin plateau, accessed by road across the Fraser River. The road winds through a small canyon and climbs to the Chilcotin, under the ever-changing big sky.

In 1979 Budge and Nancy were invited to open the stampede. In the next two days he came to appreciate the skilled horseman-ship of the stampede contestants, of all ages. There was not only bronco riding, but steer and Brahma bull riding as well. There was a cowboy breakfast on the second morning—flapjacks and fried eggs, followed by the parade with Budge and Nancy riding in a Mustang convertible. The long parade had a few floats but mainly horses and riders. They were impressed by the beauty queen contestants, all mounted and all skilled riders. At the stampede grounds Budge joined with the local politicians and dignitaries in the 'bull' throwing contest—dried cow-pat discuses. He wrote later: "I judge informality to score better than vice-regal dignity on these occasions!"

As a complete contrast, as Honorary Colonel of the Seaforth Highlanders of Canada, Budge flew to Fort Lewis in Washington State. where by arrangement with the U.S. Army, some exercises were carried out. Aside from the opportunity for joint exercises and liaison with the U.S. forces, there was a social aspect which helped cement relations between the Canadians and their U.S. hosts. Budge's rank of full-colonel is known in the U.S. Army as a 'Bird Colonel' because they wear an eagle on their epaulettes. It came as a great surprise to his American hosts to see this elderly Seaforth 'bird colonel' (and Lieutenant-Governor) joining in an obstacle course exercise, swinging on a rope across a pond, slithering through trenches and climbing obstacles. He joined the unit for the start of a night exercise, where he listened in on a Brigade "O" Group before returning to the Fort where, in the comfortable senior officers' quarters, he slept in a room marked 'General Ike Eisenhower.' Next morning he and the Brigade H.Q. officers were taken out to the battleground in a U.S. gunship helicopter at treetop height—a battle lasting into the next night. A highlight of the trip was a full-dress parade of the Canadian units, complete with both pipes and drums and military bands, one of them the band of the U.S. 9th Infantry Division.

His next engagement was near Kamloops, to attend a National Scout Jamboree. Budge still lent support to the scout movement and was keenly interested in taking in the activities laid out for this event. The jamboree was held at Rush Lake on the eastern extremity of the Douglas Lake Ranch and had over 2000 scouts and 500 leaders present. It was attended by, among others, Charles 'Chunky' Woodward, owner of the ranch and president of the family owned Woodward's departmental stores. He had with him his sons John and Christopher (Kip) and the ranch manager, Neil Wooliams. The Mayor of Kamloops, Micheal Latta was also present. Budge paid particular attention to the activities as he went around visiting the various groups. With his eye for detail he concluded that there should be a critical appraisal of these before the next jamboree.

Time was found for fishing on one of the ranch's many lakes. Budge was accompanied by cattle boss Mike Ferguson, who had spent over forty years working at Douglas Lake. The ranch covers 164,000 acres, with grazing rights on another 220,000 acres of Crown land. This combined acreage provides grazing for over 25,000 head of cattle. The ranch was founded in about 1884 and is the third oldest company in B.C. In size it is the largest ranch in North America and the 4th largest in the world.

The late 'Chunky' Woodward took to ranching early in life and was never happier than when at Douglas Lake. He was a first-class horseman, particularly with the quarter-horse, named because of its speed over a quarter-mile course. It is also used for 'cutting' or separating a cow out of a herd and in 1964, at the invitation of the Duke of Edinburgh, 'Chunky' took some members of the Canadian Cutting Horse Association over to Britain where they gave several exhibitions.

September 1979 marked the end of Budge and Nancy's second summer at Government House. Despite their obvious popularity, there was still some self-criticism. Budge wrote: "People have been very kind, without exception, in their comments about our performance in this office—which does make it all so much easier.

I still, fairly often, stop to wonder at this appointment. Such an ordinary man, lacking in so many things. But in the main I enjoy it—and that is important. The top of the list now is that everything possible be done to retain Nancy's happiness and good health, without which we have nothing."

Over the previous two years the new Provincial Law Courts were being constructed in Vancouver. It was designed by internationally known architect Arthur Erickson, who has many major buildings to his credit. Originally the courts were to be designed as just one more downtown tower. Instead, it is lateral and covers three city blocks, rising to a maximum of only seven levels on the east side. With a sunken restaurant area and public ice rink, a feeling of spaciousness has been added to the down-town core. The northern extremity adjoins the old Law Courts which now serves as the Vancouver Art Gallery. The most unusual feature is a huge, sloping glass roof on the west side covering terraces that can be used for functions. The building is innovative, highly imaginative, but not without its critics.

Legal dignitaries were gathering in Vancouver for the official opening on September 6. The previous day a U.B.C. Faculty Club dinner was held to honour Lord Denning, British Law Court's Master of the Rolls (A high office in British legal terms) Budge showed his adaptability and quick thinking. He had been assured that he was not on the speaker's list and was looking forward to a relaxed night when he saw his name on the programme to speak before the honoured guest. He spoke impromptu of the 'majesty and splendour' of Lord Louise Mountbatten's funeral in Westminster Abbey that very morning and then brought it round to Canada's ties with the monarchy, ending with Quebec's importance within the fabric of Canada and how important this was for national unity.

On the day of the Law Court's official opening Budge had a double bill. He spoke at the dedication in the afternoon and again in the evening at the Law Society Bencher's Dinner. As a non-lawyer in a gathering of distinguished barristers, he had worked extra hard on the dinner speech. One interesting twist to the evening was that the Master Treasurer of the Benchers, and chairman for the evening was lawyer Harry Rankin, an ex-corporal in the Canadian Seaforths who had served in the battalion for the whole war, being wounded in action and Mentioned in Dispatches. By 1979 he was a longtime Vancouver alderman, an avowed socialist—and sometimes inclined to be irascible! This evening he rose to the occasion as a jovial and amusing host.

In his speech Budge alluded to the close relationship between the embodiment of the Monarchy in Canada and a legal system with roots based in British common law: "It has been said of Canada that our development to the full stature of nationhood has been retarded by our tendency to cling to mother's apron strings in England, but in recent years we have learned to accept the fact of our independence. We're recognizing our own particular problems as never before, and we're making serious efforts to deal with them. Canada now takes its place as a new world entity wherein old world cultures and customs are enshrined in a modern context."

In his own role as representing the Crown, Budge pointed out that one reaction to the Monarchy is that many people see it as an encroachment on Canadian independence, or they misunderstand it altogether:

> "Some of my correspondents tend to misconstrue the executive title, Lieutenant-Governor in Council, imputing great powers to me and, in consequence blaming me for things they don't like—which may perhaps be of some help to my hard-working Government! A recent letter from the B.C. Penitentiary asked, 'Why did you appoint judge so-and-so—he's a fink. Please see that he's dismissed as soon as possible.'
>
> The problem is that few Canadians are fully aware, if aware at all, of our system of Monarchy and its implications and benefits to all Canadians, whatever their Province or origin and they need to know more about it."

In closing he was able to bring to his audience a sense of British Columbia's legal history and, at the same time pull-off a surprise. He referred to the province's first Supreme Court Justice, Sir Matthew Baillie Begbie as "one of our earliest gifts from the United Kingdom—a rugged individualist for those rugged times and one of the more colourful figures in the early history of our province. By contrast we have here today as our honoured guest, Lord Denning, an innovator of the law on a world scale. May I then take advantage on this great occasion, in memory of my late father-in-law, Reginald Symes, barrister and solicitor of Vancouver, to present to Mr. Justice Nathan Nemetz, Chief Justice of British Columbia, for his new chambers, a memento much prized by Reginald Symes. Signed in Barkerville in 1883 by Matthew Baillie Begbie it is a parchment calling one Charles Wilson to the Bar. Charles Wilson was later the senior partner in Wilson, Wheeler and Symes."

During his term at Government House Budge entered into some areas of social responsibility quite outside the normal purview of his office. It is coincidental that so soon after the Law Court opening his attention turned to youths in trouble with the law. On the evening of September 19, in company with then Victoria Alderman Robin Blencoe and a social worker, he went downtown dressed inauspiciously to meet and talk with some of the 'street kids.' He had asked the press to let him be free of any publicity so that he could pursue it at his own pace, in his own way, and they honoured this request. This venture was partially in response to some property damage at Government House, garden chairs and tables thrown in the pool, tree limbs broken off and even vandalism on the vehicles.

Budge met the kids on the street and in coffee shops. Not all were at that time in trouble with the law, but by their life-style the potential was there. All of them suffered varying degrees of maladjusted home life yet Budge saw signs of ability and decency in most of them, if they were given a chance. They had no idea who Budge was and tried to make him 'streetwise', offering him dope to sell. However, once the word was out and they learned who he was, the trouble at Government House ceased. One of the boys, 15 year old Michael had, the day before, successfully got himself off a B&E charge (one of many), without the benefit of a lawyer. Budge was particularly impressed by him.

By the end of September Budge had contacted a number of groups and individuals and had arranged a lunch to discuss ways of helping the kids. The Victoria Kiwanis Club also offered their support. Budge told them his idea was a 'ladder' programme—"a ladder reaching from the downtown street corners and alleys, to the achievement of useful and rewarding citizenship; the first rung to be easy of access and as inviting as possible." One positive step was to arrange for some of them to come on the next spring cruise on H.M.C.S. *Yukon* as uniformed naval cadets. Budge sought out Michael and asked his help in recruiting others for the cruise. At a later meeting at Budge's request they talked about his schooling, which had been very patchy, but at the 'New Directions' School he had made some effort, although he had not attended for some months. Budge took the trouble to see the principal of the Central High School and arranged for him to go back, at the same time getting permission for Michael to go on the cruise.

The most important event before year's end was a return to Ottawa for a meeting with Governor-General, the Hon. Ed Schreyer. In discussions on an agenda for a meeting of Lieutenant-Governors arranged for January 1980 he agreed to consider including Budge's theme of the Crown in Canada, but did not support his pursuit of encouraging Quebec to discard the phrase accorded to Elizabeth II—"Queen of a Foreign Country."

It was disappointing for Budge that at this second meeting he reluctantly concluded that there was not much more empathy between them than he felt with Premier Bill Bennett. He decided that over the next three years communication between them would be an interesting exercise. There would, however, soon be another opportunity at the Lieutenant-Governors' meeting. After a lunch with Bill Bennett a few weeks later, Budge concluded that he was virtually alone in his campaign to ensure the Monarchy remained a Canadian institution.

Budge had long contemplated organizing an event which had never been accomplished before—a family gathering—a Bell-Irving 'clan gathering'—a reunion of all the Canadian branches, complete with a family tree for each one: a page for H.O.'s off-spring; one for Dr. Duncan's; one for William's and one for Adriana's, representing the Kerfoots. After much correspondence and planning, and with Christmas and New Year festivities behind them, on Saturday January 12, 1980, a total of 225 were present at Government house. The one who came the furthest and was also the oldest present was Sister Mary Amanda (Anna Bell-Irving), a daughter of William Bell-Irving. She was eighty-five and came over from her English convent (Budge called her the 'flying nun'). Most of the Kerfoots still lived in Alberta and were well represented. A large number of relations met each other—indeed, learned of each other's existence for the first time. It was a tremendous effort and produced the results Budge had aimed for—a wonderful family reunion. It is quite certain that no similar event has ever been held at Government House.

Later in the month Budge returned to Ottawa for the meeting of Lieutenant-Governors at Rideau Hall. At that time the provinces were represented by: Gordon Winter – Newfoundland; Joseph Doiron – Prince Edward Island; John Elvin Shattner – Nova Scotia; Hedard Robichard – New Brunswick; Jean-Pierre Coté – Quebec; Pauline McGibbon – Ontario; F.L. (Bud) Jobin – Manitoba; C. Irwin McIntosh – Saskatchewan; Frank Lynch Staunton – Alberta and Budge – British Columbia.

In addition to several 'housekeeping' items of business, there were two important ones; the first on the question of whether Lieutenant-Governors should become ex-officio members of the Order of Canada. Pauline McGibbon, who was already a member spoke strongly in favor of the proposal as did Ed Schreyer who pointed out that Lieutenant-Governors were already distinguished Canadians in the first place, in order to have been appointed in that role. Budge spoke against any 'free issue', stating that he would prefer to earn the Order in some other capacity. The idea did not come to fruition and it was a full two years after leaving office before Budge was appointed to the Order, although he has been instrumental in putting forward other Canadians he deemed worthy.

The other item, also an initiative of his, was a re-design of the Lieutenant-Governors' Standard. While driving with the Union Jack fluttering on the hood of his car, Budge had come to believe that a better symbol could be designed for the Queen's Provincial Representatives. His thought was to have a flag that would provide some uniformity for all the provinces, other than the central crest.

The idea received unanimous support. After several revisions a design was approved by the Queen and gazetted by a Federal Order in Council on February 1, 1982. The background is Royal blue with ten maple leafs encircling the provincial crest surmounted by a St. Edward's crown. Only Quebec and Nova Scotia differ, in that Quebec's crest is in a plain white circle, with a Tudor crown. Nova Scotia's is a Union Jack with the emblem inside a circle of 18 green maple leafs and no crown.

There was general acceptance of Budge's proposals on the Crown in Canada, though in several respects his approach to the role of Lieutenant-Governor differed to that of other office-holders. This was in part because in his early life there had been a distinctly British influence, giving him a clearer perspective of the ties to the United Kingdom. Never having been a politician he was attuned to moments when pure politics invaded an occasion. This was evident when on February 29 he opened the 2nd Session of B.C.'s 32nd Parliament. In his journal that day, noting that the Throne Speech took roughly thirty minutes to read he commented:

"I found it hard to read because it is full of rather cheap politicking; boasting of what has been done and what will be done—but in generalities. I wish the government would develop a more dignified approach to their P.R. Perhaps a touch of modesty once in a while would make the speech sound better."

The opening was followed by a State Ball at Government house, an event which had a definite Bell-Irving innovative touch. There were almost 1000 guests, in Budge's opinion too many for comfort, though the H.M.C.S. *Naden* band saved the evening with their superb playing and, unlike previous years, there were intervals for rest and conversation. At midnight an Eightsome Reel was danced, by two sets of Seaforth officers and their ladies and one set from Government House, which included Budge and Nancy and Michael and Sharon Roberts. Budge soon began thinking of ways to improve the following year's occasion.

For many months preparations had been going on in Amsterdam to commemorate the 35th anniversary of the liberation of the city. On May 1 Budge and Nancy flew there, joined by veterans from Vancouver and Edmonton, including John Stagliano and wife, and Major Ollie Mace. It was an exciting trip, with a plane full of old wartime friends to talk to up and down the aisle.

Arriving at Amsterdam airport there was a large reception to welcome the vets, complete with a military band. Amsterdam was twinned with Toronto and a small delegation from there was led by Mayor John Sewell. Toronto's part in the week's celebrations was overshadowed by the presence of Vancouver's Seaforths who had prior claim by their part in the liberation.

It was an unforgettable week, especially for Nancy who thirty-five years later was able to witness at least in part the way Amsterdam took the liberating Canadians—and her husband—to their hearts. Budge and Nancy stayed at the home of the Burgomeister, William Polak, and a businessman lent them his Daimler and chauffeur for the week. On the first full day, Saturday May 3, there was an afternoon canal cruise followed by an Amsterdam Philharmonic Orchestra concert. Opera singers sang pieces by Verdi, which affected Budge very much as they were among his favourites. By contrast the Amsterdam Police brass band played light music, at one stage inviting the crowd to form a conga line around the concert hall.

On the Sunday morning an ecumenical service was held at the Westerkirk, one of Amsterdam's most significant churches, dating from 1631, and the burial place of Rembrandt. The service was officiated by a Dutch Protestant minister, a Canadian Forces Catholic priest and the Chief Rabbi of Amsterdam. In the evening a "Silent Procession" walked from Weteringcircuit to Dam Square where wreaths were laid at a newly dedicated monument. Later the Burgomeister presented Budge with a citation.

The highlight of the week was the parade, taking the same route as on May 8, 1945 when the Canadian Seaforths entered the city. Just as then, the crowds were so thick that the parade often came to a stop for several minutes. Several wartime army vehicles had been rounded up including a jeep painted exactly as Budge's was in 1945. Holding onto the windshield he rode standing, wearing the kilt, a World War II design battledress tunic and Balmoral bonnet. The crowds pressed forward shouting "Thank you, thank you for liberating us." Many had tears in their eyes—and so had the veterans. There were young people, not yet born when the war ended, passing notes and flowers to Budge. He wrote:

> "We finally reached Dam Square. The veteran vehicles were drawn up in line. School choirs sang songs in English to us, specially written for the occasion. Nancy, with the Polaks and other V.I.P.s were in the stands in front of us. The crowds in the square grew steadily denser as they converged there following the parade. The Burgomiester spoke to them and his message was to "To Amsterdam's Canadians, the heart of Holland is saying thank you." I was given a white dove to release upon conclusion of my remarks as a renewed symbol of Victory, Peace and Liberation. It was joined by thousands of pigeons released immediately afterwards."

Budge was later given two photographs, remarkably alike, one of him giving his speech in Dam Square in 1945 and one of his speech in 1980. The veterans were invited to the Palace to be greeted by members of the Royal House of the Netherlands, among them Princess Margriet, born in Canada in January 1943. Queen Beatrix was now on the throne as her mother, Juliana, had abdicated in favour of her elder daughter just days before the commemoration, and was now once again titled Princess Juliana (in September 1948 Queen Wilhelmina had abdicated in favour of Juliana). It was most unfortunate that riots had broken out in Amsterdam during the new Queen's induction, totally at odds with the fervour over the arrival of the Canadians.

Aside from the commemorative aspect of the events in Holland, there was a very personal moment for Budge. It was the dedication of a tulip in his name. He and Nancy were taken to the beautiful 80 acre Keukenhof Gardens, constructed in the 1830's. They had evolved into a place to demonstrate the hundreds of varieties of spring bulbs grown by Dutch nurserymen. In a conservatory in the centre, Budge was presented with the *General Bell-Irving* tulip, which he had the honour to baptize with champagne.

One of the last events was a wreath-laying ceremony at the Canadian War Cemetery at Groesbeck, attended by members of the Dutch Royal household, the Canadian and Dutch ambassadors, the Canadian Minister of Veterans' Affairs the Hon. Dan MacDonald and two of Canada's senior Armed Forces officers, Admiral Falls and Lieutenant-General Turcot. The minister had lost his left arm and leg at the Senio River and Budge was particularly impressed with him. He thought how suitable it was to name a veteran to the post.

(One sad note was that many of the friends Budge had made in 1945, the Velthorsts, Dudok Van Heels and Van Woudenburgs had died in the intervening years but he was able to meet Rita, the Velthorst's unmarried daughter, and the son of the Dudok Van Heels, Robin and his family.)

Next stop was London where, on May 13 Budge and Nancy attended a service in St. Paul's Cathedral dedicated to holders of the Most Excellent Order of the British Empire. Within the splendour of St. Paul's hymns were sung, accompanied by the band of the Welsh Guards. Trumpeters played in the gallery to mark the Queen's arrival and departure. The ushers were scarlet uniformed soldiers from the Brigade of Guards. The thought came to Budge that he had not dwelt enough on the magnificent heritage Canada had received from the British Empire.

Their last appointment in London was to Buckingham Palace where they had been invited to drinks with the Prince of Wales. He was in shirt-sleeve order in the uniform of the Parachute Regiment, having just returned from a visit to their headquarters. This was their third meeting with the Prince and they were more impressed each time, viewing him as 'forthright and obviously with it.'

From the Palace they headed straight for Heathrow to return to Victoria where within two days they boarded H.M.C.S. *Yukon* for the spring cruise. On May 16 they were met by Rear-Admiral Michael Martin, Commander, Maritime Forces, Western Command and Captain Neil Boivin of the *Yukon*. Although the format for the 1980 cruise was similar to previous ones, there was one big difference in that there were several Victoria 'street kids' and an equal number of Duke of Edinburgh award winners on board. A chief-petty officer was in charge of the whole group, assisted by an N.C.O. cadet from the Seaforth Highlanders. While agreeing with the philosophy behind this unusual arrangement, Neil Boivin's main concern was that if anything untoward happened, money missing or something going astray, the street kids would be blamed, but fortunately no such incidents were reported.

After Budge inspected the guard on the quarter deck, the *Yukon* slipped her moorings and headed out, bound for Campbell River. As the cruise progressed there were the usual civic lunches and legion hall visits, Indian villages, parties on the ship for both adults and children, but one event stands out. This was a Nisga'a Tribal Council meeting held on board ship in the Nass Estuary.

Taking a ship into the Nass Estuary required considerable skill, as the navigable passage for a large ship is narrow, with rocks on one side and very shallow water on the other. A ship could end up either hard on the rocks or hard on the mud, which is very shallow towards Kincolith village. There were many occasions when Budge was filled with admiration for Neil Boivin's skill in handling his ship.

On May 20, with the ship safely anchored, local chiefs came aboard for the first council meeting ever held in the presence of a Lieutenant-Governor. Most of those present represented various townships of the Nisga'a and their concerns covered Indian representation on the local hospital board to asking for more effluent studies before opening up a planned new mine, the Kestrel. Most of the discussion, of course, centred upon the land. Budge put up a suggestion that a conservation programme be set up for the Nass Valley, which extends northeast from the estuary taking in Greenville, Canyon City, New Aiyansh to Cranberry Junction on the New Hazleton-Stewart Road. It is one of a number of spectacular gorges between high mountain ranges, in which considerable mining and forestry activity takes place. Land ownership has long been contentious.

This was born out by the reading matter presented to Budge following the meeting. It included a 1913 "Nisga'a Declaration to His Britannic Majesty in Council"; "A Forestry Proposal of the Nisga'a Tribal Council"—October 1978; "A Fishery Proposal of the Nisga'a Tribal Council"—March 1980. The other document was an "Aboriginal Rights Position Paper."

Budge was pleased that a number of the visitors gave passionate speeches on the great significance of this visit by a Lieutenant-Governor as the Queen's Representative aboard a Royal Canadian Navy vessel. The chiefs donned ceremonial dress, then Herbert Doolan and Henry MacKay presented a pair of decorated canoe paddles to Budge, who was dressed in his Windsor uniform with a Nisga'a ceremonial cloak across his shoulders.

This meeting was significant in that it took place before the federal government and several provincial governments began looking at land claims in earnest, with a serious view to settling them both monetarily and with concrete proposals over stewardship of the land. One of the first to be signed as an Agreement in Principal in February 1996 was the Nisga'a claim, covering 1,930 sq. kilometres (approximately 10% of their original lands) and granting mining, forestry and fishing rights. One of the main proposals, along the lines of Budge's suggestion to look at conservation was a section on environmental assessment and protection, which is to be set by the Nisga'a but must meet or exceed both federal and provincial government standards. The Act will give the Nisga'a Nation self-governance, along with $190 million over 15 years to upgrade the region's infrastructure and living conditions. This includes a road which will finally connect Kincolith to Greenville and New Aiyansh. The fifty-six reserves would disappear to be replaced by a Nisga'a government and four village councils. A study: "Regional Socio-Economic Assessment of the Nisga'a Agreement in Principle" was released in December 1996 laying out the agreement in detail. The agreement was finally initialed on August 4, 1998 at a ceremony in New Aiyansh, though there is considerable opposition in some quarters. There is no doubt much of the talk around the table that day in 1980 was, in many ways a precursor to later, more specific talks. Budge's note—"I do want to do something for the Nisga'a and this meeting will be a useful base" was no idle thought.

At the end of the Tribal Council meeting the ship proceeded down the coast and Captain Boivin ordered a mortar-firing practice, after which the 3 inch ack-ack gun was fired at a drogue towed by a jet from Comox Air Force base. There was also a man-overboard drill. As a canvass dummy was thrown over the side Neil Boivin told Budge, "The ship is yours!" and left him to carry out the orders to manœuvre both the ship and the whaler that was lowered to retrieve the 'man.' A whaler was lowered overboard to help in the rescue and there was one difficult moment when it cut across the Yukon's bow too closely. The captain's immediate concern was whether Budge was aware of the ship's momentum—which he was—and fortunately no collision resulted. The rescue was carried out successfully.

On May 23 they reached Esquimalt, where Admiral Martin was waiting to come on board to greet them. By their third year in Victoria Budge and Nancy had met Admiral Martin and his wife Pat on many occasions, both formal and informal and a very close friendship had grown between them. Mike Martin stood out in a crowd; confident, urbane—just the sort of man that Budge would have been happy to see service with had fortune dictated such an occurrence. He had begun his career as a midshipman in 1944, joining the Royal Canadian Navy College (an establishment known until recently as Royal Roads Military College before closure by the federal government. It is now a university). It was then a single service college. He served with the Royal Navy for various courses early in his career and later attended staff college at Greenwich in S.E. London. In a long career he had commanded mine sweepers, frigates and destroyers as well as important shore-based positions. He served three years in Washington, D.C. with the Canadian Defence Liaison Staff. After commanding the 2nd Canadian Destroyer Squadron Mike Martin was promoted Rear-Admiral in 1977 and commanded the Canadian Marine Forces Pacific Command.

Unfortunately for the navy, by the early 1980's both Mike Martin and Neil Boivin had retired, the Admiral eventually joining the B.C. Ferry Corporation. Among other things, having seen the Victoria 'street kids' on his ship Neil became interested in youth work and kept a fatherly eye on Michael for some time, meeting for coffee and having him to his house until Michael moved away from Victoria. Neil was posted to Brussels on a Navy assignment and they lost touch. Michael was interested in becoming a fighter pilot but Neil warned him that he did not have the educational requirements and would have to first work very hard to get it. Also he might not have the physical requirements and would have to be prepared for a possible disappointment.

Neil applied to an organization that worked with street kids but at the end of a long interview in which he told the panel that he believed discipline is a matter of setting bounds, he never heard from them again. His naval training would have made him a good prospect as he would have encouraged the problem youths in positive ways. Instead Neil has for many years helped out with the physically handicapped, and has taught many to swim.

On June 29 Budge joined officers and other ranks of the R.C.N. to mark the 70th birthday of the Royal Canadian Navy and the presentation of a new "Queen's Colour, Maritime Forces Pacific." Starting at 10.30 a.m. the guard of 100 sailors paraded in front of the Legislative Building. After a 15 gun salute Budge, dressed in his Windsor uniform joined Admiral Martin to inspect the guard. The old Colour was paraded and marched off and the new one was marched on. One novel touch was that the old Colour guard wore old-style naval uniforms and were bearded. It was a unique and infrequent occasion; the old Colour, with the white ensign, had been presented 21 years before and was now being replaced by the maple leaf flag, after which it was enshrined in the Garrison Chapel of Christ the King.

Switching back to the military, on August 3 Budge and Nancy began a European and Mediterranean tour as guests of the Canadian Armed Forces. It would culminate in a great honour for Budge—taking the salute at the Edinburgh Tattoo. The first stop was the Canadian Forces base at Lahr, Germany where part of the force was a battalion of the P.P.C.L.I., who had invited Budge to both Lahr and Cyprus. While at Lahr Budge met officers and men of the Royal 22nd Regiment (with whom he had fought alongside in Italy). He then went on in turn to the Royal Canadian Horse Artillery and the Royal Canadian Dragoons. He was impressed with the various C.O.s, all of them young and keen, each proudly taking him on a tour to meet their men and demonstrate equipment capabilities.

At 05:40 next morning they boarded a Hercules transport aircraft for the flight to Cyprus. The flight was memorable in that the Hercules flew right down Italy's Adriatic coast at a relatively low altitude and he looked down on the battle locations that the 2nd Canadian Infantry Brigade had fought over; Ortona, the Savio, San Martino and San Fortunato among them. At 14:00 hrs they touched down at Akrotiri and as the door opened were met by a blast of heat, to which they would be exposed for the next few days. In Cyprus was another battalion of Patricias commanded by Lieut. Colonel Brian Vernon, as part of the United Nations peacekeeping role. While in Cyprus, by express permission of the C.O., Budge wore a P.P.C.L.I. tropical uniform.

After inspecting an honour guard he was taken to a "B" Company sector briefing by the Company Commander, Major Ken Nette. He then had coffee with the junior ranks before moving forward to the Company positions on the line. Budge wrote:

"It was very interesting to see the Turkish and Greek posts, often very close to the United Nations posts—all armed but at present no shooting. The buildings close to the line are for the most part badly shot up. It seemed quite absurd that the Greeks and Turks would be prepared to sit endlessly glowering at each other, with no apparent urge to get on with making peace for 'One Cyprus.' In the meantime it is costing the participating nations a lot of money."

The next day, visiting "A" Company's forward positions, Nancy went along. In each they were briefed expertly by a junior rank, often a private. One or two locations were virtually 'eyeball to eyeball' with the Turks. When Budge went to raise his camera, he was immediately stopped and told that taking a photo would almost certainly result in the Turks firing at them. Nevertheless his departing waves were returned in a friendly fashion.

While in Cyprus the British Contingent held a parade to present medals to various unit members. The parade was staged as only the British military can, with a precision that looks deceptively easy, and it was a highlight of the visit. There was only one military band, that of the 3rd Battalion, Royal Green Jackets, part of the British Rifle Brigade, who march at an exhausting pace. There was also a squadron of the 13th/18th Royal Hussars and some odd Royal Engineers and R.E.M.E units as well as armoured vehicles and helicopters. The show caused Budge to comment:

> "The staging, the timing, were immaculate. The advance in review order was timed and controlled by the band faultlessly. The General Salute following the advance included a machine gun "feu de joie" by the armoured reconnaissance vehicles from left to right by each troop—splendid. Then the march-past in columns was led by the Royal Green Jackets at the double with officers at the salute. A short double pace, all exactly in step and dressing in column maintained.
>
> I enjoyed the event to the point of being virtually speechless. I thought how good this sort of thing is for both participant and spectator. We in Canada can stand a lot more of it. We shouldn't lose it. Somehow or other we should persuade the politicians; produce the capability; demonstrate it to the people at home to

whet their appreciation and bring our services to a proper level of respect in our own country."

Before leaving the island they climbed Mount Olympus and visited various ancient sites, crossing into the Turkish area to do so, travelling across the sun-baked central plain then through the mountains. They visited the temples of Apollo and Aphrodite, hers perched high on a hill looking out to the sea. Following a formal farewell regimental dinner, early on August 14, Budge and Nancy departed Cyprus for Lahr. The flight to the U.K. took them once more over Italy, this time offering a clear view over the central and western part of the country, all the way from the heel up to Milan in the north.

A train journey from London's Euston Station took them to Lockerbie where a small family reunion was arranged with the Scottish cousins at Whitehill. Sharp at 3 p.m. on Saturday August 16 a staff car arrived from the Edinburgh Headquarters of Scottish Command, to pick up Budge and Nancy, while the relatives followed in their own cars. They were taken to Gogar Bank House, the residence of General Sir David Young, KBE., CB., DFC., General Officer Commanding Scotland and, along with this appointment, also Governor of Edinburgh Castle. He and Budge had first met when Sir David was Director of Infantry. While attending a Canadian Scottish Regiment dinner in his honour, he had stayed as a guest at Government House. (The DFC is an unusual bravery decoration for an army officer. Although commissioned into the Royal Scots, at one point in his career Sir David joined the Glider Pilot's Regiment. Pilots were trained to fly powered aircraft and during the early 1950's Malayan emergency with the communist regime and the start of the Korean War, volunteers were requested to fly the Air O.P. spotter planes to assist field artillery units. Sir David was awarded the D.F.C. for leadership in continuous air operations against the Malayan terrorists.)

After dinner a chauffeur-driven Daimler took Budge and Nancy to the forecourt of Edinburgh Castle, where for many years the Edinburgh Tattoo has taken place. They were escorted to the Royal Box, from where Budge took the salute from each of the various military contingents on the programme. Strangely it was to some extent an anti-climax to him. Having many times been part of military parades and tattoos over the years he found the scale of the Edinburgh Tattoo too big. That is not to deny the quality of each performance, the groups coming from all over the world to perform. There were marching bands from the U.S.A. and a rifle and bayonet drill team from Rutgers University. That year among the pipe bands was one from Wellington, New Zealand. There are usually at least two pipe bands from overseas—British Columbia's Delta Police Pipe Band performed in 1994, the same year that Scotland lost the Gordon Highlanders, being amalgamated with the Queen's Own Highlanders and renamed The Highland Battalion (Seaforths, Camerons and Gordons).

Budge wondered if some of the groups really belonged at a Highland Tattoo, but part of the problem could be blamed on the shrinking number of Scottish regiments available to Sir David, making it necessary to swell the ranks with other performers.

After a busy Sunday: a morning service at St. Giles Cathedral, visiting a B.C. Native art exhibition, "Legacy", and a London Philharmonic Orchestra concert in the Usher Hall, it was time to leave Edinburgh, and return to Lahr for the flight back to Ottawa by military transport. It was an uncomfortable flight as the seats were already filled with travelling military personnel, including those near the flight deck that were meant for V.I.P.s. They settled for some in the rear in front of restless children, who jiggled Budge's seat as he was trying to write. Characteristically he noted:

> "I suppose if we want to operate in a vice-regal manner we should have an A.D.C. running interference for us at all times. But I think not—I don't think either we or our 'office' lose anything at all by our operating as ordinary persons, which we normally are, particularly when outside B.C. and more or less incognito."

On August 19 they were once more back at Government House, exhausted and jet-lagged, but pleased that so much had been packed into the trip and everything had gone so well. One month later to the day, Budge took part in an Order of Canada presentation by His Excellency, Governor-General Edward Schreyer. It took place in the Vancouver suburb of Port Coquitlam and was presented to an extraordinary young man, Terry Fox. At eighteen years old and attending S.F.U. he had lost a leg to cancer, but fitted with an artificial leg he still ran and played basketball. The idea came to him that he would run across Canada to raise money for cancer research through pledges. His effort was phenomenally successful but the cancer returned half-way through the run and Terry was flown back to Vancouver for more treatment. At the ceremony Budge sat next to him and found this brief contact very inspirational. The Governor-General was himself very moved and set a simple, warm tone to the ceremony. Unfortunately Terry Fox died on June 28, 1981, just nine months after receiving his award. Budge and Nancy were honoured to be asked by the Fox family to attend a private funeral.

With three fine sons of his own, Budge was touched that this young man gave of himself to help other people in their fight against cancer. He wrote:

> "Terry's life and death have made all Canadians stop and think. What are our objectives? What is it all about? As a direct result of his example; of his demonstration of the infinite capacity of man, I have felt a little stronger, more capable, more determined to be useful. I am sure this reaction must be spread right across Canada. What a great deal this splendid young man did for Canada. For myself, I am only too aware of my weakness, fallibility; the tendency to let things pass, to go back to mediocrity and one must work on it continuously."

(A memorial to Terry was built at the west end of the B.C. Place Stadium in downtown Vancouver, where a permanent flame burns until cancer is beaten)

Terry's life was in many ways a contrast to the young people on the Victoria streets who Budge was trying so hard to help. His loving parents had provided him and his two brothers and sister with a stable, loving home life. Budge was mindful of this contrast when he recalled the recent spring cruise on H.M.C.S. *Yukon* and how well Michael and the others had behaved. Michael, now returned to school and another boy, Jack had been to see Budge just the week before. Jack had worked in the steward's pantry on board and had been complimented by the staff, but now he was badly in need of direction and Budge hoped to find a means of getting it to him to help set a new course in life. He hoped that the story of Terry Fox might be an inspiration to them.

Some of the more hardened delinquents had been sent to a residential home, the Malahat Life-Centred Learning Hospice, where the age range was from 12 to 18, both boys and girls. Some were narcotic addicts and had been arrested for various serious offences such as prostitution and even manslaughter. In early November Budge and Nancy went to the centre, the first of several visits at its location just off the Malahat Highway, the highest section of the road between Nanaimo and Victoria. Its location is isolated, though with easy access to the main highway. Some of the staff had young children in a nursery on the premises and the interplay between the children and the delinquents was having a beneficial effect. The Director, George Bullied, asked Budge's help in obtaining a fish-boat to train the boys in becoming deck-hands and to provide a bit of adventure in their lives. The advice offered was to stay in his own field and to contract out any boating venture. He found a retired fisherman who still had his boat and rented it on a per diem basis with the man as instructor. Five of the boys became fishermen. Budge was so impressed with what he saw at the house that he invited everyone from the Malahat Centre to Government House for a pre-Christmas lunch on December 8.

When the day came, Budge and Nancy entertained more than 40 people with Budge carving the turkey at one end of the long table and comptroller Doug Hanbury carving a ham at the other. They noticed how demonstrative the children were, and it was a memorable time for all of them. Budge also invited the Hon. Grace McCarthy along so that she could see first-hand the efforts of one individual in making a difference. Sixteen years later George Bullied is still full of praise for Budge and Nancy's efforts to bring something special into the lives of the young people in his care. He had financed Malahat House himself, as he had done previously with Twin Valley School in Wardsville, Ontario but unfortunately, when a few years later interest rates hit 18% he could no longer keep up the mortgage on the Malahat house and it was repossessed.

By a coincidence he had served in the latter part of WW II and Korea with the P.P.C.L.I., by that time as a sergeant. His C.O. in Korea was none other than Colonel Jim Stone, DSO. George at 70 years of age is now helping with drug rehabilitation projects in downtown Eastside Vancouver.

Budge's last major duty in 1980 was to open a short December session of the Legislature. He read a fourteen page Speech from the Throne and again it was, in his opinion oozing politics, especially an item, 'The Six Basic Aims of British Columbians' which contained nothing at all to inspire the populace. It caused Budge to comment—

"Wouldn't it be great if we had some politicians with the fire in their bellies of Henry V before Agincourt!"

(Another Budge witticism around this time was after a speech to the Men's Canadian Club of Victoria: "In this business one tends to develop a thick skin rather than a swollen head.")

Although he was aware of one particular aspect of his role that was seldom called upon, known as the Royal Prerogative, he was equally aware of the remote circumstances that might require it. The Royal Prerogative is given to the Lieutenant-Governor in case a Provincial Government action was "clearly against the wishes of, or contrary to the best interests of the people." The subject came up in a conversation with Mel Smith, then Deputy Minister to the Hon. Garde Gardom, Minister of Inter-Governmental Relations. The prerogative still remains and the most likely circumstances in which it might be used would be if (A) a government were defeated in an election but the Premier was not willing to resign or to recall the Legislature, or (B) a minority government was defeated on a motion and refused a dissolution of the Legislature.

At a later meeting with the minister himself, Garde Gardom expressed his concern that the government, with a small majority might easily be defeated in such a manner. He was sure that the leader of the Opposition, the New Democratic Party's Dave Barrett, would be "hot foot" to Government House demanding such action.

Budge wrote:

> "From his remarks it would seem that the Cabinet is unsure of what I might do in case of such an emergency. Neither do they want me involving myself in such 'political' matters as the continuity of Canadian unity; Federal-Provincial relations, etc.
>
> Nothing or nobody will quash my interest and involvement in the future of our country, regardless of criticism.
>
> With regard to possible emergencies in the B.C. Legislature, I am sure I could cope, but let's take steps to make sure I wouldn't be stumped, under any circumstances."

(Although, because of the balance of parties in the Legislature in 1980 the government was alert to the possibility, there has never been a situation in British Columbia where the Lieutenant-Governor was forced to take that drastic step. When in April 1991 Premier William Vander Zalm resigned it was a political decision forced on him through a personal involvement in a rather unusual real-estate transaction in which a considerable sum of money changed hands in the proverbial plain brown envelope. Its after-math led to the decimation of the Social Credit Party, the once proud party of both Bill Bennett and his father W.A.C. Bennett. Lieutenant-Governor David Lam was not directly involved as there was no dissolution of the Legislature. A new party leader/premier was chosen from within the sitting members.)

Christmas Day 1980 was a memorable one, spent at Donald's chalet at Whistler in the company of all three sons. All of them had settled into careers. Donald, at 29 had married in September of that year, having attained his M.B.A. at Harvard Business School where he met Ellen McGaffigan of Boston. They had married there but planned to live in Vancouver where he would seek employment. Roderick continued as a federally employed fisheries biologist but had become interested in the Seaforth Highlanders of Canada once he had finished his rowing career. He met the criteria for an immediate commission and was gazetted 2nd Lieutenant on January 1, 1981. Hal was still with A.E. LePage as a commercial leasing salesman but later joined the Real Estate Division of Public Works Canada.

When Ellen and Donald returned to Vancouver he brought with him a new hi-tech idea. It was a computer design system which could be used by both architects and engineers using 3-D imaging. It was possible to 'turn' the drawing on the screen in order to see it from all angles, a process which he had helped to develop, and its design capabilities had a huge potential for those professions. He had decided to form a company in Vancouver to market this concept to be called Vancouver Drafting Services Ltd. By this time the shares in Bell-Irving Investments Ltd. had reached $120.45 and Budge proposed to purchase the non-family shares to raise money for investment in Donald's new venture. At that price it was not hard to persuade the other shareholders to sell.

The sum of $95,000 was raised of which $90,000 was invested in Donald's new company, as part of a capitalization of $500,000. The outlook for business was so good that an increase from the initial share price of $10 to at least $15 per share was forecast within a very few months, thereafter increasing by 15% per year for at least the following three years. Unfortunately by June 1982 because of a downturn in the number of projects in both architecture and engineering, Donald's company became a victim. Also a newer, faster system known as 'CAD' was coming onto the market. With a serious cash-flow problem, the company was wound up, though equity was sufficient to repay investors at least 50% of their original investment. Donald and Ellen returned to Boston, where he joined Digital Equipment Corporation, a hi-tech company and in a short time became part of the management team.

On May 18, 1981, the third anniversary of Budge's appointment as Lieutenant-Governor, a B.C. Rail tour of Central British Columbia was begun. It replaced the spring cruise and allowed an opportunity to take in several places not previously visited. Between the ski-resort town of Whistler and the town of Lillooet, the track winds through spectacular country, between high mountains and alongside glacier-fed lakes. There are one or two 'whistle-stop' locations before the country opens up to ranch-land for the next several hundred miles. One of the more interesting people they met in Lillooet was 'Ma' Murray, a pioneer and longtime editor of the *Bridge River-Lillooet News*. She had remained editor well into her eighties but by this time was at least 94 years old and was in a nursing home.

A side-trip was taken to the restored town of Barkerville, scene of B.C.'s most famous goldrush of 1860 which largely resulted in the birth of the towns along the route. In its time it was as significant as Dawson City was to the Yukon goldrush but did not have an equivalent of Robert Service to immortalize the location in verse. Nevertheless much has been written about Barkerville, especially the presence of educated black people who came from the U.S. to fill several professional roles in the town. Like Dawson City, much of Barkerville has been restored. It also marks the start and finish of the famous wilderness canoe circuit on the Bowron Lakes chain. The town of Tumbler Ridge was also visited. Like Kitimat a few years earlier, it is a new town created out of the wilderness, this time to serve a huge coal-pit created primarily for the Japanese market. The tour ended at Fort Nelson, high up in B.C.'s north-east corner, where again the coast-mountain range is a serrated line against the western horizon. Fort Nelson is also served by the Alaska Highway.

In July 1981, it was back to scouting when Budge attended an international jamboree at Kananaskis, Alberta. There were over 24,000 scouts there and while it lasted the site was the 8th biggest city in Alberta. The jamboree was timed to coincide with the Calgary Stampede so that as many scouts as possible could attend it. There were several groups of Girl Scouts from various parts of the world. Allen Ball, Boy Scouts Commissioner for Victoria and Assistant Provincial Commissioner extended an invitation to Budge, who readily accepted, but insisted on being treated as a regular scouter. He arrived to find a tent had been assigned—a regular 6' × 4' × 4' high, complete with camp cot. A sign outside read "GOVERNMENT HOUSE." Attending from England was Lord Baden Powell, grandson of Lord Robert Baden Powell, founder of the Boy Scout movement. B.C. was well represented, with several senior scouters present, but Budge was anxious to meet as many boys and leaders from out of province as possible. Accompanied by Allen Ball and Lord Baden Powell, they toured the sub-camps and had an especially humorous reception at those of Newfoundland and Nova Scotia.

At the former they were made 'Honorary Newfies'. For this privilege they had to stand on a podium, eat a whole capelin, a fish very much like an oolichan but extremely salty. This was followed by a drink of 'screech' (which among other unrecognized liquids contained some rum) and then finally a dipper of Atlantic sea-water was poured over them. The Nova Scotians let them off lighter, the main item being the presentation of a scallop shell on a string to use as a sporran. Scouters from other provinces were surprised and envious that B.C. had their Lieutenant-Governor present—and he was obviously enjoying himself. During his stay Budge was presented with the Silver Wolf Medal, an honour bestowed for significant services to scouting.

As he watched some of the camp activities, Budge discussed with the various leaders ways to improve the programmes to entice more of the very boys that scouting could benefit; the under-privileged and those on the street. Part of the problem was that they were so removed from the values of the movement that it would take, in the words of Allen Ball, a quantum leap. Some Venture Scouts did start a programme, which met with moderate success.

The jamboree provided a good opportunity to visit the Alberta branch of the Bell-Irving family, descended through Williamina's daughter Adriana, who married William Duncan Kerfoot. The Kerfoots had prospered in ranching and after the jamboree Budge and Nancy headed to Providence Ranch in Grand Valley, near Cochrane to meet James Duncan Kerfoot. His brother William had been killed at Ortona over Christmas 1943, serving with the Loyal Edmonton Regiment, one of the few battles that Budge missed. He did not know until much later that his second cousin had died at Ortona only months before he took command.

There was a bronze plaque to William set into a rock overlooking the valley, which Budge was taken to see. James (Jim) had been a major in the Indian Army and had served in Burma, where he was wounded. Adriana had six children and her son Archie, Jim's uncle was still alive, a healthy eighty-two year old. He was able to give Budge other aspects of family history from the Kerfoot side. The reason that Williamina, with her daughters Jane and Sarah are buried in the Stony Indian cemetery at Morley is that it began as a white cemetery, but when the Stoney Reserve was expanded, the original cemetery was encompassed by it.

Seven of Adriana and William's eight children had married and their descendants now numbered over fifty. While at the ranch Budge and Nancy met again many relatives who had been at the gathering in Victoria. They also met several of the neighbours and Budge was a little taken aback when one rancher took him to see his guns and pointing to the ammunition said "these are not shot cartridges, they're bullets—and we're ready for the Government!"

Budge left Cochrane with a painting of Heidelberg by Jane Bell-Irving and an H.O. watercolour, slightly torn, of a pastoral scene with cattle. Back in Victoria he found that a premiers' conference had been arranged. It would be hosted by Bill Bennett and much of the activity would take place at Government House and its overuse by the government for political purposes gave Budge much to ponder:

> "The constant use of Government House is a pity from our point of view. It most certainly detracts from the image of the Crown's presence in B.C., but I read it as an inescapable fact of life in Canada, 1981.
>
> I wonder about the Crown. I have been preaching; trying to sell it as a Canadian institution and part of our heritage. We do certainly need something solid, above politics ... still, we are solidly a democracy and the key to it all is the electorate. We are not yet united as one people; one Nation. The peoples' wants are local, not national. They do, however, have a common dislike of all governments."

While the conference took place at Government House, a Pasley holiday was enjoyed, all the more so because their sons appeared frequently, often all together to help out with the chores that Budge had set himself. He began to relax and to take stock, especially as he was now well into the third year of his appointment. The rest made him realize how much he was looking forward to retirement, not to vegetate, but to enjoy some reading, but of equal importance to become more involved in projects and causes that interested him. Having sold their boat, *Shieling*, Budge realized he could not, after all be without one and purchased a smaller boat, which he named *Jenny*. He called her a mixed blessing because she needed work and was not reliable, at least in the beginning and always seemed to be breaking down.

Back at Government House on August 24, they settled down to the usual round of events and ambassadorial visits throughout the late summer and into October, when Budge received an unusual request. It was presented at a meeting with U.B.C. President Douglas Kenney, Chancellor J.V. Clyne and Law Professor Charles Bourne. Would Budge take on the role of 'Visitor' to the University? The function of Visitor was perhaps best described as a type of ombudsman or final appeal court in any problem of protocol within the university body. A Visitor was not involved in any legal wrangle or activity which might lead to court proceedings, but mainly to interpose in matters concerning such things as disputes over procedural or academic matters between members of the faculty and students, or perhaps between faculties.

The position was provided for in the B.C. Universities Act and the three U.B.C. representatives thought the tradition should be preserved as a better route than going to court in such matters. There might, however, sometimes be a need for legal counsel and the choice of lawyer should be the Visitor's, though paid for by the university. Budge had one advantage in that although he lacked legal training he had sat on various military courts martial and had been one of the principal members of the Kurt Meyer trial. He was willing to take on the Visitor role.

In November 1981 a request came from the University of Victoria. The case concerned a law student who, failed in his marks, was appealing for a reconsideration. The university was at first reluctant to use a Visitor, but finally decided that it might be preferential to the Courts. On April 22, 1982 Budge gave his judgement, helped by Donald Clancy of the Attorney General's Department as counsel. It was almost two years since the student had contested his failure to receive a passing grade in first year law and he had shown great persistence in taking it through the University Senate Appeals Committee.

At the Visitor's hearing the student was represented by counsel Robert Higginbottom, and the university by Dean of Law Lyman R. Robinson. The proceedings were chaired by Senate member Dr. W.R.

Gordon. The first challenge was from the university on the rights of the student to appeal to the Visitor. Backed by his counsel, Budge gave his opinion that both his standing and jurisdiction were satisfactory. On examining all the evidence he found:

1) That no member of the university had been in breach of any rule or regulation of the university. 2) That the grades given and the reported failure, subject to an opportunity to write supplementals were of sound academic judgement. 3) As Visitor he would not therefore interfere in the Law Faculty's original failing grade given to the student.

Budge did not enjoy having to turn down the student, though unknown to him the man was already a qualified architect who had reasoned it would be a good idea to have a law degree as well. Donald Clancy gave assurance that it was the right decision. Budge submitted a detailed 'finding' on the case so that the student could at least be aware of his rationale.

(Donald Clancy is now Mr. Justice Clancy of the B.C. Supreme Court and Robert Higginbottom is now Mr. Justice Higginbottom, a Provincial Court Judge.)

In November 1981 Budge and Nancy returned to the still struggling Malahat Life Centred Learning Hospice, whose progress they had followed since the previous year's Government House Christmas party. The facilities had been extended, which they were shown with much pride and then a play was put on, with many of the young delinquents showing considerable talent.

There was one young lady, not yet seventeen who had taken to street prostitution. She had been ordered by the courts to spend six months at the Malahat Centre and her time was now up. She was crying and upset and her next destination was to be a receiving house in Victoria, where there was a 10 p.m. curfew weekdays and midnight at weekends. Inmates could not consume drink or drugs on the premises yet had to remain out and unsupervised during the day. Neither George Bullied or the Bell-Irvings thought it a very good arrangement so they took the unusual step of taking her back to Government House on a temporary basis, buying her shoes and clothing and taking her with them on some of their out of town functions. Despite the problems of her early life she had a sweet nature and they thought this could be worked on to assist in her redemption—if they could get through to her. Doug Hanbury and his wife Lois took the girl in as a foster-child which, at first worked well, and she began to attend the local High School.

Again a Christmas lunch was provided at Government House but, unfortunately she was not present, having stayed only a few weeks with the Hanburys before departing to take to the streets of Vancouver. George Bullied found her and brought her back to the Malahat where she remained recalcitrant and determined to keep to prostitution. There was no hint of gratitude to either the Bell-Irvings or the Hanburys, although Nancy offered the suggestion that she could phone them any time.

George's deep conviction that he must try to help these young people was commendable but it must have been very disappointing when some did not respond even with input from the Lieutenant-Governor.

On December 18 Hal's wife Susan presented Budge and Nancy with their first grandson, to be christened Henry David—the sixth born in an unbroken line. At the other end of life's journey was Peter Traill, now ninety-five, who Budge visited on Christmas Eve. Although he was declining rapidly Peter still had all his faculties and it saddened Budge to see his old mentor wishing for the end and insistent on a cremation 'with no frills.'

January 1, 1982, marked the beginning of Budge and Nancy's last full year as Lieutenant-Governor and Chatelaine. Budge gladly donned his 'black and stripes' with medals, to visit City Hall and five militia messes before a total of 885 guests began arriving for the Government House levee. There was, unfortunately one guest too many. They could have done without the one who stole Nancy's bonsai pine tree, a present from the Japanese Consul-General.

The first full item on Budge's calendar was a visit to the 3rd Battalion, P.P.C.L.I., engaged in field exercises at Wainwright, Alberta. Arriving at Edmonton Budge changed into Arctic gear to face the -20 degree weather in which the exercise took place. The battalion was fully mechanized and it seemed to him that too much dependence was placed on the 'Grizzly' armoured troop carrier. It had good mobility and was without doubt efficient, but carrying ten men and equipment was crowded inside. A toboggan and tent secured to the turret made it unturnable, which was shortsighted when the turret was an essential part of its fighting capability, Budge noted:

> "As an infantryman of a more simple era I'm nervous about being so dependent on vehicles and having men packed into very vulnerable 'small cans.'

Were I commanding I would want much more drill on the business of contact—very fast mounting, dismounting and deployment. The stowing of gear should be worked out to maximum efficiency. Kept in proper perspective, the Grizzly is a useful tool, but first allegiance should be to the troops' physical shape and stamina—only then the reliance on a vehicle.

The rations strike me as fancy Yankee stuff—not solid enough for a fighting man to live on for too long. They'll need a square meal every day or so."

Budge's overall impression of the personnel was good—from the C.O. down, but he could not forget the lessons he had learned under fire and it made him all the more aware that none of these men, including the brigadier in charge of the exercise, had ever heard a shot fired in anger—and therefore the training lacked realism. He felt he could quickly become a 'damned nuisance' and decided that he had come to the end of his usefulness in such matters. He was nevertheless tempted by an offer from Brigadier Cotter to visit Suffield where a Patricia company would later be training with a British tank regiment. Budge was disappointed to be taken back to Wainwright officers' mess for the night instead of being offered a sleeping-bag and tent in the battalion lines. He was, after all, only eight days from his 69th birthday!

A long-planned Lieutenant-Governors' meeting in Victoria took place on February 7th to 10th. There had been several changes since the previous one. The Hon. Pauline McGibbon of Ontario had stepped down and replaced by the Hon. John Aird; Budge's old Lorettonian friend Gordon Winter had been replaced by the Hon., Dr. William Paddon. The Hon. Pearl McGonigal now represented Manitoba. It was another credit to Budge and his chatelaine that the conference was hailed as a success and this was amplified at a private luncheon in early April with Senator Ray Perrault. After passing on the Prime Minister's congratulations for the splendid job he was doing the senator broached the subject of an extended stay in office. Budge thanked the senator for the confidence shown in him, but declined.

Prime Minister Pierre Elliot Trudeau had been pre-occupied for some time with a far-reaching plan that, in a very direct sense would have a bearing on Native issues. It was to patriate the Constitution from the United Kingdom. Following the results of the Quebec Referendum on Sovereignty Association of May 20, 1980, he decided that the federal government should proceed unilaterally, if necessary, to achieve (1) the patriation of the constitution (2) the adoption of an amending procedure and (3) adoption of a charter of rights. On October 6 of that year he introduced into the House of Commons a "Proposed Resolution for a Joint Address to Her Majesty the Queen respecting the Constitution of Canada." Its purpose was to seek agreement from both the British House of Commons and House of Lords by laying before them a bill contained within the resolution.

In Canada a joint committee from the Senate and the House of Commons was convened to scrutinize the amendments, and to hear and receive submissions. Although the resolution was passed by both chambers in April 1981, only Ontario and New Brunswick were prepared to accept it unconditionally. The other eight provinces challenged it all the way to the Supreme Court. By a majority of seven judges to two the Court's verdict was that the consent of the provinces was not required by law, yet by six to three the Court also stated that a 'substantial degree' of provincial consent was required and two out of ten provinces was not enough.

Following a further round of discussions between the Prime Minister and the Premiers, with many more amendments, on November 5, 1981 a final version was agreed, although Quebec still dissented. While Budge played no direct part in these events, he followed them closely and noted that in all these months of discussion, one major element had been left out; the rights of First Nations people. Native concerns had been totally ignored during the whole proceedings and they were beginning to get very angry about it. Even to the very last, Premier Bennett had gone on record as saying that native concerns should not be singled out. He could not have been unaware that his own Lieutenant-Governor had taken a great personal interest in these very concerns.

After an unsuccessful last minute effort to win Quebec over by offering an opting-out clause, the resolution was passed by the Senate on December 8. It was then sent to Britain where the House of Commons passed it on March 8, 1982 followed by the House of Lords on the 25th. With no more changes Royal Assent was given on March 29. This was most fortunate as April 17 had already been arranged for the Queen to come to Ottawa to co-sign a Proclamation with Pierre Trudeau.

Festivities began in Ottawa on Friday April 16 with a concert at the National Arts Centre performed by an all Canadian cast in the presence of the Queen and Prince Philip. After the show the stage was used for a dinner hosted by then Secretary of State the Hon. Gerald Regan. He made a short speech in which he proposed a toast to 'Our country, Canada.' Budge had no objection to this, but asked him why there was no toast to the Queen. The lame reply was that it would have upset some people who were already smoking. Budge felt angry and disappointed that with Her Majesty already in the capital (though not at the dinner) she could be treated in such a way. A later explanation during a more relaxed discussion with Gerald Regan brought forth an even stranger explanation—'the Ottawa/Ontario political environment.'

The next morning was clear as Budge and Nancy set out for the signing ceremony, she in a new wide-brimmed straw hat and he in morning coat, medals and top hat. The ceremony was held outdoors, on a dais set in front of Parliament Hill's Centre Block. The crowds had gathered and after the Governor-General and Prime Minister had taken their places, at 11 o'clock the Queen arrived. The Royal Standard was raised on the Peace Tower to a trumpet fanfare and a 21 gun salute was fired by the 30th Field Regiment, R.C.A. The Guard of Honour was provided by the 3rd Battalion, Royal 22nd Regiment. The Queen took her place and the Prime Minister delivered a short address. The Proclamation was placed on the signing table by the Clerk of the Privy Council, Michael Pitfield. Her Majesty signed it and—at that moment it began to pour with rain—a deluge. Budge noted:

> "Some umbrellas and raincoats appeared, but although most of us outside the covered ceremonial platform were soaked through in five minutes, I was glad to note that virtually all the crowd stood fast, totally disregarding the rain.
>
> Fanfare! P.M. signs the Proclamation, followed by Minister of Justice Jean Chretien and Registrar-General Andre Ouellet. Proclamation was then read to the crowd by Under Secretary of State, Mrs Huguette Labelle. The Queen addressed the Nation, after which Her Majesty left the platform. Nancy and I walked back to the Chateau Laurier to change into dry things."

While they were in Ottawa, arrangements were being finalized for a late-May four day trail-ride across Douglas Lake Ranch, at the invitation of Chunky Woodward. Budge had wanted to see the country and in seeking Chunky's advice the answer came back that the ranch would provide horses and the trip would be set up down to the last detail. It had been long anticipated and he looked forward to this opportunity to ride across the range-lands of this historic ranch. The party consisted of Budge, Chunky and Carol Woodward, Deputy Attorney-General (and occasional A.D.C.) Dick Vogel, David Harris, A.D.C. for this trip, Kamloops Mayor Mike Latta, cattle boss Mike Ferguson and the Vancouver Province's Victoria Bureau reporter, Barbara McClintock, who had grown up on the prairies and was an accomplished rider. Nancy, Emily Latta and Judy Ferguson travelled in a van, joining the riders for the evening meal. Meals were prepared by a talented native Indian cook named Sharon. The horses varied from registered quarter horses to the stolid trail-riding variety. Budge's horse was Douglas, a rangy sorrel who, Barbara McLintock described: "... carries the Vice-Regal burden with such care and caution that you can't help thinking he understands the importance of his rider."

The saddles were of course western and, despite his capable horse, this proved to be Budge's undoing. He was used to an English saddle and ended the first morning in agony, so stiff that after lunch he could not remount his horse. A quick return to the ranch house for a soak in the hot-tub was a great help, but he stayed out of the saddle for the rest of that day. Bliss came next morning when an English style saddle was delivered and any further discomfort was avoided for the rest of the ride.

The next day there was a scheduled meeting with members of the Spahomin Creek Reserve. The day started out—and remained—wet, cold and windy. The rain came in sheets on the open part of the trail and only hot coffee prepared in flasks before starting out kept them warm. Arriving on the reserve they found a delegation led by Len Marchand, M.P.—one of the few native Indians in the House of Commons (now recently retired Senator Marchand). Budge was presented with an 'address' written in English but read in a native dialect. Budge later found it to be mainly complaints written in strong language on the treatment of First Nations people by white Canadians. He acknowledged it briefly and said he would reply in more detail later. However the meeting was in other ways friendly enough. The food was provided by the Indians and was very appetizing, with bannock bread, salmon and a large pot of stew, served on paper plates which barely held together in the heavy rain.

As the ride continued, the weather improved and there were lakes for fishing, waterfalls to lunch by, miles of spectacular scenery, with rolling grassland interspersed with pockets of pine trees and the big western sky overhead. There were herds of cattle and cowboys in their typical western garb driving cows and calves across the hills into the corrals for branding. Budge recalls one lunch stop where they looked down into a lush green meadow with grazing cattle, while all around were blue and yellow wild flowers.

At the end of the fourth day they reached the distant Courtney Lake corral where, after the horses were collected in their trailers the party were taken to Corbett Lake Lodge for a pre-arranged dinner. They were joined by several leading citizens of nearby Merritt including several wealthy ranchers. Two brothers, Irish-Australian owners of the nearby Stump Lake Ranch, were ranchers on an international scale with ranches in Australia and California.

In June came the last cruise, this time in H.M.C.S. *Restigouche* commanded by Commander Douglas Henderson. The itinerary was not so far north, anchoring at Squamish, Gibsons, Powell River, Cortez Island, Courtney-Comox, Nanaimo and back to Esquimalt. The Gibson visit was significant in that it is where the internationally known serial *The Beachcombers* was made and a landmark in the town is Molly's Reach, the cafe sitting above the dock where much of the action in the serial takes place. On Cortez Island they visited the Cape Mudge Indian village, of the Kwakiutl clan, where they were entertained to a ceremonial lunch by Chief Harry Assin and members. An enjoyable part of the visit was the Kwakiutl museum which had some fine examples of native carving and artifacts, as well as a display of old photographs, fortunately all retained by the village.

With the last cruise behind them came the realization that the end of their term was less than a year away. Youth still continued to be a major concern of Budge's and after the cruise he was invited to H.M.C.S. *Quadra*, at Comox, a naval cadet training establishment. It provided an intensive two week programme for cadets from across the country, many of them girls. There was some sea-time in naval vessels but one of the most interesting programmes was 'drown-proofing.' Cadets were tied by wrists and ankles and placed floating in 56 degree water for 30 minutes. There were seven young women this time, one of whom being slight would sink and then resurface, with no sign of panic and grinning broadly every time she came up. When all had passed, their bonds were cut and by tradition they threw the fully-clothed instructors into the water.

For Budge a highlight of the visit was to see the previously delinquent Michael, now in charge of a division of the two-week contingent and one of the best leaders in camp. He had turned into a fine looking young man and Budge was very pleased. By December he had enrolled at Camousen College to complete Grade 12 and in a talk with him at Government House Budge got him seriously interested in an armed forces career, though warning him that it must not be a 'flash in the pan.'

Budge's last year in office coincided with a difficult financial period for the Province. The economy had begun to falter during the latter half of 1982 and by mid-summer it was turning out to be one of great labour unrest, with four major sectors poised to strike; the waterfront, the fishing industry, the civil service and the construction sector. With interest rates reaching 18% through 1981 and early 1982, many other sectors were affected as well. The Finance Minister had forecast a $730 million deficit and Premier Bennett introduced severe austerity measures, causing cuts to be made to many progammes. This included the entertainment budget at Government House.

At a meeting with Budge on July 28 he suggested cancelling a number of functions that had been planned to the end of the year. Later the order came to cancel State balls and dinners. After 1983 even garden parties and the Christmas celebrations with the Salvation Army band were cut. None of these have ever been re-instated. The only items not cut were dinners for Cabinet ministers and senior civil servants. Cabinet was divided on the wisdom of cancellations. The Premier's thought was that having asked people to tighten their belts it would not look good to have a ball or large dinner. The Hon. Grace McCarthy believed such functions should still go ahead, as most guests were ordinary citizens from all over B.C. being recognized for their services to the community.

The Hon. Hugh Curtiss, from his perspective as Minister of Finance at that time, agreed with the Premier. He saw the symbolism of cancelling these events as a vital way to get the restraint message across. Because of the economic downturn, the worst in thirty years, Hugh Curtiss advocated deficit financing as the only way to keep the province running. He was obliged to make frequent trips to the bond-rating agencies, trying to hold on to B.C.'s good reputation with them.

Nevertheless he sympathized with Budge's point of view in trying to preserve the Vice-Regal stature of Government House and that of the office-holder. He recalled that Budge was far more enquiring of government procedures than any other Lieutenant-Governor he had dealt with and frequently phoned to seek guidance on a paper that came across his desk. He said: "I would attest to his humility and caring nature. Never any arrogance, never any interference. He was, after all, the Crown's representative and countless documents were thrust in front of him for signature."

During his time at Government House, Budge was served by a number of chauffeurs and in October there was a change when Joe Bate left his employ to be replaced by John Mager, who was to that time an insurance agent in Duncan. Of considerable interest to Budge, John was also Pipe-Major of the Branch 53, Cowichan Royal Canadian Legion Pipe-Band. With John's arrival he now had the advantage of his own chauffeur/piper and batman combined. John is still at Government House, and has served three later Lieutenant-Governors.

In his continuing role as Honorary Colonel of the Seaforth Highlanders of Canada, Budge provided John with a MacKenzie tartan kilt to go with his full-dress piper's uniform. He attended as many regimental functions as time permitted, and was particularly proud to attend the November 19, 1982 Seaforth Annual Mess Dinner. Lieutenant Roderick Bell-Irving, that year's recipient of the Sword of Honour as best subaltern, gave the toast to the regiment, and the battalion had won the Sir Cassimir Gzowski Trophy, a top honour among major militia infantry units in Canada. Budge introduced the new Commanding Officer, Lt. Colonel Tony Phillips, taking over from Bill Anstis who had resigned to take up a new job with the Saskatchewan government. In his speech he reminded all present that "attaining the Gzowski trophy is not the ultimate objective, but a bench-mark on the way up!"

Soon it was Christmas—and this last one at Government House was going to be memorable. The staff party included everyone, from the temporary help to senior members, and later joined by neighbours. All were entertained by a group of wandering carollers and the Salvation Army band. Many people expressed in Budge's words, "the kind sentiment that they would like us to stay on."

On January 1, 1983 came their last Levee, with 1037 citizens coming for the occasion. Two incidents added to its memory; one was the arrival of a coach tour from Portland, Oregon—a very novel New Year's Day for them, especially as the pipe band of the Canadian Scottish Regiment entertained. The other was a young man who very politely asked Budge if he could be excused just prior to "Oh Canada" and "The Queen" as he could not bring himself to be present for either!

Budge's 70th birthday was celebrated in fine style on the 21st as a guest at the Vancouver City Police Pipe Band's Burns' Supper. Asked to give the toast to the Immortal Memory he obliged—and received a bottle of Scotch to celebrate his birthday. It was perhaps appropriate that the next day he once again visited Peter Traill, frailer than ever, but with Robert Burns' birth-date on the 25th very much in mind, he expertly quoted the Scottish bard. It was very close to seventy years since he had left Fifeshire and had met H.O. soon after his arrival in Vancouver.

Later Budge visited 95 year old General Pearkes in Victoria's Aberdeen Hospital. It was two days after the General's birthday and Budge was surprised to find that an orderly had shaved off his moustache, which he had worn all his adult life, but he was bright enough and did not seem too upset by the act. As with Peter Traill, Budge treasured the long association with his old early WW II commander and appreciated the guidance and role model he had provided. General Pearkes died on May 30, 1984.

With six months to go before handing over the reigns to a successor Budge began preparing to leave Government House. The first move was to put the Shaughnessy townhouse on the market and to give warning to their West Vancouver tenant that the home on Folkstone Way would be required by the end of April. Asked his advice about a successor, Budge suggested Robert (Bob) Gordon Rogers, a former forest company executive with a first-class community record. There was, of course, a protocol to be followed and other people would be on the list presented to the Prime Minister and Governor-General.

Budge was involved in the initial stages in another recommendation as well. At the end of February he attended a dinner for His Grace the Duke of Westminster at the Vancouver Club hosted by the Duke's company, Grosvenor International. Through this company the Duke still owns over three hundred acres of Annacis Island. The original purchase and development was begun in the days of a predecessor (a cousin), who was known throughout his life as 'Bend Or', a nickname taken from a famous race horse. His land agent, the late George Ridley, came to B.C. in 1946 scouting for land to purchase and saw the potential of this developable land in the Fraser River estuary.

The Royal Westminster Regiment did not have a Colonel-in-Chief and it occurred to Budge that as a serving officer in the British Territorial Army (Militia), the Duke would, if willing, be an ideal person for the role. Gerald Cavendish Grosvenor had joined the

Queen's Own Yoemanry in 1970 at age nineteen, serving in the ranks until receiving his commission in 1973. He succeeded to the title following his father's death in 1979 but continued in the Territorial Army and reached the rank of Lieutenant-Colonel in 1992, when he became Commanding Officer.

Budge is very modest about his role and he would have had no idea of the lengthy train of events he had set in motion. It is because traditionally a Colonel-in-Chief is usually a member of the Royal Family, though there are exceptions such as Countess Mountbatten of Burma holding the position with the P.P.C.L.I.

All ranks of the Royal Westminster Regiment were very keen to have His Grace as their Colonel-in-Chief but there were many stumbling blocks along the way, most of them in moving the request through the correct military channels in Canada. The regiment's Honorary Colonel, William McKinney, is a forceful man who likes to cut through 'red tape'. He was determined that it would go through and it did. When the final hurdles were cleared in Canada and permission was received from then Minister of Defence, the Hon. Tom Siddon, a formal request from the regiment was laid before Her Majesty, the Queen. Budge's suggestion finally came into being, but it was not until December 18, 1993 that His Grace was finally gazetted Colonel-in-Chief of the Royal Westminster Regiment.

On March 8, 1983 the Queen and the Duke of Edinburgh arrived on a long-planned visit to B.C. They sailed into Victoria harbour aboard H.M.S. *Britannia*. As they crossed the inner harbour in the Royal Barge it was windy and pouring with rain, but there was great enthusiasm from the crowds despite the weather. Her Majesty spent several days in British Columbia and a tight programme had been arranged.

The Britannia was used frequently on this visit: for a Duke of Edinburgh award ceremony with His Royal Highness present to give the awards; for a reception in Victoria and for a State Dinner in Vancouver. Both ended with the ship's Royal Marine band presenting a 'Beating Retreat' ceremony, always an outstanding performance by these hand-picked bandsmen. (With the de-commissioning of *Britannia* in December 1997, these displays could well become a thing of the past.) This Royal visit was the last opportunity for Budge and Nancy's direct involvement and it was a truly memorable one.

With barely four months to go before Budge left Government House, and with the economy reaching a crisis point, Premier Bennett announced his intention to finance the day-to-day running of the province by special warrants. The province's fiscal year begins on April 1 each year and if the Legislature is not sitting, by tradition it is recalled to pass an interim supply bill.

Because of the state of the provincial economy, coupled with the deficit financing brought in by his government, the Premier was accused of being afraid to face the opposition if he recalled the Legislature. Determined to go ahead, on April 1 Budge was asked by the Minister of Finance to sign a warrant for $699 million to keep the government in funds for about one month. It would allow 'government by decree' and effectively give Cabinet financial discretion without reference to the Legislature. A storm of protest was led by the Hon. Dave Barrett who on March 31 hand-delivered a letter to Budge claiming:

> "The legislative authority for the administration to tax the citizens of B.C. and spend their money expires at midnight this very day. Yet your government has not announced a recall of the Legislature to lay before it the required public accounting of past expenditures and the budget appropriations required for the new fiscal year which begins tomorrow. Nor has it announced the only alternative course of seeking your writ to hold an election to seek the mandate of our citizens.
>
> ... The present government appears to deem itself immune from all the restraints on spending of taxes which are inherent in our parliamentary process. It is an unforgivable breach of our province's constitutional customs and the parliamentary process by which we are all bound. There is no emergency compelling such arbitrary and undemocratic conduct."

(Ten years earlier Barrett had faced censure from Social Credit, then in opposition for trying to force closure on debate over a supply bill. The opposition rallying cry had been 'not a dime without debate.')

Budge's reply simply was short and succinct: "Might I say, in response, that I continue to find pleasure in the thought that you have confidence in my constant intention to fulfill the important responsibility of my office."

Many citizens joined in the protest when they became aware of the extent of Bill Bennett's financing proposals. Budge had several letters urging him not to sign. The late Marjorie Nichols of the Vancouver Sun, a respected parliamentary reporter suggested that the Premier was in error in claiming the right to use special warrants. One of her derisory headlines was, "How it's done in a Banana Republic." On a more serious note she posed the question of what action Budge could take. She suggested that if he refused to sign the initial empowering special warrant it would be unprecedented and would precipitate a national constitutional debate. Every provincial government would have an interest in the outcome and its aftermath. She said of Budge: "Mr. Bell-Irving, the scholarly former soldier is well versed in the powers of his high office and has let it be known that he would not hesitate to employ such powers to deal with a crisis."

Budge sought extensive legal and procedural advice. He was told there was no proper basis in law to refuse to sign and he therefore did so. The issue depended upon the interpretation of Section 21 of the Financial Administration Act and a 1981 amendment. It was this amendment which was being interpreted in the broadest possible way, as the intent of the Act was that it be used for a single, unforeseen emergency, not for day-to-day governance.

With the weight of opinion against him, on April 7 the Premier sought permission to dissolve the Legislature and Budge signed the dissolution proclamation. The writ was dropped for a May 5 election. The polls indicated that his government might do poorly but despite this, Bennett went to the people to seek approval of a tough restraint programme, made abundantly clear during the election.

The constituency of the Hon. Hugh Curtiss was Saanich and the Islands, so he was one of the few M.L.A.s who came to the Legislature frequently during that time. As Minister of Finance until the dissolution (and again in the new government), next to the premier, he was more involved than anyone in the day to day running of government. He was acutely aware of Budge's grave concern about this situation, especially as from April 1 to June 23, when the new Legislature sat, the special warrants continued. By that time the total amount had climbed to over $1.4 billion.

Budge scrutinized each one carefully and challenged some—a diking programme for flood control and a highway improvement programme in the Municipality of Burnaby. The question was whether these were justifiable as an emergency or whether they could wait to be passed in due course by the new sitting. The ministers responsible scrutinized them and with slight amendments Budge gave assent. There was always the unarguable answer that it would be cheaper if done immediately.

All this did not spoil the remaining weeks in office. There was a strong desire by those who had been closely associated with Budge and Nancy during the past five years to pay tribute, especially his Aide-de-Camps. They and their wives arranged a dinner in his honour at H.M.C.S. "Discovery". His tenure was all the more meaningful for them because of his own military background which provided a common bond. He wrote:

> "This was 'the occasion' of our Government House career. It was an extraordinary and, I hardly feel justified demonstration of appreciation and affection, and obviously as much for Nancy as for myself."

Budge was presented with a teak glass-topped coffee table under which, mounted on green baize were the cap badges of his Aide's regiments and units, with their individual names engraved on a brass plaque by each badge. They surrounded an enamelled facsimile of the Lieutenant-Governor's flag. It was a most striking personal reminder of a very special group. Nancy's gift was a brooch in the form of the Lieutenant-Governor's flag, engraved in Sterling silver. A similar event was held by the Victoria based Aides the following week at the Union Club.

On April 18 came another landmark; the first night in their retirement abode, high up on West Vancouver's Folkestone Way. With its panoramic view to Vancouver Island in the west, to 10,000 foot Mount Baker far to the east, they knew at once it was the right choice. An unusual feature of the apartment is a loft with the same commanding view and here Budge made his office. The addition of built-in bookcases in the loft, the hallway and two sides of the living area soon made it a very special home—and a place to entertain the increasing number of grandchildren: Roderick's daughter, Miriam, from his first marriage, Neil and Charlotte from his second marriage to Alison, Hal's sons David and Stephen, and Donald and Ellen's adopted daughter Ali.

On Election Day, May 5th, the Social Credit Party was returned to power with a substantial majority, 35 seats to 22 for the New Democratic

Party. During the run up to the election the N.D.P. under Dave Barrett appeared to be doing well, stressing the dire consequences of cutbacks. As well as the Liberals and Conservatives, several smaller parties fielded candidates that year, the Green Party, Western National Party, Western Canada Concept Party and the Communist Party, but none of them won enough votes to affect the outcome.

The Legislature re-opened on June 23 with great fanfare. The Honour Guard was made up of both the Seaforth Highlanders of Canada and the Canadian Scottish Regiment. Budge read his last Speech from the Throne, 40 minutes long and laying out much of the government's plans for the next four years. Just before going into the later reception, Premier Bennett informed Budge that he had just heard from the Prime Minister that Bob Rogers had been confirmed as the next Lieutenant-Governor of British Columbia.

(The election had a serious aftermath. Despite the Social Credit majority, both in the number of seats and the popular vote, following release of the government's austerity measures, the B.C. unions showed their considerable power. Taking the name from the recent Polish experience they formed a 'Solidarity Movement' resulting in massive labour unrest, many walkouts and a general strike came very close in the late fall. In mid-November the Premier invited Jack Munro, tough-talking President of the I.W.A., to a meeting for one-to-one discussion on the situation. After several hours of bargaining an accord was reached and the government was compelled to give way on several of its planned cutbacks and anti-union bills. The meeting was held in the Premier's riding of Kelowna and became known as the 'Kelowna Accord.' It did not please all union members and some regarded Munro's actions as a sellout.)

Of Budge's last official functions, two of them were military. The first was a Sunset Ceremony on the lawns of the Legislative Building by the 3rd Battalion, P.P.C.L.I. in the presence of Colonel-in-Chief Lady Patricia, Countess Mountbatten of Burma. A special treat for Budge was the fact that as well as the band of the Patricia's there was also the band of the 3rd Battalion, Royal Green Jackets, with their bugle band, that had so impressed him in Cyprus a few years before.

The other one, though not related to his office, was the 40th anniversary of the Sicily landing, on July 10. Over two hundred veterans attended a church service and parade. Padre Roy Durnford, D.S.O. with his motto "Working to beat Hell", had passed on in June 1971, though he was very much in the minds of the veterans*. The service was taken by the Rev. Harry Lennox, a much revered Vancouver clergyman. The turnout of wartime officers was impressive; Syd Thomson, Jim Blair, Borden Cameron, Dunc Manson, Davie Fulton, David Blackburn, Donald Clark, Jim MacLean and Farrel Taaffe. Ex-C.S.M. Joe Duddle, D.C.M., with two artificial legs, sat in the front row of the spectators.

Captain Rainse Ireland (formerly R.S.M.) turned the parade over to Budge, who marched it passed General Bert Hoffmeister. Budge then fell out, joined the saluting base and Captain Ireland took them past again to salute Budge. He wrote, "Nancy had a tear in her eye, but I was unable to console her, as I had one too."

On the evening of July 14, Budge and Nancy hosted the last of a series of eight private dinner parties at Government House, held for the benefit of many old friends who would not normally have had an opportunity to be entertained there. This time they invited Bob and Jane Rogers and generously placed them where they normally sat themselves. It was the last Bell-Irving function. The next morning at 11.30 Robert Gordon Rogers took the oath of allegiance and was sworn in as British Columbia's 24th Lieutenant-Governor. In Budge's final speech, delivered as the immediate past office holder he said:

> "May I record, before this company, our grateful thanks to the officers and staff of Government House who have served this office, and us, so very well for the past five years. Mr. Premier we commend and thank the Government of B.C. for their continuing support of this office, this house, of which we are all so proud—and for your support of us personally. I use the plural 'us' advisedly because there have been two of us all the way.
>
> We have seen a potential value and importance in this office—in the Monarchy as a Canadian institution. It has for us been a worthwhile challenge—and we have had a growing desire, a hope that we

---

* Roy Durnford had remained a padre and went to Korea from 1950 to 1952. When he returned it was to the military H.Q., B.C. Command for six years, followed by two years as assistant to Dean Northcote Burke at Vancouver's Anglican Christchurch Cathedral. He and his wife Mary then moved to Quebec where he was padre to St. Andrew's Veterans Hospital at St. Anne's de Bellevue. They returned to Vancouver where he took up the post of Padre at Shaughnessy Veterans Hospital. Roy Durnford died of a heart attack on June 25, 1971, though he had been suffering from Parkinson's disease for some time.

might in time be succeeded by a man, bigger than I, yet blessed as I have been, with a natural-born chatelaine. Today, all our hopes have been realized. All British Columbians are most fortunate that this great institution is in the capable hands of His Honour Robert Gordon Rogers, and his charming lady, Jane. Nancy and I will go home now—Happy."

POSTSCRIPT

BUDGE'S RETIREMENT FROM GOVERNMENT HOUSE did not signal the end of his involvement in the affairs of the Province or of Canada and in 1985 he was awarded the Order of Canada for his services to the country. He continued to be active with the Seaforth Highlanders of Canada, among other things serving on the ex-commanding Officers' committee. On September 29, 1990 Budge received his Honourable Discharge certificate, completing fifty-seven years service with the regiment, though he is still a welcome member of the officers' and sergeants' messes. An ongoing concern of his has been the fate of the Canadian militia, as cut-back has followed cut-back and he has taken every opportunity to make his views known on the need for a strong volunteer presence in the armed forces.

He has served on several other committees and important decision-making panels. One of these is the Seymour Demonstration Forest in the North Shore Mountains, which Budge is credited with helping to preserve. He has served on the advisory committee and also on the angling committee, which did an in-depth study of stream protection. Bob Cavill, Administrator of Watershed Management called Budge a 'crusader' for his work in the preservation of streams and his vision for the overall management of the area. His input was appreciated by the professional staff, who had the delicate task of dealing with municipal politicians that did not always appreciate the difficulties of watershed protection. In March 1998 Budge was honoured for his work with the demonstration forest by the Steelhead Society of B.C., when he was presented with the Cal Woods award.

Budge has maintained his interest in the Scout movement, serving in various volunteer executive capacities over the years since his early involvement, begun through his sons. He remains the Honorary President of the B.C. and Yukon Provincial Council and is an Honorary Member of the National Council.

Donald Bell-Irving and his wife Ellen returned to Boston where he took up the position of Marketing Division manager with the Digital Equipment Corporation and in December 1987 they adopted a Korean baby girl, christened Ali. Donald and Ellen established their own 'Pasley Island' off the Maine coast, purchasing a property on Pole Island, where they built a house. He also brought electricity to the island, after a long battle with the local power authorities, for which his neighbours were eternally grateful. Tragically, Donald died of a brain tumour in March 1992. Ellen and Ali continue live in Boston and are in frequent touch with Budge.

On April 7, 1997 Budge and Nancy celebrated sixty years of marriage, with a large reception at the Seaforth Officers' Mess; a truly joyous occasion. Sadly, Nancy died only a few months later, on July 24, after a long debilitating illness which she fought bravely, and was patient and gracious to the end.

Budge's most recent involvement is with the Disabled Sailing Association of B.C., of which he is Honorary Chair. His interest in the association came about through meeting Vancouver City Councillor Sam Sullivan at a dinner. In 1979, when he was nineteen years old, Sam had a serious skiing accident which left him a quadraplegic. With only limited use of his hands, he was determined to master as many solo activities as possible including sailing and ultra-light flying. The Disabled Sailing Association had its beginnings at Vancouver's Expo '86, when then British Prime Minister Margaret Thatcher presented a British designed 'Sunbird' 15 foot sailing dinghy to Rick Hansen, the British Columbian paraplegic athlete who completed a round the world 'Man in Motion' tour from March 1985 to May 1987, (the dinghy was received on Hansen's behalf by his sister Christine). In 1989 Rick Hansen donated the dinghy to Sam Sullivan to develop sailing programmes for the disabled. With the gift of the Sunbird, Sam founded the Disabled Sailing Association. A dinghy has since been designed especially for the association by Don Martin and is called the Martin 16. With 'add on' controls it can be operated by quadraplegic sailors with only 'sip and puff' ability.

Sam's achievements impressed Budge so much, he offered to help in any way he could, and not only promotes the organization whenever possible, but with the help of the Chief Herald of Canada he has given the English version of his motto, "Nothing is Impossible" to the association. There are now 12 chapters throughout North America and there are currently over 2000 disabled people who take part in sailing, including racing, many of them children. There is an annual regatta in which these sailors from all over North America compete for the "Mobility Cup." Budge is proud of his part in this worthy endeavour.

APPENDICES

I | The Situation on the West Coast at the Outbreak of War in 1914

In the confusion of the outbreak of war it was rumoured that two German warships, the "Nurnberg" and "Liepzig" of Admiral Von Spee's China Squadron were sailing up the Pacific to bombard Victoria and Vancouver. There were several prominent Germans still living on the west coast and they came under suspicion, with accusations of both spying and sabotage.

None of the rumours proved true. The Leipzig came no closer than San Francisco and Nurnberg no closer than Hawaii. Von Spee sailed across the Pacific to Coronel, where on November 1st, 1914 he met a British cruiser squadron under the command of Admiral Sir Christopher Cradock. The British were defeated and Cradock died in the sinking of his flagship, the "Good Hope." Both the Leipzig and Nurnberg played decisive roles in this battle.

It was fortunate that the rumours were false because the only ship of any size based in Esquimalt was the twenty-three year old light-cruiser H.M.C.S. "Rainbow", purchased with the "Niobe" from the Royal Navy in 1910 for about $200,000. Her only armament was two six-inch guns and four 12-pounders. Anticipating the arrival of German ships she was sent on patrol in the Pacific. Victoria's defence was left to a few shore batteries with inadequate, outdated guns. Provincial Premier,

Sir Richard McBride was determined to do something about the situation. Following a meeting of key citizens on July 29, 1914 to discuss the situation he took it upon himself to purchase from a Seattle shipbuilding company, J.V. Paterson, two submarines built for the Chilean navy that were no longer required, or could not be paid for. Against a deadline imposed by the approaching declaration of war, McBride purchased them for $1,150,000. After some haggling the federal government reimbursed the province.

As a precaution the Admiralty ordered the cruiser H.M.S. "Newcastle" from the China Station to join the "Rainbow" at the Esquimalt base. She arrived on August 30th with the Japanese heavy cruiser "Idzumo" and placed under the command of Captain Fredrick Powlett of the "Newcastle."

This then, was the state of affairs around the time that war was declared. The two submarines offered an opportunity to increase the naval power of this, then far-flung outpost and they were brought up from Seattle under such a cloak of secrecy they were almost shot at by the shore batteries, who were fortunately stopped in time. It may have been cause for embarrassment to the premier that the submarines were of very little use. Many years later Budge was fortunate to track down one of his father's old crew members, Dick Macaulay, who aside from being a crew member on the "Ivy Leaf" actually worked on the submarines. He said the engines and batteries gave a lot of trouble and he had the terrifying experience of being inside one of them when the bows sank, and the vessel took on a 45 degree angle with the stern still on the surface. It was only quick action by other naval personnel that avoided a tragedy.

2 | Shooting Down the Seaplanes

Torpedo carrying German seaplanes began to take a more important part in activities around the eastern end of the English Channel. The Admiralty could not be convinced they were responsible for the destruction of anti-submarine nets and, on June 11, 1917 Henry set out to see if he could catch them red-handed. He took on five German seaplanes and won his first D.S.C. Admiral Sir Reginald Bacon, Senior Officer in Charge of the Dover Patrol, described the action in Vol. Two of his *Dover Patrol 1915-17:*

"Lieutenant H.B. Bell-Irving, R.N.V.R., arrived early at his patrol-station and heard sounds of machine-gun fire. He saw five enemy planes flying low in line ahead, firing at each cable support buoy as they passed it. He gave the order to man the guns and open fire. One shot hit the first seaplane amidships, bringing it down. The second machine immediately landed close-by and the drifter fired two more rounds at this machine, whose pilot was endeavouring to pick up his damaged comrade. They also fired more rounds at the machines still circling overhead. Lieutenant Bell-Irving chased the machine on the water, as it taxied eastward. This craft was in trouble as it could not go straight, one of the floats having been hit by the drifter's fire.

The firing-pin of the drifter's gun had broken; the gun layer changed it; fired three more rounds at the machines in the air, who cleared off, and five more rounds at the machine in the water, which stopped. The yacht "Diane", which had come upon the scene, took the two aviators prisoner, and endeavoured to tow the damaged machine, but unfortunately they were unsuccessful in getting it into the harbour."

In this action the gun-layer was also decorated, receiving the D.S.M. for his accuracy in damaging the two enemy planes.

3 | Nan's Dover Letter Re Friendly Gunfire

Nan was amused to find that there was a Town Crier whose job it was to warn the town's inhabitants when a practice was scheduled for the heavy guns on the harbour front. He did not always get the timing right, as Nan pointed out in a letter: "As I write the big guns are practising. The windows are rattling in fine style—they do make a terrific din and shoot nearly across the Channel. The guns are not far from the house and the old town crier, who is at least 80 is going around with a bell and announcing in a cracked voice that there is to be a gun practice. He wears a black frock trimmed with gold and a tall hat also much trimmed with gold. He uses a large dinner bell.

He has never got the time right yet; consequently numerous old ladies spend the afternoon shut in their rooms with cotton wool in their ears and nothing happens. Next day they are frightened into fits when the guns fire quite unexpectedly. They then get cricks in their necks looking for German aeroplanes!"

4 | Mick and Duncan's Crashes

In December 1915 Mick and Duncan were wounded within days of each other and were both transferred to London to a private hospital run by Lady Ridley in her large house. It was exclusively for officers of allied forces. Duncan was flying as an observer at the time in another squadron and received a skull fracture.

They both recovered well, though Duncan took longer. He did not return to active service for three months after which he began pilot training. By the middle of May he had earned his wings and was posted to 60 Squadron in France. It gained a reputation for the skill and daring of its pilots.

In early July 1916 Mick was wounded again, this time in the head while on a photo-reconnaissance flight. He passed out, regaining consciousness just in time to crash-land inside the British lines. His observer was also wounded and died soon after. By a remarkable coincidence he landed a few hundred yards from where Roderick was in charge of a burial party. The bullet had entered Mick's skull and lodged in the brain. Again, unbelievably, no vital parts were touched though he suffered some memory loss for a time. He was nursed by his sister Isabel who had joined the nursing staff at Lady Ridley's and he recovered sufficiently to return to Canada. Having been awarded a D.S.O. and an M.C. he was given a hero's welcome. While in Canada the bullet in his brain shifted, causing blackouts and some loss of peripheral vision. He was sent to Johns Hopkins Hospital in Baltimore where Dr. William Dabney successfully removed the bullet.

(Some years after WW II Budge was in Holland and was interviewed on the radio. A short time later he received a letter from a woman in Brussels, who asked him if he was the Major Bell-Irving who had had the bullet removed from his brain in 1917, because she was the operating room nurse and had picked the bullet from off the floor where Dr. Dabney had dropped it after removal.)

In September 1916 Duncan shot down an observation balloon. Because of the ground defences placed around balloon sites it was considered the equivalent of shooting down three aeroplanes. Duncan was awarded the Military Cross. Two months later he received a bar to this decoration for shooting down two enemy aircraft and damaging a third while escorting bombers. He was wounded in the leg and once again taken to Lady Ridley's where Isabel still nursed.

In August, 1917 Duncan was appointed a flying instructor and second-in-command of the Gosport Flying Training School. The instructors, all experienced combat pilots, were given their own fast Sopwith Pups and he was so impressed with its handling that on the first flight he began a series of stunts, including an upward spiral. The Pup spun out of control though Duncan would undoubtedly have regained it had his foot not jammed in the rudder bar. For the second time he fractured his skull and damaged his foot so badly it was thought that an amputation might be necessary. Instead he ended up with a permanent limp.

In January 1918 Mick was involved in another flying accident. After the successful removal of the bullet in his brain he was given command of one of the first Canadian R.F.C. squadrons at Camp Borden, though he was not yet allowed to fly. Later he returned to Britain and was appointed liaison officer with responsibility for all matters affecting Canadians in the R.F.C. On a visit to Gosport he persuaded Duncan's successor to let him take the special advanced flying course. While performing a difficult stunt his plane crashed and he was badly injured, once more to his head. One leg was so badly smashed that it was amputated above the knee. From this time Mick's flying days were over and as soon as he was sufficiently recovered, he returned to Canada. It must be remembered that to be a successful fighter pilot required more than a normal share of the dare-devil spirit and there was never any suggestion that the brothers were taking unnecessary risks or wasting machines in these accidents.

5 | The Death of Major Roderick Bell-Irving

The counter-attack began at 5 a.m. and Cuvillers was taken by 8 a.m. Things were so quiet in the village itself that preparations were begun for breakfast. No.1 Company Commander, Captain R.C. McIntyre, decided to make a reconnaissance to ascertain if all was as well as it appeared. He saw a large group of advancing enemy in sufficient numbers to outflank the battalion, whose companies were spread out on a wide front. In the ensuing defensive fight three of the four company commanders died. Only Captain McIntyre survived. By the time they had once again secured the position only seventy-eight men were not wounded.

Kerans returned to the battalion H.Q. in Cuvillers where he found R.S.M. Kay hurriedly organizing men against the advancing enemy. In the meantime heavy machine-gun fire was heard coming from the Abancourt ridge, high ground still in enemy hands, which was directed at the 16th Battalion's outposts and resistance lines. It was without doubt the fire in which Roderick was caught as he approached his forward men and he was not seen alive again.

6 | Henry Bell-Irving's Activities in World War II

Until March 1943 Henry had been stationed first in Weymouth and then in London where, instead of living in an officers' mess he had endured the same daily stresses, strains and dangers as the civilian population from air-raids, the blackout, rationing and acute shortages of heating fuels. He had lived in a number of civilian 'digs'; one in Chelsea, one close by Hampstead and one in central London not far from Buckingham Palace. The rooms in Chelsea had no windows left and were permanently blacked out. Raids to try to knock out the Battersea Power Station on the opposite bank of the Thames had taken out the glass so many times that the landlord gave up replacing it. It mattered not to Henry as his hours at work were so long that he seldom saw his rooms in daylight hours.

He had learned to shop and cook for himself, though in one of the locations where an Admiralty secretary also had rooms they shared their meagre rations and cooking duties. In the winters the damp and cold were intense, often with no heating available in either his rooms or his office, which was out on Finchley Road in a block of flats. He endured colds and 'flu, complained of having to wear heavy sweaters and his topcoat in the office, and the need to dry the damp out of his underwear and pyjamas by a gasfire whose jets were barely alight, yet every letter home was full of humour, jokes and observations about life in wartime Britain.

Henry was lucky, in that his relations in Scotland would sometimes send down a salmon or a game bird and eggs to help supplement the rations. He was always willing to share these luxuries with friends or fellow officers. In common with other officers of all three services he was a member of a number of London's clubs: the Royal Automobile Club, the Royal Thames Yacht Club and the East India and Sports Club. Being friendly and gregarious, his various abodes were always open to members of the Bell-Irving family and friends; Budge and Nancy, Wendy and Corney Burke and sometimes the Scottish cousins could be found there. Parties were thrown and up to twenty people would gather to share a prized bottle of whisky or gin, always in short supply unless one was 'in the know.' His comments about 'red tape' in the Admiralty or the work habits of tea drinking workman are amusing to read yet he admired the way the British always muddled through in the end.

In March 1943 Henry received a new posting and was placed in charge of a camp under construction near Warrington, Lancashire. Its purpose was to house up to 1200 seamen to train for aircraft carrier duties and the intakes were to increase each week until there was a full complement. It was the first time since arriving in Britain that he had lived in an officers' mess with regular food provided, but he missed his visits to the London clubs and the camaraderie they offered. Fortunately his job changed once more and he took on a more active role leading to "D" Day.

7 | The Macdonald/Campbell Feud
(Glencoe Massacre – February 13, 1692)

Charles I's granddaughter Mary, married William, Prince of Orange, who became William III. They reigned jointly from Feb. 13, 1689, after the Stuart James II had been deposed, but the Jacobites were still intent on winning back the throne. After the July 1689 Battle of Killiecrankie in which the clans fought for the self-styled James VIII (the 'old pretender) they won the battle but were later routed after their commander, Viscount Dundee was killed. The Highland chiefs were ordered to swear allegiance to William if they were to gain a pardon. The final date to sign being January 1, 1692.

The elderly Macdonald of Glencoe (whose patronym was MacIain) fought well at Killiecrankie, though he had a reputation as a cattle thief and rogue. He was not above helping himself to live-stock, driving them back to the security of his wild glen. One who had been a victim was Campbell of Glenlyon, an officer in the Earl of Argyll's Regiment, formed to keep order in the Highlands. The Campbells had nearly always been on the side of the English Crown—always playing safe by opting for the strongest faction.

Sir John Dalrymple, Secretary of State for Scotland, was a harsh administrator with no love for Highlanders, especially MacIain. He had no wish to quarrel with the more powerful chiefs but if one was to have a lesson then who better? Hindered by deep snow, and with unclear instructions the old man travelled north to Fort William, only to find he should have gone west to Inverary. By the time the sheriff accepted his pledge it was January 6 and Dalrymple declared it invalid. Now with the tacit blessing of the King he avowed to annihilate the chief and his people.

He sent Glenlyon with a company of the Argyll Regiment to be quartered in Glencoe. There is a code of hospitality in the Highlands still to be found. Whole clans and individual house-holds could war, fight grievances or rob each other, but if a stranger or strangers came in peace they were welcomed and given hospitality, and this was accorded the Argyll soldiers.

On the night of February 13, after a meal had been served, hosts and guests went to bed, but the order had come from Dalrymple in the name of the King. The massacre was to begin at 5 a.m. When it was finished MacIain was dead, though his two sons and many others survived, aided by a blizzard. There is a belief that many of the Argyll men did not have their heart in it and gave subtle warnings. The death-toll was 39, only a fraction of the clan, though they died savagely. Most of the women and children escaped by climbing up into a pass. Their primitive living conditions inured them to the cold and that helped them survive.

The MacDonalds were later permitted to return, but MacIain's older son Alasdair, now Chief, complained that his people were in a poor state and half starved. The King was dead by 1702 racked by consumption and officially Glencoe was forgotten. The years have not dimmed the memory and that is why the MacDonald soldier ordered any of that name to stand fast and why Pipe-Major Essen was careful about the tunes he selected.

8 | Operation "Mincemeat"

The planted corpse of "Major William Martin" of the Royal Marines convinced the Germans that in fact the invasion of Sicily was a decoy and the real target was the large Mediterranean island of Sardinia. The corpse, with a briefcase attached was put into the sea from the Royal

Navy submarine "Seraph" on the afternoon of April 30, 1943 and was found by a Spanish fishing boat the same day. German intelligence soon obtained the information.

'Martin' was supposedly killed in a plane crash while carrying documents designed to make the German military intelligence think that plans for an attack on Sicily were fakes to throw them off the real target of Sardinia.

In October 1995 after sixteen years of work by amateur researcher Roger Morgan he discovered the corpse was that of Glyndwr Michael, a 34 year old drifter who had committed suicide in a bombed out London warehouse. So real was the persona of Martin, he had a letter and photograph from his fiancé Pam (actually Jean Gerard Leigh, a clerk in M.I.5), an engagement ring bill, theatre tickets and even an irate letter from his bank manager!

Charles Chomomdeley of MI5 and Commander Ewen Montagu of Naval Intelligence, intercepted German military communications and were able to advise Winston Churchill "Mincemeat swallowed whole"—so whole that German troops were moved from Sicily to Sardinia. The 'Major' was buried at Huelva and Roger Morgan is hoping that a plaque showing his real identity can now be displayed. A book "The Man Who Never Was" was published and revealed the story, followed by a film of the same name. Both were pre-dated by a novel written by former British cabinet minister Duff Cooper. His novel "Operation Heartbreak" was so close to the real story that the government threatened to have him prosecuted under a breach of security clause. However he threatened to name Churchill as his source and the case was dropped.

9 | The Hitler Line and "D" Day Dodgers

The Hitler Line battle began at 06:00 hrs on May 23, 1944 and was one of the bloodiest of the Italian Campaign. German resistance was tenacious and every unit of the 2nd Canadian Infantry Brigade suffered casualties, including a high proportion of officers. It was essentially a one day battle, but will live in the memories of all who took part. The Seaforths alone lost three officers and forty-nine other ranks killed and over one hundred wounded. Fifty were taken prisoner.

The term "D Day Dodgers" is alleged to have been coined by Lady Nancy Astor, one of the first British women members of Parliament while visiting the 8th Army in 1944. The inference was that the men were deliberately avoiding service in France, a rather strange idea when fighting conditions were at least as severe in Italy. However the men fought back with humour and a song was composed, sung to the tune of "Lilly Marlene":

> "We are the D Day Dodgers, out in Italy,
> Always on the vino, always on the spree,
> Eighth Army skivers and their tanks,
> We go to war in ties and slacks,
> We are the D Dodgers, in sunny Italy."

10 | The Ortona Christmas – 1943

There was a tremendous contrast between Christmas 1944 and the previous one at Ortona. The capture of Ortona (December 21-28) was one of the toughest battles faced by the 2nd Cdn Inf Brigade and the first that involved hand-to-hand fighting, gaining ground foot by foot. Their opponents were the 1st Parachute Division. The Seaforths were commanded by Acting Lieutenant-Colonel Syd Thomson, who had well proved his leadership qualities and had returned from the Senior Officers' School just weeks before. There was no let-up in the fighting even on Christmas Day and Borden Cameron, aided by Padre Durnford did his best by serving one company at a time as they were pulled from the fighting for barely an hour. The meal was served in a church on the edge of the town which had miraculously escaped major damage. It was barely yards from the most intense fighting and many men came into the church having lost comrades only hours or minutes before pulling out. Nevertheless a full Christmas dinner was served on white table cloths with china and cutlery scrounged from the many ruined houses around them. The men were battle-stained, unwashed for several days, with stubble on their chins, but at least for a brief time they were allowed to forget the battle still going on so close.

The sounds though, could not be drowned out and the 25 pounders continued to fire overhead while close combat machine gun fire and grenade explosions continued.

One of the best eye-witness accounts of the day was by Corporal Roy Thorsen, a professional journalist who was a fighting soldier with the Seaforths, but who had agreed to send reports back to his paper, the Victoria Daily Times. He wrote:

> "The scene of the Christmas Celebration was a lovely, centuries old church, surrounded by ruined buildings.
>
> On arrival at the House of God equipment and arms were laid out in the courtyard. Before them, his head bared, stood the Padre, Hon Major Roy Durnford, a popular, highly respected figure. A smile of welcome for all lighted his face, bronzed by the Sicilian and Italian sun.
>
> After voicing a few words of prayer and asking God's blessing for the courageous men who had fallen, the Padre asked the soldiers to join him in singing carols, which we did with gusto.
>
> ... as the troops entered the church they were literally stopped in their tracks in astonishment at the wonderful interior picture greeting the eye. A great galaxy of glittering candles glow with the brilliance of a make-believe wonderland. Long tables laden with Christmas fare to make mouths water that for so long had endured greasy canned stews and hardtack biscuits. Before the dinner ended members of the pipe-band filled the church with the skirl of their pipes.
>
> The Padre was at the door to shake each man's hand as we left to return to the grim reality of the torn-up town, still potent with danger from secreted snipers and booby-trapped buildings."

INDEX

A

Abbeville, 187, 241-241
Admiralty 15, 17, 19, 23, 143
Agira, see Monte Fronte (Grizzly Hill) action 160-165, 166
Akehurst, Lt.-Col. J.F.R., D.S.O. 233
Alaska 5, 24, 33, 60, 95, 290, 312
Aldershot 113, 119, 121; *Malplaquet Barracks* 113, 114; *Delville Barracks* 118, 119
Alert Bay 16, 73, 89, 90, 91
Alexander of Tunis, Field Marshal 193, 195
Nicholas II and Alexandra, Tsar and Tsarina of Russia 28
Alberta Pacific Timber Co. 74, 78
Amsterdam 226-231, 232, 268
Anderson, Tom, R.S.M. 97
Andes, Royal Mail Ship 115, 116, 117
Andrew, H.R.H. Prince 279
Andrew, Lt.-Col. M.W., D.S.O. 243, 244
Anglo British Columbia Packing Co. Ltd. (the A.B.C.) 6, 12, 16, 24, 29, 40, 57, 61 *U.S. subsidiaries* 6; *ABC Naval Flotilla packer boats: Holly Leaf, Ivy Leaf and Fir Leaf* 15, 16, 89, 91, 93; *Daisy Leaf* 69, 71, 72, 73
Annacis Island 263, 325
Appeldoorn 226

Argyll, Duke of 136
Armstrong, Major Gordon 232, 236
Arnisdale (Loch Hourn) 45, 46, 47, 136
Arrandale Cannery 60-65, 69-73
Attlee, the Rt. Hon. Clement 273

B

Bacon, Admiral Sir Reginald 19
Baden Powell, Lord Robert 313
Ball, Allen 312, 313
Bankside (near Lockerbie) 3
Barrett, the Hon. Dave 268, 270, 310, 327
Battle of Britain 120, 125
Battle of the Rivers 213-220
Basford, the Hon. Ron 271
Bassett, Major John 215, 217, 223
Bastin, Major Leslie 234, 238
Begg, Lieut. E.G. 152
Belgium 17, 121, 224
Bell, Thomas 1
Bell-Irving, Adrianai, 7, 296, 313
Bell-Irving, Aeneas 7, 12, 14, 15, 27, 29, 32, 127, 264
Bell-Irving, Alan Duncan (Duncan) 7, 14, 20, 22, 25, 26, 30, 33, 43, 111, 127, 127, 129, 257, 259
Bell-Irving, Ali 329
Bell-Irving, Anita Helen 7, 21, 29, 32

349

Bell-Irving, Anna 296
Bell-Irving, Annie (Nan) 13, 14, 17, 19, 21, 23, 27, 29, 31, 36, 187; *death of Nan* 270
Bell-Irving, Ann Helen (Nancy) 36
Bell-Irving, Bella (cousin Shum) 45, 48
Bell-Irving, Charlotte 329
Bell-Irving, David 329
Bell-Irving, Dollie 45, 48
Bell-Irving, Donald Reginald 258, 264, 266, 311-312
Bell-Irving, Dr. Duncan 1, 2, 3, 4, 5, 21, 282, 296
Bell-Irving, Duncan Peter 5, 15, 21, 40
Bell-Irving, Ellen (née McGaffigan) 311
Bell-Irving, Elizabeth 128
Bell-Irving, Ethel (née Hulbert) 4
Bell-Irving, Eva (née Peircy) 50, 51
Bell-Irving, Gordon 32, 128
Bell-Irving, Helen Beatrice (Beatrice) 7, 11, 32
Bell-Irving, Henry (forbear) 2
Bell-Irving, Henry Beattie (Henry) 7, 8, 10, 11, 13, 14; *joins R.N.V.R. as Sub-Lieut. on B.C. Coast* 15-17; *war service in Dover* 17-30; *returns to H. Bell-Irving Ltd.* 32, 33, 36, 40, 48, 50, 53, 55, 61, 73, 93, 111; *arrives in U.K.* 125, 139-140, 166, 186-187; *on staff of Senior Naval Officer in Normandy Landing* 188-189, 230, 235, 236; *death of Henry* 264
Bell-Irving, Henry David 317
Bell-Irving, Henry Ogle (H.O.) 1, 2, 3, 4, 5, 6, 7, 8, 9, 10, 11, 13, 14, 15, 17, 21, 25, 29, 31, 32, 33, 34, 39, 40, 42, 43, 48, 49, 50, 51, 56, 57, 58, 68, 72, 259
Bell-Irving, Henry Pybus (Budge) 1, 2
   Chapter One:
     born Jan 21, 1912 14; *Dover* 17-26; *Crystal Palace* 26-30
   Chapter Two:
     returns to Vancouver 31; *attends first school* 34-35; *attends Shawnigan Lake School* 36-38; *attends Loretto School* 40-58
   Chapter Three:
     Works at Arrandale Cannery 60-66, 68-74; *attends U.B.C. (meets Nancy Symes)* 66-67; *joins Seaforth Highlanders* 75; *in lumber industry* 74-88
   Chapter Four:
     Knight Inlet Cannery 89-94; *in office of H. Bell-Irving Co.* 94-108; *marriage to Nancy* 101; *prelude to war, camps at Sydney and Vernon* 102-106; *last holiday before war declared* 106-108
   Chapter Five:
     Mobilization 109; *small arms course in Esquimalt* 110; *on advance party to Britain* 111-118; *with the Seaforths in Britain* 118-137
   Chapter Six:
     Preparation for Sicily invasion 139-143; *arrives on beach* 145-149 *Leonforte* 153-157; *rescues Private Wood* 157-159; *wins D.S.O. at Grizzly Hill, Agira* 163-166; *Booth Force operation* 167-169
   Chapter Seven:
     Invasion of southern Italy 176-179; *first thoughts on Lines Bros.* 179; *promoted to Lieut.-Col. and returns to England* 182-193; *commands battle school* 185-187; *brother Roderick killed in action* 186-187
   Capter Eight:
     Takes command of the Loyal Edmonton Regiment 191-203; *returns to Seaforths* 203; *discovers best use of PIAT as anti-tank weapon* 204-205; *PIAT successfully put to the test* 207-210; *Operation Chuckle* 212-213; *fun on the canal bank* 216-220; *Brigade in Holland* 223-227
   Chapter Nine:
     Leads unit in the Ijssel River battle 224-225; *leads battalion in liberation of Amsterdam* 227-231; *promoted to Brigdier* 232; *command of the 10th Canadian Infantry Brigade* 232-242; *leads victory parade in Amsterdam* 235-236; *sits as member of court-martial in General Kurt Meyer trial* 242-245; *returns to Canada* 246

Chapter Ten:
: *Joins Lines Bros. as North American manager* 248-256; *returns to Vancouver to set up Bell-Irving Realty* 257; *business expands and opens up branches* 258-267; *becomes active in Scout movement* 264-265; *sells Bell-Irving Realty to A.E. LePage Ltd., remains as Chairman of western arm* 267; *elected President of the Vancouver Board of trade* 268; *sworn in as B.C.'s 23rd Lieutenant-Governor* 273

Chapter Eleven:
: *First Royal Canadian Navy cruise on H.M.C.S. MacKenzie* 275-276; *Mountbatten, Countess as guest* 278; *visits Scotland as guest of honour at military parade in Elgin* 280-281; *criticized by Rafe Mair for Christmas message* 283; *Michael Roberts begins duties as private secretary* 284; *first visit of Prince of Wales* 285; *sworn in as an honorary chief of Nisga'a Nation* 288-290; *opens new Law Courts in Vancouver* 293; *re-visits Amsterdam for 35th anniversery celebrations of liberation* 298-300; *attends Nisga'a Tribal Council meeting on board H.M.C.S. Yukon, in the Nass estuary* 301-302; *visits Cyprus as guest of the Princess Patricia's Canadian Light Infantry* 304-306; *takes the salute at the Edinburgh Tatoo* 306-307; *visits home for delinquent youths and sets up meetings to try to offer guidance* 308-309; *guest at international Scout jamboree in Alberta* 312-313; *attends patriation of the Constitution ceremonies in Ottawa* 318-320; *takes part in long trail-ride on Douglas Lake Ranch* 320-322; *the Queen and Prince Philip visit Victoria on H.M.S. Brittania* 326; *Budge embroiled in with problems relating to Premier Bennett's austerity measures* 327-328 +330; *hands over to the Hon. Bob Rogers* 331-332

Bell-Irving, Henry Symes (Hal) 253, 264, 266, 317
Bell-Irving, H. & Co. Ltd. 6, 13, 31, 32, 33, 40, 50, 57, 88, 109, 179, 194, 257
Bell-Irving, Ian Malcolm 128, 247
Bell-Irving, Isabel 7, 21, 33, 57, 128, 260
Bell-Irving, James Jardine (J.J.) 5, 50, 54
Bell-Irving, Jane 1, 314
Bell-Irving, John 1, 5, 11, 45, 46, 48, 57
Bell-Irving, John Darg 32
Bell-Irving, Margaretta (née Ogle) 1
Bell-Irving, Marie Isabel del Carmen (née Beattie) known as Bella 4, 7, 8, 19, 22, 23, 31, 52, 57
Bell-Irving, Malcolm (Mick) 7, 14, 22, 25, 26, 30, 31, 32, 43
Bell-Irving, Mary McBean 7, 32, 128
Bell-Irving, Mary McBean (Molly) 19, 31
Bell-Irving, Miriam 329
Bell-Irving, Monica (née Marpole) 32
Bell-Irving, Monica Ruth 32
Bell-Irving, Nancy (née Symes) 67-68, 71, 75; *attends Newnham College Cambridge* 75-78; *visits Germany* 80-81; *returns to Vancouver* 87-88; *marriage to Budge* 101; *to Britain with Budge* 111-113; *volunteer work in Britain* 120; *life in wartime England* 126; *begins driving canteen truck* 129; 131, 171; *concern over Nancy's pregnancy* 172; 179, 182, 183, 185; *Nancy returns to Canada* 194; *meets Budge in Montreal on his return from Europe* 246; *assists Budge in setting up Lines Bros.* 248-249; *joins him in Montreal* 255; 271, 275, 276; *responsibilities as Government House chatelaine* 277; 279, 288, 291, 292; *joins Budge for Amsterdam liberation anniversary* 298-300; 306, 309, 317, 329
Bell-Irving, Neil 329
Bell-Irving Realty 260-266
Bell-Irving, Richard 7, 13, 14, 26, 31, 32, 50, 57, 68, 88, 94, 95, 128, 237
Bell-Irving, Richard Morris 31, 128
Bell-Irving, Robin 5, 15, 112
Bell-Irving, Roderick 258, 264, 266, 324
Bell-Irving, Roderick Keith Falconer 31, 54, 102, 104, 114, 128, 135, 139, 171-172;

351

shot down and killed in action over France
186-187; *Budge visits grave* 240-241
Bell-Irving, Roderick Ogle 7, 9, 13, 14, 21,
25-26, *killed in action* 27-30
Bell-Irving, Ruth 14, 16, 24, 31
Bell-Irving, Sarah 1, 314
Bell-Irving, Stephen 329
Bell-Irving, Wendy 19, 21, 31, 102
Bell-Irving, William 1, 3, 296
Bell-Irving, Williamina (née McBean) 1,
3, 7, 313
Bennett, the Hon. W.A.C. 270, 311
Bennett, the Hon. William 270, 277, 280,
296, 311, 323, 326, 328, 330
Berlagebrug (Berlage Bridge) 227, 228
Biddlecome, W.E. Sgt 114
Blair, Major J.W. 128, 149, 170, 331
Blair, R.M. Lieut.-Col. 75
Black Watch (Canada) 203, 211
Bogert, Brig. M.P., D.S.O. 203, 227
Boivin, Captain Neil, R.C.N. (Retired)
300-303
Bone, Captain David, Merchant Navy
140, 142, 143
Bonner, Robert Q.C. 171, 179-180, 261
Booth, Brig. E.L. 167-169
Bourne, Prof. Charles 315
Bredin, Lt.-Col. W.B. 243, 244
British Army:
    Cameron Highlanders, 4th Territorial
    Batt. 122
    Combined Operations 136
    Commandos 132, 137
    11th Royal Horse Artillery 167
    51st Highland Division 144, 224
    56th Division 205, 231
    (Malta) Brigade 144, 159
    Royal Artillery 15, 137
    Royal Engineers 33, 128, 137, 305
    Royal Green Jackets 305
    13th/18th Royal Hussars 305
    12th Royal Tank Regiment 197
    Seaforth Highlanders 170-171, 184
    10th Infantry Brigade 193
    Welsh Guards, 2nd Battalion 121
    8th Army (the 'Desert Rats') 135, 143,
    144, 178, 193

B.B.C. (British Broadcasting
    Corporation) 165
British Expeditionary Force 121
British Resistance Organization 131
British Seaforth Association 119
Brooke, General Sir Alan 139
Buckingham Palace 30, 211, 236, 300
Bullied, George 308-309, 316
Burke, Cornelius (Corney) 112, 128, 172,
264
Burns, Robbie (Seaforth Sgt's Mess
    annual dinner) 97, 137
Burns, General E.L.M. 192
Campbell, Clan 136
Canadian Army:
    1st Canadian Corps 191
    1st Canadian Infantry Division 106,
    108, 110, 112, 123, 125, 140, 167, 191,
    list of regiments in Division 199
    1st Canadian Infantry Brigade,
    comprised of: the Royal
    Canadian Regiment; Hastings
    and Prince Edward Regiment;
    48th Highlanders 160, 166
    2nd Canadian Infantry Brigade 110,
    129, 140, 142-143, 146, 170, 176, 191,
    193, 199, 202, 304 – comprised of:
    Seaforth Highlanders of Canada
    (72nd Regiment) 9, 25, 29, 34, 57,
    75, 86, 95, *last camps* 102-106; *mobilization 1939*, 109-110; *in Britain*
    117-143; *action in Sicily* 147-173;
    Leonforte 153-157; *Agira* 160-166;
    Salso River 166-169; *Happy Valley
    rest camp* 170-173; *Italian Campaign
    begins* 176-179; *Decorata cross-road
    action* 180-181; *Budge returns to
    command unit* 203; *Savio River
    battle* 206-211; *last battle in Italy*
    219-220; *enroute to Northern Europe*
    223-224; *in action on the Ijssel River*
    225-226; *cessation of fighting* 227;
    257, 280, 324, 330
    Seaforth Anti-Tank Platoon 135, 162,
    168
    Princess Patricia's Canadian Light
    Infantry 75, 110, 143, 148, 160, 162,
    214, 278, 317-318, 326, 330

Loyal Edmonton Regiment 110, 133, 143, 151, 154-156, 160, 166, 187; *under Budge's command* 191-203; *the capture of the San Fortunato Ridge* 200-202, 216, 313

3rd Canadian Infantry Brigade comprised of: Royal 22^e Regiment 199, 304, 319; Carleton and York Regiment; West Nova Scotia Regiment 199, 203

10th Canadian Infantry Brigade 232-242 comprised of: Algonquin Regiment; Argyll & Sutherland Highlanders (Canada) 233-234; The Lincoln and Welland Regiment, 233; The 29th Canadian Armoured Reconnaissance Regiment (South Alberta Regiment) 232-233; The 10th Canadian Independent Machine Gun Company (New Brunswick Rangers) 234

4th Armoured Brigade 233, 234

5th Canadian Armoured Division 190

British Columbia Dragoons 216

British Columbia Regiment 234

Canadian Scottish Regiment (16th Battalion) 18, 25, 29, 324, 330

British Columbia Regiment (Duke of Connaughts) 99, 209

9th Field Ambulance Unit 133

Le Regiment de la Chaudiere 239

Princess Louise's Dragoon Guards 228, 231

The Calgary Highlanders 235

The Royal Canadian Dragoons 235, 304

The Royal Canadian Horse Artillery 239, 304

The Royal Canadian Regiment 235

Royal Canadian Artillery: 2nd Heavy A.A. Regt. 127; 2nd Light A.A. Regt. 236; 7th Medium Artillery Regt. 168; 3rd and165th Field Regts. 168; 30th Field Regt. 320; 1st Anti-Tank Regt. 235; 90th Anti-Tank Battery 161, 167; The Royal Westminster Regiment 325-326

12th Armoured Regiment (see Booth Force) 167

Canadian Military Hospital No 15, 120, 131

Campbell, Lt.-Col. C.S. 243

Cameron, Captain Borden 214, 331

Canadian Fishing Co, 53

Canadian Pacific Railway 3, 5

Canadian Real Estate Board 268

Carrington, Private G.V. M.M. 207

Casablanca Conference 144

Castle Camp, Inverary 136, 137, 138

Cattolica Rest Camp 197, 200, 212

Chamberlain, Neville (British Prime Minister) 104

Charles, H.R.H. Prince 285, 300

Charles Edward Stuart, Prince 41, 47

Chartwell 125

Churchill, Winston (British Prime Minister) 100, 123, 125, 144, 169, 175

Circassia, Landing Ship, Infantry (Large) 140-146

Clancy, Mr. Justice Donald 315, 316

Clark, General. J.A. 96, 112

Clark, D.M. Brig. 99, 131, 203, 331

Clark, General Mark 178

Clarke, Lieut. Col. R. P. (Slug) 184, 192

Clyde, River 60, 117, 143

Clyne J.V. 276, 315

Cochrane, Alberta 7, 313

Coffin, Lieut. Col, A.F. 233-234

Coleman, Lieut. Col. Rowan 187, 233

Collison, Colin 69, 72, 73

Collison, Dr. 69

C.B.E. (Commander of the British Empire) 97

Connolly, Jay (author of Rough Diamond) 36, 37

Constitution, patriation ceremony 318-319

'COOV LISIMS' – The Rock (Budge's Nisga'a name) 289

Croix de Guerre (French bravery decoration) 30, 110

Creighton, A.V. Lt.-Col. 99, 129, 190

Cromb, Corporal James and Private Charlie 153

353

CROMWELL, (German invasion codeword) 125
Curtiss, the Hon. Hugh 280, 323, 328
Cyprus 304-305, 330

D

"D" Day, 189-190
"D" Day Dodgers (see also Appendix 9) 190, 227
Dam Square, Amsterdam 230, 299
Davidson, Lieut. D.W. 115, 129
Davidson, Marci 129
Davies, St. John 34
Dean, Lt.-Col. D.G. 243
Denning, Lord (Britsh High Court official) 293, 294
Dewar family 114, 115
Dieppe 134, 137
Discovery, H.M.C.S. 35, 329
D.S.C. (Distinguished Service Cross) 19, 23, 30
D.S.M. (Distinguished Conduct Medal) 169, 212
D.S.O. (Distinguished Service Order) 29, 30, 97, 110, 161, 169, 170, 172, 184, 190, 201, 220, 233, 236, 309
Dixon, Commander Gar 272, 273, 284
Douglas Lake Ranch 292, 320-322
Dover 17-26, 36, 75
Dover Patrol 17-26; Dover Drifter Patrol 17
Duchess of Richmond 112
Duckitt, Thomas 272, 273
Duggan, Captain J. 201
Dunkirk 122
Dunlap, Air Marshal C.R. 187
Durnford, Hon. Major the Rev. Roy 145, 170, 212, 218; *awarded the D.S.O.* 220-221; 226, 331
Dutch resistance fighters 228, 230-231, 235

E

Eastbourne 133, 157
Edenbridge, Kent 124
Edwards, Bert 263
Edinburgh 3, 51, 54, 76, 306
Edinburgh Castle – Edinburgh Tattoo 306-307
Edward VII His Majesty King 9
Edward, Prince of Wales 30
Elgin, Morayshire 280
Elizabeth, Her Majesty (the Queen Mother) 123
Elizabeth II, Her Majesty, Queen 279, 281, 287, 296, 319-320, 326
English Channel 17, 18, 19, 20, 128, 144
Erickson, Arthur 293
Ernaston, SS 22
Esquimalt 15, 16, 103, 275, 280, 303
Esson, Pipe-Major E. 136, 166

F

Fairweather, Lieut. Col. David 181, 280
Fairweather, Sgt. George 181
Ferrie, Lt.-Col. C.C. 128, 131
Fieldhouse, Private R.E. 150
Florence, 194, 195, Ponti Veccio Bridge 194
Focke-Wolfe 190 – German fighter aircraft 133, 157
Ford, Sir John 278
Forin, J.D. Lt.-Col 121, 125, 131, 147, 148, 149
Foster, Maj-Gen. H.W. 243, 244
Fotheringham, Pete 61
Fox, Terry 307-308
France, 6, 15, 17, 25, 30, 31, *Germany wishes to reclaims The Saar* 80-81, 106, 108, 122, 195
Fraser River 5, 10, 24, 33, 78, 263

G

Gardom, the Hon. Garde 280, 310
George V, His Majesty King 30
George VI, His Majesty King 123, 236
Germany 3, 14, 28, 80, 81, 108

German Army:
- 30th Corps 227, 15th Panzer Grenadiers 154, 159; 104th Panzer Grenadier Regt. 159; 10th Army 197; 4th Parachute Regt.197; 26th Panzer Division 199; 29th Panzer Grenadier Division 199, 202; 100th Mountain Division 199
- Panther, Mk 5 German tank 115, 162, 208; Tiger Tanks 201, 204

Glasgow 3, 22, 46, 48, 141
Glendale Cannery, Knight Inlet 89-94
Gibson, Brig. T.G. 191, 203
Glendinning, Major Howarth 214, 224
Gordon Highlanders 307
Gordon, Dr. W.R. 315-316
Gort, General Lord VC, DSO, MC 121
Gothic Line 196
Government House, Victoria 1, 67, 275-332
Gray, Gordon 267
Greenlees, Dr. J.R.C. 41-57, 68, 142
'Grizzly Hill' (see Agira) 159-166, 170
Grover, Bryan 268
Grosvenor Laing 263; Grosvenor International 325

H

Haig, Field-Marshall Douglas 103
Hanbury, Doug & Lois 316
'Happy Valley' 169-173, 176
Harling, Lieut. James 162-165
Higginbottom, Mr. Justice Robert 315, 316
Hindenburg Line 25, 27
Hitler 100, *causes turmoil in Europe* 102, 121, 230
Hitler Line 187, 590
Hitler Youth 220
Hoffmeister, B.M. Major-General 78, 117, 1121, 127, 129, 132, 135, 141, 142, 147-149, 151, 152, 154, 160, 165, 167, 170, 176, 179; *promoted to command 5th Canadian Armoured Division* 190, 331
Hogan's Alley 97, 257
Holland 30, 121, 224-232

Home Guard, Britain's part-time army 129 (see also British Resistance Organization 131)
Hong Kong 13, 45, 50
Hube, General, (Commander of 14th Panzers) 173
Hudson Bay Co. 5, 86
Hunter, Private R.H. 150

I

Ijssel, River 224-226
Ijssel Meer (Zuider Zee) 227, 237
Inverailort Castle 137
Inverary Castle 136; Castle Camp 136
Iredale, Isabel (Betty) 262
Irving, Mary 1

J

Jardine Matheson 1, 13, 44, 50
Jardine, William 5
Johnson, Brig. I.S., D.S.O. 243

K

Kaiser Wilhelm 30
Kakobau, Sir George 278
Kelowna Accord 330
Kenney, Dr. Douglas 315
Kerfoot, James Duncan 313
Kerfoot, William Duncan 7, 313
Kerfoot, William Duncan (II) 313
Kesselring, Field Marshal 173, 193, 195, 199
Keukenhof Gardens 300
Kincolith 69, 70, 287-288, 301

L

Lachine 250, 251
Lam, the Hon. David 311
Land Commission Act 269

Law Courts, dedication 293-294
Law, Mary 272
Leckie, Colonel R.G. Edwards 9
Leger, the Hon. Jules 272, 281, 283
Leonforte 153-157, 159
LePage A.E. Ltd. 258, 266, 271
LePage A.E. (Western) Ltd. 267, 271
Leslie, Lieut. Col. Tom 102
Lieut. Governor's Standard 297
Limpsfield, Surrey 123, 125, 127, 128, 129
Lines Bros. Ltd. 113, 179, 195, 238, 247, 251, 253
Lines Bros. Canada Ltd. 250-256
Lines, Arthur 249, 255
Lines, Moray (Sandy) 252, 253
Lines, Walter 113, 194, 247, 249, 250, 253, 254, 255, 256
LION and TIGER, code names for objectives 160-162
Lovat, Brig. Lord, 24th Chief of Clan Fraser 137
Loch Fyne 136, 140
London 5, 15, 21, 26, 29, 36, 55, 56, 85, 87, 96, 118, 124, 127, 139, 281, 300
Lonsdale, C.W. 36, 37
Lord Roberts School 35
Loretto School 11, 15, 35, 36, 40-58, 59, 62, 67, 68, 74, 142
Lough, J.R.S. Brig. 75, 97, 98, 99
Lower Mainland Regional Planning Board 269
Ludendorff, German Army General 27, 30
Lynch, Major Stewart 207, 209

M

McBride, Private J.G., M.M. 153
McCarthy. the Hon. Grace 280, 309, 323
McClintock, Barbara 321
McCreery, General Sir Richard L. 8th Army C. in C. 208
Macdonald, Lt.-Col. B.J.S. 243, 244
MacDonald, Captain W.K., M.C.152, 168
MacDougall, Major Frank 201

MacDougall, Captain Robert L. (author, A Narrative of War) 153 155-157, 161, 176, 250
McGaffigan, Ellen 311
Magee, Brian 267
McGibbon, the Hon. Pauline 279, 297, 318
MacKenzie, Pipe Major Hector 8-9
MacKenzie, Dr. Norman 261, 262
MacMillan, H.R. 78, 88
MacMillan, H.R. Export Co, 78-88, 117
MacMullen, Captain James 181
McNaughton, A.G.L. General 113, 124
MacNutt, Sgt. 111
Mace, Major O.H., D.S.O. 215, 226, 298
Maginot Line 106
Mair, Rafe 283
Maitland, Ian (15th Earl of Lauderdale) 50, 51
Maitland, Ivor 50; Maitland, Sylvia 50
Makerstoun House, 50, 51, 54
Malahat Life-Centred Learning Hospice 308, 316
Mallaig 45, 46, 48
Malone, Major Dick 142
Manson, Duncan 128, 155-156, 331
Martin, Rear-Admiral Michael R.C.N. (Retired) 300, 303
Mary, Her Majesty Queen 30
Matthews, Bill 89-94
Matthews, Major J. 8
Meade, Cpl. D., M.M. 165
Mediterranean Sea 15, 175, 195, 223
Mercer, Captain A.W. 151
Merchiston Castle School 3
Merritt, Lt. Col. Cecil V.C. 97, 99, 105, 134
Merritt, Captain F.W.I. (Bill) 38, 152, 154
Metauro River 195
Metcalfe, Sgt. W.A. 157, 159
Messina, Strait of 176, 211
Meyer, General Kurt 242-245
M.C. (Military Cross) 30, 97, 110, 121, 165, 184, 184, 207
M.M. (Military Medal) 153, 165, 207
Milkbank 2, 3, 6, 7, 29

Miller, Donovan 276
Milne, 'Gramps' 34
Money, Captain Gordon 162, 168
Monte Luro (Gothic Line) 196-197
Montgomery, General B.L. (Monty) 133, 143, 170, 176, 178
Montreal 87, 111-112, 246, 248-256, 264
Mount Marino and Mount San Giovanni 195
Morley, Alberta 7
Mountbatten, Lord Louis 278
Mountbatten, Lady Patricia 278, 326, 330
Munich Agreement 104
Munro, Jack 330
Murray, Dr. Ronald 78, 85-86, 87, 88, 142
Mussolini, Benito 51, 144, 163

N

Nageleisen, Lieut. D.A. 225
Naples 191
Naden, H.M.C.S. band 298
Nass River 60, 288
Neilson, Private C.E. 169
New Democratic Party 268, 269, 270, 329-330
Newnham College, Cambridge 76, 78
Newth, Mel 266, 268
New York 4, 21, 55, 85, 245, 248, 250
Nichols, Marjorie 328
Nicholson, the Hon. Jack 273
Nicholson, Lt.-Col. G.W.L. 172, 176, 196
Nisga'a 73, 74; *creates Budge as an Honorary Chief* 288-290; *tribal council meeting on H.M.C.S. Yukon* 300-302

O

Operation 'Chuckle' 212-213
Operation Husky, (codeword for invasion of Sicily) 143, 172, 175
O.B.E. (Order of the British Empire) 218, 236, 300
Order of Canada 297, 307

Ortona, (see Appendix 10) 190, 204, 225, 304, 313
Owen, the Hon. Walter Owen 271, 272, 273

P

Palmer, E.W. (Ted) 258
Paris, 48, 123, 223
Pasley Island 11, 35, 52, 59, 75, 76, 77, 104, 106, 107; *sold to a syndicate* 259-260
Passchendaele Dinner 96, 212
Pearkes, General George VC, DSO, MC, Croix de Guerre 110, 120, 122, 130, 273, 325
Pearson College 285
Peck, Col. V.C 25, 27
Peebles, Sgt. Robert 204
Penman, Sgt.-Major D.R. 164, 165
Perrault, the Hon. Raymond 318
Philip, H.R.H. Prince 279, 326
PIAT, anti-tank projectile 114, 135, 161, 162, 202, 204, 205, 207-210
Piazza Armerina 151-152
Piedmonte d' Alife 191-192
Pieve Sestina 207-210
Pipe Band, Canadian Seaforths 9, 117, 133, 136, 166
Portnuff, Captain J.C., M.C. 205-207, 212
Protocol for Lieut. Governor 276-278
Pybus, Captain Henry 13

Q

Queen Elizabeth, Cunard Line 245
Queen's Own Highlanders 280, 307

R

Rankin, Harry 293
Regan, the Hon. Gerald 320
Reid, Private G.A. 156-157
Restigouche, H.M.C.S. 322

Rhine, River 224
Rideau Hall 281
Rines, Alfred 35
Rivers, Private C.A. 168-169
Roaf, Captain J.H. 123
Robb, Hugh 32, 128, John 128, David 128
Roberts, Brig. J.A., D.S.O. 243
Roberts, J. Michael 284-285
Robinson, Prof. Lyman R. 315
Rocky Mountain National Parks 265
Rogers, the Hon. Robert Gordon 325, 330, 331-332
Rogers, Mrs. Jane 332
Rome 191, 210, 213
Rommel, Field Marshal Erwin 121, 133, 173, 201
Ross, Mrs Phylis 273
Rotterdam 226
Roy, Dr. Reginald 116, 118-119, 124, 139-140
Royal Air Force 102, 128, 140; (226 Squadron) 146
Royal Canadian Air Force 128; (417 quadron) 173
Royal Canadian Navy 15, 75, 116, 127-128
Royal Flying Corps 15, 18, 22
Royal Military College, Kingston 44, 99
Royal Naval Volunteer Reserve 13, 15
Royal Navy 17, 116, 128, 137, 139
Royal Vancouver Yacht Club 39, 87, 172

S

Salso and Troina Rivers battle 166-169
San Fortunato Ridge 199-202, 204, 304
Savio River 206-211
Sayle, Audrey (Realty) 262-263, 272
Schreyer, the Hon Edward 281, 283; 296, 297, 307-308
Scotland 1, 6, 20, 42-57, 60, 76, 139, 280-281
Scottish Command 306-307
Scouts, 264-265; *jamborees* 292, 312-313
Seaforth Armoury 95-97, 115-116
Shawnigan Lake School, 36-39
Sherman, British tank 165, 235

Sicily 133, 141, 211, 225, *Sicilian Campaign* 142-170, 175
Siegfried Line 224
Simon Fraser University 266
Simonds, General G.G. 167, 179
Skye, Isle of 45, 46
Small Arms School, Hythe 111, 113
Smith, Private E.A. (Smoky) V.C. 208-211
Social Credit Party 268, 270, 327, 329
Solidarity movement 330
Sparling, Brig. H.S., D.S.O. 243
Stagenhoe Park 114-115
Stagliano, Cpl. J. 209-211, 240, 241
Staples, Major Tony 215
Steele, Sir Samuel 282
Stenhauer, the Hon. Ralph 279
Stephen, Ken 268
Stevenson, Lieut. Col. J.B. 112, 114, 119, 122, 128
Stone, Lieut. Col. J.R., D.S.O. 191, 201, 203-204, 309
Stoney Indian Reserve, Morley, Alberta 7, 314
Story, Cpl. R.R. M.M. 153
Sutherland, Hon. Donald M.P. 96
Sweeny, Ben 21, 33
Sweeny, Sedley 31, 33
Switzerland 9, 48, 49, 56, 57
Symes, Aileen 67
Symes, Reginald 67, 252, 255, 294
Symons, A.R. (Randy) 263

T

Taplow, Robert 5
Terry, Corporal F.W., M.M. 163-165
The Road to the Isles 46-47
The Strands 6, 33, 34, 52, 57
Thomas, Captain E.W. 147, 154
Thompson, Sgt. K.P. D.C.M. 208-212
Thompson, Lieut. Col. Syd D.S.O., M.C. 147, 180, 184, 190, 203
Titania, Hudson Bay Co. ship 5
Toronto 248, 251, 267, 271, 283, 298

Toronto, University of 54, 56, 58, 59, 66
Traill, Peter 99, 247, 259, 260, 317, 325
Treaty of Locarno 100
Trudeau, the Rt. Hon. Pierre Elliot 271, 272, 284, 318, 319
Tupper, Cpl. Gordy 153
Tweedsmuir, Lord 96
Tweedsmuir, Captain Lord John 131, 132

U

Union Steamship Co. 19, 60, 86
United Kingdom (Britain) 5, 10, 17, 20, 35, 36, 76, 95, 108, 120, 124, 125, 128, 223, 245, 280, 318
U.S. Army; 7th Army 144
University of British Columbia (U.B.C.) 59, 66-68, 76, 262, 269, 276, 315

V

V1 'buzz'bomb and V2 rocket 190
Vance, E.H. Sgt-Major 111
Vancouver Board of Trade 8, 268-270
Vancouver Club 75, 264
Vancouver Island 32, 53, 73, 102
Vancouver Real Estate Board 261, 263
Vanheel, Dudok 239, 300
Van Straubenzee, Lieut. Col. 197
Van Woudenberg, Henk and Ebba 229, 300
V.E. Day, (May 8 1945) 226-229
Velthorst, Herbie and Lucy-Mary 228-229, 300
Vernon, 105
Victoria I, 4, 29, 32, 102
Victoria, University of 315-316
V.C. (Victoria Cross) 25, 97, 110, 121, 209-211
Vogel, Richard 321

Vokes, Brig. (later General) Chris 124, 142, 143, 154, 160, 162, 167, 179; *commands 1st Canadian Infantry Division 191*; 200, 212, 245

W

Walker, Walter 61, 69
Webster, Sgt. F., M.M. 165
Wallace, the Hon Clarence 273
Welsh, Major 'Tiger' 163
Watson, Lieut. David R.N. 21
Westminster, His Grace the Duke of 263, 325, 326
West Vancouver 258, 262, 267, 282, 329
White Hill 2, 45, 46, 47, 51, 306
Wilhelmina, Her Majesty Queen 236
Williams Lake Stampede 291
Wilp 225
Wilson, Lieut. Marriot 162, 165
Winter, the Hon. Gordon 42, 273, 278, 296, 318
Women's Canadian Club of Vancouver, 129
Women's Voluntry Service (W.V.S.) 136, 137
Wood, Private F.L. 133, 157-159
Work Point Barracks 75, 110
Worthington-Evans, Lady 126
World War I (the Great War) 14-30, 115
Wotherspoon, Lieut. Col. G.D. (Swatty) D.S.O. 232, 235, 237, 264
Women's Royal Naval Service, (WRENS) 140
Woodward, Charles (Chunky) 292, 321

Y

Young, General Sir David (Retired) G.O.C. Scotland 306
Yukon, H.M.C.S. 300-303, 308

BIBLIOGRAPHY

The Dover Patrol 1915-17 -Vol. II – Admiral Sir Reginald Bacon (Hutchinson & Co.).

History of the 72nd Seaforth Highlanders of Canada – Bernard McEvoy & Capt. A.H. Finlay, M.C. (Cowan and Brookhouse 1920).

The Loretto Register – 1925-1964 – (T. & A. Constable Ltd. 1966).

The Seaforth Highlanders of Canada 1919-1965, – Dr. Reginald Roy (copyright the Seaforth Highlanders of Canada 1969).

Blood, Tears and Folly – Len Deighton (Jonathon Cape 1993).

Merchantman Rearmed – Captain David W. Bone (Chatto & Windus 1949).

A Narrative of War – From the Beaches of Sicily to the Hitler Line with the Seaforth Highlanders of Canada, 1943-1944, – Dr. Robert MacDougall (The Golden Dog Press 1996).

The Canadians in Italy – 1943-1945, Vol. II – Lieut. Colonel G.W.L. Nicholson (the Queen's Printers 1956).

The D-Day Dodgers – Danial G. Dancocks (McClelland & Stewart Inc. 1991)

A City Goes to War – G.R. Stevens, OBE (Charters Publishing Co. Ltd. 1964) (A history of the Loyal Edmonton Regiment).